Secrets of the Ser... Bloodline

The Unveiling of Profound Esoteric Mysteries

by Tau Tia L Douglass

Purple Peacock Publications

Secrets of the Serpent Bloodline: *The Unveiling of Profound Esoteric Mysteries*

First Published June 2013 – Revised October 2013

By Tau Tia L Douglass

Published by

Purple Peacock Publications
Suite 333
Vaynor House,
Vaynor Road,
Milford Haven
Pembrokeshire
SA73 2NB
UK

Telephone: +44 7961938387
Email: mail@purplepeacockpublications.info
Web: http://purplepeacockpublications.info
Web: http://serpentbloodline.info

ISBN 978-0-9576564-0-6

We have made every reasonable effort to trace ownership of all copyrighted material and to secure permission from copyright holders, and/or to cite the sources. If you believe that there has been an oversight or omission, please contact Purple Peacock Publications, Suite 333, Vaynor House, Vaynor Road, Milford Haven, Pembrokeshire, SA73 2NB, UK.

Text, graphics and images are ©Purple Peacock Publications 2013
Unless otherwise stated.

Cover Design by Purple Peacock Publications.

Printed through Lulu Publishing Services.

All rights reserved. No part of the publication may be reproduced, stored in a retrieval system or transmitted in any form by any means, electronic, mechanical, photocopying, recording or otherwise, except brief extracts for purpose of review or educational use, without written permission of the publisher.

Acknowledgements

First the foremost I want to thank my Mum for all her help. I doubt this book would ever have got done without your help, thank you so much for being there for me, I love you.

Thanks Tau Graham Suddick for all your help, not just with the book and everything related to the Church and Order, but for being here and helping when I needed it most.

I would also like to thank all my Sisters and Brothers within in the Order, the Outer Order and the Church. You have all played a part in getting this book out. Whether it is was words of encouragement when I needed the morale, by helping fund the project, by giving me advice or by helping with other things to do with the Order, Church & Movement that has freed up more of my time for working on this book. You are all such wonderful people and I feel very lucky to have you in my life.

I want to thank all of those from my past and present who have been an endless source of inspiration. Whether you think of me as your enemy, acquaintance or friend, you came into my life for a reason. I regret nothing and I have learnt a lot about myself through both the good and bad experiences.

I want to say thank you, and also sorry, to all those who I managed to get a information from. When you told me things you had sworn under oath to never reveal, and you maybe thought wrongly, that I was a member of your Order. I am a researcher, I may have appeared to be something I am not at times in the past in order to gain trust. Although I don't agree with sneaking about, I felt at the time it was a means to an end.. The end being I would have detailed information from the horses mouth so to speak. I am often asked how I can say anything about an Order or religion I have never even belonged to. Well my research is how and I won't reveal my tactics here, but it did work. So if you are angry at me for revealing things you told me in private, sorry, however I am not the one who is the Oath Breaker.

Special Thanks To Contributors

Angela Marie Schumacher, André Heyrman, Kiarna Steart, Patrick Cook, Suzanne Berg & Gemmol Lewis.

Secrets of the Serpent Bloodline - The Unveiling of Profound Esoteric Mysteries

Secrets of the Serpent Bloodline - The Unveiling of Profound Esoteric Mysteries

Foreword

This is my first book and to begin with I didn't know it was going to be a book. As I was discussing these topics, I found I was asked the same questions over and over. I found I was having to repeat myself so much. So I decided to make articles about things as people asked me about them. I also made articles about the research others had been doing into DNA etc. I was constantly asked for a book and so I decided to compile the articles, and add to it some musing from my own magick diary, some teachings on how to get started with the Great Work and more about our bloodline and the teachings passed down through the underground stream.

You can read the book like any other book in some parts. In other parts you will find you will use it more for reference. I hope you enjoy the book, but if you get to a part with too many facts and figures that bore you, don't give up on it – just skip that bit and maybe when everything starts to make more sense you can come back to it in the future.

You might not have any interest in DNA and genetics, and no idea how all that works. Don't worry, you can just skip all that and read the bits you are drawn to.

At times you might read something and not want to believe it, that is also fine. Just carry on learning what you can from the book and leaving those bits you feel you are either not ready to hear or don't feel right for you. No matter who you read on subjects like this, there will always be bits and pieces you don't like. Don't let that take away from all the things you can learn here.

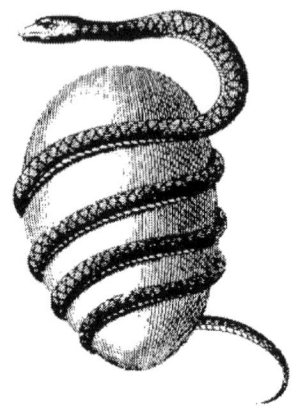

Secrets of the Serpent Bloodline - The Unveiling of Profound Esoteric Mysteries

Introduction

The Children of The Serpent

Thousands of years before Sapiens were created using our genes mixed with those of simians, we were exploring the planet. Our red headed ancestors were building stone circles, underground caves, mounds and pyramids. There is no part of the planet we have not been to long before Sapiens were even thought of. We painted our homes with elaborate images, we were in tune with nature and never took more than we needed, and always gave back to the Great Mother.

We are the Shamans of old, performing beautiful ceremonies under the full Moon as we played our tribal drums and other instruments. Later when the less intelligent Sapiens started to breed without foresight and conquer with greed, they tried to wipe us all out. They thought peace loving nature worshippers were less intelligent than them with their dog eat dog culture. They wanted to murder all the 'red headed giants' and make sure no one knew the truth about the past. Only now the Sapiens are finally catching up in intelligence to us, they know about DNA, and the truth about us is finally being revealed.

Respect our ancient bloodline, we were here a long time before you, and if you listen to us, rather than demonising us, you might just learn how to live in harmony with nature, like we used to. Then the Great Mother can heal.

Who are we? Sapiens have given us many names, all of which are meant as insults, or have come to mean insults, we are Neanderthals, Fairies, Witches, Seers, Dragons, Vampires, Watchers, Anunnaki, Magickians. We are the Spiritual Royalty, Shamans, Titans, Cloud People, the teachers of Gnosis and Sophia. We are the children of the serpent, the grail children.

Secrets of the Serpent Bloodline - The Unveiling of Profound Esoteric Mysteries

Contents

Liber I

Part 1: Origins & Genetics of our Shamanistic Ancestors

Chapter 1
Holy Grail	17
Blood Type Origins	21
Blood Type Personalities	22
Which is the vainest blood group of them all?	24
Original Hair, Eyes and Skin Colour By Blood Group	25

Chapter 2
The Divine Feminine Returns	29
Female Bonds & Intuition	33
The Sacred Holy Herb	33

Chapter 3
Ancient Shamans	35
Y DNA I2b1 – More Research & Notes	41
Merovingian Royalty	45
Melusine	46
Neanderthal V Cro-Magnon	47
Ramses II	48
Ramses III	49
Akhenaten	50
Psychopaths	51
Ancient Bloodline	53

Chapter 4
Rh negative Health & Genetics	55
Child Blood Type Calculator	56
Blood Group Compatibility	57
Risks During Pregnancy Regarding Rh Status	58

Are you a Secretor or a Non-Secretor?	59
Enforced Immunization of ALL Rh Negative Women!	60
Rh Disease! Since when is a different species a disease?	62
Mules Are Rh Negative!	63
Spiritual Royalty Genetics	65
DNA of Rh Negatives	65
Signs and Symbols of the Grail Bloodline	66
What Did Jesus Really Look Like?	66
Rh Negative Eye Colours	68
Evil Eye Talisman	71
Are You Related To Neanderthals?	72
Rh Neg Blood Linked Diabetes Type 1 in Sardinians	80
Ancient Red Heads In USA	85
Scots May Be Directly Descended From Neanderthal Man	87
Wisdom Teeth & Rh Negatives	90
Sumerian Gods & Goddesses	91

Part 2: Awakening Spirituality

Chapter 5

Truth	93
Theolalite	94
Gnostic Theolalites	96
The Four Pillars of Gnosis	100
The Alchemical Process	101

Chapter 6

Awakening Process	105
Naive Enlightenment	106
Enlightenment	107
Higher Self	109

Chapter 7

Reptilian Brain	111

Self Pity Monster	112
Relationships	115

Chapter 8

The Law of Attraction	117
Holy Grail Elixir	118
Probationers & Oath Breakers	120
Life In Numbers	122
11 & 333 Magick Numbers	123
The Great Mother & The Great Work	127
Gold	129
Holy (Blessed) Water	130

Chapter 9

Magick Paths & Traditions	133

Part 3: Occult Knowledge

Chapter 10

Eagle & Snake	149
Serpent, Eagle or Simple	151
Ancient UK Tribes	152
Anointing & Sacraments	153
Septimontium	155
Agape	158
Druids, Wicca (Witchcraft), OTO Origins	161
Mayan Human Sacrifice	167

Chapter 11

Ancient Temples	169
The Underground Labyrinths & Cities	169
Venus of Laussel	170
Bee Goddess	171
Black Stone - Black Madonna	178
The Truth About The Mitre	179

Lilith	182
Hieros Gamos	183

Chapter 12

Incubi and Succubi	185
Long Hair Truth	186
Peace Sign	187
The Crucified Serpent of Knowledge	189
The Alchemical Salamander	190
Satan & Lucifer	191
Forbidden Fruit	192
The Peacock Angel	192
Witches Broom Origins	193
Magick With A K	193

Chapter 13

Astrotheology	195
Astrological Ages	196
The Aeons	196
Time Cycles	199

Liber II

Part 1: Magick Minds

Chapter 1

Chakras	203
Clairvoyance	206
ESP	209
Remote Viewing	210
Psychometry	216

Chapter 2

Dream Realm Analysis	217
Scrying	219
Enochian Magick	221
Banishing Ritual	223

Ritual Magick	224
Incense Making	227

Chapter 3

Qabalah	235
Sigilisation	244
Spells	245
Potions	247
Tarot	250

Part 2: How to kick-start your own Journey

Chapter 4

Awakening Your Senses	255
Meditation Techniques	257

Chapter 5

Guided Meditations	263
Basic Correspondences Chart	263

Chapter 6

Five Tibetan Rites	271

Part 3: Ritual

Chapter 7

Banishing & Protection Rituals	275

Chapter 8

Scrying The Aethyrs	281
Planetary Magick	287
Making a Sigil	288

Chapter 9

Wheel of The Year	291
Ceremonies To Try	291

Liber III

Part 1: Mind of a Mystic

Magick Diary & Blog Entries	299

Part 2: The Order

The forming of the Order	383
True Herstory of the Templar Knights	384
The Knights Hospitaller Templar Cross	385
The Title Tau	386
Crosses Before & After Names	388
Bafomet	389
Liber OIO	391

Part 3: The Hidden Church

The Church of St Mary & St John	393
Orders & Societies	394
Mission	397
History	398
The Mitre & Vesica Piscis	402
Seminary	403
Esoteric Comparative Theology Course	403
Celtic Gnostic Mass	405
Support Truth	407
Be The Solution	409
Festivals	411

Part 4: Mary Magdalene & The Hidden Teachings

Mary Magdalene Poem	415
Truth About Mary Magdalene & Her Children	417
The Hidden Teachings of Mary Magdalene	421
Knowledge from the Underground Stream	433
Mana	434

Liber I

Secrets of the Serpent Bloodline - The Unveiling of Profound Esoteric Mysteries

Part 1: Origins & Genetics of our Shamanistic Ancestors

Chapter 1

Holy Grail

Do you know your blood type?

The blood that flows through your veins contains your life force, and your blood group type can tell you a lot about your ancestors.

Do you have O Rh D Negative Blood?

O Rh D negative blood - or blue blood - sangre azul in Spanish, is a very ancient bloodline. I am sure you have heard the stories about the Holy grail and Mary Magdalene moving to the South of France with the children of Jesus. Behind all stories there is some truth, and when you start to join the dots with bits and pieces of information that we do have, a story unfolds.

The Spiritual Royal Bloodline.

If you can forget all you have been taught, and open your mind to new ideas for a moment you will be amazed how easily you can allow yourself to see the big picture. There are many secrets that have been kept from us, and as more people become aware of their own inner divinity, the truth that has been hidden for thousands of years is finally coming to the surface.

There used to be a tribe of highly advanced beings on the earth. You can look and find stories about them. They were the red headed Gods and Goddesses of legend. They lived in peace and harmony on Earth. Men and women worked together and they created a beautiful vast Kingdom - Eden? Atlantis? Hyperborea? Take your pick. They had no need for wars or conflict, because they lived in a heaven on Earth. Some say they were alien to the planet, however they just evolved separately from other humanoids. And although they evolved quicker than others, this was not because they are alien, it took them thousands of years to get to that point, the others just hadn't caught up yet.

There were other beings on the Earth who evolved separately to these Gods & Goddesses, they were a simian race and not very intelligent. Some of the Gods decided to created a new race using their own genes mixed with the genes of the simians. The Gods knew about DNA and how to genetically alter things.

Eventually they created some new beings that were half God and half simian beings, modern humans were born. They liked their new creation so much, they decided to take them as wives. The humans were so much smaller than the Gods, with narrow hips, and so they struggled giving birth to the children of the Gods. A new line was born with more of the genes of the Gods, but the mixing had caused some aggression and mental problems.

The Gods did love their new creations, and taught them many things. However some of the Gods disagreed with what had been going on, and this interference with nature and ordered all the new humans to be killed so they couldn't breed.

A flood wiped out most of the mixed humans, but some survived.

The Gods watched as the humans evolved, and the humans adored the Gods as spiritual leaders - Kings and Queens. There was peace for a long time, as the Gods taught the humans how to grow things and build cities. They taught them about how the female body was in tune with the Moon, and how it effected everything on Earth. Their calendars were all Luna, and they venerated the females as creators and leaders. Because the calendars were Luna, they had 13 months in a year.

Some of the males from the purer mixed line humans began to get jealous of the women and their power within the tribe, they decided to rebel and take over. They no longer wanted the spiritual teachings of the Gods and rejected them, took over their tribes and started wars with other tribes. They worked at hiding the true history about the Gods/Goddesses and matriarchy. They worked at suppressing women and any form of spirituality they could not use to control and manipulate people. They wanted as much land and control as possible.

They created a religion that focused on one God, the Sun and male energy. They changed the calendars to Solar and 12 months, and said 13 was an evil unlucky number.

By this point the humans and the Gods had become more or less the same size, only the Gods still had wider hips, bigger heavier bones and remained matriarchal, but had to go into hiding.

Jesus and Mary Magdalene

Now we get to the time of Jesus and Mary, who were of the royal spiritual blood of the Gods, both with red hair, pale skin and O Rh negative blood. Mary Magdalene was the real teacher, Jesus was her partner, they belonged to a secret Order that taught the truth, which is passed down secretly to it's members.

Because it was not allowed for women to be spiritual teachers in the new patriarchal society, Jesus did take most of the credit for Magdalene's work.

They were hated for trying to free people from the dogma they had been programmed to believe, and escaped to the south of France where they raised a family. The locals saw them as the spiritual leaders they were, and kept them safe for many generations.

The stories of Jesus dying on the cross and many other stories are all allegory, and are not talking about Jesus the man, they are talking about the Sun in the wheel of the year and the four seasons, divided by a cross.

Morocco & Basque Region

The family spread out from the Middle East through Egypt, to Morocco and down to the Basque area of Spain, moving down to Castile, and the Spanish royal family carry this bloodline and have the sang grail, royal blood or blue blood, as did many of the royal families in the past. The Thracian royals also carried this bloodline.

The ancestors also moved from the Basque area to the UK and Ireland, and became later known as the Picts - painted ones. They were eventually drove to the north of Scotland when other tribes invaded. The Picts carry the royal bloodline and created the Kings and Queens of Ireland and Scotland, and carried the truth still passed in their secret rituals and ceremonies.

Do you have Pictish ancestors?

There are some genes that identify Picts. Y DNA lines are Haplogroups J and I. mtDNA haplogroup H & U.

If you are of blue blood you will have the red hair gene. See how red hair has been demonised for generations? In Egypt and other countries red haired people have been killed because of their magickal powers. In other places called Witches, evil, marked by the Devil. All because those controlling the world as it is now, never want the truth about our origins getting out and meaning they can no longer control people with their lies. The truth about the Witch hunts - the true spiritual royalty who carry the secrets from the past had to be removed, so the truth could never get out. But some of us have survived.

The bloodline families can be traced back to Ramases in Egypt, the red headed King.

Blood type analysis

I am using the term God and human, to differentiate between the spiritual leaders of old who created modern humans, and humans of today.

O Rh negative - Pure blue blood of the Gods, very rare.

O Rh positive - Mixed, God and human. The most common blood of modern humans. This is most likely the first humans created by the God/Human mix.

A Rh negative - Mixed, God and human type 1. Very rare.

A Rh positive - Human type 1. Very common.

B Rh negative - Mixed, God and human type 2. Very rare.

B Rh positive - Human type 2. Very common.

AB Rh negative - Mixed, God, Human types 1 and 2. Very rare.

AB Rh positive - Mixed, Human types 1 and 2. Very rare.

All Europeans and most people in the world have some of the blood of the Gods, but the traits show up most in those with Rh negative blood. And just because you have say B positive blood, it does not mean that you don't have some of the traits, because European type 1 & 2 humans would have done very well to not be mixed with some who did carry the genes, but because the Rh negative genes are recessive more people are born positive. To be of the pure O Rh negative bloodline it would mean your ancestors are all also O Rh negative, which is why it is so rare, but higher percent of pure blood still survives in certain areas, and in some of the old royal families.

So what does all this mean?

It means that our current leaders are making a bad job of things because they are not spiritual beings. They only care about themselves and selfish gain of power and money. They want to keep everyone dumb and doing as they are told, while they have all the benefits.

However, the children of the Holy Grail and waking up and finding each other again. They know the world is out of balance, and if we continue on this current path we will destroy our Mother Earth and all life on her.

The time has come for us to awaken from our slumber, join together the old tribes and bring peace, harmony and balance back.

You will know if you are one of the Grail Children, you will recognise yourself as a Theolalite.

Currently the only Church with valid apostolic succession which has been founded by true spiritual royalty is The Church of St Mary & St John (a spiritual church, not religious). If you feel a calling to Minister, or work towards your own inner truth and enlightenment you can find out more here http://churchsmsj.org/

Blood Type Origins

Homo Erectus, this is where B positive blood came from and before that Gorillas.

Homo Heidelbergensis, this is where A positive blood came from. Before that Chimpanzees. The genes of these ones were used with a small percent of Neanderthal genes to create the Cro-Magnons. The Cro-Magnons were created as a warrior race, who were supposed to be big and strong, and good for working. However, a little knowledge is dangerous, and they soon took over completely, killing off as many Neanderthals as they could. The Neanderthals were the tribe Kings and Queens, the Shamans... The ones who had decided to tamper with genes, had created monsters, unspiritual war-like Cro-Magnons brought patriarchy and war as they created a new - dog eat dog - culture.

Cro-Magnon, these have mainly A positive blood. Neanderthals were the Ones that created, communicated & educated the Cro-Magnons before they rebelled against their creators.

Neanderthals, these are where O neg blood came from. All rh negs carry this blood group, if you are A, B or AB neg you carry it recessively. If you are O positive, you also carry it recessively, and most other Europeans do, even if you are A or B positive.

Blood Type Personalities

Type O Positive
People with the Type O positive blood group, are said to be creative, confident and quite popular, they enjoy being the centre of attention. Type O positives are also outgoing and very social, though mostly initiators, they may never get to finish what they start. They tend to be a little too defeatist and this can lead to problems for them. They have a tendency to be addictive personalities, where drugs and alcohol may become a problem if not kept in check. Also watch the 'poor me' victim mentality.

Type O Negative
People with the Type O negative blood group, are said to be ultra creative, reserved when they have to be, but very direct when passionate about something. Type O negatives are born leaders, they are the genius of the all the blood groups with their high intelligence, inventors, entrepreneurs, spiritual and artistic. Often admired by their peers for their knowledge and wisdom, yet hated and despised by those who are jealous. If not careful the O negatives can become very withdrawn, as they tend to not be able to make sense of their less mentally and spiritually developed peers.

Type A Positive
People with the Type A positive blood group, are said to be very trustful, honest and conscientious to a fault. Type A positives are also known to be perfectionists, they might seem outwardly calm but tend to be a bag of nerves within. Type A are also artistic and are sometimes shy and sensitive too. A positives are good workers, who get the job done, but tend to feel a sense of superiority over others, this can lead to power struggles and greed. Try to keep this in check.

Type A Negative
People with the Type A negative blood group, are said to be open and honest, and very outgoing. Type A negatives are also known to be very professional in their dealings. They appear more cool, calm and collected than they are often feeling inside, they tend to be very good at covering their anger with passive aggressive behaviour. Type A negatives are sometimes very talented in their field and love to compete, they live to conquer anyone in the same field and bring them down. On the surface they can seem very popular, but dig a little and you could find very shallow friendships, as one too many have felt their wrath or their knife in their backs. Try to avoid being so ruthless in your dealings, and you will be much happier in life.

Type B Positive
People with Type B positive blood group, are strong willed, goal oriented, they always finish whatever they start, whether in perfect timing or in excellent fashion. People with Type B positive blood group, always seem to find their own way in life. Not ones to band together, they are very much out for themselves and what they can gain from others. If not careful can tend to use things like religion to control others. Try to think more of others than yourself sometimes, this can help you find a sense of peace.

Type B Negative
People with Type B negative blood group, are very strong willed, can think of many goals, but don't often finish what they start, this can lead to them feeling like a failure at times. People with Type B negative blood group tend to shy away from the limelight, yet when they develop a passion about something they will take centre stage to fight for what they believe in. The stubbornness they show can often cause them more harm than good, and at times they just need to admit they are wrong.

Type AB Positive
Those with a Type AB positive blood group, are an interesting lot indeed, though they are trustworthy and honest, its been said that they seem to have a split personality! Type AB blood group like helping people, they are outgoing and confident but they can be shy too. Sometimes greedy, sometimes good workers. This group are hard to judge.

Type AB Negative
Those with a Type AB negative blood group, as AB positives these are an interesting lot indeed, but even more so, as they also have some of the negative traits. Though they are trustworthy and honest, its been said that they seem to have a split personality! Type AB blood group like helping people, they are outgoing and confident but they can be shy too. They often have a very confused and chaotic inner voice, which can sometimes make them contradict themselves.

Which is the vainest blood group of them all?

The winner is O positive.

In the past statistics showed that B positive, followed by B negatives to be the most vain of all the blood groups. These were short term statistics and now the research has had time to mature.

After a longer term the results have now changed. Now clearly leading is O positive, closely followed by A positive, A negative, then a big gap followed by B negative, O negative, AB positive, B positive and lastly, who are the least vain of all, is AB negative. This shows how statistics can be deceptive if not given long enough to mature.

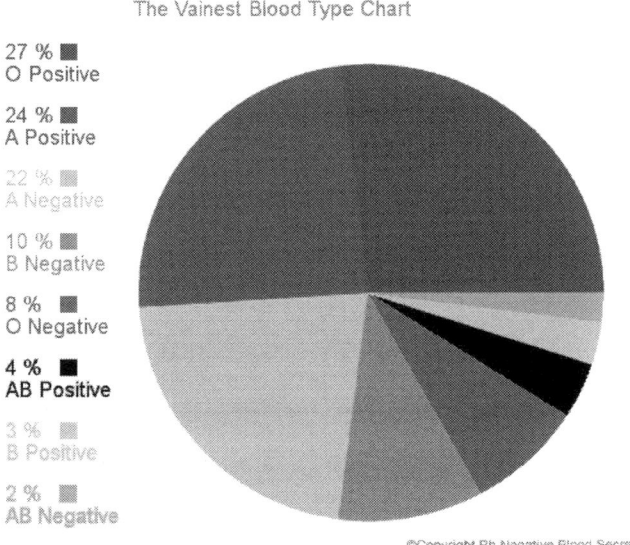

Secrets of the Serpent Bloodline - The Unveiling of Profound Esoteric Mysteries

However, seeing as O positive is the most common blood group, these results could be seen as not really fair, especially as AB negative is the most rare, and came lowest in the results.

So in reality the rare blood group A negative which scored very highly, could actually be the most vain.

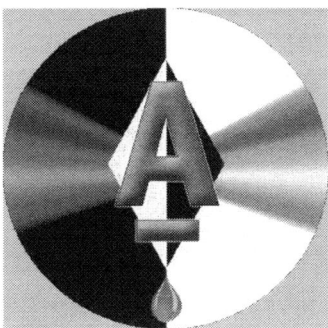

What is your blood group? Do you think you are vain? Maybe you think this article is about you?

Original Hair, Eyes and Skin Colour By Blood Group

To help explain why we look the way we do. Please remember that because of how mixed most people have now become, not everyone is going to fit perfectly into these. The only group who are consistent in looks would be those families who have been consistent in only breeding within their own pure group of O negatives only, as these are the only blood group that isn't mixed with others through genetic engineering.

O Rh D Negative - The Most Ancient Blood Group.

Light Strawberry Blonde - Dark Auburn hair colour, with all the shades in-between. Babies can be born with white hair which turns more of a copper auburn shade as they get older. Babies can also be born with pale copper, turning more into a medium auburn as they get older.

Hair can be wavy or very curly, but rarely completely straight.

Skin colour is always white, from a very pale snow white through to a pale pink or peach.

Eyes are blue, grey or rarely violet. Because O negatives normally have mood eyes they can change to any colour, but these are the normal colours.

O Rh D Positive - The Second Most Ancient Blood Group.

The first genetic experiment of the O negatives mixing their genes with those of ancient simians created these people.

Hair colour can vary greatly and can be more or less any colour, from blonde straight through to black woolly hair.

Skin colour is also the most diverse in this group, from pale white through to black.

Eyes can be any colour at all.

The biggest effect on the looks of these people is dependent upon where they live in the world. The ones who were placed in hot countries evolved to have black skin and wooly hair, the ones in cold climate will have remained pale skinned. The black skin was needed for these people because without the protection of the hair that simians have all over their bodies, they would easily burn in the Sun, so black skin, despite what we are told, is part of evolution for those living in climates that required it.

A Rh Positives Blood Group.

These were a later experiment of the Neanderthals, taking some of their own genes and mixing it with chimpanzee genetics. They became the Homo Heidelbergensis, then with more experiments and breeding they became the Cro-Magnons.

Straight light blonde through to dark brown hair is dominant in this species.

Skin can be very pale to light olive.

Eyes are predominately green/hazel.

Because these were placed mainly in Europe they retained pale hair and skin.

A Rh D Negative Blood Group.

These are generally the same as A Rh positive in looks, but can also have some of the O negative looks as they are carriers of the O negative genetics.

B Rh D Positive Blood Group.

These were a results of experiments taking Neanderthal genes and mixing them with those of gorillas.

They became Homo Erectus, and still in some remote parts of Africa full blooded Homo Erectus can still be found.

They have black hair and black skin, and paler brown skin in some areas, and in other areas they became oriental looking. The genetic differences happened over long periods of time, creating the different looks. However 'Native' American Indians today, still very much look like an oriental Asians.

Because gorilla skin is very black, most of this line are very black, however with experimentation and genetic engineering some became paler skinned. Some Neanderthals also chose to breed with these creating paler skinned ones through the generations.

They have brown eyes only.

B Rh D Negative Blood Group.

These are generally the same as B Rh positive in looks, but can also have some of the O neg looks as they are carriers of the O neg genetics.

AB Positive and Negative Blood Groups.

These are the most mixed of all and can acquire looks from any of the above groups.

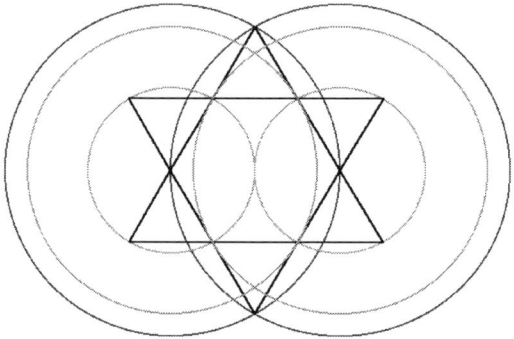

Secrets of the Serpent Bloodline - The Unveiling of Profound Esoteric Mysteries

Chapter 2

The Divine Feminine Returns

For thousands of years patriarchal religions have told us that men came first and that women came from a man. That men are complete and women are animals, and second class citizens. That women are incapable of being Divine, or being Priests.

However, before we had patriarchy, we had matriarchy. All the ancient tribes were led by women, women were the first Shamanistic spiritual leaders, who taught dream analysis and how to use herbs to cure aliments. They were also completely in tune with nature. Their bodies following the 13 month cycles of the Moon, menstruating in the dark Moon, and at the most fertile in the full Moon.

They taught how to open your mind to amazing experiences using psychotropic drugs, mainly magic mushrooms. This led to mushroom adoration in some tribes, as part of their various nature worship activities.

The Priestesses taught about the different seasons, the movement of the Sun, Moon and the planets. They could predict when things were going to happen, by closely following these teachings.

These women would produce female clones of themselves using parthenogenesis. Special ceremonies would be carried out to achieve this under the full Moon. The women knew that they were the most fertile during the full Moon and so called it - being impregnated by the Moon Goddess.

Celebrations would happen at certain times of the year, mainly Beltane, as this was supposed to be the most fertile time of the year. Not only in nature, but their own bodies, which are part of nature.

Females do have a prostate and are capable of ejaculation.

See http://en.wikipedia.org/wiki/Skene's_gland

Also see http://davidpratt.info/sex2.htm

The Virgin Birth

The first male was born after a mutation on one strand of the sex chromosome.

Humans have 23 pairs of chromosomes. 22 of these are equally matched. The exception, pair number 23, the sex chromosomes, are matched in the female (XX) and mismatched in the male (XY). We say mismatched because the Y-chromosome is shorter than its matching X-chromosome. The Y-chromosome has been called the male chromosome and the X-chromosome has been called the female chromosome. These names are not completely accurate descriptions but they have found their way into common usage. Because the Y-chromosome is shorter than the X-chromosome and is found only in males, some genes present on the mismatched X-chromosome are present without any matching alleles. Thus, genetic defects on the Y-chromosome affect only males.

Females have complete and matching DNA strands, however males don't.

Enlightenment

Because women have two complete strands, they can become balanced and in tune with nature very easily. When trained their bodies again naturally line up with Luna cycles. They can easily learn how to open all their energy centres (chakras) and become enlightened.

Unfortunately most women have forgotten how to do this, because the teachings have been purposely hidden from us. It is also easier for women of certain ancient genetics to activate this within themselves, as they can easily tune into their genetic memories. Other women will struggle more.

A male however, is missing some of his DNA, and to activate this within himself he needs the help of a Priestess (a woman with fully open chakras). The Priestess is trained in Tantric arts and knows how to pass the energy on to a man under certain conditions and the male has had training in how to receive this energy. Once he has received this energy, this replenishes the shortened strand, as the Kundalini energy goes up his spine and activates his pineal gland. Again, men of certain genetics can do this much easier than others.

Religions like the Catholics will say that women don't have chakras, and that is why they can't be Priests. Again complete lies and betrayal of all women. Men all start out as female in the womb, only when the mutation occurs do they turn into males. All humans have chakras, and if women didn't have them men wouldn't be able to activate theirs either.

The Grail Bloodline

After many years of males being born, some of them decided they did not like women having all this power over them. They were unenlightened, and didn't want to be enlightened by women, they began to resent women, and became brutal and war like. They raped the Priestesses, and stole all their teachings and destroyed all evidence of it, so that women would no longer be able to know the truth about their own bodies and the Divine qualities of them.

Patriarchy was born. The men took the teachings and became the Priests. They suppressed women, as they didn't want them to ever find out the truth about enlightenment, and the male's need to receive it from a woman.

However, some kept the true teachings by passing this information on by word of mouth to their children, and their children also passed it on. These teachings became the underground stream of knowledge. They secretly venerated the Goddess, and gained amazing powers and enlightenment. If any of these secret Orders were discovered they were destroyed by the Priests. Those who were passing these truths were hunted down and burnt as Witches and heretics.

Some families still display their secret knowledge in symbolism in their family coats of arms. Parthenogenesis is shown in symbol form as fish, mermaids, dragons, salamanders, snakes and lizards.

Symbolism of Goddess Worship

The Priests made sure no one would dare to worship the Goddess, by demonising everything to do with it. The feminine side was seen as left, so no one was allowed to use their left hand. Even today the Italian word for left is sinistra (sinister).

Lucifer was used as reference to Goddess worship as it secretly meant Venus the morning star.

Venus traces a perfect pentacle across the ecliptic sky every eight years. When our ancient ancestors, 'Serpent Bloodline' who were Gnostics, discovered this Venus and her pentacle became symbols of perfection, beauty and love. The Greeks used her eight year cycle to organise their Olympic games. Indeed the very first symbol used for the games was a pentacle. This was later changed by Christianity.

If you draw a pentagram, the lines automatically divide themselves into segments according to the Divine Proportion. The ratios of the line segments in a pentacle all equal PHI. This is the reason the symbol is associated with the Divine, beauty and perfection. The Sacred Geometry of nature, again is all about the Goddess, Mother nature, who created us all.

Satan - also another name for the Goddess, represented as Sirius the Dog Star, that represents Isis.

What about the mention of other Gods?

Gods and prophets throughout the ages have been created to represent whichever age we happen to be in and they are all based on the original Astrotheology teachings of the Goddess.

Each Astrological Age brings with it a new era where major changes happen on the Earth.

Sumer, Mesopotamia era was in Gemini, this is why we have the stories about twins or brothers (Enki & Enlil), one good, one bad, who battled to control the Earth.

These Gods and prophets are all allegory for Astrotheology.
http://en.wikipedia.org/wiki/Astrological_age

The Priests wrote the bible, and myths all based round these. But then told people it is evil to look to the stars for answers, they did this to keep you dumb and unaware, while they used these lies to control everyone.

The Divine Feminine is returning, and we will at last have the truth revealed. At last we can have equality and harmony, where women no longer have to be suppressed and men no longer need to feel threatened by women, because we will work together at bringing balance.

Female Bonds & Intuition

Why do women have such strong bonds with their children and husbands?

The Mother of a child takes some of their DNA when pregnant with them, which is why when you have a child with a man, you are also taking his DNA into you and becoming part of his family. This DNA stays in you and is your genetic connection to your children. This is why a Mother can know when something is wrong with their child. They say it is instinct or intuition, it is the genetic connection.

The same is also true for the man the woman has had children with, because she has some of his genes, it is the same. A man can not take the woman's genes this way, which is why a man never has as strong a bond with his wife, as she does him. Most men would move on very quickly if their wife died, but how many female widows ever move on and marry again if they loved their husbands? I would make a guess on not many.

Cannabis - The Sacred Holy Herb

Since marijuana affects the chemical centre of the brain, it changes the hormone levels in the body. In men it decreases the level of testosterone. This could sometimes lead to the enlarging of breasts. In women it increases testosterone. Could this be the missing part of the parthenogenesis puzzle?

Maybe this was used during the ceremonies to change the chemical balance within the females at certain times of their cycle, and this would trigger the process? Then if they continued to use this during their pregnancy it would increase the testosterone in the foetus, therefore leading to a mutation of the X chromosome to a Y, leading to the birth of the first male.

Baphomet symbolises cannabis, the Templars venerate it.

As a man has to activate his feminine side for the Great Work, having cannabis will help do this, as it reduces his testosterone poisoning.

Atbash cipher, was used in translating the word Baphomet, it transposed into the Greek word "Sophia", which means "Wisdom" and is also synonymous with "Goddess".

Baphomet = Goddess & Cannabis = Enlightenment = Gnosis & Sophia.

There is more on the true origin of Bafomet in Liber III.

Chapter 3

Ancient Shamans

Who were the first Shamans?

The first Shaman's appeared in the Tigris, Mesopotamia area. These people evolved separately from the other two main species of humans, in old accounts by the other humanoids they were called the Gods, the Giants and the Watchers. They were actually Neanderthals.

These Shamans had a dream culture which was when spirituality was first being discovered.

All religions are based around seven different things:

- Mushroom worship
- Tree/Nature worship
- Fertility
- Elements – Fire, Water, Earth, Air
- Astrotheology - Planets
- Serpent
- Ancestors

Most religions are a good mix of all of them. The evolutionary origin of religions refers to the emergence of religious behaviour during the course of human evolution. When humans first became religious remains unknown, but there is credible evidence of religious behaviour from the Middle Palaeolithic era (300-500 thousand years ago) and possibly earlier.

During human evolution, the hominid brain tripled in size, peaking 500,000 years ago. Much of the brain's expansion took place in the neocortex. This part of the brain is involved in processing higher order cognitive functions that are necessary for human religiosity. The neocortex is responsible for self consciousness, language and emotion. The relative neocortex size of any species correlates with the level of social complexity of the particular species. The neocortex size correlates with a number of social variables that include social group size and complexity of mating behaviours. In chimpanzees the neocortex occupies 50% of the brain, whereas in modern humans it occupies 80% of the brain.

Robin Dunbar thinks that the critical event in the evolution of the neocortex took place in archaic homo sapiens about 500 thousand years ago. His study indicates that only after the speciation event is the neocortex sufficiently large enough to process complex social phenomena such as language and religion. The study is based on a regression analysis of neocortex size plotted against a number of social behaviours of living and extinct hominids.

So what could have caused this expansion?

This first occurred when our early ancestors discovered 'magic' mushrooms. They produce similar hallucinogenic-type effects to LSD when you eat them. The most common form is a species called psilocybe semilanceata or 'liberty cap', while the other more potent variety is amanita muscaria or 'fly agaric'.

Our ancestor would have come across these and other types of psychoactive as they were foraging for food. At first they won't have made the connection to the effects and what they just ate, however once they did, you can be sure they would have decided to worship these divine fungi. Evidence of this still remains today in our current religions, myths and traditions.

Toad stools and stories of pixies and fairies in the woods are in our tales and myths. And of course the whole Christmas traditions were first found in Germanic and Scandinavian origins. The tribe spiritual leaders would go into the forests on their reindeer sleighs and collect the magic mushrooms. He or she would choose a tree in the Sun and as he/she picked the mushrooms would leave them to dry in a pine tree, while they carried on collecting more. On returning to the village they would call round to see everyone and give them the mushrooms for their special ceremonies. So right there we now know the origins of the Christmas tree with things decorating it and Santa, calling round with the gifts of mushrooms for the special occasion.

You can find sacred mushroom symbolism and images in all kinds of religious art. From paintings and stained glass windows in churches, to the vestments of priests and bishops.

These mushrooms would have given the consumer some amazing spiritual experiences, as anyone who has taken them will know. Of course I am not saying everyone should run out and try it. Eating mushrooms you find yourself can be fatal, there are a lot of poisonous ones out there.

So eventually their minds would expand over time and I do believe this is the missing link in human evolution.

A dream culture was set up around this, and the mind expanded massively, these early red headed Gods with their mushroom cults and secret teachings were the spiritual guides to the other humanoids, and were taken as the Priestly caste, and later when patriarchy took hold they became the Priests of Aaron, during the emergence of the Jewish religion. However slowly the other species were taking over and imposing restrictions on the knowledge, to gain power.

Patriarchy tried to restrict the Neanderthal gene.

"Human societies everywhere on Earth have lived for thousands of years with gender roles. In fact humans have separated tasks between men and women ever since the stone age. Men went hunting or warring while women were gathering, taking care of the children or sewing clothes from animal skins. Hormones influence the specialisation of the brain. This is why men and women think and feel differently. Gender role division runs deep into our genes.

Gender equality is something that appeared in Northern Europe. Medieval Norse societies were already much more egalitarian, socially and sexually, than any other part of Europe at the time. Even though women's rights activism has now spread through most of the Western world and has reached other countries since (e.g. China, thanks to communism), the only societies where women can really aspire to act and be treated like the equal of men are only found in Nordic countries.

Now what is interesting is that Neanderthals did not practice gender role division, like Homo Sapiens. Both men and women went hunting together. Some specialists have argued that could be why Homo Sapiens ultimately got an advantage over Neanderthals, as women had spare time to make clothes, build tools or make pottery vessels, becoming technologically superior to their distant cousins.

If gender roles are genetically determined in modern humans, how come that out of all humans in the world some came to act differently, more like Neanderthals. Maybe a percentage of the Scandinavians have always behaved this way justly because they inherited the "gender equality" gene from Neanderthal. It does not mean at all that they are the modern Neanderthals, just that they inherited at least this gene. It only takes one accidental mating with a Neanderthal at one point to spread some of their genes through a Homo Sapiens population. If it is useful it survives natural selection, even if only locally.

There is overwhelming evidence that modern humans inherited at least some genes from Neanderthal. Maybe that it less than 0.1% of our genome, but it is there. Blue eyes and red hair could very well have come from Neanderthal too. Why not the gender equality gene ? I am not even arguing the existence of such a gene. It is evident from the archaeological evidence about the difference of lifestyle between Homo Sapiens and Neanderthal. It could not have been cultural. Some animals also have gene for gender equality (e.g. ducks), while others are genetically determined for role separation (e.g. lions).

Had gender equality been characteristic of many human societies on Earth for centuries, we could argue that the gene might have spread worldwide.

Secrets of the Serpent Bloodline - The Unveiling of Profound Esoteric Mysteries

However I think that this phenomenon is more limited to people of Scandinavian descent, who spread the gene through most of the Western world at varying levels with the Viking invasions. Gender equality is not so much cultural as genetic. Parts of Europe closely related to Scandinavia, be it the Baltic, the Netherlands or East England all have a higher tendency to gender equality. Conversely, the most genetically distant countries (Greece, Southern Italy) also have the most marked gender division."

From http://www.eupedia.com/forum/showthread.php?24893-Do-modern-Europeans-partly-descend-from-Neanderthal

MtDNA haplogroup H & U carry the Neanderthal gene which makes us want equality, this isn't a bad thing like he is trying to make out, it means we are balanced spiritual beings, and not half brained like Patriarchal Cro-Magnons.

Feminism has been used against us though. Now instead of one parent working and another staying at home to look after the children and everything there, now both have to go out to work just to survive. Something went wrong somewhere, it has been used to create more working slaves, more stress, and less time for us to think and work on ourselves spiritually.

He also goes on to say "Neanderthal blood would have passed through y-haplogroup I. I2a2 being strong in the Balkans, this is where you should look. E-V13 replaced a lot of older I lineages in the southern Balkans, but did marry with native women of haplogroup U4, U5, H1, H3, etc. The same is true in North Africa. All native men of European descent have been killed or made not to pass their Y-DNA, but over half of maternal lineages in northern Morocco and north-west Algeria are of European descent. Neanderthal genes can pass just as well through mothers as fathers. Y-DNA is only one side of the story. "

They stopped Haplogroups J & I men from breeding, and that is why we are so rare, and Rh negatives so rare, because they are the carriers of this blood.

The above is valuable research, it shows why Neanderthal men are so rare and have the Y DNA J and I, who were the Priests of Aaron, they were the shamans, the spiritual royalty, along with their mtDNA H and U wives.

Hugh Montgomery says:

"There are two Haplogroup J1 CMH lineages:

12-23-14-10-13-15-11-16-12-13-11-30

and

12-23-14-10-13-17-11-16-11-13-11-31

These are TRUE Priestly Jewish lineages

In "Cohen Modal Haplotype" (CMH) haplogroup J2

12-23-14-10-13-17-11-16-11-13-11-30

This is a Jewish lineage related to the CMH. There is no question J2 is Semitic and there is little question that it is Jewish -- though those who have it might not, today, be followers of the Jewish religion."

J2 info here http://en.wikipedia.org/wiki/Y-chromosomal_Aaron

Source: Extended Y chromosome haplotypes resolve multiple and unique lineages of the Jewish Priesthood by M.F. Hammer, D.M. Behar, T.M. Karafet, F.L. Mendez, B. Hallmark, T. Erez, L.A. Zhivotovsky, S. Rosset, K. Skorecki, Hum Genet, published online 8 August 2009.

Southern J haplogroup and the northern I haplogroup both descended from IJ and are therefore closely related, closer in fact than either is to haplogroup R.

I and J are almost the same and at times the experts have difficulty in deciding whether a sample is one or the other.

They may also interchange.

Nevertheless the experts have decided to differentiate the two.

I is found in Scandinavia and North Germany as well as in the British Isles mainly in former Viking areas.

I is also found in Sardinia, and Croatia and elsewhere in the Balkans.

J is found amongst Arabs, Jews (ca.30%) and Mediterranean Peoples.

As we said I and J in some respects may be considered almost the same.

I is the oldest haplogroup in Europe...It is thought to have arrived from the Middle East as haplogroup IJ ....and developed into haplogroup I .. Nowadays haplogroup I accounts for 10 to 45% of the population in most of Europe. It is divided in four main subclades.

The Jewish or Aram Connection of I2* and I2?

Haplogroups I1 is associated with Northern Europe and I2 with the south.

I2* is close to the breakoff point with I1 and Ken Nordvedt suggests it may be specifically Jewish, Aramaic, or Hebraic.

Sasson Margaliot suggests all I2 may hail ultimately from Aram which he defines as Armenia, Georgia and Turkey.

This brings represented countries to: Iran, Georgia, Armenia, Turkey, Jordan. And as well we have Mediterranean examples from Greece to Iberia; eastern Europe, as well as western Europe. Only Scandinavia is very weak in representation. There is a strong Jewish cluster. Are most all I2* ultimately connected with various diasporas of the Jews? I don't know, but it is a possibility. Evidence in the negative is that variance ages for some clades of I2* look older than Jewish history.

If the Picts (also Britons) had really been related to the ancient Hebrews then they should exhibit either directly the same DNA haplogroup as the Jews/Hebrews (typical groups are "J", "J2", or "E3b", etc.) or more likely a typical "cousin" haplogroup - if they had been genetic cousins - and the closest is the "I" haplogroup and its derivatives ("I1b" and "I2b"). And indeed - the Clan Chieftains, those who claim, based on their traditions, their Pictish descent exhibit an unusually high percentage of "I1b" and "I2b" haplogroups, up to 20%, although their overall concentration in Scotland is rather low. The small overall percentage would indicate a very ancient origin, "flooded" / "overwhelmed" in later centuries by the Gaelic, Viking, Norman, Danish, and Anglo-Saxon "invasion" (a mix of the "R1b", "R1a", "I", and "I1a" haplogroups).

Yet there is another factor which contributed to "blurring" the representative genetic map of the old Scotland - a massive emigration from the Highlands, especially the Chieftains and other nobility in an attempt to save their lives when the Clan systems was supposed to be "wiped out" - and the old Picts were especially the target. Why..?? They usually were the "carriers" of the old traditions of freedom in Scotland (Declaration of Arbroath, religious independence, etc. etc.).

"I2b1 (M223) has a peak in Germany and another in eastern Sweden, but also appears in Russia, Greece, Italy and around the Black Sea. Haplogroup I2b1 has been found in over 4% of the population only in Germany, the Netherlands, Belgium, Denmark, England (not including Wales or Cornwall), Scotland, and the southern tips of Sweden and Norway in Northwest Europe; the provinces of Normandy, Maine, Anjou, and Perche in northwestern France; the province of Provence in southeastern France; the regions of Tuscany, Umbria, and Latium in Italy; and Moldavia and the area around Russia's Ryazan Oblast and Republic of Mordovia in Eastern Europe. Of historical note, both haplogroups I1 and I2b appear at a low frequency in the historical regions of Bithynia and Galatia in Turkey, possibly descendants of the ancient Thracian tribes which are historically recorded to have immigrated to those parts of Anatolia from the Balkans (Mysians, Thyni, Bithyni and Phrygians)."

http://en.wikipedia.org/wiki/Haplogroup_I2_(Y-DNA)

J2 and I2 are basically the same, and definitely come from the same Neanderthal roots, the very first shamans, spiritual royalty. The female lines are mtDNA H and U.

So despite the disinformation about Neanderthals and them being extinct, they live on in us, all Europeans and some Asians carry their genes, and those from certain families who have kept their bloodline pure, are more so.

Y DNA I2b1 – More Research & Notes

R1b DNA is NOT the spiritual royalty line. I have been saying this for years, I am direct line from the High Stewards and my Father is I2b1. The Douglass clan site and Stewart sites all say the DNA for our families is R1b, this is a lie, and it is because it is the most common and it pleases the most people, and it means more people will get tested and pretend they are of the bloodline.. nope you are being conned. Male line is I2b1 or J2, no other. Here are some who are trying to explain to the R1bs but they won't listen of course - all taken from the Stewart DNA Yahoo Group:

"Belinda,

What you are missing is that R1B1* anything at some level, are all connected. You may have to go back a long way but they will connect. Now they all can't be Stewarts can they? Common sense tells us that some of them had to assume the name.

I am afraid you have snared yourself, the I2b1 Stewarts can demonstrate that they are all related, one common ancestor. They have low recurrence of surnames outside of Stewart, R1B1 does not. Some of the surnames that do show up on the I2b1 tests I have seen are all associated with the real Stewarts. One of the things that are expected is that there will be an occurrence of Non matching surnames. But one of the things that also would be expected with a family such as the Stewarts is non-matching surnames with connection to the family. The Stewarts often changed their name and are connected to such families as the Douglass, Napier, Lennox (Same as Napier), Menteith, Fleming, Maxwell, Grahams, Kennedy, etc,..etc,. Some of these names should show up as close matches. There is an I2B1 Stewart who has such matches, explain why?

Dr. Samuel Stuart"

"Belinda,

Problem is we are not talking about modern times, we are talking about over a thousand years ago, I2b1 was dominate. So it really doesn't matter what you find there now, does it? Was Flaald born in 1980?

I will tell you what gave me the Idea about the I2b1 Stewarts. The examination of the available I2b1 DNA, by Joe Anderson Phd. M.D. Associated Grad study Genetic research. I asked him to look at some stuff and he did, that is what he told me.

Mutation rates are far more varied then you obviously think they are. You can have huge drift in just 4 generations. Although DNA can be stable for hundreds of years. A mutation rate of 3 or more, every one hundred years is in the realm of possibilities. You have not read about the studies the Chinese have done that is obvious.

I have reviewed your theory from Ryk's site, as well as here. I have read most of your old post's. You seem to go in any direction the wind blows, as long as its your direction.

I also know that the descendant you are talking about from Alexander 4th is your relation, isn't he Belinda? So if you were proved wrong you wouldn't be a Stewart would you? You have no creditability or at the very least are very, very bias. Doesn't leave room for objectivity, does it?

I will tell Dr. Anderson you said he is wrong about I2b1, because you have a preferred theory. May I tell him what your degree is in? Mine is in Anthropology.

Last this is supposed to be about Stewart DNA in general. Not just R1b1*, *which you spend all your time on and put for the promotion of your theory for, dismissing everything else. When someone brings up something that doesn't agree, they are attacked and called names.*

Bottom line, you have no proof, end of story.

Dr. Samuel Stuart"

"**Four reasons why the I2B1 are descended from the High Stewards**

There have been many things said to me over the last month such as I am arrogant, mistaken, that I have not proven anything (even though I have), that the balance of evidence is against me (in spite of a lack of evidence to prove that), and that I'm argumentative and disrespectful (since when is providing proof disrespectful and argumentative). The word genuflection was used and I assure you I do not worship my family on bended knee. Many of you have said that you do not care if you are descended from the High Stewards but your reactions say otherwise. I must say the idea of digging up my ancestors just so people who have no proof of relation to them can see if they are related does not sit well with me or others. All of you should be working toward what this project was supposed to be about, finding your connections to each other and were your families come from. Not trying to prove that you are descended from the High Stewards. If your names were Smith something tells me that this project would be working towards its goal, instead you spend your time arguing and saying that you have proven that you are descended from the High Stewards, when you have proven NOTHING! All I have been trying to do is present my information. When I do though, I am told I am wrong. Nobody wants to tell me how, just that I'm wrong. Well, when I started my Family history project some years ago I set out to prove it wrong as I believed it was all B.S., as every Stewart has stories. I was unable to prove otherwise and nobody else has been able to prove otherwise either. So I would like to present my information and evidence of my descent from King Robert II one more time for the benefit of everyone but especially for the Stewarts in the I2B1 haplotype and perhaps this will make it a little clearer.

#1. My family History and Documents which can be found at www.theroyalhouseofstewart.com

#2. There are other Stewarts who can connect to the branch of Minto, although they lack the one document that absolutely proves their connection (There was a will that laid out the family descent but it was lost in the archives). There are many other records that indicate that they are from this line of Stewarts, including a family history written in 1807 and even George Edson, editor of the SCM, also states that they are undoubtedly from the Stewarts of Minto, and their DNA is the I2B1 haplotype. The Minto Stewarts are KNOWN to be from the High Stewards, again, not assumed but known.

#3. I can show how the Napier Family, who matches my DNA, connects to the Stewarts. Their Family history is documented to 1634. This history states that they were directly descended from John Napier 7th of Merchiston who was a mathematician and the inventor of Logarithms. The Following information about the Napier family comes from the Scots peerage.

John Napier 7th of Merchiston had 12 children, and his eighth born child by his 2nd wife Anne (Agnes) Chisholm, Daughter of Sir James Chisholm of Cromlix had a daughter named Margaret Napier. Margaret Napier married James Stewart 11th of Rosyth in 1606. The Napier to whom I match with in DNA is the descendant of a John Napier who was in all indication the child of the Stewart of Rosyth family (Grandson of John Napier 7th of Merchiston) and took the name Napier, his mother's name. This matches to their family history of being descended from John Napier 7th of Merchiston (only through a daughter) and explains why their DNA matches mine. The Stewarts of Rosyth were known, not just assumed but KNOWN, positively to be of descent from the High Stewards.

#4. The Stewarts in the I2B1 Haplotype group form a very definable tree. This is not the case with the Stewarts in the R1B1 haplotype as many of them are related simply by the fact that they share the same Haplotype. This does not tie them to the High Stewards. It is only that they are related by Haplotype and the relation to each other may go back to time long before the Stewarts were ever in Scotland. Being that the R1B1 is the most common Haplotype in the U.K. and shared by more surnames than you can count, it is very likely that a large number of these Stewarts would not be descended from the high Stewards and would be among the many that took the name for varying reasons. I might add that history disagrees with the assumption that most Stewarts alive today descend from the High Stewards; the only real way the theory that Belinda Dettmann came up with works is if most are descended.
So in summation if someone can show me how I am wrong, I would like to know. I would also like to know who among you has as much documented evidence and is able to show how each different surname match on your DNA connects to your family. So, unless of course you completely dismiss my family history and my DNA (as is continually done even though no-one has any proof otherwise.) then you know that the so called "origin" for the High Stewards is I2b1.

These four examples presented here are more evidence, for all, that the I2B1 Haplotype are indeed Stewarts, the proof is in the pudding, so to speak.

Douglas Stewart"

So as you can see, I am not the only one who knows this, so why are the R1bs so insistent that they are the true line?

Merovingian Royalty

The Merovingian Royals are a popular talking point. A lot of things up on the net, have some truth. Though remember it is hidden in allegory. Sea Monsters?? Just think about it.

When researching Royalty, especially in modern times you are researching for those who were put up as leaders by the real 'Spiritual Royalty', those who have the bloodline that has been kept pure and the knowledge passed down through generations of their families. They can trace their lines back to the Aaron Priests and much further back.

The Royals of old were spiritual royalty. Then the Roman Catholic Church was set up by those who are not of the bloodline, and they used their power to enthrone Kings and Queens who would be compliant to their wishes and their greed, lust for power and land. If one of the royal heads didn't do as they wanted, they would poison them, or remove them in some other way.

The Royals were given their power by the Priests, and still do to this day.

So if you are searching for true Spiritual Royalty, look to the Gnostics - the Bishops or (Tau) are the ones carrying the secret spiritual teachings. That is what the Mitre is, a crown. They have had to hide, because the RC Church was determined to wipe them all out and force everyone to go through their Church for spiritual teachings. The RC Church still dress in the robes and ceremonial wear of the Priests of Aaron, who in turn got their robes from the Goddess, and all the clothing, symbols and sacraments have hidden meanings. They put it right in your faces, without you even knowing the hidden truth. The Roman Catholic Church is purposely withholding these teachings from you.

The spiritual royalty can be traced through DNA and blood types. O Rh negative is the most pure blood and Y DNA lines are Haplogroups J and I. mtDNA haplogroups H and U. These lines can be traced back through Pictish Royalty, Merovingians, Cohen Priests and Egypt Royalty.

There is so much more, but know this, you have been lied to, you have been programmed. Some people don't want to know the truth, because it isn't easy to break through all the lies and false ego programmed into us since the day we are born. But it is possible.

Slowly the teachings have been released all over the world, in many forms and though most through allegory, many set up as 'new' teachings when really they are very ancient, some is made plain and easy for anyone seeking to understand, but not fully, as science, as of yet can not explain these things. Not in this cycle. Those of the bloodline can, and slowly release more and more of the teachings.

So why not just come out with the truth? Tell everyone?

The teachings had to be kept hidden, to survive. Look what happened to the Templars and Cathars? Look how many lies have been told about them since? History is always made by those who win. They can demonise anyone they want to, and call a Saint anyone they want to.

The real spiritual work for you only truly starts when you are initiated into the Mysteries. However, YOU are the only one who can lead yourself to the truth. And the first step to that is realising that everything we have been told about history is a lie, our origins, religions, traditions. You have to allow yourself to put aside everything you already think you know and let go of the false ego, and when you finally really do mean it, your Higher Self will start to guide you to the truth.

Melusine

I don't think this book would be complete without mentioning the famous Melusine. Stories about her and her bloodline are deeply embedded into the tales of the 'new' royals. The royal families of modern times are all mixed. This becomes even more obvious when you see the Salin Laws (deeply patriarchal) brought in by Clovis I, who was the first King of the Franks. The Franks and Saxon lines mixed and formed a strong Cro-Magnon patriarchal line. But they started to lose their magick and intuition. They wanted more of the bloodline families genes.

Enter Pressyne, mother of Melusine, she was a female of the pure Serpent Bloodline, a full blood. Elynas, the King of Albany married Pressyne, in order to make the bloodline purer, and pick up some 'magick' from the bloodline families. They tell tales of her being a fairy who is a Dragon or Serpent, depicted as a Mermaid. They had three daughters together, Melusine being one of the most well known. She married Raymond of Poitou, France and so the legends go that those who descend from this line are from the Devil.

There are many tales about Melusine, you can look them up for yourself. But they are all allegory for the pure blooded females of the Serpent Bloodline, that the mixed royals are very proud to descend from.

The males in this mixed royal line are Y DNA haplogroup G2a, a cousin line to the Serpent lines, but not 100% pure, but much purer than the R1b lines.

Neanderthal V Cro-Magnon

Are you more Neanderthal than Cro-Magnon?

- Neanderthals have bigger, heavier bones, wider feet, wider knees, wider hips.
- Neanderthals have veins that run through top of arm, rather than through the middle.
- Neanderthals have O neg blood, Cro-Magnon A Pos.
- Neanderthal have red hair, Cro-Magnon Blonde.
- Neanderthal tend to be left handed, Cro-Magnon right handed.
- Neanderthal females tend to have large breasts and precocious puberty.
- Neanderthals tend to have savant abilities, dyslexia and dyscalculia.
- Neanderthals tend to have longer bodies than Cro-Magnon, and shorter arms and legs.
- Neanderthals have lower body temperature than Cro-Magnons. The world is set up for Cro-Magnons and Sapiens, which is why those of us with a lot of Neanderthal genes are effected so negatively by vaccinations and medications.
- Neanderthals tend to have above average IQ, though some might struggle at school because school teaches you to learn the way Cro-Magnons and Sapiens do. Rather than the Neanderthal way, who prefer to learn by doing, rather than reading and repeating.
- Neanderthals tend to be artistic and musical. Cro-Magnons are more planned and structured.
- Neanderthals are free with feelings and are very open. Cro-Magnons tend to keep their feelings to themselves and can be seen as secretive.
- Neanderthals prefer circular thinking, Cro-Magnons prefer linear thinking.
- Neanderthals have very big round eyes, Cro-Magnon eyes are smaller.
- Neanderthal men have very strong muscular arms.
- Neanderthals love water and feel at home in it, Cro-Magnons are usually OK in water, but Homo Erectus struggle to swim.
- Neanderthals have a large gap on their jaw, behind the third molar, Cro-Magnons don't.

These are extremes of the two, because most of us are very mixed we could show bits from both.

I am sure more needs adding to the list, so it will expand in time.

Ramses II

All over the internet many sites claim that Ramses II had B negative blood, they do this without any kind of proof and merely copied and pasted from someone else's mistranslation. It has since been copy and pasted on to hundreds of blogs. This article is to put this myth to bed once and for all.

Seeing as Ramses II is a direct line back to my own family it shocked and annoyed me to find people making the claims that Ramses II has B type blood, as this is the blood of Homo-Erectus lines, not our Neanderthal lines, which are O negative. So I did my own research and found the source of this disinformation.

The study on the Mummy of Ramses II was done by some French Scientists in 1985, who produced their results in a paper:

La Momie de Ramsès II: Contribution Scientifique à l'Égyptologie (1985). The results showed that Ramses II of Egypt had red hair and was HLA-B27+. HLA-B27+ causes Ankylosing Spondylitis, Psoriatic Arthritis and many other auto-immune diseases.

However in a general news report about this it was mixed up with the following research - Jean Bernard, who was Director of *the Research Institute of leukemia and blood diseases,* President of the *Academy of Sciences* and a member of *the French Academy,* in his book *Blood and History* (1983), shows that the blood test used to characterize the populations, suggesting the passage where the mummy of Nakht:

The blood groups, hemoglobins, enzymes, remain the same (except for rare exceptions) from birth to death. Beyond death. An examination of the mummy of Egyptian Nakht weaver, who lived in the time of Ramses II, showed that the blood belonged to the weaver B.

This doesn't translate very well, but he isn't talking about Ramses II having B blood, he is talking about the Weaver, a servant, of his time having B blood.

Untranslated it reads: Les groupes sanguins, les hémoglobines, les enzymes, restent les mêmes (sauf rarissimes exceptions) de la naissance à la mort. Au-delà de la mort. L'examen de la momie du tisserand égyptien Nakht, qui vivait du temps de Ramsès II, a montré que **le tisserand appartenait au groupe sanguin B**. (The Weaver belonged to the blood group B).

You can find this information here:
http://www.ankhonline.com/revue/histoire_afrique_acquis_recherche_ankh.htm

You can also find out about the weaver here:
http://tim-theegyptians.blogspot.com/2011/03/coffin-of-weaver-nakht.html

This is why is always important to check your sources before copy and pasting.

Ramses III

Some sites are reporting that, based on some mutations that have been revealed, Ramses III haplogroup is I2b, which would make sense, seeing as he has the red hair gene and HLA-B27 antigen, which is found in those with O Rh negative blood and this haplotype. His mtDNA is H, which is also no surprise.

However, other sites are now starting to claim that:

"Based on his 13 STR markers tested, the probabilities are that he belonged to haplogroup E1b1a (aka E-V38, the Black African branch), although there is a faint possibility that it is E1b1b (E-M215, the Northeast African and Mediterranean branch)."

Why would they be implying he is haplogroup E? Other than their need, yet again, to prove that everyone is 'out of Africa' and make the old claim that the Pharaohs were black.

The mutations that have been made available are not complete, but when put in a DNA predictor they come out as I2b.

"From the values posted, Whit Athey's Haplogroup Predictor suggests (99.0% probability; equal priors) an I2b haplogroup (FTDNA) also called I2a2" (ISOGG)

So now as the ignorant spread disinformation around the web, some of us know the truth.

Akhenaten

Akhenaten was the first in the line of Cro-Magnon infiltrators in Egypt who attempted to wipe out all forms of Goddess worship and force everyone to worship a male God and the Sun disk only.

What is clear is that he was Cro-Magnon, and not pure Neanderthal like Ramses. King Tut's blood type was A2 with antigen MN. A2 is a much rarer subgroup of A. It was once the sole provenance of European populations, having its highest frequency in the Scandinavian lands. This fits perfectly with him being half Neanderthal, a mixed Cro-Magnon.

But our families knew what to do, they gained their trust and secretly worked their way back up through the military and as a High Priests of Amun (basically same thing as RC Church these days) and eventually regained power in the 19th Dynasty when Ramesses I gained back the title of King, his Father was Seti.

He and his wife Queen Tia set about restoring the old ways. The 19th Dynasty were much loved and respected. Eventually though through war, corruption and infiltration the High Priests of Amun gained full control of the whole of Egypt, and the true spiritual royalty were forced to move on. The great era of Egypt was over, as Amun-Ra worship took over completely, and still does today in the form of the Roman Catholic Church & Freemasonry.

While not regarded as a dynasty, the High Priests of Amun at Thebes were nevertheless of such power and influence that they were effectively the rulers of Upper Egypt from 1080 to c.943 BC, after this period their influence declined. By the time Herihor was proclaimed as the first ruling High Priest of Amun in 1080 BC--in the 19th Year of Ramesses XI—the Amun priesthood exercised an effective stranglehold on Egypt's economy.

The Amun priests owned two-thirds of all the temple lands in Egypt and 90 percent of her ships plus many other resources. Consequently, the Amun priests were as powerful as Pharaoh, if not more so. One of the sons of the High Priest Pinedjem I - would eventually assume the throne and rule Egypt for almost half-a-decade as pharaoh Psusennes I - while the Theban High Priest Psusennes III - would take the throne as king Psusennes II--the final ruler of the 21st Dynasty.

Psychopaths

Many are against abortions, however Rh negative women don't have a lot of choice about that really do we?

If a positive male tries to infect us with his simian genes our body would reject it naturally.

This is why the *RhoGAM* vaccination is so wrong, not only does it cause auto-immune problems for the woman, the children are born autistic or have other mental issues. If the problems they are born with aren't obvious they can be psychopaths. You can not mix two species without problems.

Because our bloodline are naturally peaceful and matriarchal, if we breed with aggressive patriarchal species, we create very confused people who in their own minds are in a constant battle. One half wants to be spiritual, peaceful and loving, but the other part wants to rape and pillage, and be very dominant and aggressive.

Pure Bloodline families don't have any aggression, even if someone pushed us over the edge we just don't have it in us to kill someone. This is seen as a weakness by the Cro-Magnons, and they despise those like us because of this. They can not understand someone who is loving and caring unconditionally, like dolphins and other creatures. That we would rather be shot dead than hurt someone else. Can you imagine how frustrating it is to live in a world of violent, selfish nasty people when you are not like that yourself? How could you? I wonder if you wouldn't think twice about killing someone if they tried to kill you? If you are mixed you will have a constant battle in your mind.

Psychopaths do too, but because they don't want to be hurt by others they decide to remove the kind loving side altogether, and become even more overly aggressive and selfish than the others who are mixed.

They think that Dolphins and other animals are dumb, because they would let you kill them. So they instantly think we are dumb for being passive.

They do not see the strength in compassion, can you?

We are an easy target because we are loving, caring and spiritual, most of us have been genocided, we had to all split up and mingle with others. It was no longer safe in our caves and mounds, because the Cro-Magnons would not leave us alone, they wanted us all dead. They hate the fact we wanted to live in harmony with nature, and keep trees and forests.

They also didn't like the fact we created them with our genes mixed with those of simians.

The Hidden (Occult) Church passed the teachings down for generations and it is only now that some of us are starting to bring the truth back out into the public. Those who know the truth, who used to hunt us all down and kill us, burn us at the stake etc, can't do that as easy because people are more educated, and they know that the lies they spread about us being evil witches, possessed by demons and in league with the devil is all lies.

At least most do, there are still some who want to hunt us down and kill us, because the likes of Alex Jones and David Icke keep telling people that our bloodline goes round murdering people. When in reality it is them, or those like them who know the truth, the mixed ones who are so bitter and twisted about not being pure or Divine, and see being that way as a complete weakness.

Only our bloodline can rebuild Eden, Heaven on Earth, but that would remove all their power and control, so they won't allow it.

We have the hidden teachings of Mary Magdalene safe here and this is one teaching I think you should see, it is teaching number II and can be found in Liber III along with some other teachings from Mary Magdalene.

Now our families work towards getting the land for this
http://theomerla.weebly.com/

So that our clans can live together the way we used to, in peace.

Ancient Bloodline

Hitler talked about A Rh positive blood being of the superior race, and wanted to wipe out anyone who carried the Rh negative genes, the Jews have a high percentage of Rh negative blood. He felt inferiour to Rh negatives, as when he did studies he was amazed at the intelligence they showed above his more easy to control and less bright 'superior race'. He wanted to covert the occult teachings for himself, the teachings about true spirituality that our ancient tribes had passed down for thousands of years.

Karl Marx and Friedrich Engels specifically wanted to exterminate Scottish Highlanders, Bretons, Basques, South Slavs, and Czechs. All have a higher percentage of Rh negative or carry it recessively. Their excuse was that they are from an earlier 'primitive' population.

Yes that is true, O rhesus negative blood was the first blood of humans. The ancient shamanistic tribes that inhabited the earth a long time before we created the rhesus positives when we mixed some of our genes with simians. If anyone dares to mention the differences we are told to shut up, that we are being racist. Yet there are obvious differences and a lot of them.

Why do they hate us so much and say we are primitive? Even though they themselves carry some of our genes within them?

It is because our tribes were peaceful nature loving matriarchal clans, who lived in harmony with nature, and who didn't want their version of civilisation, e.g. Cities, pollution, industry, mass produced foods, patriarchy, war, money, greed and all the other things that have ruined our beautiful planet.

Will they succeed in wiping us all out, as they continue to destroy our Mother Earth? Or will we be able to stop them before it is too late?

You don't have to be Rh negative to care about your planet and your children, and grand children's future.

Secrets of the Serpent Bloodline - The Unveiling of Profound Esoteric Mysteries

Chapter 4

Rh Negative Health & Genetics

This section is all about putting the pieces of the genetic puzzle together, not only with my own knowledge, but by backing it all up with various other sources, from scientific papers, the research of various Doctors, Anthropologists and those who have come to the Gnosis themselves.

Over the years many have found me and my sites because they started to research their blood type. Often they have read strange stories and theories on various internet sites which state if you have O Rh negative blood you are an alien, or the spawn of the Devil, a reptilian and all kinds of strange ideas.

By the time they found me, they were often so taken in by one of these theories that a lot of them were unwilling to face the facts. After all, being told you are an Angelic Being or Starseed Alien sounds so much more alluring and egocentric, than being told you evolved here on earth, and actually you descend from a species of people that have been ridiculed and insulted for thousands of years.

However, some were willing to listen, and those are the ones with more of the genes, the ones who had activated their Serpent side, more than their egocentric side, and were willing to look into it more fully themselves.

Before we go on I am just going to mention blood type diet briefly here, because in truth there is far more research and help related to this from various other sources. A quick internet search will lead you to many.

Those with O type blood are supposed to thrive on protein and are to avoid all grains if possible.

Those with A type are better to remain on a vegetarian diet to have optimal health.

Those with B type do well on a good mix of all things, but are especially suited to diary.

AB types are the same as B, but should avoid eating too much meat because they carry the A protein too.

Child Blood Type Calculator

Blood Type Genetic Basis:

In genetics, blood type gene has two alleles, each allele has genotype A, B or O. The A and B are dominant, and O is recessive. So allele A combined with allele O is type A.

Similarly, BO is type B, AA is type A, BB is type B, OO is type O, and AB is type AB.

If both parents have type A blood, then the alleles could be AA or AO, thus the allele A frequency is 75%, allele O frequency is 25% for both parents.

So the chance of alleles OO is 25% × 25% = 6.25%,

alleles AA is 75% × 75% = 56.25%,

alleles AO is 75% × 25% = 18.75%,

alleles OA is 25% × 75% = 18.75%.

Since AA, AO and OA are blood type A, and OO is blood type O, thus their child has 6.25% chance to be blood type O and 93.75% chance to be blood type A.

The +/- is called the rhesus factor, with + being dominant, and - being recessive.

So if both parents are -, the kids are always -, otherwise the kids might be + or -.

Child Blood Type Estimate Table:

		Father's Blood Type			
		A	B	AB	O
Mother's Blood Type	A	A/O	A/B/AB/O	A/B/AB	A/O
	B	A/B/AB/O	B/O	A/B/AB	B/O
	AB	A/B/AB	A/B/AB	A/B/AB	A/B
	O	A/O	B/O	A/B	O

Parent Blood Type Estimate Table:

		Child's Blood Type			
		A	B	AB	O
One Parent's Blood Type	A	A/B/AB/O	B/AB	B/AB	A/B/O
	B	A/AB/O	A/B/AB/O	A/AB	A/B/O
	AB	A/B/AB/O	A/B/AB/O	A/B/AB	Impossible
	O	A/AB	B/AB	Impossible	A/B/O

Blood Group Compatibility

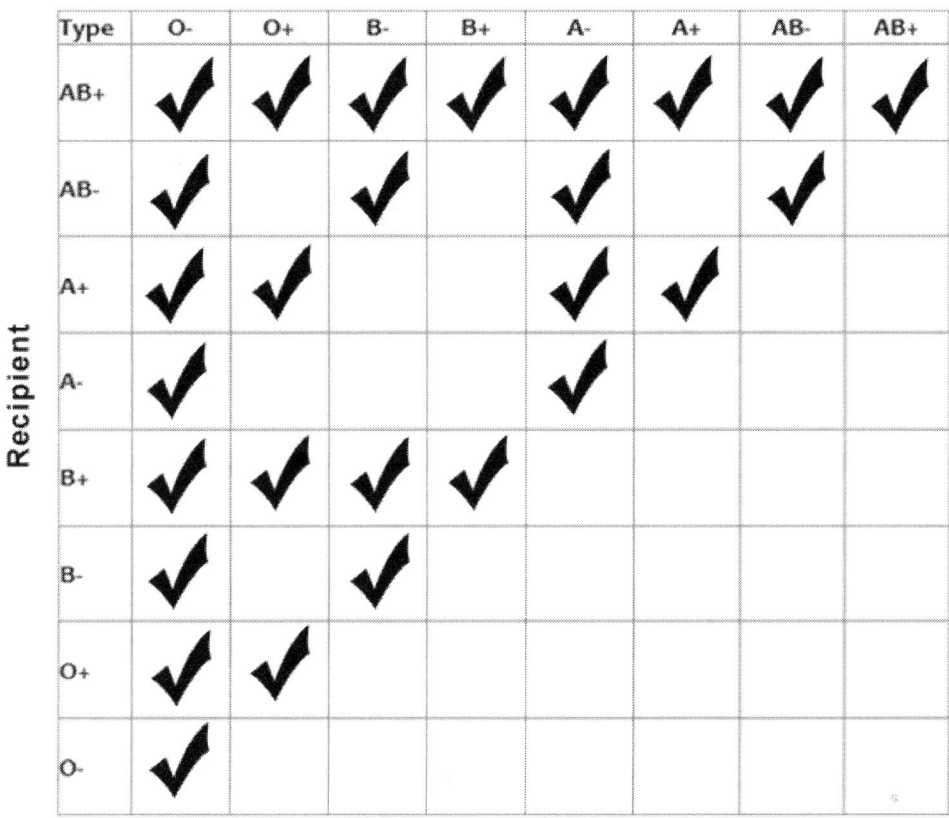

Secrets of the Serpent Bloodline - The Unveiling of Profound Esoteric Mysteries

Risks During Pregnancy Regarding Rh Status

There seems to be a lot of confusion where Rh status and pregnancy are concerned, so I thought I would make a chart for you to check against.

You have to remember though, that problems only occur when the positive baby or the positive Mother passes their own blood to a negative Mother or baby.

To avoid all problems completely you should only have children with someone who is the same Rh status as you. This is also not taking into account all the other factors in blood like Kell, Duffy and others which can also effect pregnancy.

Parent	Baby	Baby +	Baby -
Mum + Dad +		No problems for baby or Mum.	Potentially problems for baby if the Mother's blood is passed to baby.
Mum + Dad -		No problems for baby or Mum.	Potentially problems for baby if the Mother's blood is passed to baby.
Mum - Dad +		First baby will be fine. The subsequence babies if positive may be rejected by the Mother as they are seen as a foreign object or disease, and during the birth of the first positive baby they may have developed anti-bodies against positive blood, if some of the babies blood passed to them. If they have the anti D this is supposed to prevent this happening, however the women will have auto-immune diseases triggered from the injection and the babies could be born autistic.	No problems at all, the baby will be fine and no injection is needed.
Mum - Dad -		Not possible, the baby will be Rh negative.	No problems for baby or Mum.

©Tau Tia L Douglass 2013

Are you a Secretor or a Non-Secretor?

You may know your blood type – but do you know whether or not you're a secretor or a non-secretor? Most people have no idea that this blood typing sub-system even exists, but in truth, knowing which category you fall into can help you to make the most of your health.

The concepts of secretors and non-secretors were first introduced to the public by Dr. Peter D'Adamo's book Eat Right 4 Your Blood Type. In his book, Dr. D'Adamo posits that differences in blood type make people respond differently to various diets and medical treatments, and are the reason why some people are more vulnerable to certain illnesses and maladies than others. Each blood type, he says, has a distinct chemical reaction to lectins – substances found in foods. When a person eats a food containing lectins that are incompatible with his or her blood type, those lectins target a certain area and cause blood cells in that area to clump (or agglutinate), leading to uncomfortable symptoms. Continuing to ingest the offensive food will make the person susceptible to disease in the areas where the agglutination occurs.

Whether you're a secretor or a non-secretor is completely independent of your blood type, but just as important when it comes to understanding any metabolic dysfunctions and immune susceptibilities. Simply put, a secretor is a person whose body secretes its blood type antigens into its fluids – saliva, mucus, etc. A non-secretor does not. (Approximately 80% of the general population are estimated to be secretors.) And while no one blood type is better than the others, it is thought better to be a secretor than a non-secretor. The ability to secrete blood type antigens into your bodily fluids offers enhanced protection against outside factors such as potentially harmful microorganisms and the lectins from the food you eat. Secretors also have a more accommodating intestinal environment in which beneficial probiotic bacteria can thrive, since blood type can be used as a food source for such bacteria. Non-secretors on the other hand, because their bodies don't infuse their fluids with blood type antigens, have tendencies toward:

- Higher rates of oral disease, including more cavities – and, interestingly, habitual snoring
- Digestive problems, such as inflammation and ulcers
- A more prevalent rate of autoimmune disorders, such as multiple sclerosis
- Lungs that are more susceptible to environmental factors and cigarette smoking
- A greater risk of diabetes and heart disease
- A greater risk for recurrent urinary tract and Candida (yeast) infections
- An increased association with alcoholism
- More difficulty breaking down dietary fat and properly metabolising calcium
- An increased intolerance to carbohydrates

Your "secretor/non-secretor" status, in conjunction with your blood type, also determines the viscosity and clotting time of your blood. So you see? Since many of your bodily functions and responses are influenced by your secretor status, knowing which you are can be a valuable tool in determining how to take the best care of yourself – and how to feel better than ever.

Source 3rd MAY 2009
http://proactivemedicine.blogspot.co.uk/2009/05/are-you-secretor-or-non-secretor.html

Secretor Status

Antigens are present in the blood and, in most individuals, in bodily fluids such as saliva. If antigens are present in your bodily fluids, you are known as a 'secretor'. If they are not present in your bodily fluids, you are a 'non-secretor'. This fact is important for the diet, so it is important that you find out your secretor status.

Some researchers have found a correlation between Rhesus status and Secretor status. If you are unable to determine your Secretor status, a general rule of thumb is that Rhesus + usually denotes a secretor, and Rhesus – usually denotes a non-secretor. This research has not been sufficiently documented at this stage, so if possible and if available in your country, a test for secretor status should be done at the same time as the test for your blood type.

Secretors are shown as '1' and non-secretors as '2', for example, A1 (secretor) or A2 (non-secretor).

Source 2010 http://www.weight-tips.co.za/utlhealth/bloodtype-&-diet.htm

Enforced Immunization of ALL Rh Negative Women!

Many Rh negative women are coming forward with their experiences of having been given the Anti D vaccination when they were pregnant. Many are saying that their children have autism and all kinds of other health problems, that they feel were caused by having this injection in the first place. In some cases it wasn't even necessary, as both the Mother and Father were Rh negative.

So finding the following medical article claiming that all women who are Rh negative should be given this injection is very worrying indeed:

SS5-3: Rh Haemolytic Disease of the Newborn: A Major Public Health Problem.

Alvin Zipursky MD, FRCP; Vinod Paul MD, PhD

Background: Rh haemolytic disease of newborn infants is preventable by administration of anti Rh (D) gamma globulin to Rh negative women post-partum; as a result Rh disease has been virtually eradicated from developed countries.

Objectives: To provide evidence that Rh isoimmunization and consequently Rh haemolytic disease of the newborn occurs in low income countries.

Methods: The evidence has been obtained by determining the annual total distribution of anti-Rh (D) gamma globulin world-wide. That information combined with data on total births and prevalence of Rh negativity provides indirect evidence of the total number of women who have received anti-Rh (D) gamma globulin and thereby the number who have not received protection.

Results: It is estimated that annually over one million women did not receive anti-Rh gamma globulin and as a result over 100,000 babies are born with Rh haemolytic disease resulting in stillbirths, neonatal deaths or bilirubin induced brain damage (kernicterus). In many countries Rh negative women are not identified. One approach to solving this problem has been in the state of Bihar, India where there is now a program to determine Rh groups of 34 million girls, ages 0-18.

Conclusion and implications for public health practice: This serious public health problem is preventable and programs should be developed for the prevention of Rh is immunization in all women at risk and thereby the eradication of Rh haemolytic disease of newborn infants.

What the article fails to identify is that two Rh negatives can have children perfectly normally, with no problems at all. And is it the positive blood that causes problems, not ours!

Rh Disease! Since when is a different species a disease?

Diseases vs. traits

While the science of genetics has increasingly provided means by which certain characteristics and conditions can be identified and understood, given the complexity of human genetics and culture, there is at this point no agreed objective means of determining which traits might be ultimately desirable or undesirable. Would eugenic manipulations that reduce the propensity for risk-taking and violence, for example, in a population lead to their extinction? On the other hand, there is universal agreement that many genetic diseases, such as Tay Sachs, spina bifida, Hemochromatosis, Down syndrome, **Rh disease**, etc. are quite harmful to the affected individuals and their families and therefore to the societies to which they belong. Eugenic measures against many of the latter diseases are already being undertaken in societies around the world, while measures against traits that affect more subtle, poorly understood traits, such as risk-taking, are relegated to the realm of speculation and science fiction. The effects of diseases are essentially wholly negative, and societies everywhere seek to reduce their impact by various means, some of which are eugenic in all but name. The other traits that are discussed have positive as well as negative effects, and are not generally targeted at present anywhere.

From http://psychology.wikia.com/wiki/Eugenics

How dare they imply that just because Rh negatives have problems when breeding with positives, that is means we should all be wiped out, like it is a disease! Since when did being a different species mean you have a disease? If Rh negatives only breed with their own kind there is no problem with the birth at all.

There is a witch hunt out against us that never went away. They won't be happy until everyone last one of us has been wiped out.

Mules Are Rh Negative!

OK so you know how these memes start.. Some ill-informed person decides to start a rumour without checking the facts, and then posts it up on the internet. Soon it is all over, and people copy and paste is everywhere and the source of the disinformation is soon lost.

However, being as this book deals in facts only I thought I would put to bed the idea that mules have Rh negative blood once and for all.

Animals have different blood and antigens to humans. Animals do get Haemolytic disease which can be caused when human Rh negatives and positives have children together. However that does not mean to say it is the same antigen that causes it in animals too.

> Neonatal isoerythrolysis (NI) is an immune-mediated haemolytic disease seen in newborn horses, mules, cattle, pigs, cats, and, rarely, in dogs. NI is caused by ingestion of maternal colostrum containing antibodies to one of the neonate's blood group antigens. The maternal antibodies develop to specific foreign blood group antigens during previous pregnancies, unmatched transfusions, and from Babesia and Anaplasma vaccinations in cattle. Cats are unique in that blood type B cats have naturally occurring anti-A antibodies without prior exposure, and their kittens that are type A develop haemolysis after nursing. In horses, the antigens usually involved are A, C, and Q; NI is most commonly seen in Thoroughbreds and mules. Neonates with NI are normal at birth but develop severe haemolytic anemia within 2-3 days and become weak and icteric. Diagnosis is confirmed by screening maternal serum, plasma, or colostrum against the paternal or neonatal RBC. Treatment consists of stopping any colostrum while giving supportive care with transfusions. If necessary, neonates can be transfused with triple-washed maternal RBC. NI can be avoided by withholding maternal colostrum and giving colostrum from a maternal source free of the antibodies. The newborn's RBC can be mixed with maternal serum to look for agglutination before the newborn is allowed to receive maternal colostrum.

Source: http://www.merckvetmanual.com/mvm/index.jsp?cfile=htm/bc/10203.htm

On these fantasy sites they also use the fact mules are sterile as a way of comparing it to Rh neg women having trouble to have babies with Rh positives.

A mule is the product of two different species (a horse and a donkey) mating with each other. Mules are always sterile because horses and donkeys have different chromosome numbers.

For the mule, having parents with different chromosome numbers isn't a problem. During mitotic cell division, each of the chromosomes copies itself and then distributes these two copies to the two daughter cells. In contrast, when the mule is producing sperm or egg cells during meiosis, each pair of chromosomes (one from Mum and one from Dad) need to pair up with each other. Since the mule doesn't have an even number of homologous pairs (his parents had different chromosome numbers), meiosis is disrupted and viable sperm and eggs are not formed.

Neanderthals and the simians they mixed genes with did have different amount of chromosomes, but the two smallest ape chromosomes were combined into a single, larger human chromosome.

Most ape and human chromosomes are identical. The 9th and the 14th ape chromosomes, when combined, are like a palindrome of the human 12th chromosome. That is, when viewed on a chromatic scale, if the ape chromosomes (9 + 14) are joined and flipped over, the result would look just like the human #12 chromosome.

That's what makes apes so genetically close to human beings, despite the difference in the number of chromosomes, and once the chromosomes had been joined and Sapiens were created it was possible for them to breed with Neanderthals. Some of the Neanderthals did breed with the new Sapiens, and that produced the Cro-Magnons. It was harder for them to reproduce this way, but was possible, even though the Rh factor was different.

Even though Neanderthals and the simians started out not being able to breed with each other, after the genetic engineering it was possible. The Sapiens could of course breed very easily between themselves.

Two people with Rh negative blood can have children normally, as can two Rh positives. The only problems occur when the parents are incompatible and it doesn't matter which way round it is.

Like so:

Father	Mother	Result
Rh Negative	Rh Negative	Normal
Rh Positive	Rh Positive	Normal
Rh Positive	Rh Negative	Problems
Rh Negative	Rh Positive	Problems

Spiritual Royalty Genetics

The following are genes showing that you have a link back to the true Royalty, the Spiritual Royalty. Melanocortin 1 receptor gene (red hair gene), HLA-B27 antigen, Rh D negative blood, CCR5-Δ32, DNA Y Haplogroups I2b1 & J2. mtDNA haplogroups H and U.

Carrying the CCR5-Δ32 gene means you are immune to AIDS and The Black Death. It is also said to carry protection against Smallpox and Ebola.

Also if you try you will find you can get a link directly back to one of the bloodline families.

If you are of the Spiritual Royalty Bloodline you will have the traits of a Theolalite.

You can search for clues on your family crests and coats of arms. Stars, boars, lions, fleur-di-lys, snake, bee, reptiles, dragons, mermaid, shells, roses and various others.

DNA of Rh Negatives

The originating haplogroups of the O Rh negative blood which are proven lines, meaning families who have kept records of their clans, and know they are Bretons, Gaels & Picts are as follows:

Y DNA Haplogroups I2b1 & J2. As as well as other lines in the I and J haplogroup, and mtDNA haplogroups H and U.

However, it is important to realise that blood type is NOT passed through Y DNA or mtDNA, it is passed through Autosomal DNA.

Because the genes that cause Rh negative blood are recessive, anyone who has bred with someone from one of our families in the past, could end up with Rh negative blood, and their DNA groups will not be that of the bloodline families.

Someone with AB+ blood could also have some of our other recessive traits if someone in their family history bred with one of our bloodline, so they might for instance have red hair and blue eyes.

People who don't understand genetics and DNA run about claiming their DNA line is the origin of Rh negative blood, without realising that they only have Rh negative blood because someone in their family at one time bred with one of the bloodline families, who are the origin of this blood. If they were one of the bloodline families, they would already know about it.

Signs and Symbols of the Grail Bloodline

The Unicorn is symbol of the patriarchal Grail line. The equivalent traditional symbol of the male was a blade or a horn, usually represented by a sword, sometimes an arrow. In the Old Testament's Song of Solomon and in the Psalms of David, the fertile unicorn is associated with the kingly line of Judah - and it was for this very reason that the Cathars of Provence used the mystical beast to symbolise the Grail bloodline. There is much confusion about the female line, as it has been well hidden. However names with water in them, mermaid symbols, hearts, stars, shells, chalice and swans all represent the female line. And despite the disinformation, the fleur-de-lys is to represent purity within both patriarchal and matriarchal lines. A crown represents those who reached Kether – illumination, this later lost true meaning. The colour black used in names and crests is related to Alchemy – the black or royal arts. They are named the black arts since before 'Kemet' in Egypt, which means black. In those days it was not seen as something evil, just as esoteric teachings. The word Kemet has nothing to do with black skin. It was based on the Goddess Isis who was considered the Black Sun.

If you are of the bloodline, please feel free to join us by applying to join our Outer Order.

What Did Jesus Really Look Like?

We are often asked about the physical appearance of Jesus, and well being that he was one of the Serpent Bloodline it is very easy to figure out.

Under our videos we constantly get comments from people implying that we are lying for even suggesting that Jesus had red hair and blue eyes. They claim that Jesus was a black man, like some claim the Egyptian Pharaohs were black too. Well with DNA testing we have established this is completely in correct, however we don't have a mummy of Jesus to test, and the Turin Shroud has been proven a medieval fake several times over.

Others imply he would have been olive skinned because he was from the Middle East. However seeing as some of us can trace our family lines directly back to Jesus and have -- you guessed it - red hair, blue eyes and O Rh negative blood, it is easy for us to accept. In our other articles we also explain that Tigris is the area where our bloodline has its origins. But for all those who can not accept it, lets look at some things that would suggest that Jesus did indeed have red hair and blue eyes.

Firstly, he is a direct line descendant of King David, lets look into the physical characteristics of King David.

Secrets of the Serpent Bloodline - The Unveiling of Profound Esoteric Mysteries

David was born about 1030 BC. He was "ruddy, and withal of a beautiful countenance, and goodly to look to" (I Samuel 16:12). Ruddy means more than a rosey-cheeked boy. The Hebrew is ארמים ('admônîy), meaning red hair.

And that is not all, it goes further back into the royal line with the grandson of Abraham, Esau, twin brother of Jacob.

At the birth of the two brothers, "came out red, all over like a hairy garment." (Genesis 25:25).

Red hair seems to run in this family. Also notice that through history, within the old royal families, red hair was common among them. Yet not in the general public.

Of course there are many more not mentioned here including: Queen Boudica, Queen Elizabeth I, Mary Queen of Scots, Lettice Knollys, red-headed cousin to the queen on the Boleyn side and famous beauty. Ramses, Anne Boleyn, Richard the Lionheart, Marie Antoinette or Cleopatra. Red hair dyeing is sometimes practised in Islam, because it is reported that Muhammad had red hair.

Some of the oldest Clowns would often have red wigs and paint their faces white. It is because street entertainers of that era would have mocked royalty often, and seeing as the royals all had red hair and pale white skin, this was why they dressed like that, in an emphasized way.

Even today clowns mock those with red hair and pale skin. i.e.: The clown from the movie IT and Ronald McDonald.

Back to Jesus.

How was Jesus described by those who actually saw him?

Few people are aware that in the archives of Rome there is a physical description of Jesus. It is contained in a report written during Jesus' lifetime by a Roman, Publius Lentulus, to the Emperor Tiberias. It reads as follows:

'There has appeared in Palestine a man who is still living and whose power is extraordinary. He has the title given him of Great Prophet; his disciples call him the Son of God. He raises the dead and heals all sorts of diseases.

He is a tall, well-proportioned man, and there is an air of severity in his countenance which at once attracts the love and reverence of those who see him. His hair is the colour of new wine from the roots to the ears, and thence to the shoulders it is curled and falls down to the lowest part of them. Upon the forehead, it parts in two after the manner of Nazarenes.

His forehead is flat and fair, his face without blemish or defect, and adorned with a graceful expression. His nose and mouth are very well proportioned, his beard is thick and is the colour of his hair. His eyes bright blue, clear and serene. Look innocent, dignified, manly and mature.'

Conclusion

No accounts from anyone or anything you show them will persuade some people. I have just tried to show how the royal line to which he belongs do have red hair and blue eyes, so why wouldn't he?

Rh Negative Eye Colours

It is said that eyes can never lie, that when you look into someone's eyes you can see their true spirit. There are so many different colours and shades of eyes but Rh negatives do tend to have lighter eyes in general. They also tend to have mood eyes - changing colour depending on their mood and what they are wearing.

I decided to do a survey to find out the most popular eye colours in Rh negatives and then a survey out in the public where anyone could answer. Because all eye colours are made up from brown and blue, and the colour in between those is green. I decided to make the survey more fair we should group certain shades in to one of these three groups, as follows:

Brown Eyes - Amber, Black.
Green Eyes - Hazel, Olive.
Blue Eyes - Grey, Violet.

Here are the results within the Rh negative study group.

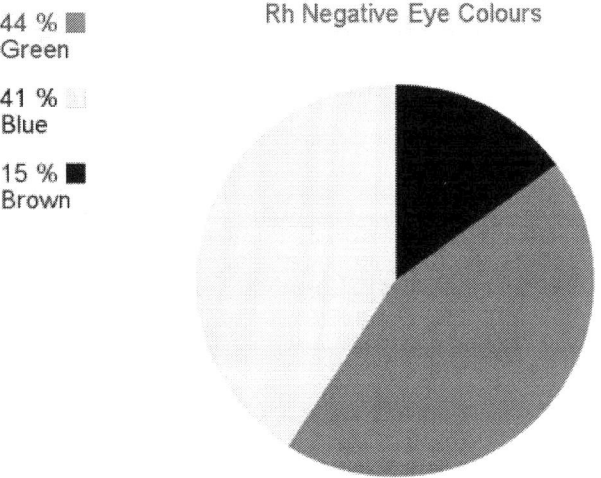

Secrets of the Serpent Bloodline - The Unveiling of Profound Esoteric Mysteries

As you can see in the Rh negative study group green is the highest, closely followed by blue and brown is the lowest. This points to the original Rh negatives having blue eyes. Brown is the dominant eye colour which normally over rides any other colour, then green, then blue. Seeing as blue is so high here it shows that those with Rh negative genes do carry the blue eyed gene strongly, as all green eyed people also carry it.

Here is the chart for the general public results, within Europe, Scandinavia, America and Australia.

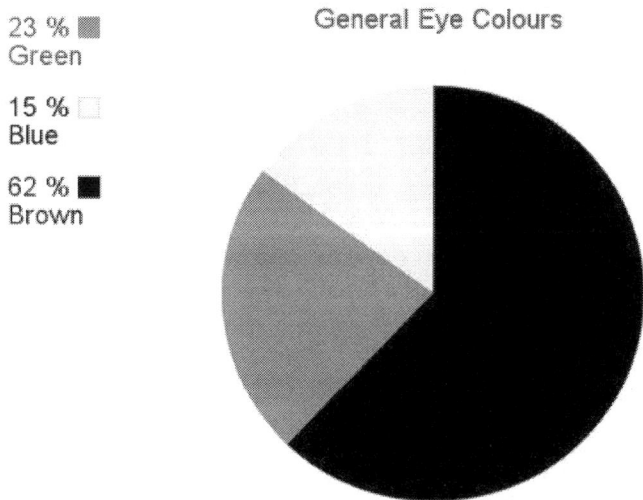

These results are harder to get a good picture from because it isn't a worldwide survey and seeing as the vast majority of the world has brown eyes. However this is including areas with the highest number of blue eyes.

What is interesting is how people seem to think that green eyes are rare, however there are lot of places in the world where the people have green eyes, and these areas show where our ancient bloodline families have visited the most, as the genes are still strong there, because as I said, all people with green eyes carry the blue eyed genes. Obviously after time an area left behind will slowly lose all green and blue eyes completely, so long as people are breeding with people with brown eyes, as they are the dominant genes.

We all have the same two eye colour genes. What gives us different eye colours are which variations of these genes we have.

Secrets of the Serpent Bloodline - The Unveiling of Profound Esoteric Mysteries

One of these genes is called HERC2. It comes in two variations, brown and blue. The other gene, called gey, also comes in two versions -- green and blue.

Your eye colour depends on which combination of these versions you have as shown in the chart:

HERC2	Gey	Eye Colour
BB	GG	Brown
BB	Gb	Brown
BB	bb	Brown
Bb	GG	Brown
Bb	Gb	Brown
Bb	bb	Brown
bb	GG	Green
bb	Gb	Green
bb	bb	**Blue**

So you can see how difficult it is for someone to have green or blue eyes, especially blue.

Here is a map of all the places in the world where people carry the green eyed gene.

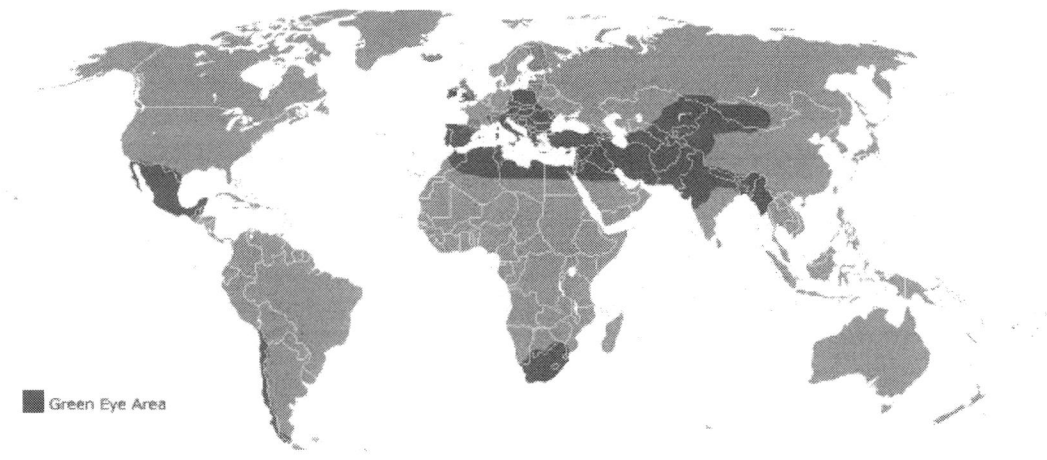

Most of the other areas are all brown eyed areas completely, with only Europe, Scandinavia, America, Russia and Australia having some blue eyes.

Secrets of the Serpent Bloodline - The Unveiling of Profound Esoteric Mysteries

Evil Eye Talisman

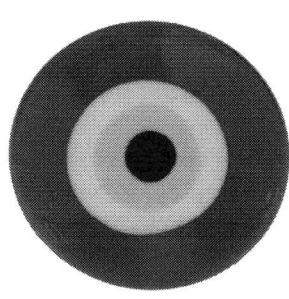

Our ancestors, keen to try to keep the lines pure, did start a bit of a thing about our blue eyes.

They would say that green eyes were the evil eyes of jealousy, now why would they say that?

Green eyes happen when the genes of those with blue eyes are mixed with the genes of those with brown eyes, so someone with green eyes carries genes for both brown and blue eyes, and seeing as Cro-Magnons are a mix of Homo Heidelbergensis who had brown eyes, and Neanderthals with blue eyes, many of them did have green eyes.

So Cro-Magnon's predominately had green eyes, and were the ones who tried to kill us all because of their envy.

So we created blue eyed charms to protect against them. You will see them all over in many countries. Most not even realising the true origin. Of course wiki readers get a few clues, but never the full truth, as always.
http://en.wikipedia.org/wiki/Evil_eye

Also see http://en.wikipedia.org/wiki/Hamsa

The hand of Mary, including the eye of Mary, the Divine Mother of the Grail bloodline.

Are You Related To Neanderthals?

Asks Dr Pinna

"If you have a "RED GENE" freckles, light skin, reddish hair, that is a sign. High intelligence is also a Neanderthal trait. The Neanderthals had large craniums and therefore more brains. They survived through the Ice Ages which required the ability to adapt to hunger and to be able to kill large animals. This meant they had good skills in team work."

By David Noel

From a combination of old and new evidence, it appears that at last we have a satisfactory answer to the age-old question of 'What Happened to the Neanderthals?'. If the current reasoning is correct, their descendants are still with us, and we call them the Basques.

Robert J Sawyer has recently published his book "Hominids" [2], a fictional account of an interaction between Sapiens humans and Neanderthals, but drawing on the latest scientific research about Neanderthals.

This research included studies of DNA extracted from bones of Neanderthal remains. The account mentions five months of painstaking work to extract a 379-nucleotide fragment from the control region of the Neanderthal's mitochondrial DNA, followed by use of a polymerase chain reaction to reproduce millions of copies of the recovered DNA.

This was carefully sequenced and then a check made of the corresponding mitochondrial DNA from 1,600 modern humans: Native Canadians, Polynesians. Australians, Africans, Asians, and Europeans. Every one of those 1,600 people had at least 371 nucleotides out of those 379 the same; the maximum deviation was just 8 nucleotides.

But the Neanderthal DNA had an average of only 352 nucleotides in common with the modern specimens; it deviated by 27 nucleotides. It was concluded that Homo sapiens and Neanderthals must have diverged from each other between 550,000 and 690,000 years ago for their DNA to be so different.

In contrast, all modern humans probably shared a common ancestor 150,000 or 200,000 years in the past. It was concluded that Neanderthals were probably a fully separate species from modern humans, not just a subspecies: Homo neanderthalensis, not Homo sapiens neanderthalensis.

Looking now at the evidence for the theory that the Basques are descended principally from Neanderthals, everything suddenly falls into place, and the supposition becomes almost self-evident.

Location: The 'home country' of the Neanderthals is well known to have been western Europe. One source says that they "dominated this area for at least a quarter of a million years". Many of the best Neanderthal specimens have originated from the Iberian Peninsular. The Basque Country, lying on the western side of the Pyrenees and on the border between Spain and France, fits in neatly with this location.

Note: According to more recent sources Neanderthal originated in the Tigris area, and have been found in Israel. This is not to say a lot of them didn't settle in, or were pushed into the Basque area. The Basque area is where Neanderthals bred with the first humans they created mixed with simian genes, creating Cro-Magnons.[11]

The Basques are well-known to have distinctive body characteristics. Kurlansky says "Ample evidence exists that the Basques are a physically distinct group. There is a Basque type with a long straight nose, thick eyebrows, strong chin, and long earlobes" [1].

Basque skulls tend to be built on a different pattern. In the early 1880s, a researcher reported *"Someone gave me a Basque body and I dissected it, and I assert that the head was not built like that of other men"[1].*

These qualitative differences are indicative, but quantitative evidence, with presence or absence of features, or items being present in different numbers, has greater weight in deciding whether specimens belong to the same or different species. Powerful quantitative evidence comes from a consideration of blood factors.

Human blood is classified according to various parameters, the most important of which are ABO and Rhesus characteristics. In ABO, blood may contain the 'A' factor (giving A-group blood), the 'B' factor (B-group), both 'A' and 'B' (AB blood), or neither (O blood). The A and B factors act like antibodies, and if blood containing one or both of them is transferred to a person whose blood does not already contain them, adverse reactions occur. Group O blood contains neither antibody and can typically be transferred without reaction to any recipient.
Some 55% of Basques have Group O blood, one of the highest percentages in the world [3].

Secrets of the Serpent Bloodline - The Unveiling of Profound Esoteric Mysteries

Even stronger evidence comes from the **Rhesus factor**, discovered only in 1940. The blood of most humans (and, apparently, all other primates [6]) contains this factor, and is called Rhesus-positive or Rh+ blood. Blood lacking this factor is called Rhesus-negative.

The Basques are well-known to have the highest percentage (around 33%) of Rhesus-negative blood of any human population [2], and so are regarded as the original source of this factor. In the United States,**some 15% of the 'European' population are Rh-negative**, while the percentage in the 'Asian' and 'Black' population is much less than this.

Possession of Rh-negative blood can be a major disadvantage for a human population. A Rh-negative woman who conceives a Rh-positive child with a Rh-positive man will typically bear her first child without special problems. However, because of intermingling of fluids between mother and foetus, the first pregnancy builds up antibodies to Rh+ blood in the woman which typically attack the blood of her subsequent Rh+ children, causing them to miscarry, be stillborn, or die shortly after birth (infant haemolytic disease [6]).

Note: If Rh negatives breed only with each other, there are no problems at all.[12]

The scenario so far then is this. Around 600,000 years ago, in southern Europe, a species of man separated off from the ancestral line, and we call this species Homo neanderthalensis, the 'N-people'. The blood of this species contained none of the factors A, B, or Rh.

Note: Neanderthals evolved and came out of Tigris area, not Africa.[11]

Much later, possibly around 200,000 years ago in Africa, the main human line had picked up the A, B, and Rh factors (possibly from other primates, the Rhesus factor is named after the Rhesus monkey or macaque), and by then could be classed as Homo sapiens, the 'S-people'.

In competition between related species or races, antibodies in their blood are a powerful genetic advantage for those who possess them when competing against those who don't. History has many examples of European settlers who quite unintentionally won out against native populations because the latter had no antibodies against diseases such as measles which the Europeans brought with them.

In the present scenario, a woman of the N-people (Basque, Rh-) who partnered with a man of the S-people (non-Basque, Rh+) would be likely to bear no more than a single child of the partnership. 'Mixed marriages' in humans are not usually genetically disadvantageous, but in this case they would be. The effect would be a continuing reduction in the N-people population as 'mixed' couples produced only a single child, half the nominal population-maintenance rate.

There are other physical characteristics of humans which are typically associated with Rh-negative blood, but which in the present scenario would be regarded as belonging to the N-people. These include early maturity, large head and eyes, high IQ [6], or an extra vertebra (a 'tail bone' — called a 'cauda'), lower than normal body temperature, lower than normal blood pressure, and higher mental analytical abilities [5].

http://drpinna.com/neanderthals-and-basques-14808

Rh Negative Blood & HLA B27

By Matt McGrath

In the human immune system, the HLA (human leucocyte antigen) family of genes plays an important role in defending against foreign invaders such as viruses.

The authors say that the origins of some HLA class 1 genes are proof that our ancient relatives interbred with Neanderthals and Denisovans for a period.

"Getting these genes by mating would have given an advantage to populations that acquired them."

At least one variety of HLA gene occurs frequently in present day populations from West Asia, but is rare in Africans.

"The HLA genes that the Neanderthals and Denisovans had, had been adapted to life in Europe and Asia for several hundred thousand years, whereas the recent migrants from Africa wouldn't have had these genes," said study leader Peter Parham from Stanford University School of Medicine in California.

"So getting these genes by mating would have given an advantage to populations that acquired them."

Dr. Pinna says:

The HLA gene which provides our white cells in our immune system with the ability to recognize viruses and perhaps cancers was a gift from our Neanderthal ancestors.

Neanderthals interbred with Europeans and Chinese but not with Africans. This is very important from a medical point of view.

Since the HLA (HUMAN LEUKOCYTE (WHITE CELL) ANTIGEN) protects against viruses, we find the most deadly viruses in Africa. For example, the famous EBOLA virus. Why? Because Africans do not have the ability to defend against and eradicate this virus. The viruses found in Europe and China are rather mild, such as mumps, measles and German measles. Also, Africans have less defenses against cancers caused by viruses. Here is a report from the Guardian, U.K:

"The difference is that a disproportionate number of cancers in Africa are caused by infections, such as the hepatitis viruses (B and C), which cause liver cancer, or the human papilloma virus (HPV), which causes 98% of cervical cancers. The worldwide average for infection-related cancers is about 22%; in Africa, the figures are much higher: 40% of cases in women and 30% in men."

European and Chinese interbreeding with Neanderthals was a gift from God. Not only did it give us red hair and big brains, but also a way to fight viral infection.

http://drpinna.com/neanderthal-genes-boosts-our-immune-system-23305

HLA B27 & Arthritis

Arthritis is a term for any of more than one hundred diseases that produce swelling in a joint, accompanied by pain and stiffness. The most common forms of arthritis are osteoarthritis (the degeneration of a joint) and rheumatoid arthritis ("the great crippler," inflammation of a joint that erodes bone and cartilage). Other forms include ankylosing spondylitis (inflammation of spinal joints, mainly affecting young men), infectious arthritis (caused by invading microorganisms), and chronic Lyme arthritis (which appears in some people who contract Lyme disease). Lupus, an autoimmune disease, also has elements of arthritis, with painful and often swollen joints.

Neanderthal skeletons show signs of arthritis, as do Egyptian mummies. Ancient Greek and Roman physicians wrote detailed descriptions of arthritic conditions and methods of treatment. In fourteenth- and fifteenth-century Europe, gout became common among members of the upper classes, and an outbreak of rheumatoid arthritis swept through the masses of Europe during the Industrial Revolution. By the early nineteenth century, rheumatoid arthritis had been recognized as a distinct condition, separate from gout. Augustin Landre-Beauvais gave rheumatoid arthritis its first complete clinical description in 1800; in 1859 Alfred Garrod (1819-1907) distinguished gout by the presence of uric acid.

While the disease had been known for centuries, its cause remained unknown. Some thought arthritis was the result of an infectious disease, such as gonorrhea or tuberculosis. In 1900 two physicians, Frederick J. Poynton (1869-1943) and A. Paine, discovered a bacteria in a group of children afflicted with rheumatism. They speculated that rheumatic arthritis could be the result of an immune reaction to an invading micro organism. In 1940 researchers found a rheumatoid factor, an antibody-like substance, in the blood of arthritis patients. Further study showed that rheumatic infections were caused by a group A streptococcus, so the rheumatoid factor was indeed an immune system response to that bacteria. Current research focuses on the relationship between specific genetically coded HLA molecules (an element of the immune system) and the occurrence of various types of arthritis. For example, the HLA-B27 molecule is common in people with ankylosing spondylitis.[14]

HLA B27 & CCR5-Δ32

According to Randall Johnson at the Baylor College of Medicine in Houston, *"Only 7% of the US population tests positive for the HLA-B27 gene; this gene, found only in persons with Rh-Negative blood, can trigger the immune system to operate overtime at WARP SPEED in times of medical emergency."*

Note: HLA-B27 is also sometimes found in those who are Rh negative recessive.

The HLA-B27 Genetic Marker is said to have protective properties that guard against the progression of HIV. It is said, **that people with this gene do not have the right proteins for the HIV virus to bind with.** The HLA-B27 Marker is most often found in people with O- Blood.

CCR5-Δ32 is a deletion mutation of a gene that has a specific impact on the function of T cells. At least one copy of CCR5-Δ32 is found in about (5-14%) of people of Northern European and in those of Northern European descent. There also is a small minority (1%) with the same mutation amongst Southern Europeans or Balkan Peninsula. It has been hypothesized that this allele was favoured by natural selection during the Black Death for Northern Europeans.

The allele has a negative effect upon T cell function, but appears to protect against smallpox and HIV. Yersinia pestis (the bubonic plague bacterium) was demonstrated in the laboratory not to associate with CCR5. Individuals with the Δ32 allele of CCR5 are healthy, suggesting that CCR5 is largely dispensable. However, CCR5 apparently plays a role in mediating resistance to West Nile virus infection in humans, as CCR5-Δ32 individuals have shown to be disproportionately at higher risk of West Nile virus in studies, indicating that not all of the functions of CCR5 may be compensated by other receptors.

While CCR5 has multiple variants in its coding region, the deletion of a 32-bp segment results in a non functional receptor, thus preventing HIV R5 entry; two copies of this allele provide strong protection against HIV infection. This allele is found in 5–14% of Europeans but is rare in Africans and Asians.

HLA-B27 is an inherited gene marker that is associated with a number of related rheumatic diseases. They share in common, certain features like spinal and peripheral arthritis, skin and GI disorders, anterior chamber eye disease, psoriasis like skin lesions, as well as inflammation and joint pain. This gene is found with highest prevalence in patients with ankylosing spondylitis, reactive arthritis, and patients with the combination of peripheral arthritis and either psoriasis or inflammatory bowel disease.

Neanderthals have been found with skeletal deformities known to be caused be ankylosing spondylitis and Arthritis.[13]

CONCLUSION

Neanderthals carried HLA-B27 which offers protection from certain diseases, however it also causes autoimmune diseases. CCR5-Δ32 deletion is also linked in with O negative blood. They originate in Neanderthals and are not often found in Africa. If you have Rh negative blood, you are blessed with some of the genes from our most ancient families.

Research by Tia Douglass & Andre Heyrman of NADA.

REFERENCES

[1] Mark Kurlansky, The Basque History of the World, Penguin Books, New York, 2001.

[2] Robert J. Sawyer, Hominids, Tor Books, 2002.

[3] FAQs About Basque and the Basques, www.cogs.susx.ac.uk/users/larryt/basque.faqs.html

[4] David Noel, Matrix Thinking, BFC Press, 1997. Chapter 104, Syston Boundaries and SIOS. Also at: www.aoi.com.au/matrix/Mat04.html

[5] The Rh-negative Factor and 'Reptilian Traits', www.reptilianagenda.com/research/r110199a.html

[6] Blood of the Gods, www.geocities.com/ask_lady_lee/rhneg.html

[7] Philip Lieberman, Eve Spoke: Human Language and Human Evolution, W W Norton, 1998

[8] What is Basque?, www.clan-blackstar.com/research/basque.html

[9] Basque Pronunciation, www.eirelink.com/alanking/collq1.htm#Pronunciation

[10] Homo neanderthalensis, www.modernhumanorigins.com/neanderthalensis.html

[11] List of Neanderthal sites, en.wikipedia.org/wiki/List_of_Neanderthal_sites

[12] What does it mean to be Rh negative? www.betterbirth.com/rh-negative

[13] La Chapelle-aux-Saints 1 (also known as "The Old Man") is a partial skeleton of the species Homo neanderthalensis,en.wikipedia.org/wiki/La_Chapelle-aux-Saints_1

Rh Negative Blood Linked To The High Amount of Diabetes Type 1 in Sardinians

Type 1 diabetes among Sardinian children is increasing: the Sardinian diabetes register for children aged 0-14 years (1989-1999).

Casu A, Pascutto C, Bernardinelli L, Songini M.

Source

Department of Internal Medicine, Azienda Ospedaliera Brotzu, Via Peretti, Cagliari, Italy.

Abstract

OBJECTIVE:

The Sardinian type 1 diabetes register represented the basis to determine the most recent trends and the age distribution of type 1 diabetes incidence among Sardinians <15 years of age during 1989-1999. Part of the data (1989-1998) has been already published by the EURODIAB Group with a lower completeness of ascertainment (87%). The geographical distribution of type 1 diabetes risk was also investigated.

RESEARCH DESIGN AND METHODS:

The new cases of type 1 diabetes in children aged 0-14 years in Sardinia were prospectively registered from 1989 to 1999 according to the EURODIAB ACE criteria. The completeness of ascertainment calculated applying the capture-recapture method was 91%. Standardized incidence rates and 95% CI were calculated assuming the Poisson distribution. Trend of type 1 diabetes incidence was analyzed using the Poisson regression model. Maps of the geographical distribution of type 1 diabetes risk for the whole time period and separately for 1989-1994 and 1995-1999 were produced applying a Bayesian method.

RESULTS:

A total of 1214 type 1 diabetic patients were registered yielding to an overall age- and sex-standardized incidence rate of 38.8/100000 (95% CI 36.7-41.1). There was a male excess with an overall male-to-female ratio of 1.4 (1.3-1.8). The increase of incidence during the 11 years analyzed was statistically significant (P = 0.002) with a yearly increasing rate of 2.8% (1.0-4.7). No evidence of an effect of age and sex on this trend has been found. The geographical distribution of type 1 diabetes relative risk (RR) showed that the highest risk areas are located in the southern and central-eastern part of the island and the lowest risk in the northeastern part, even if most of these differences were not statistically significant. This geographical distribution seemed to remain mainly the same between 1989-1994 and 1995-1999.

CONCLUSIONS:

The homogeneity of diabetes risk and the increase of incidence over the age-groups in the Sardinian population stress the role of an environmental factor uniformly distributed among the genetically high-risk Sardinians.[1]

Sardinian DNA

About 42% of the Sardinians belong to Y-chromosome haplogroup I. The second most common Y-chromosome haplogroup among Sardinian male population is the haplogroup R1b (22% of the total population) mainly present in the northern part of the island. Sardinia also has a relatively high distribution of Y-chromosome haplogroup G (11%), which is also found in the Caucasus, the Pyrenees and the Alps, in particular Tyrol area. Other haplogroups show lower frequencies.

Note: These health problems then seem to be related to the I haplogroup and Rh negative blood parts of the island, but not R1b areas.

The most common mtDNA haplogroups in Sardinia are H (H1 and H3) and V who are also particularly common in the iberian peninsula. Some subclades typical of Sardinia and rare in the rest of Europe are:

The subclade U5b3a1 of Haplogroup U (mtDNA), about 4% of the female population in Sardinia belongs to this haplotype. One other interesting anomaly is the presence of H13a of Haplogroup H (mtDNA) is present on the island at around 9.2%. As this is an extremely rare subclade normally present in the Caucasus, its worthy of further investigation.[2]

**RH blood groups and diabetic disorders:
is there an effect on glycosylated hemoglobin level?**

Hum Biol. 2000 Apr;72(2):287-94.
Gloria-Bottini F, Antonacci E, Bottini N, Ogana A, Borgiani P, De Santis G, Lucarini N.

Recent cloning of RH genes has elucidated their structure, suggesting that RH proteins are part of an oligomeric complex with transport function in the erythrocyte. This observation prompted us to investigate a possible relationship between the RH system and the glycosylated hemoglobin level (Hb A(1c)) in diabetes. This compound is considered an important indicator- of glycemic control in diabetic disorders. We studied 278 subjects with non-insulin-dependent diabetes mellitus (NIDDM) from the population of Penne, Italy. Glycemic and glycosylated hemoglobin (Hb A(1c)) levels are associated with RH phenotype. Glucose and Hb A(1c) levels are increased in DCcEe subjects and decreased in ddccee subjects as compared to the mean values for other genotypes. Sex, age at onset of disease, duration of disease, and age of patients were also considered. Correlation analysis suggests that these variables influence glycemia directly and Hb A(1c) indirectly. The RH system, on the other hand, seems to influence the Hb A(1c) level directly. Preliminary data on 53 children with insulin-dependent diabetes mellitus (IDDM) from Sardinia seem to confirm the relationship between RH and Hb A(1c) observed in NIDDM. Since glycosylated hemoglobin is found inside red blood cells, the relationship between RH genetic variability and Hb A(1c) level suggests that RH proteins may influence glucose transport through red cell membrane and/or hemoglobin glycation.[3]

Type 1 Diabetes is linked to other genetic traits of Rh Negatives through SNP data:

SNP Rs2476601

This SNP, located in the PTPN22 gene and also known as R620W, or 1858C>T, may influence Rheumatoid Arthritis and other autoimmune diseases, including but not limited to, multiple sclerosis, Crohn's disease, celiac disease and type-1 diabetes.

In an expanded follow-up study of >6,000 controls and 6,000 patients, the heterozygote odds ratio for type-1 diabetes for this SNP was recalculated to be 1.98 (CI 1.82-2.15). [PMID 17554260]

rs2476601 was confirmed in another 2007 study to be a risk factor for RA [PMID 17804836]

[PMID 16490755] confirms the association of rs2476601 rheumatoid arthritis.

[PMID 15674368] two copies of the PTPN22 R620W allele more than doubles the risk for RF positive RA.

rs2476601 shows a 0.75 (r squared) correlation with rs6679677, a SNP in the RSBN1 gene associated with rheumatoid arthritis. [PMID 17554300]

[PMID 17934143] Confirms association of rs2476601 with type-1 diabetes in a Sardinian population of 490 sporadic patients (794 families).

[PMID 18301444] In study of 332 Norwegian patients plus a meta-analysis, the rs2476601(A) allele was linked to autoimmune Addison's disease. (p=0.003)

[PMID 18305142] rs2476601(A) has a higher relative risk in type-1 diabetes cases carrying lower risk HLA class II genotypes than in those carrying higher risk ones ($p=1.36 \times 10^{-4}$ in a test of interaction).[4]

Linking PTPN22 with HLA-B27 which is associated with many autoimmune diseases, where as the SNP is associated with various others including Diabetes.

Confirmation of the genetic association of CTLA4 and PTPN22 with ANCA - associated vasculitis.

(PMID:19951419)

Carr EJ, Niederer HA, Williams J, Harper L, Watts RA, Lyons PA, Smith KG

Cambridge Institute for Medical Research, University of Cambridge School of Clinical Medicine, Addenbrooke's Hospital, Hills Road, Cambridge CB20XY, UK.

BMC Medical Genetics [2009, 10:121]
Type: Journal Article, Research Support, Non-U.S. Gov't
DOI:10.1186/1471-2350-10-121

BACKGROUND: The genetic contribution to the aetiology of anti-neutrophil cytoplasmic antibody (ANCA)-associated vasculitis (AAV) is not well defined. Across different autoimmune diseases some genes with immunomodulatory roles, such as PTPN22, are frequently associated with multiple diseases, whereas specific HLA associations, such as HLA-B27, tend to be disease restricted. We studied ten candidate loci on the basis of their immunoregulatory role and prior associations with type 1 diabetes (T1D). These included PTPN22, CTLA4 and CD226, which have previously been associated with AAV.

METHODS: We genotyped the following 11 SNPs, from 10 loci, in 641 AAV patients using TaqMan genotyping: rs2476601 in PTPN22, rs1990760 in IFIH1, rs3087243 in CTLA4, rs2069763 in IL2, rs10877012 in CYP27B1, rs2292239 in ERBB3, rs3184504 in SH2B3, rs12708716 in CLEC16A, rs1893217 and rs478582 in PTPN2 and rs763361 in CD226. Where possible, we performed a meta-analysis with previous analyses.

RESULTS: Both CTLA4 rs3087243 and PTPN22 rs2476601 showed association with AAV, $P = 6.4 \times 10^{-3}$ and $P = 1.4 \times 10^{-4}$ respectively. The minor allele (A) of CTLA4 rs3087243 is protective (odds ratio = 0.84), whereas the minor allele (A) of PTPN22 rs2476601 confers susceptibility (odds ratio = 1.40). These results confirmed previously described associations with AAV. After meta-analysis, the PTPN22 rs2476601 association was further strengthened (combined $P = 4.2 \times 10^{-7}$, odds ratio of 1.48 for the A allele). The other 9 SNPs, including rs763361 in CD226, showed no association with AAV.

CONCLUSION: Our study of T1D associated SNPs in AAV has confirmed CTLA4 and PTPN22 as susceptibility loci in AAV. These genes encode two key regulators of the immune response and are associated with many autoimmune diseases, including T1D, autoimmune thyroid disease, celiac disease, rheumatoid arthritis, and now AAV.[5]

Conclusion

PTPN22 rs2476601 is associated with HLA-B27 which in turn is associated with Rh negative blood and all the related health problems, including but not limited to: Type 1 diabetes, autoimmune thyroid disease, celiac disease, rheumatoid arthritis, multiple sclerosis, Crohn's disease, psoriasis, ankylosing spondylitis.

These health problems are particularly virulent in those with Y DNA I and mtDNA H.

Sources

[1] Type 1 diabetes among Sardinian children is increasing
-ncbi.nlm.nih.gov/pubmed/15220238
[2] DNA of Sardinians-nature.com/ejhg/journal/v11/n10/full/5201040a.html
[3] Diabetic Disorders linked to Diabetes Type 1 -
generativemedicine.org/wiki/wiki.pl/Rhesus_(Rh)_Blood_Group
[4]SNP Rs2476601 -snpedia.com/index.php/Rs2476601
[5]Linking PTPN22 with HLA-B27
-http://europepmc.org/articles/PMC3224698/?report=abstract

Ancient Red Heads In USA

A cave near Lovelock, Nevada, (about 80 miles north east of the city of Reno in that state) has produced several sets of mummies, bones, and artefacts buried under several layers of bat excrement - the desiccated bodies belonged to a very tall people - with red hair. Once again, only White Nordics fit the bill with regard to stature and hair color.

In fact, red-haired enemies feature in local Indian legends - or what were thought legends until the discovery of the Lovelock mummies. (The locals Indians are the Paiutes, the same ones who object to the scientific investigation of the Spirit Cave Mummy). According to these legends, the red haired enemies centered on these tall troublemakers whom they called the "Si-Te-Cah."

Significantly, the name Si-Te-Cah means "tule eaters" - tule being the fibrous reed which is the base material of the mats in which the Spirit Cave Mummy was buried. Tule is no longer found in the region and was likely imported along with the people who used it.

According to the Paiute, the red-haired peoples were warlike, and a number of the Indian tribes joined together in a long war against them. According to the Indian legend, after a long struggle, a coalition of Indian tribes trapped the remaining Si-Te-Cah in what is now called Lovelock Cave. When they refused to come out, the Indians piled brush before the cave mouth and set it aflame. The Si-Te-Cah were incinerated.

Sarah Winnemucca Hopkins, daughter of Paiute Chief Winnemucca, related many stories about the Si-Te-Cah in her book "Life Among the Paiutes."

On page 75, she relates: "My people say that the tribe we exterminated had reddish hair. I have some of their hair, which has been handed down from father to son. I have a dress which has been in our family a great many years, trimmed with the reddish hair. I am going to wear it some time when I lecture. It is called a mourning dress, and no one has such a dress but my family."

In 1931, further skeletons were discovered in the Humboldt Lake bed. Eight years later, a mystery skeleton was unearthed on a ranch in the region. In each case, the skeletons were exceptionally tall - much taller than the surrounding Amerinds.

There is a small display on the Si-Te-Cah in the Lovelock museum today, but it ignores the evidence which indicates that the Si-Te-Cah were not Amerinds. The Nevada State Historical Society also displays some artefacts from the cave.

The Nevada State Museum went public with its findings on the Spirit Cave Mummy in 1996. Immediately the issue sparked a furor, with the American Indians demanding that the corpse be reburied in accordance with tribal custom - falsely claiming the Spirit Cave Mummy as one of their own.

The Amerind tribe involved, the Paiutes, laid claim to the corpse under an American law, the Native American Graves Protection and Repatriation Act of 1990, which allows for the return and reburial of bodies of "Native Americans".

An extended legal dispute arose over the issue of to whom the corpse actually belongs. As part of the legal wrangling, the Paiute have consistently refused to allow DNA testing of the corpse.

This is not the only case where American Indians have blocked the study of obviously non-Amerind remains. Another case, that of Kennewick Man was similarly held up by Indian objections; and in 1993 another skeleton was found near Buhl in the state of Idaho.

Retrieved 16th July 2003 from http://www.freerepublic.com/focus/f-news/946813/posts

Neanderthals were in America, and all over the globe a long time before the other humanoids were created. How ironic is it that the 'Native' Americans say America is their land, when they killed our people there a long time ago?

To the Neanderthals it is like being slaughtered by our own children, and it is a very hard thing to come to terms with. Especially as the acts of the white Cro-Magnons means we are grouped together with them as 'white' and told we are the same, so not true.

Scots May Be Directly Descended From Neanderthal Man

When this article was published back in 2001, it shocked a lot of people, as people were used to Neanderthals being portrayed as stupid cave dwellers. Well Neanderthals might prefer to live underground in caves and mounds, but they aren't stupid.

By Tom Peterkin.

FROM William Wallace to the goalposts at Wembley, Scots have a fearsome reputation for causing trouble.

Now, a team of scientists may have discovered the explanation-we inherited Neanderthal genes.

Experts in evolution from Oxford say the key lies in the red hair for which Celts are famous.

The team studied the origins of the gene which causes red hair and discovered it is older than the first Homo Sapien settlers to come to Europe from Africa around 30,000 years ago.

This strongly suggests the gene must have been present in Neanderthal man, who was living in Europe long before the arrival of Homo Sapiens. The Oxford team says this points to interbreeding between Neanderthals and the new settlers, an idea which has previously been dismissed. It was originally believed that Homo Sapiens, because they were more sophisticated, simply drove out the Neanderthals to the point where they became extinct. The conclusion the team draws is that the red hair, freckles and pale skin which characterise Scots are most likely the genetic legacy of a long-dead species, known for being hairy and having prominent brows and receding foreheads. Around 10% of Scots are redheads, while an additional 40% of the population with other hair colourings carry the gene responsible for red hair.

Dr Rosalind Harding, of the Institute of Molecular Medicine at the John Radcliffe Hospital, in Oxford, calculated the age of the ginger version of the gene, known as the melanocortin 1 receptor (MC1R), by using a complex model that looked at its mutation rate.

She found that the gene was present 100,000 years ago-at least 70,000 years before Homo Sapiens' migration into Europe from Africa. Harding maintains that the gene could not have originated in the sweltering heat of Africa, because natural selection would not have allowed the survival of a trait that predisposes humans to skin cancer.

Studies have revealed that carriers of the gene are five times more sensitive to ultraviolet light than others and therefore far more likely to contract skin cancer. Given that the gene is so much older than the earliest anthropological records of Stone Age Homo Sapiens, who were responsible for the spectacular cave paintings produced around

30,000 years ago, Harding believes that MC1R must have originated in the Neanderthals.

"The gene is certainly older than 50,000 years and it could be as old as 100,000 years," she said. "An explanation is that it comes from the Neanderthals-the other people that were here before modern man came out of Africa."

Harding believes that the prevalence of the ginger gene in so many of today's population provides evidence that early Homo sapiens bred with the Neanderthals and that many of today's humans are descended from unions between the two species.

So does that mean it is possible that Scottish redheads are directly descended from the Neanderthals? "It seems to be the logical conclusion to what I am saying," said Harding. "But I don't know if people are going to like me for saying that."

© The Scotsman Publications Ltd.

Source: SCOTLAND ON SUNDAY 15/04/2001

Wisdom Teeth & Rh Negatives

Tails, extra nipples and wisdom teeth are throw backs. The more simian genes someone has, the more likely they are to have those things, as they are less evolved than the ancient tribes. In the past Neanderthals used to have wisdom teeth, a long long time ago, now none do. But those with more simian genes still have them.

Wisdom teeth were for our ancestor's early diet of coarse, rough food – like leaves, roots, nuts, grass and things, they are no longer needed. The more evolved you are, the less likely you have them. If you don't have room for them, but they try to come through, you are more evolved than those who grow them normally.

Neanderthals do have a gap on their gum line behind their last teeth, top and bottom, but the wisdom teeth are simply not there.

From surveys done 70% of those with Rh negative blood had never had wisdom teeth at all. 25% had some or all of them come through and had to have them removed. Only 5% had grown them normally.

Sumerian Gods & Goddesses

These statues date back to roughly 2500 BC. History records that they must have been "in awe" due to being in the presence of their god. (That's how they explain the wide-eyes, anyway.)

However, note that Incan legends record that giants with huge blue saucer-shaped eyes, white skin and red hair that supposedly built their giant stone monuments found in South America.

Also note the huge brow bridge of these wide-eyed people. That fits the Neanderthal skull. The larger brain capacity also fits Nazcan skulls. Many of them cone-headed in shape.

You look at these facts carved in stone and decide for yourself. Remember that Neanderthal skeletons were found alongside Jewish skeletons in Israel, making them contemporaries! Also the Jewish Cohen Priests share the Neanderthal DNA, who were seen as the Priestly Caste, where as the other Jews have some Neanderthal genetics, but not as many.

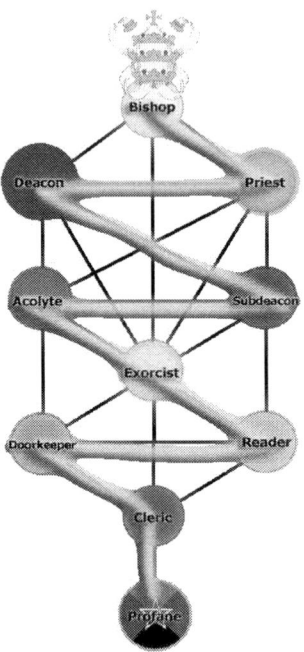

Secrets of the Serpent Bloodline - The Unveiling of Profound Esoteric Mysteries

Part 2: Awakening Spirituality

Chapter 5

Truth

As posted to the Temple of Theola site.

People do get confused on what type of group we are, are we Pagan? Are we religious? What do we believe?

We are spiritual, not religious and we believe that all good spiritual paths lead to the same place - enlightenment. Enlightened beings don't feel the need to label themselves. They have their inner 'Divine light', they become Theolalites, and that is all that word means.

Truth is our only belief.

We are not here to 'prove' anything to anyone. If someone decides to take what they learn here further then fine, if not, that is fine too. You might find something that resonates with you.

We are not here to force our views on to anyone. We are not in some kind of competition to decide who knows the most, or who is the most enlightened, because all that kind of nonsense is removed from you when you have your own inner peace. You stop searching and are just happy to share your own knowledge and listen to the view of others.

New age/spiritual groups are notorious for taking advantage of those seeking answers, we don't do that, we are NOT a 'New Age' group, our teachings go far beyond recorded his-story. We just encourage you to use your own intuition about things. No one else can give you answers, you have to find your own answers. It might be easier to sit back and listen to someone else's views and just believe that, but that is dangerous, and that is how extremist cults are formed.

You can only ever find answers within yourself, not from anyone else.

Question everything and everyone.

What are someone's motives for telling you something? Is it to massage your ego? What good does that do in the long run? You might feel important and better for a while, but you will still be empty inside, until you find your own truth and stop living by your false ego, which is created by others.

Does this person feel the need to 'prove' their powers to you? Do they give you false hopes about things? Do they have books to sell? Do they ask for money from you, and I don't mean for just covering the cost of meetings or paying for their time to help you. If you put value on money and believe that by paying more for something, you can get better results, you are the fake 'Gurus' dream come true. They will massage your ego and tell you what you want to hear, why? So you will keep going back with more money. You aren't going to want to pay someone who tells you the truth, and says you have to sort yourself out because no one else can do it for you, are you?

The truth often hurts, and we don't want to hear it. But remember those who tell you the truth, because in the future when you accept it and start to do something about it, they are likely to be the only ones who will be there for you still. By that point you will probably have no money left because you gave it all to fake Gurus, and they are suddenly no longer interested in you. You will have lost all your friends, from being an egomaniac and they got fed up of you going on and on about what your teacher has told you about how fantastic you are. And then one day the truth will finally dawn on you, and you will remember who told you the truth. And you will no longer fight it, you will work towards YOUR truth, and no one else's.

We are here for you, when you have stopped living in your false ego and are ready to find the TRUTH - There is nothing at as freeing and empowering than TRUTH.

Be the solution http://templeoftheola.org/be-the-solution.html

Theolalite

What are Theolalites?

They look like you or me, you could not tell by their looks. But upon looking into their eyes or being in their presence, you would soon recognise them.

They aren't like others, they can be seen as secretive and reserved, sometimes even stand offish. However, if you got to know one you would learn so much from just being in their presence.

They are highly spiritual beings, who have no need for jealousy, envy or gossip. They actually find this abhorrent and can't understand why others would want to be like that. When a friend is doing well, they are genuinely pleased for them and most of the time have probably helped them get there, without taking any credit.

They work selflessly for others, never asking for praise or admiration. And although some might see them as aloof and acting as if they are above others, they don't mean to give that impression...

They simply don't know how to act round 'normal' people, as they are far from normal.

Do Theolalites have any special abilities?

Theolalites are born with powers of telepathy, remote viewing, psychic, psychometry and various other 'gifts'. As children they grow up believing everyone is like this, and it can be a real shock to them when they realise they are the only ones. They are often bullied by others as children, and this quite often continues into adulthood, as others don't tend to trust those who can read them like a book. They can look into your soul and see your true spirit and although they don't like a lot of human behaviours, they forgive them for their faults, because they realise they're not as advanced as them.

Am I a Theolalite?

Theolalites reading this article will instantly recognise themselves.

- Have you always felt like an outsider no matter which group of people you have tried to fit in with, and find all the back stabbing and bitching so petty?
- Do you have just a few very close friends, and find others come and go all the time, but you just don't click with them?
- Do you find jealousy and envy abhorrent, and live your life wanting to help others on their own spiritual paths?
- Do you sense the hurt and pain in others, so strongly it can be unbearable at times?
- Do you find yourself knowing what others are thinking?
- When you touch an object or enter a room, do you pick up vibes?
- Do you find yourself having a strong need to find others like you?
- Do you want the world to be a better place, and can only see it happening if people develop spiritually?

If you answer yes to most or all the questions above, you are probably a Theolalite.

Can anyone become a Theolalite?

Some are born awake, aware and balanced, unfortunately others have to work at it. The very fact someone wants to work on becoming better and more spiritually advanced means you have a much higher chance than someone else just chosen at random.

So well done, you have made a massive step towards change and spiritual evolution already.

Currently the only Church with valid apostolic succession which has been founded by Theolalites is The Church of St Mary & St John (a spiritual church, not religious). If you feel a calling to Minister, or work towards your own inner truth and enlightenment you can find out more here http://churchsmsj.org/

Gnostic Theolalites

What are Gnostic Theolalites?

A Gnostic is one that seeks Gnosis (Knowledge). A Gnostic doesn't need labels because true independence is being Gnostic. Originally, Gnostics simply called themselves, "Knowledge seekers" as Gnosis means Knowledge, the idea being, if Truth is ONE, then all Knowledge Seekers who GENUINELY seek the truth, should eventually end up at the same view, but by their own paths.

Theolalite is just a word to describe someone with Gnosis, who has full connection to their own Higher Self. Theola=Divine, Lite=Light. They carry the Divine spark within them, ignited by their compassion and the truth.

Despite what people say about Gnostics they are pre-Christian and it isn't a religion, it is a way of life - that of seeking knowledge and wisdom, which leads to spiritual enlightenment or illumination. When you are enlightened, you can see the big picture, you can see the connection in all things and you realise that all spiritual paths lead to the same place. So some people don't call themselves a 'Gnostic' until after they have reached enlightenment.

There were Gnostics about before the age of Pisces (the fisher King & Queen - Christianity), before the age of Aries (the ram - Jewish religion), before the age of Taurus (Holy bull or cow worship - Minoan, Hindu, Egypt), before the age of Gemini (Twins - Sumer twins Enki and Enlil). They are the holders of the secrets from the underground stream.

Because we are now entering the age of Aquarius, the age of enlightenment, many more hidden (occult) truths are being revealed to the general population than ever before. Aquarius is represented by a man or woman with a pitcher, pouring out water on to the world from the heavens. That water represents enlightenment.

For every age something new is worshipped by the general population. Religions are built up around these things because humans generally have always needed to be guided to live life happily, because we know about death. Animals don't know they are going to die, so they don't worry about it. But because humans became conscious of this, as the neo-cortex expanded, it led to them spending their whole life worrying about it. To make people get on with their life in peace they were told stories and myths, things that would reassure them that if they led a good and noble life, they would go to somewhere wonderful when they left this place. Or that if they behaved like animals, they would be reincarnated as an animal. This worked on many levels. It kept people happy, it kept them from fearing death and it made them be good people through fear that if they did bad things they would be punished for it in the afterlife, or come back as a slug or something.

At the end of every astrological age there is the time of upheaval and upset. Many are starting to reject the old ways that they have always been taught, and are looking for something new. This is when the new age comes in and the old deity is symbolically killed, so the new deity can take over. This is why Moses told the people to slaughter the golden calf, as bull and cow worship was to end, and the new age of Aries was to be brought in. At the end of each age of course, there will always be those who try to cling on to the past and are scared to move forward. This is why all the old religions are still about for us all to see, those religions are stuck in the old ages and the people never learnt how to evolve from those old teachings and move on.

The same will happen at the end of this age. Those still following Christianity will refuse to let go of the old ways and move forwards towards Aquarius and the new ways of enlightenment. In the new age those who accept it will be able to see all of this above as truth, they will realise that all the religions were created for each age, and they will accept responsibility for themselves and their own actions, without the need of an authority figure or deity to tell them what to do. They will become a Priest or Priestess themselves, they will connect to their own Higher Self in the new coming age. They will gladly seek out Gnosis and Sophia (wisdom) and will enjoy learning and helping others.

In the past all through ancient times, only a selected few were given this Gnosis and these teachings. Everyone else was expected to follow the teachings of that age, and never become enlightened themselves. Sometimes this was because they didn't have the Will or intelligence to know any different, or because the Mystery School was taken over by people who wanted to use Gnosis to control others and gain power for themselves. For having a little of this knowledge can lead to problems... For instance, if someone was to join a Mystery School, learn a few things, then decide they don't want to learn anymore, all they want to do is take what they do know and control others with it. Then they go along and create a cult, give people a bit of knowledge, but because they haven't connected to their own Higher Self. All they do is create more confused people in the world, and more power hungry control freaks, who will twist the truth to get what they want. The Roman Catholic Church are a good example of this. They have a lot of the knowledge about all these things, but they choose to use it against people, instead of using it to help people. They have not connected to their own Higher Self, so they can't help anyone else. They choose instead to demonise anything that could enlighten people.

What do Gnostic Theolalites believe about Jesus?

Jesus was the member of a Mystery School, the Order he belonged to taught about enlightenment and Gnosis. He never proclaimed to be a God, he taught that we all have the Divine spark within. His 'followers' where simply those he was teaching what he himself had learnt. Because Jesus and his wife Mary Magdalene had built up such a large following it was becoming difficult for those who were trying to control people with the religions they wanted them to follow. The power hungry unenlightened ones decided to come up with a plan that could be used to control everyone. The new age of Pisces was dawning, and so they decided to take Jesus the man, and turn him into the new God of the Pisces age. They took his true teaching and changed them, told people he was the God, and these are his words and teachings (the bible), and forced people to follow them. Anyone who refused was slaughtered. Jesus, Magdalene and their family were forced to flee to South of France, where they kept the true Mystery School teachings and passed them down in the underground stream. Everyone was told he had died for their sins and they should all repent etc. The masses were deceived and a lot of them still are today.

Why do Gnostic Theolalites wear the same robes as Catholics?

The Church of St Mary & St John is bringing the esoteric truth to the mainstream, as holders of the secret knowledge of the ages, we celebrate each age and each aeon. Because we are still in the age of Pisces, the Bishops who have reached enlightenment, will wear a Mitre to represent this age. When we are in the new age it will be something different again. Within our Templar Order we have Fisher Princes, Princesses, Kings and Queens too.

As for the robes, these are pretty much the same in whichever tradition you follow. A Tau robe (alb) and a cloak (cope) are the same things, worn by Ceremonial Magickians, Christians, Witches, Wiccans, Druids etc etc. Where do you think they got that idea from? The same Mystery Schools of course.

Just like the Dogon Tribe in Mali had Gods that were half fish and half man. These people where visited by strangers who came from the sea, in ships, and they were tall and white, and they had a fish head on, they told them about the stars and special rituals. Sound familiar? Again, from the Mystery Schools.

As well as the theme for each Aeon, there were always other Gods and Goddesses to represent the planets and other stars. It was only after the introduction of patriarchy by Zoroaster, that religions started gradually all venerating just one male God.

All the Mystery Schools at one time were run by Priestesses, men came to them for enlightenment and teachings. Later when patriarchy took over the men were only allowed to join and learn the truth if they were castrated (this is no longer done, however many religions still insist on celibacy) and dressed up in the robes of the Goddess, imitating women, which Priests still do to this day. The Church of St Mary & St John does not insist on celibacy of its Clergy.

When will the new age be here?

The new age is now dawning, and within The Church of St Mary & St John's Celtic Gnostic Mass and within our own Mystery School, we celebrate the Aeons and the Ages. We also do something special that helps bring in the new age and celebrates that the new age will be about enlightenment for all, which will in turn create balance, equality and finally bring the truth to all.

Is what you teach the same as the new age movement?

Yes and no. A lot of people have a few pieces of the puzzle, they have taken bits and pieces from all over the place, but not many have found the full truth. In so much as, some of them might believe they are teaching the full truth and others know they are selling lies, but like to make money out of spirituality, and they know that the truth doesn't sell, so they make up stories. The only thing you have to remember on your journey, as you seek out the truth, is that it can only truly be found within. Anyone who guides you to anywhere but there, is guiding you the wrong way.

The Four Pillars of Gnosis

The four pillars of Gnosis are the foundations of the Gnostic knowledge - they are Art, Science, Philosophy and Mysticism. Knowledge and wisdom are cultivated through the intelligent combination of these areas of study within us - they are a medium of expression for the consciousness itself.

Art - Art is the world of the imagination and of inspiration. The esoteric art has always expressed the internal, mystical reality of a person. This is referred to as the "Royal Art of Nature". It provides direct teachings to the consciousness of a person who is receptive to them and is a type of food for the soul that is perceived through the imagination and illuminates the heart.

Science - Science is about study, experimentation and verification. Gnosis is in this sense a science as it is about experimenting and verifying for yourself. The science of Gnosis contains many areas of study, including:

- Psychology: the functions of the mind, the subconscious.
- Kabbalah: the internal dimensions of nature, the astral world.
- Alchemy: working with and developing our internal energies, transformation.

There are also other areas such as the tarot, astrology, chakras, meditation etc. They are mystical sciences for us to study and verify in our own way.

Philosophy - Philosophy is the love (Philo) of wisdom (Sophia). It is about the questions to our very existence - who are we, why are we here and where are we going? Gnosis is a living philosophy where we allow the inner questions, the spiritual impulses, to direct our questions and our search for knowledge. This is what constitutes the Initiatic Philosophy - learning to comprehend and develop the path of self realisation within our own life.

Mysticism - Mysticism is the direct experience that illuminates the consciousness and is in fact the one that completes all the other pillars. Gnosis itself is a mystical study and therefore meditation forms a large part of our studies. Mysticism also includes working with our dreams and learning to perceive and strengthen the connection we have to our own internal Being. It is a practical study where an effort is directed to allowing the consciousness to experience the inner nature of things beyond the mind, body and emotions.

The Alchemical Process

Alchemical Stage 1 - Earth

What is the first thing you encounter when you close your eyes? Blackness. When you enter your inner world, you enter into darkness. This is the first experience, and the first stage of the Great Work. here the operation of putrefaction takes place. Here the fixed gets dissolved by the volatile. By becoming aware of the volatile mind, the bodily consciousness diminishes. In alchemical symbols Nigredo is always indicated by something black: the raven, the raven's head, the dark jacket, darkness, the night, the Solar or Moon eclipse, the tomb, hell, and death.

When the Matter has entered the stage of blackness, it is called lead or Saturn, or the head of Moorish one.

Putrefaction, the process during the phase of blackness. In the picture a skeleton and a black raven. The cut off tree stump to the right is a symbol that sometimes appears in alchemical engravings to symbolize that the old self has to be cut off and a new self will spring up (the new growth symbolized by the fresh sprout on the trunk).

The skeleton is standing on an eclipsed sun. The sun is the Inner Light, the Divine Self, that is hidden by the blackness of our every day, normal behaviour and being. It is obscured by the physical consciousness we all have. Therefore that what obscured our Divine Self has to be putrefied and purified in order for the Divine Self to shine in all its glory.

Alchemical Stage 2 - Water

The white dove is a symbol for the stage of Whiteness or Albedo. Often the early stages of this are shown as being in a bath or vat of water. Becoming aware of your inner world, is like being in water. In this picture the King and Queen, or Sulphur and Mercury, or Moon and Sun have been elevated into the air. Here they have attained the state of Whiteness or Albedo, indicated by the white dove, and the star.

This is the perfect putrefaction, when all blackness has disappeared and the colour white appears. Then it is said that life has conquered death, that the king has been revived, that earth and water has become air, that the child has been born, that Heaven (the Volatile, the Female) and Earth (the Fixed, the Male) have married. It is the realm of the Moon.

When one has purified there awareness of Self, during meditation, by eliminating thoughts, or otherwise, then at a certain point, light appears. This can be but is not necessary a visual light inside oneself. The light that appears is also metaphoric for an absolute clear, pure awareness of Self. It is something that cannot be described. One does not indeed experience the darkness anymore that is there when one closes the eyes.

Alchemists say that in Whiteness, the Matter has attained a degree of Fixedness that fire cannot destroy. In that state one is in a very fixed position, that is, very stable, very much in the here and now, in total clarity of Self.

Philosophers say that when one has attained this stage, one needs to destroy the books because they become superfluous. From this point on one needs to continue this purification of awareness to the next stage of yellowness.

Alchemical Stage 3 - Air

Citrinitas – the yellowness; the solar dawn or awakening. Now the light is no longer reflective as in the lunar light of Albedo. Its nature is direct and it is all pervading. It is sometimes referred to as the original Light or the Light that is pure, creative Intelligence.

It is said that the only true knowledge is revealed to us when this Light becomes conscious in us.

Stage three begins with the "yellow death". There is a dying away of the "lunar light" to the point of complete darkness, which is in fact "black light," a light so bright we cannot see it as our inner sight is veiled and it appears as darkness. It is a complete dying of the dualistic state of mind that perceives subject and object as separate.

The "yellow death" signals the end of the influence of the "lunar light," as the consciousness is transformed into "solar light." This "solar light" awakens the sense of revelation and revelatory knowledge. Inner knowing is not arrived at by study, reflection or deep thought; it is to be experienced as a direct revelation.

Since stage three has moved clearly into the mystical realms, there is no way to describe this, it has to be experienced. However, the intuitive knowledge that we often receive in life, whether in a dream or in a flash of realisation, gives us at least a hint of the power of the "revelatory light" or "solar light."

In this sense, we could say that our intuition is an expression of the eternal mystical knowledge, a level at which everything is already known. This is referred to as Pure Intelligence. Our Higher Self provides this intuition. In order to know something of this stage we must rely on the illuminations of those exceptional few human beings who have recorded their experiences.

Alchemical Stage 4 - Fire

The fourth and last phase is characterized by the colour red. When the yellowness has been made, it needs to purified further, sublimated, until the Matter becomes totally Fixed and is completely stable. Then we have the Red Sulphur, the red stone, the Red Elixir, the Stone of the Wise.

When the Divine Light (Theolalite) has emerged during meditation, one needs to make it last. This demands a continued effort of holding one's attention to this pure awareness, not only for the length of the meditation session, but also during every day life. At a certain point the pure awareness of one's Divine Self (Theolalite) will be permanent.

This time a winged Sun figure rising from a tomb. The tomb is a often used symbol for the phase of Blackness. The figure to the right is the Goddess Diana, a symbol for the second phase of Whiteness, symbolized by the Moon. The figure on the left is the God, symbolized by the Sun of the third phase of Yellowness. The bow and arrow is a symbol for Fixing the volatile. In other words when Yellowness has been reached, one needs to Fix the Matter (like an arrow pins down something) until it become totally Fixed.

Jesus was an Alchemist

Reading the above it might seem obvious how religions have used the alchemical process Jesus went through and taken it literally.

The alchemical process is played out by our Sun everyday and on a larger scale every year. It is born, it dies when the Moon comes out and is reborn. The same way Jesus was born a King, he lived a pure life, and he met Mary Magdalene his Queen (Moon/White Dove), the two merged during Hieros Gamos (the star) where his all old self dies and he found his Inner Light. He then rises from his tomb reborn - illuminated.

Chapter 6

Awakening Process

As we begin our awakening process one of the first things we begin to notice is the differences between the new way of thinking and being, and the old way. Though the new way has its pitfalls, you will definitely prefer it because of one very important thing—it enables you to pull yourself out of mental, emotional and physical distress created by victimhood.

Our awakening process causes us to lose friends, friends who wish to stay victims. As we move further towards enlightenment, we no longer resonate at the frequency of victimhood. Therefore, our friends and loved ones find no safe harbour in their friendship with us anymore. This is difficult for you even though you understand it. We are no longer mentally in step with the rest of the world.

Maybe many times you wondered if you were losing your mind. When you look at those you know who are living in unaware lives, seemingly unaffected by the changes you are experiencing, You wonder which of you is sane and which isn't. As your world continues to separate into two different worlds, one being asleep and the other on the upward spiral to enlightenment, the idea of differing realities becomes very real to us. You might look at your asleep companions and wonder how in the world they can continue to live their lives oblivious to the changes taking place around them. To say they are asleep is an understatement. And though this understanding might help your state of mind, it most definitely does not bring relief and comfort to your heart. You feel the separation acutely.

You hurt from the knowledge that you have less and less in common, less and less to say to one another. You are drifting apart like two ships passing in the night and there is nothing that you are willing to do about it. For to do something about it would be to either let go of your present path and return to a total asleep life that would leave you emotionally and spiritually dead, or try to convince them to awaken and begin the spiritual path so that we can have something in common that is of interest to you both - something that makes both your hearts sing. As you can see, neither is a worthwhile option. The first one hurts you and the second one hurts them and breaks the universal law of free will.

So they might say you are crazy and need to check into a mental hospital. You can console yourself by thinking that one day, they might 'get it' too.

And until that time comes, you must let go of my desire to be accepted by them.

Sometimes they put forth some pretty convincing arguments, so convincing in fact that you might find yourself giving yourself another good old-fashioned reality check. You might ask yourself 'why I am doing this?, why I am willing to hold on to nothing in order to attain a goal that I have no guarantee that I will reach, or that when and if I do, it will be all that I was told it would be?'

You will run through the facts in your head that you have accumulated for just such an occasion. You remember that you were told that it would not always be easy—that the path is narrow, rocky and full of pitfalls. You also remember those days when you have just come through another lesson and feel that blissful state of peace, or the prosperity that suddenly arrives unannounced but oh so welcome, or the synchronicities that bring some new friend and companion to your doorstep. Just a few of those memories and you are once again able to see and feel that this path, this goal is worth it, and you pull yourself together and continue on.

Naive Enlightenment

What is Naive Enlightenment?

When you are on a spiritual path, many cycles happen, before you get to complete enlightenment. The very thing that starts us on a spiritual path is normally what is called "Naïve Enlightenment" This is when we suddenly realise the world isn't how we first thought it was, we start to see the bigger picture, we have awoken up to realise we have been living a lie and trying to conform to our false ego, which is created by those around us.

At this point we often feel euphoric, and completely enlightened, and the signs of this are easy to see for those further down the path. The newly awoken being who is going through Naive Enlightenment will often think they are God, the messiah and feel they can do no wrong and they know everything there is to know.

Your mind works at high speed, new information is coming to you with ease, you feel magickal and wonderful.

But wait, before you start shouting about being the messiah or acting like a 'know it all' take a chill pill, because you are about to face one almighty fall.

Dark Night of the Soul - The Abyss

There then follows a time of chaos and confusion, you can't understand why no one else can see the truth you can see. You might start to try and convince others of your 'truth' and no matter what you do they won't listen to you. Some might listen and they might also think you are wonderful for teaching them the truth, and this only delays the hell you are going through. Depression sets in, all your new found magickal powers abandon you, and you feel more alone and down than you have ever felt before.

So how do you get out of it?

You learn to swallow your pride, you admit you were wrong, that you don't really know everything and you forgive yourself for your mistakes. You focus your intent completely on finding the true you, your Higher Self, your Holy Guardian Angel. Create a ritual or meditation to perform everyday to invoke your Angel, but you must want to give up your old ego and all it's needs and wants to be massaged by others. Your Angel, the true you, knows when you are not serious, and it will never come back and make everything wonderful again, unless you are willing to look inside once more - the truth is inside you and you can never find the truth outside yourself.

Enlightenment

What is enlightenment?

I am asked this often, everyone wants to know what it actually means, what will I feel like when enlightened? Will I be a good person who can do no wrong? Will I have reached perfection?

You will feel the same as you do now, only you will no longer be striving to find out the truth, because you will have it. Being enlightened will not mean you can do no wrong, and that everything you say or do is correct. Some will use the new found knowledge for bad things and to control others. If you are not careful on your path and rush in and find out the truth too soon, it can lead to insanity. The Aspirant can't deal with the truth if they are ill prepared and instead of seeing the truth and moving forward, they get depressed, or angry and filled with resentment. So they use their new found knowledge as a way to abuse others. Those who are well prepared can see the beauty in the truth, find inner peace and happiness.

Jesus said, *"Everyone who seeks should continue seeking until he finds. When he finds, he will be troubled at the contemplation of Truth, but when he has passed through the time of trouble, he will be astonished at the brightness of the Light, for the Way of Truth is the Pathway to the Eternal Godhead, and the price of the beatific vision is the wringing of the soul. The person who desires to rise above all things must descend below all things, for the way to the heights passes through the depths of anguish, which generate the fires of Life. The person who has suffered and found Life is blessed."*

I get asked often - if you know the truth, isn't it elitist to keep it to yourself and not just tell someone?

Well the example above is good enough reason to avoid at all costs someone ill prepared from finding the truth. Everyone must find their own path to truth. Mystery schools and Orders can only point in the right direction, and show you things that can help you, they can not do the work for you, this you must face alone.

We all have a set of daemons to face, parts of psyche that we don't like, so try to avoid acknowledging. We know that drinking too much is damaging to us, or lying, or stealing.. Our hearts know this, and these daemons that control these behaviours will do all they can to latch on to you forever, if you let them, and it is so much easier to let them.

What is a Daemon?

dae·mon (dē'mən) Gr *daimōn*, divine power, fate, god, in - *dā(i)-*, to part, divide, tear apart. daemon "spirit," from Gk. daimon "deity, divine power; lesser god; guiding spirit, tutelary deity" "one's genius, lot, or fortune;" from PIE *dai-mon- "divider, provider" (of fortunes or destinies), from base *da- "to divide". Used (with daimonion).

Daemons are divided parts of our minds. Sections of our minds that when tapped into can give us Divine powers.

Ceremonial magick is a way of summoning these daemons and banishing them, one by one, so that you are free from all the problems these cause to you. But you must face them to banish them for good. Often when starting out on this path many an Aspirant will get so far, then a big bad ugly daemon will appear that they have to face, and they feel they can't. They will use any excuse to not face it, they will blame their spiritual teacher, they will blame their job, they will blame their loved ones, their health.. anything to allow them an excuse to back out and keep the daemon latched on to them.

Secrets of the Serpent Bloodline - The Unveiling of Profound Esoteric Mysteries

If you manage to face all your daemons and banish them, you then get the chance to summon wonderful daemons from your psyche, ones that can do wonderful things - like learn a new language, become a great Musician, a Poet, a Writer, Scientist and Artist.. anything you can imagine. All these daemons are within you already, you just need to summon them to make the most of those parts of your brain you are not yet using.

All the answers are within you, not outside of you.

Once enlightened you don't stop learning, but you start learning at a fantastic pace. There is a difference between being enlightened to the truth and knowing everything, no one can ever know everything, we never stop learning. And it is an enlightened person who will ask for help and guidance from others on a topic they know nothing about.

Don't be afraid while on your journey to ask for help and guidance, but always follow your own intuition about what is right for you.

Devote yourself and your work to your Holy Guardian Angel/Higher Self, invoke them everyday, they will guide you to where you are supposed to be and eventually everything will fall into place.

Higher Self

Some might get upset at me for saying Angels and Demons are not separate from us, they are not outside ourselves. There does exist outside ourselves astral entities, and that is a whole different matter. Also the Archangels which have been invoked and empowered over many many years have also become astral entities themselves, but humans created them. The Angels and Demons that others have created, just like Deity Archetypes, can be invoked so you can benefit from their attributes. However this is not a pure way of working with magick, as you are using entities others have created and it can never be as pure as something you create yourself.

Within each of us their exists our Higher Self, or as some call it, Holy Guardian Angel or Future Magickal Self. You first have to find out it's name, and yes it does have one, and it has a symbol key that is used to invoke it in the beginning. First you find the symbol, but you probably won't even realise it is the key to your Higher Self until later. Once you have realised this is your key, you use it everyday to invoke your Higher Self, until eventually you will be given their name. Your Higher Self can be male or female, or alternate.

Once you have your own Higher Self's name, or Holy Guardian Angel, it is the most powerful thing ever. I sometimes forget just how powerful. The other day I had lost my purse, and I couldn't remember when I had it last. I thought I might have left it at the Vets. I looked all round the usual places. I was just about to give up and ring the bank to say I lost my card. Then I stopped for a moment and I called my Higher Self by name to tell me where it was. I was told to look in the office, and there it was... sat on my desk. I never put it there! and would never have thought about looking there! but my Higher Self knew. I thanked my Higher Self and sent her love and adoration, this is important.

Until someone has this connection themselves, they won't understand this, but I can assure you it is possible and it is most amazing thing ever, and not just for finding stuff, all kinds of things that have to be experienced for yourself, words can not describe it.

Now of course a Christian's mind set will be, 'oh my goodness she has been possessed by a demon'. They have cut themselves off from true spirituality by believing the Divine and evil are something outside themselves. A Gnostic Theolalite has learnt to look within.

Setting Your Body Clock

This is a test that anyone can do. Before going to sleep, as you are in bed settling down, ask your Higher Self to awaken you at the time you need to wake up.

Look at your clock and say to your Higher Self - 7 hours from now (or however many hours it is) I will wake up naturally and feel refreshed, rested and ready to start my day.

Then turn out your light and go to sleep. You should find yourself waking up exactly on time, if not a few minutes before the time you wanted. However if you do have to get up for work or something, make sure you have a back-up alarm set for 10 mins after the time you want.

This might not work on your first attempt, but if you do this every night, it will. You will find you can ask for any wake up time and it will happen.

Often these things just take a little practice, but are well worth the effort.

Chapter 7

Reptilian Brain

What is the Reptilian Brain?

The reptilian brain (also called R-Complex or Archipallium) is responsible for self preservation. It is there that the mechanisms of aggression, survival and reproduction reside. It also controls some involuntary actions and the control of certain visceral functions (cardiac, pulmonary, intestinal, etc), indispensable to the preservation of life.

How does it effect me?

When on our spiritual paths, we will have to question our own beliefs constantly, it is all part of the process, however....

What happens in our brains when someone disagrees with a belief we have taken on as truth?

The small nut sized amygdala (there are two, one on each side of the brain) among other things is the centre for identification of danger, (fear headquarters) and is fundamental for self preservation. When triggered, it gives rise to fear and anxiety (through the R-complex) which leads an animal or human into a stage of alertness, preparing for "FIGHT or FLIGHT."

This is triggered when someone says something to upset a belief system we have, we get angry and aggressive and often start to hate the person for ever even mentioning it. So we either attack them trying to bring them down and belittle them, or we run away.

How can I avoid reacting this way?

Becoming aware of these responses is important to our enlightenment, as fear can only damage our hearts. When you are aware of these reactions, you can learn how to control them, and not let it have a negative effect on you and others.

So when someone says something that you don't agree with, don't take it personally, they are not attacking you and they are entitled to their own views about things. Calmly listen to their side, then put your side across, that way you might both learn something from each other, instead of becoming enemies.

Self Pity Monster

What is a Self Pity Monster?

There is no doubt about it, you will have come across one or more of them. Today's culture is set up to pander to them.

A Self Pity Monster will see that you are in a good mood, feeling happy and cheerful. They will work out a way to make you miserable and feeling sorry for them, or trying to prove yourself to them.

An example being - imagine you just had some fantastic news, you got engaged, or found out you got a new job, or something else that makes you feel on top of the world. The Self Pity Monster (also known as a Psychic Vampire) will see you and how happy you are, and because they are in victim mode and feeling horrible, they can't stand to see you happy, so they will do one of two things - They will either:

1. Start complaining about a problem they have, either with their health, their job, their relationship, or some other problem. Anything at all. Instead of feeling so happy for you their friend they need to take that energy from you, drain you of it, and feed themselves. Instead of waiting for another time to talk about something with you that is troubling them, they will hit you with it and complain when your energy is most high.

2. Attack you in some way to make you feel guilty for being so happy, either by accusing you of being a bad person for laughing and joking and being happy, or think up a reason why you are not allowed to be happy. Maybe it is the anniversary of their Aunties death or something? It doesn't matter what, they will think up some way to make you feel bad and miserable.

It's all Me Me Me!

A Self Pity Monster spends all their time feeling sorry for themselves. They will ring you up and talk at you for hours and hours about all their problems, and not stop for a moment to even ask how you are, and if they do ask - when you try to reply, maybe saying you have a cold or something. They will cut you off and talk over you about how when they have a cold, it is always so much worse than whenever anyone else has one. They will go into competition with you about illnesses and how hard done to they are. They talk like they are the only human in the world who has ever suffered. It is all me me me with these people.

Sulking Episodes

Don't think for a moment you can dare to not give the Self Pity Monster your full undivided attention at all times. If you are out at the pub with a group of friends with a SPM and you are talking to others and enjoying yourself, the SPM will walk out and start sulking. You won't know where they have gone, so one of you will go and look for them. When you find them they will say they don't feel well, or just keep saying nothing is wrong, but refusing to come back and join you. Then everyone feels guilty for carrying on and forgetting them, so everyone makes a fuss (their intention in the first place) and they will have ruined the night. If you think this is just a one off try going out with them again, and again, you will soon notice the same pattern happening time and time again.

Alcohol Abuse and Mental Disorders as Excuses

Another tactic of he SPM is to get blind drunk and start hurling abuse at others or causing fights, again more attention seeking tactics and the next day they will be all sorry and say it wasn't them, it was the drink.

If they notice you getting wise to the their tricks and manipulation they will change tactic for a while, they will say they have learnt the errors of their ways and they want to change and get help. Of course the trips to Alcohols Anonymous or a Therapist won't last long, as they will realise that the people there won't make them the centre of attention and put up with their self pity. So it will soon all stop and they are back to square one.

Self Pity Monster and Relationships

A SPM will jump from one relationship to the next very quickly, as they can't be on their own. They need someone else to drain energy from. It won't much matter how unsuitable the person is for them, they will jump into bed and into a relationship with them right away.

They will accuse their partner of things, make them feel guilty, force them to prove themselves to them. They will expect them to put up with their mood swings and bad behaviour.

That person is then in for a very rocky ride until they realise what is going on and dump them. The SPM can be a very hard person to escape from. They will threaten to commit suicide if you leave them, they will threaten to hurt your family members, they will threaten to smash up your car, anything at all. They are very dangerous people to get involved with.

Traits of a SPM

* superficial charm
* self-centred & self-important
* need for stimulation & prone to boredom
* deceptive behaviour & lying
* conning & manipulative
* little remorse or guilt
* shallow emotional response
* callous with a lack of empathy
* living off others or predatory attitude
* poor self-control
* promiscuous sexual behaviour
* early behavioural problems
* lack of realistic long term goals
* impulsive lifestyle
* irresponsible behaviour
* blaming others for their actions
* short term relationships
* varied criminal activity

What should you do if you are involved with a SPM?

If you recognise these symptoms in someone, do not approach them with this information. Just make your escape as quickly as possible. A SPM can not be talked round, they can not be reasoned with, they will attack you if you turn against them, aggressively. They will spread rumours about you and do anything they can to get pity from others and make you out to the bad person.

Drained used up people who have been in the path of destruction on a SPM will be very run down and often will find all this very hard to deal with. But don't give up. It might seem like the lies the SPM is spreading about you will turn everyone against you, but any who are worthy of your friendship will stick by you, and those who don't really know you and listen to hearsay, well they aren't worth knowing anyway.

Relationships

When thinking about wanting to find someone to be in a relationship with, you have to ask yourself some important questions and be truthful with your answers.

Why do you want a relationship? and saying that you have a lot to give is lying to yourself, even if it is true - that isn't the real reason.

You know there is some kind of selfish desire involved.

Maybe you search high and low for someone who 'ticks all the boxes' on your want list.

They have to look like this, or act like that, or be into this. They have to want sex all the time, they must be rich. Or whatever, some selfish desires will be there. Admit them, write them down and study them.

It might be as simple as wanting to find someone to share holidays and experiences with, but you can get that from a friend.. Think carefully about what it is that you think you really 'need'. Is it really just a 'want'?

You could waste your whole life trying to find that one special person, and put your life on hold until you do. Or you could be realistic and realise no Prince Charming or Beautiful Princess is going to come along and make your life fantastic and perfect and wonderful..... You are responsible for your own happiness, no one else is.

So why waste time worrying about if you will or won't meet someone? Just get on with your life, and find happiness alone. Because one thing is for sure... While you can't be happy on your own, you will never be happy with another. They will never be perfect enough, or ever live up to your expectations. You would probably end up being over-bearing, or even possessive, because you rely on them for your happiness, and it just isn't healthy.

When we learn to let go of the things we think we 'need', and instead change them to - 'It would be nice, however I am going to get on with my life and dreams, with or without that.'.... It will change your life for the better.

Secrets of the Serpent Bloodline - The Unveiling of Profound Esoteric Mysteries

Chapter 8

The Law of Attraction

Why the law of attraction is wrong and dangerous?

A child who is born in a war zone, who tries the law of attraction, gets no help from anyone.

Middle class and rich people who use the law attraction are much more likely to achieve their goals, and that is because they are surrounded by opportunities.

However the law of attraction tells us to believe we already have something, and when we do that, we think we already have it so give up trying, so are less likely to achieve our goals. Sigils (you will find out about sigils later on) are much more effective than the law of attraction can ever be.

The dangers of believing in the law of attraction are the same as believing in reincarnation, which creates unfair caste systems. We arrogantly think that just because we were born into a wealthy family, it must mean we deserve it and people who are poor and live in terrible conditions, do so because they are paying for all the bad things they have done in another life. These myths are created to control us, and stop us getting ideas above our station, and they make us heartless towards the suffering of others. But it sure does make the rich westerners feel better about all the poverty people have to put up with in other countries.

Holy Grail Elixir

Do you want to gain the Magick powers of Illumination?

- Do you want to be able to lucid dream at any time of your choosing?
- To be able to remotely view any location you choose?
- To be able to enter different trance states and levels of deep meditative relaxation at Will?
- To be able to slow down your heart or speed it up at Will?
- To be able to travel the astral planes whenever you want?
- To have an inner knowing truth, peace and harmony?
- To be able to read others thoughts?
- To be able to pick up on different vibrations?
- To have precognitive dreams?
- To know the past and the future?
- To excel in your chosen field?
- To be able to see the auras of others?
- To be able to climax instantly whenever you want to, or stop yourself from climaxing at any time?
- Do you want to be able to perform powerful rituals?
- Do you just long for the truth that has been hidden for so long?

Many Aspirants spend their whole life trying to gain these powers, where as some are born with them.

Why do some of us find it so hard to gain these powers, where as to others it comes naturally?

The answer lies within our genetic make-up and especially in our blood. Some may become excellent Adepts in the way of the Mysteries, but they still can't seem to master these Magical Arts. That is because they are not genetically created to experience these things.

But there is a way - The Holy Grail - an Elixir which can only be created by Adepts of certain genetics and bloodline. The Aspirant joins the Adepts Order, and the chosen ones are given these powers by drinking the Elixir. The Elixir is only given to those who have spiritually cleansed themselves with Magick Training and are ready to receive these powers without doing harm to themselves or others. The Initiation is never easy on the Aspirant if they are ill prepared. They are monitored closely, any sign of mental illness or other issues in their life, and the Aspirant is refused Initiation.

Over the generations of these secret teachings being passed down, some Aspirants who never made Initiation have set up orders of their own, without ever having had the Elixir. They do not know this secret, and yet fool new comers who are looking for ways to gain the magick powers, into joining their Orders, Groves and Covens. However these Orders contain no Holy Grail knowledge, and amount to little more than social clubs for the dispossessed. They don't seem to care if they never gain the powers and spiritual truths, because they have been accepted by the group and made to feel special, and one of them.

No amount of their claims will ever hold true, because they have no real truth. They only have bits from here, bits from there and a lot of fake doctrine that means not much more than what the exoteric Churches are teaching already.

The Truth is hidden and kept sacred, for in the wrong hands it would lead to disaster. In the right hands, those of the Adepts who are spiritually clean of false ego and dogma, can use the power for the good of all.

If you long for these powers, and have the Will to want to do good in the world, then if you are lucky you might be invited into one of these closed Orders and you too could become an Adept.

However, the Adepts can not be tricked, they will know if you have bad intentions and want to use the powers for selfish gain and false ego reasons, and you won't make it past the outer circle.

If you have these powers already, and you have done no training, then you have the correct genetics to be able to create the secret Elixir yourself. If you are not aware of your family history, who your ancestors were, then it might interest you to look. It would also be advisable to learn the truth yourself, and join with others like you. You have lost your way from the knowledge, but will be welcomed back in by those true Adepts and their knowledge shared with you. Find your way back to us..

Probationers & Oath Breakers

You might be wondering why you can't just go to an Occult Mystery School and join up right away? You might wonder why you have to first get to know the others in the Order and them you, for at least three months. Then be taken on as a Probationer for one year.

The first three months is the time when you get to know more about those within the Order you want to join, and they get to know you. If someone turns up and is in a rush to quickly join, it means they haven't thought it through properly. They haven't looked into what it means to be part of an Order and they are very likely to lose interest before the three months are up. This weeds out those who like the idea of being in an Order and the mystique that it creates, and someone serious about the work ahead.

If they are still keen after three months, and the Others within the Order all agree, the Aspirant is taken in as a Probationer. They are given a basic set of tasks which help at activating the magick mind, these are often very similar in all the different Orders, as there are tried and tested methods for this. The Aspirant is also given a reading list and usually invited to most of the Orders ceremonies, although not all. The Aspirant signs an Oath, promising their own Higher Self that they will do the Great Work to completion within this Order, gaining support from and helping support the other members within. They are also sworn to keep secret all they have seen, talked about and heard within the Order and at the ceremonies.

A magical oath is a promise. When a person vows not to reveal the secrets of a magical order - in which case, when the promise is broken, that organisation may impose sanctions on the individual, such as expelling them from the group.

But more importantly, a magical oath is a promise to one's inner or higher self, and as such, is a very potent magickal tool. Breaking that oath robs you of that tool, by proving to yourself that you are incapable of making a binding promise. It sets a precedent in your subconscious mind that you don't have the willpower to see something through that you had intended. Basically, it makes you magickally impotent.

In every case of an individual breaking his or her magical oath there is evidence of the consequences borne out in his or her life, in severity proportional to the magnitude of the breach. Some spectacular falls come about as a result of deliberate and egregious oath-breaking.

The Order the oath-breaker has been expelled from need make no punishment on to them, as they have then become the victim of their own actions.

Think seriously about signing any Oaths, as they are a lesson to you and a real and true promise to your own Higher Self. Think about your real reasons for wanting to join an Order.. Is because of an egotistic reason? Is it because you are attracted to someone in the Order and fancy your chances with them if you join? Is it because you want to learn magick that you can use to influence others? Or is it just because you want to do the Great Work and become a better, more balanced Being?

Unless it is the latter, you are not ready for the commitment.

The Probationer will be 'tested' by the others in the Order. This is to find out how serious they are about belonging to the Order and to stop any traitors in their tracks. The tests can be varied in nature, but work well in providing the others a clear view of the intentions of the Aspirant and whether or not they are likely to be an oath-breaker. They might be trusted with a 'secret' that only they are told, and if this information gets spread around, then the oath-breaker is found out.

When you are trusted enough to join the Order proper and come to know the other members fully, you are initiated and welcomed in, this is when the 'real' work begins. If you are rejected from an Order as they feel you are not right for them, don't be upset by this. It just means that one or more of the members felt you weren't right for the group. Remember you are about to be let into the lives of these people and find out all the weaknesses, their fears, the things they have been through on their journey and they will help you on yours, there has to be perfect trust within an Order.

In conclusion - Don't sign oaths you aren't willing to keep, if you break it you are magickally impotent. Think very carefully before applying to join an Order.

Life In Numbers

The number of man is 666

The number of woman is 333

Each digit represents a stage of our life.

The idea is to add the numbers together to become God/dess = 9

Now lets look at the journeys both men & women take

To get to enlightenment we need to get to 9

For a woman this is straight forwards

3+3+3= 9

For a man this is more difficult

6+6+6=18

To become complete the man needs his 1 = wand/sword/penis

And 8 which here = an hour glass woman on her back she is infinity

The Stages of Life

For women:

3= Childhood

6= Adult woman - who at this time can use her powers to help enlighten men=6

9= Older woman who is wise and teaches others

For a man:

6= Childhood

12, 1+2= 3= Adult male who at this time must seek a woman and gain enlightenment. 3=women

18, 1+8=9= Older man who has used his 1 to reach wisdom & knowledge

Also see the Hieros Gamos article.

11:11 & 333 Magick Numbers

The Importance of the Divine numbers 11 & 3

The number 11 has always been important in my life. I was born at 11:11, my life path number 11, the way I write my name is 11 (Tau Tia L Douglass = 11), the name of our Mystery School Order is 11 (Ordo Infinitus Orbis = 11). As well as my birth number being 11 my conception date number is also 11. The magick number is 11.

All numbers are special and there only truly 9 numbers. 11 is the magick number though, which is why it isn't reduced when working out your life path number. During my life as well as 11, 3 has been important and as a child I would say it was my lucky number, it just seemed to fit and it is my birth month, seeing as I was born in March. As I got older I went from 3 to 33, then eventually 333. I even get 333 from my birth numbers like so: I was born at 11:11 and my birth number is 11. In binary 11=3 so my 3 11s become 333.

Interestingly when 'Divine Feminine' is put into the Numegalogy program 11:11 appears, find out more here: churchsmsj.blogspot.co.uk/2012/11/1111.html

Of course we also must remember that 3 is the Divine trinity of the Aeons, being that of the Mother - 1st Aeon, Father - 2nd Aeon and Divine Child of balance and androgyny - 3rd Aeon, which we are currently moving towards. "The number 11 means, in the Tree of Life, the Sphere of Daath. In the Hebraic Language Daath means "knowledge" or "Abyss", being the Sephira located in the limit between the Superior Triad (Kether, Chokmah and Binah) and the Sephiroth located at the more manifested world. Daath is where takes place phenomenon usually known as the "Black Night of the Soul", when the adept stands at the mental state represented by the daemon Choronzon whose number is 333. Transpass this state of the mind is essential to reach the consecration of the Great Work. To reach Daath is necessary, first, to make contact with the Holy Guardian Angel, who conducts the adept and helps him to reach the Abyss safely." Crowley, Aleister; *Magick in Theory and Practice*, ©1991 Castle Books.

This system used by Thelemites, does again seem to demonise the Divine Feminine, as all other patriarchal religions, as they claim Choronzon is an evil Angel of the Aybss who must be defeated, and the number they give this Daemon is 333 - The Divine Feminine completion number.

11 and 333 again, very important numbers to everyone, not just me. But they show up in my life and my own charts constantly. The 11:11 normally starts to appear for people when they are starting to make contact with their HGA, it is only after they start to recognise this that they move on to the Daath, and if they are very lucky they get through it and move on to Binah, Chokmah and Kether. The time between Chokmah and Kether is VERY challenging too, sometimes more so than the abyss, it is the path of the fool.

The number 11 also has the symbolism of the union of the Microcosmos and the Macrocosmos, as the sum of the 5 and the 6, being the 5 related to the Pentagram and the 6 related to the Hexagram. So, 11 joins the meanings of both the correlations and means the All.

During ceremonies we knock a certain amount of times, or ring a bell, stamp our foot or staff on the ground. The most generally useful and adaptable battery is composed of 11 strokes. The principal reasons for this are as follows: " "Firstly", 11 is the number of Magick in itself. It is therefore suitable to all types of operation. "Secondly", it is the sacred number par excellence of the new Aeon. "Thirdly", it expresses the great Work, in every one of its aspects. "Lastly", it is possible thereby to express all possible spheres of operation, whatever their nature. This is effected by making an equation between the number of the Sephira and the difference between that number and 11. For example, 2 Degree=9Square is the formula of the grade of initiation corresponding to Yesod. Yesod represents the instability of air, the sterility of the moon; but these qualities are balanced in it by the stability implied in its position as the Foundation, and by its function of generation. This complex is further equilibrated by identifying it with the number 2 of Chokmah, which possesses the airy quality, being the Word, and the lunar quality, being the reflection of the sun of Kether as Yesod is the sun of Tiphareth. It is the wisdom which is the foundation by being creation. This entire cycle of ideas is expressed in the double formula 2 Degree = 9Square, 9 Degree = 2Square; and any of these ideas may be selected and articulated by a suitable battery." Crowley, Aleister; *Magick in Theory and Practice*, ©1991 Castle Books.

The 11th Tarot card is Justice, the Ruler of the Balance which is ruled by Libra. The 3rd Tarot card is The Empress, and this is the card that always show up to represent me in readings and it is a special card to me. The tree number of The Empress is 14, the day I was born on and it being the 3rd card, it is extra significant to me, my birthday being 14th March. The Empress is ruled by Venus and water. Pisces being my Sun sign, which is also water.

How to work out your own birth number

I have explained above how important the numbers 11 and 3 are in general, but I also went into details about how those numbers came up on my own path, so you can see examples how things start to fit together. Once you know what your numbers are, you can see how things fit together for you. It is exciting how things just seem to fit. The things in your life that you felt drawn to and never knew why? Maybe you can find some answers once you start looking.

Always start with day first, then month, then year.

Here is an example of how it is calculated.

If your birthday is 13th October 1977.

Day: 1+3=4

Month: 1+0=1

Year: 1+9=10 1+0=1 and 7+7=14 1+4=5 then 1+5=6

You always add the digits together all the way as you work it out.

You then have your birth number: 416

This number is important to your life, and once you open your eyes you will see how important it is..

Try searching for the number in Google, and finding out the Gematria associations with it. You might find this site useful http://www.gematrix.org

Another site that is useful is http://www.billheidrick.com/works/hgemat.htm

It will work out which words and ideas correspond with your birth number. Please realise that it can only show you what others have searched for themselves in the system. There might be some nonsense, but there might also be some gems.

For instance when my birth number is put in, which is 533, in the Jewish Gematria it comes out with Supreme Being. Well you can't argue with that can you? People who are determined to misinterpret me and what I do are always accusing my of thinking I am a prophet or something. Well all women are Goddesses, I am no different, but I am sure it will give them something else to have a go at me about.

The simple Gematria comes out with - *Always Fight With All Your Might For What Is Right* and *All False Prophets Will Have To Answer For Their Sin* I do believe we shouldn't give up doing the right thing, and I also try my best to expose these gurus and religious leaders who abuse the trust of others. So try putting yours in and see what you can find out.

Interestingly, Theolalite in Jewish Gematria Equals: 318 as does "*Inner Light*", which is what Theolalite means.

How to work out your life path number

For your life path number you simply add all the digits of birth number together.

So using our example from above of 416.

4+1=5 5+6=11

If your number is two digits you normally add those together too, but because this has worked out as 11, it stays as 11, as this is the magick number.

So if you numbers were: 516 then 5+1=6 6+6=12, 1+2=3

Your life path would be 3.

Now you can look up what you life path number means, or get a detailed reading from me.

Secrets of the Serpent Bloodline - The Unveiling of Profound Esoteric Mysteries

The Great Mother & The Great Work

The Great Mother has a Soul and is alive. As are the other planets, they all have a Soul and a Spirit.

For us if we have children we leave some of our Soul here on Earth, which is why those doing the Great Work often don't want children as it means a continuation until they have died, and if they have children it continues. Once we have completed the Great Work and our Soul is no longer on Earth, we don't return to the source, we become a planet and we create our own world. Until we have stopped the rebirth cycle and done the Great Work we are trapped in someone else's world. This is something you can not even begin to understand yourself though unless you do the Great Work, as it is hard to put into words. You are not aware of going to the source, as in if your body rots in the ground and a tree grows out of your rotting body, you don't know about it, and that isn't you. But if your DNA is still in someone else still alive, you can not move on. So you could say, we are our children.

If you die and don't have children, but haven't done the Great Work, then you are just returned fully to the source, but you are not aware of it, it is just eternal sleep, so it is nothing to be afraid of. The Great Mother just uses your energy smashed into thousands of pieces to create new life. You can not create a planet without doing the Great Work, and if someone does that it means they have removed all the shadow self, or at least have full control over it. Planets are not negative, none of them are. But we can choose exactly how the planet is going to be. Some people want complete solitude as they feel completed without others being around, so they can be a fiery planet with no life on. Others, like ours, want to see new life flourish, so become a creator of new planets, eventually, if the people learn to listen to the Soul of the the planet through the Great Work, but it has many many levels to it and this is hard to explain. When you reach the point of Gnosis and full connection to Higher Self there are things you just know but can not put into words, words can not explain these things, as you just have to experience them yourself. Words are something we created, this is more than words.

I include some planetary magick sigils and rituals in Liber II, they are VERY powerful, something the Eagles have been hiding from you for years. If you remember that these planets are not just objects and are alive, and are very old wise souls, you can begin to see why this has been kept from you.

I should mention, just because someone has had children, this does not mean they should not do the Great Work. Actually they should even more so, because when someone of a line does the work, it makes it much much easier for those who come after. People don't seem to realise the true connection we have with family that no matter what we do with our life, it has an effect on our kin. This is why someone who comes from a family that say take drugs and drink all the time and are abusive, find it much harder to break free and do the Great Work, than those who come from a loving family. This is why we have our wilderness when doing the Great Work, to try to remove any negative influence from family members who try to stop us, as those who are trapped want to keep others trapped through fear and programming. If you are brought up in a family of those who do the Great Work, but choose to have children and continue the line, and they got far, then you have not much to do at all as the parent is passing that knowledge.

So love or hate your family, they do effect you and you can effect your own children too. If you choose to not do the Great Work, you are leaving a much harder job for your children. It is all about growing up, the Great Work. Because as children we feel the need to be attached to our Great Mother and are scared to leave her, but as we become an adult we feel ready to break free, and are no longer in fear of becoming a planet of our own. We feel safe and secure and without attachment, we have then completed the work.

People who do the Great Work but have children, still don't feel ready to break free, or of course they might have had them first before starting. Either way, the Great Work is for anyone who chooses to become an adult and be responsible for themselves.

Gold

Have you ever wondered why gold is so precious and sought after? Apart from the fact that is doesn't degrade or rust of course.

It is created, and only created in the last dying seconds of a stars life, when a supernova of extreme heat is happening. The explosion is only hot enough to create gold in the very heart of the star, for around a minute and supernovas only happen about once a century, making gold extremely rare. Through the death of a sun gold is made, and shot out at great speed, which is how we have some on Earth, and this is the very same way life was created on our planet. When the building blocks of life arrived on Earth from a star.

The story of the origin of the chemical building blocks of life is magickal and amazing. The ingredients were created in the hearts of ancient suns, thrown out into the universe at their deaths and eventually brought back together to form our solar system.

The elements we hold most precious were forged at the moment of cosmic alchemy during stellar deaths. Through the vast cycle of magnificent cosmic death and rebirth. Like a Phoenix rising from the ashes to create new life, our bodies when we die return to the universe, ready to create new life. How wonderful to be part of this grand cosmic play, each of us a tiny part of something majestic and wonderful.

We are all made from stars, we all come from the stars, and we all have a spark of the sun we came from inside our hearts, waiting to be ignited when we become Theolalites.

Holy (Blessed) Water

What is Holy (Blessed) Water?

Any water that someone consciously blesses with good intentions is blessed water. Water has memory, so the more it is blessed, the more powerful the effects. It is something that anyone can do, however someone who has done the 'Great Work' and has become a Priest/ess themselves has learnt how to more powerfully bless water.

How is water blessed?

A prayer or blessing is said over the water and special hand actions moved across the surface. You might wonder how chanting over water can effect it, well here are some examples of how you can see it for yourself.

If you were to take a drum and put some salt on to it, and chant over the salt, you would find the salt forming different shapes. You can try this yourself with salt, make sure you project your voice well.

You may well of heard of the experiments with water that Dr. Masaru Emoto did. Dr. Emoto developed a process in which he would freeze drops of water and take photographs of individual water crystals that formed. He found that like snowflakes, every water crystal is unique. But he learned much more than that. Dr. Emoto found that you could tell much about the nature of the water by photographing it in this way, and more importantly, that, as human beings, we can change the nature of water in many ways. Water truly does have powerful effects on us. He tested tap water from around the world and found that tap water does not form water crystals. Stagnant or polluted water does not form water crystals either, but forms unpleasant, deformed frozen structures. Rainwater, water from clean streams and rivers, water from glaciers, and water from holy places around the world form beautiful crystals when frozen.

What are the benefits of Holy (Blessed) Water?

When you know how much bad or good 'vibes' can effect water it becomes a big deal, and it will start to make sense as to why religious and spiritual people bless all their food and water before they consume it. Religious people have never been told why this is, or why Holy Water is so special, but they do know about its healing powers. They believe it is because God blesses it, however it is humans who effect it. If you were to bless your whole house with Holy Water by sprinkling it around you are bringing that good energy into your living space. If you add some to your bath water you are effecting positively all that negatively charged tap water that you are bathing in.

We ourselves are made up of about 60-70% water. When you think about this you will then realise just why someone saying nasty things to you can effect you in a big way. Someone swearing at you and telling you they hate you will be making all your water crystals turn into distorted horrible shapes, but when someone says how much they love you and care about you, your water crystals will be forming beautiful snowflake shapes.

Water is our emotions after all, it effects everything about us. Have you ever heard someone say 'I can feel it in my waters' and you never really thought about what they meant? Well we really do feel good and bad vibes within us.

Drinking blessed water has amazing healing properties, so consider using it when you are ill. But some people put salt in their blessed water, make sure it is salt free, this isn't needed anyway. The reason salt is used is because salt can take away negative energy, however if you truly bless the water properly it isn't needed.

How do I make some Blessed Water?

First take some natural clean safe to drink water, or distil some tap water and then put it through a carbon filter, distilling the water resets it ready for your positive programming. The carbon filter keeps the water neutral and stops it going acid, which distilled water can do when air gets to it, so it is important if you are going to drink it.

Next you can choose a chant to use and repeat it many times towards the water while holding your hands over it. It can be anything you want, for example: *I love you, I bless you, OM.* As long as the intention is also there, you project it and you are not just saying it, it will work.

Within our Church and Order we have our own ways of doing this which is taught to all our Clergy when they become Priest/ess and know how to correctly project the powerful energy they learn how to create and direct. During our Celtic Gnostic Mass we prepare blessed water and it is available to anyone in the Church Gift Shop. http://churchsmsj.org/

Chapter 9
Magick Paths & Traditions

AGNOSTICISM: An intellectual doctrine or attitude affirming the uncertainty of all claims to ultimate knowledge.

ALCHEMY: A ceremonial magick in which the goal is to transmute a common substance usually of little value into a more valuable substance such as lead to gold. However this is actually code for transmutation of ourselves into Divine beings.

ALEXANDRIAN WICCA: A Wiccan tradition founded by Alex Sanders in England and disputed as being the original form of Wicca instead of Gardnerian Wicca. Sanders claimed to have been initiated as a Hereditary Witch by his grandmother but critics claim many Alexandrian rituals are almost identical to Gardnerian ones, with a little ceremonial magick and Judeo-Christian mysteries thrown in. Covens usually work skyclad. The eight Sabbats are observed and the Goddess and God are revered. Alexandrian Wiccans are considered to be Traditional Witches who trace their line of initiatory descent from Alex and Maxine Sanders, through a line of Alexandrian High Priests and High Priestesses, who follow the Alexandrian Book of Shadows, and who practice the Alexandrian Tradition of Wicca.

ALGARD WICCA: A Wiccan tradition that combines both Gardnerian and Alexandrian Wicca traditions, founded in 1972 by Mary Nesnick, an American who was initiated into both Gardnerian and Alexandrian traditions.

ATENISM: Also Amenism. The Aten, the god of Atenism, first appears in texts dating to the 12th dynasty, in the Story of Sinuhe. Here during the Middle Kingdom, the Aten "as the sun disk...was merely one aspect of the sun god Re." The Aten, hence, was a relatively obscure sun god; without the Atenist period, it would barely have figured in Egyptian history. Although there are indications that the Aten was becoming slightly more important in the eighteenth dynasty period—notably Amenhotep III's naming of his royal barge as Spirit of the Aten. It was Amenhotep IV who introduced the Atenist revolution, in a series of steps culminating in the official installment of the Aten as Egypt's sole god.

AMERICAN ECLECTIC WICCA: A broad range of individuals or groups that have based their philosophy, rituals and practices on the published works of Scott Cunningham and StarHawk. American Eclectic Wiccans emphasize spontaneity and intuitive understanding of the Mysteries. Because they downplay, or discarded, the importance of Oaths, Initiations, Lineage, and Tradition many Traditional Wiccans object to these groups using the name Wicca, and believe they should be called American Eclectic Witchcraft.

AMERICAN TRADITIONAL WICCA: The groups that have no initiatory connection to Gardner or Sanders, but who have based their rituals and practices on what has been published about the Gardnerian and Alexandrian Traditions; they therefore follow a Wiccan practice based upon Gardnerian or Alexandrian without having initiatory lineage.

AMERICAN WICCA: An offshoot of Gardnerian Wicca, This tradition includes Gardnerian material and additional material supplied by the founders. Also known as Mohsian Wicca.

ANGEL MAGIC: The art of evoking and invoking Angels to harness their powers or qualities.

ANIMALISM: The doctrine that man is a mere animal with no soul or spiritual quality.

ARCADIAN WICCA: A Wiccan tradition centred around worship of the Horned God. (covens are open to both males and females).

ATHEISM: The belief that no higher power or deities exist.

ATONISM: It was High Priest, Seer & Prophet Ankh-An-Aton who dedicated himself toward the purpose of bringing back the minds of his people as members of humanity to the remembrance of those things which are of importance and towards reunion or unification with the divine creator and grower of all life.

BARDIC WICCA: A mix of Celtic Wicca and Celtic Druidry.

BRITISH TRADITIONAL WICCA: The groups of Wiccan Traditions that trace their lineage to Gerald Gardner, and/or to Alex and Maxine Sanders. Some of the British Traditional groups view Wicca as an Initiatory, Oathbound, Magick-using, Pagan Mystery Priesthood celebrating the Mysteries contained in the Legend of the Descent of the Goddess and in the Charge of the Goddess.

BRITISH TRADITIONAL WITCHCRAFT: Witchcraft Traditions tracing descent from a Hereditary, or Traditional, British source, including the Gardnerian and the Alexandrian Wiccan Traditions and their branches and offshoots. Some British Traditional Witches consider the term Wicca a synonym for British Traditional Witchcraft, while others reserve the term Wicca for the Gardnerian and Alexandrian Traditions and their offshoots and consider Wicca to be a wholly-contained subset within British Traditional Witchcraft.

BUDDHISM: The religion based on the doctrine of Gautama Buddha that says suffering is inseparable from existence and that enlightenment is achieved by the inward extinction of the self and of the senses.

BRUJERIA: A Mexican shamanistic magickal system that is an integration of Roman Catholicism and Native American lore. Practitioners are called Bruja (female) and Brujo (male); and Curandera (female) and Cureandero (male). Both Curanderos and Brujos use herbal and folk remedies.

CALEDONII TRADITION: A Scottish tradition of Witchcraft that preserves the unique festivals of the Caledonii.

CARPOCRATIAN: A sect of Gnosticism.

CELTIC RECONSTRUCTIONISM: A culturally specific and historically based pagan path that attempts to recreate the religion of the ancient Celtic peoples of Western Europe and the British Isles. It embodies a strong reverence for nature.

CELTIC SHAMANISM: A shamanic path that is based on the Faery Faith of the Celtic peoples of Western Europe and especially of Britain, Scotland, Wales, Ireland, Cornwall, Isle of Man and Brittany.

CELTIC TRADITIONALIST: A reconstruction of the beliefs and practices of the original Celtic people. Unlike Druidry, this tradition focuses more on the beliefs of the average Celtic man or woman.

CELTIC WICCA: The use of a Celtic and Druidic pantheon mixed with Gardnerian Wicca that heavily stresses the Elements, Nature and the Ancient Ones. Celtic Wicca also focuses on knowledge of, and respect for, the healing and magickal qualities of plants and stones, flowers, trees, elemental spirits, the little people, gnomes and fairies.

CEREMONIAL MAGICK: Magick that calls upon the aid of beneficent spirits and is akin to religion. Ceremonial Magick is based upon a blend of doctrines of Plato and other Greek philosophers, Oriental mysticism and Tibetan mysticism which is currently divided into three forms: Enochian, Thelemic and Eclectic. Enochian Magick originated with John Dee and Edward Kelly in the 16th century and communication with spirits involved the Nineteen Calls (or Keys): incantations in the Enchonian language, a complex language of unknown origin. This system of Magick was revived by the Hermetic Order of the Golden Dawn and studied at length by Aleister Crowley. In turn, Crowley developed the Thelemic Magick system from his studies and Ceremonial Magickians have since expanded to develop Eclectic Magick systems based on a variety of different systems, inclusive of Alchemy, Egyptology, Kabbalistic doctrines, Chaos Magick etc.. Ceremonial Magick requires a rigorous discipline and has an intellectual appeal, the mage derives power from or through the successful control of spirits, usually seen as negative spirits which are believed easier to control than positive spirits. Negative spirits may be good, evil, or neutral. In its highest sense, Ceremonial Magick is a transcendental experience that takes the mage into mystical realms and into communication with the Higher Self. Also known as High Magick, Ritual Magick, Theurgic Magick, Theurgy.

CEREMONIAL WITCHCRAFT: A tradition of Witchcraft with an emphasis on Egyptian and/or Qabbalistic Ceremonial Magick.

CHALDEAN MAGICK: The name Chaldean, in the Book of Daniel and also by many writers of antiquity, was applied to Babylonian magi who were astute in astronomy, but also practised astrology and magic.

CHAOS MAGICK: A modern magical tradition which emphasises the pragmatic use of belief systems and the creation of new and unorthodox methods. Sigils are one of the most used techniques of Chaos Magick. They work by going straight to your subconscious, where they will take effect, without your conscious, realistic brain telling you that what you are attempting is impossible. Many magicians also have personal sigils, which they continuously charge and use as a magickal signature of sorts.

DEMONISM: The worship of demons. In nonpagan religions demonism is often used to describe the belief in the existence or powers of demons. A treatise on demons.

DIANIC WICCA: A group of Wiccan traditions that focus primarily (but not always exclusively) on the Goddess. Known as the "feminist" movement in Wicca, it was first identified by Margaret Murray in 1921 in "The Witch-Cult in Western Europe". Most Dianic Wiccan traditions follow a Roman or Eclectic Pantheon that reveres Diana, but the term has been applied to traditions embracing other pantheons that are Goddess focused.

DRAGON MAGICK (Draconian): The Magickian invokes or evokes the wisdom of Dragons. It teaches you to work in harmony with dragons and with draconic energies and how to befriend draconic entities.

DRUIDRY: The paths based on the practices, rituals, and magick of Freemasonry mixed with myth. Many expressions of the tradition exist, and their differences have often been cause for dissension in the Pagan community.

DYNION MYWN: The American branch of Dynion Mwyn, a Welsh tradition named for the faery folk. It emphasizes historical lineage, religious equality, and Welsh mythology and lore. The American branch is called Y Tylwyth Teg.

EARTH MAGICK: A magickal system that draws primarily on the Element of Earth and the reverence of Nature.

ECLECTIC WICCA: Wicca traditions that combine elements from several different traditions to form their own unique system of reverence and/or magick. Many solitary practitioners are considered to be Eclectic.

EGYPTIAN MAGICK: The Egyptians used magic for both practical and religious purposes. They believed magic was a divine creation for the benefit of humanity. It was considered a field of knowledge just like architecture, literature, medicine, etc. It was just another category of knowledge to be used in coping with their environment and religion.

In our modern society, the word magic does not convey the force it did in the ancient Egyptian culture. To the Egyptians, magic was a real and potent force. It was a tangible means of communicating, manipulating, and controlling their gods. For example, their life depended on agriculture and thus the weather. Using magic to control the weather was important for their survival. Also magic was essential after death for safe passage through the afterlife.

ENOCHIAN MAGICK: A system of magick that teaches communication with angels and spirits and travel through various planes, or aethyrs of consciousness. Enochian magick apparently originated with John Dee and Edward Kelly in the 16th century and communication with spirits involved the Nineteen Calls (or Keys): incantations in the Enochian language, a complex language of unknown origin. Enochian magick was revived by the Hermetic Order of the Golden Dawn and studied at length by Aleister Crowley.

FAERY FAITH: A pagan religion based on animism, the belief that everything in this and the Otherworlds is alive and the faery folklore.

FAERY WICCA: A Wiccan Tradition incorporating the deities of the Welsh or Irish Faery Folk and drawing some theology from the Faery Faith.

FAMILY TRADITION WITCHCRAFT: A Tradition passed down within the family in an unbroken line and hence by hereditary descent. Many Family Tradition Witches do not consider their traditions Wiccan; some use the term Wicca to describe their family traditions because the beliefs and practices fit more or less closely with Gardnerian or Alexandrian Wicca. Also known as Hereditary Witchcraft.

FREEMASONRY: Is one of the largest and oldest fraternal organisations in the world. Masonic organisations are secretive Solar worship cults. It has been defined as a system of morality veiled in allegory and illustrated by symbolism.

GARDNERIAN WICCA: A Wiccan tradition founded by Gerald Gardner, and the first denomination of Wicca to make itself known publicly. The Gardnerian tradition places emphasis on the Goddess over the God, has a degree system of advancement and does not allow for self-initiation. Covens work skyclad and aim to equal numbers of male and female, paired.

GNOSTICISM: From the Greek gnosis (knowledge). A diversity of pre-Christian and early-Christian beliefs. A central tenet is the corruption of the physical world, and the ability of some to transcend it through acquisition of esoteric spiritual knowledge.

GNOSTIC THEOLALITES: The Church of St Mary & St John was founded in March 2011 by Tau Tia L Douglass. The aim is to bring the esoteric teachings out and into the mainstream. The Church was formed with valid lines of apostolic succession. On the surface it might have an exoteric look and feel, but if one was to attend a Celtic Gnostic Mass one would soon realise this is unlike any exoteric religion. The Mass is performed by both a Priest and a Priestess, the main altar divided - one half is venerating the Lord, the other the Lady... anyone with esoteric knowledge who is part of the Mass will know the true meaning. Tau Tia is the first female in apostolic succession to charter a Church and Templar Order, The Church of St Mary & St John is Herstory in the making and hope to bring balance, equality and harmony to a currently unbalanced world. Those who are part of the Church are known as Gnostic Theolalites, as they strive for perfection through the Great Work and aim to ignite their own inner Divine light. The Minor Orders are a gradual comparison of many religions and traditions, and the Major Orders are fully esoteric. Aspirants who are ordained to the Priesthood are awarded a Diploma in Esoteric Comparative Theology by the Churches own seminary. The seminary training is also available to those outside the Church.

HECATINE TRADITION: A Scottish tradition of Witchcraft that preserves the unique festivals of the Caledonii. Also known as Caledonii Tradition.

HECHICERIA: A Mexican Indian magickal tradition that reveres the pre-Columbian divinities. Practitioners are most often male and are called Hechiceros, Nuguals, or Bruho Naturaleza.

HEDGE WITCHCRAFT: A non-initiated solitary practice of Witchcraft that focuses on the traditional European, especially British Isles, role of Witch as healer, midwife and seer for a community. Highly intuitive, Hedge Witchcraft emphasizes the practical role of magick in daily living over the religious doctrine and it is acceptable for Hedge Witches to be self taught and eclectic in the spiritual aspects of their faith.

HELLENISMOS: Hellenismos is the traditional, polytheistic religion of ancient Greece, reconstructed in and adapted to the modern world. It is also called Hellenic Polytheism, Hellenic Reconstructionist Paganism, or simply Hellenism. Those who practice this religion are variously known as Hellenic polytheists, Hellenic pagans, Hellenic reconstructionists, Hellenists, or Hellenes. Hellenic polytheists worship the ancient Greek gods—the Olympians, nature divinities, underworld deities—and heroes.

HIGH MAGICK: Magick that calls upon the aid of beneficent spirits and is akin to religion. It is called theurgy, from theourgia "working things pertaining to the gods". High Magick is based upon a blend of doctrines of Plato and other Greek philosophers, Oriental mysticism, Judaism and Christianity and currently is divided into three forms: Enochian, Thelemic and Eclectic. High Magick requires a rigorous discipline and has an intellectual appeal, the mage derives power from God (the Judeo-Christian God) through the successful control of spirits, usually demons, which are believed easier to control than angels. Demons may be good, evil, or neutral. In its highest sense, High Magick is a transcendental experience that takes the mage into mystical realms and into communication with the Higher Self. Also known as Ceremonial Magick, Ritual Magick, Theurgic Magick, Theurgy.

HINDUISM: Based on the ancient Vedic literature, it is a belief system in constant transition. Populated by an almost infinite number of gods, the faith is open to adopting any or all of the gods created by younger religions. Reincarnation, and being held accountable for one's deeds (karma), are fundamental components of Hinduism. It is the third largest category of religions.

HOODOO: An American magickal system drawn from African magickal practice, Native American botanical healing knowledge and European folklore. It is often confused with Voodoo and it's practitioners are called Hoodoo, Hoodoo Doctors, Hoodoo Men/Women, Conjure Men/Women Conjurers, Root Doctors or Root Workers. Also known as Rootwork.

HUNA: The ancient Polynesian philosophical, scientific and magickal system. Huna teaches that there are three selves: lower, middle and higher that may be integrated by directing Mana properly. Practitioners are called Kahuna.

ISLAM: The monotheistic religious doctrine as revealed by the Muhammad, the Prophet of Allah. There are many sects of Islam and believers are called Muslims.

JAINISM: An Indian religion that prescribes pacifism and a path of non-violence towards all living beings. Its philosophy and practice emphasize the necessity of self-effort to move the soul towards divine consciousness and liberation. Any soul that has conquered its own inner enemies and achieved the state of supreme being is called Jina (Conqueror or Victor). Jainism is also referred to as Shraman (self-reliant) Dharma or the religion of Nirgantha (who does not have attachments and aversions) by ancient texts. Jainism is commonly referred to as Jain Dharma in Hindi and Samanam in Tamil.

JAMAICAN VOODOO: The polytheistic religion and magickal system of West African origin found in the Caribbean, South America and North America today. It recognizes that there are a multitude of gods and ghosts who each have their own myths, rites, offerings, taboos, and magical forces. Obeah is a healer god, who can also be invoked to bring illness and other calamities to one's own enemy. Also known as Obea, Obeah, Obi, Oby, Jamaican Voodoo.

JUDAISM: The religion, and culture, of the Jews. Based on the ancient Hebrew beliefs and writings (referred to as the Old Testament by other religions), current doctrine is that if every member of the faith strives to live within God's law, he (God) will fulfil his promise (covenant), and send a messiah to restore the Jews to their rightful place as the ruling class. There are many divisions within the religion, but it is overall, a fluid belief system which evolves with time. The most interesting aspect of this flexibility, is the interpretation of the holy laws in ways which "outsmart" God: allowing for less strict adherence to rules which interfere with contemporary materialism.

JUNGIAN: Relating to the theories on human behaviour put forward by the Swiss psychiatrist, Carl Jung. He perceived a duality in many aspects of the human mind. His most significant theory was that of a collective unconscious, which contains all of the "racial memories" each person is born with. Because some myths, such as a "great flood", seem to appear in all cultures, he determined that some past memories become part of our genetic code, as archetypes (symbolic representations of memories).

KABBALAH: Is a discipline and school of thought concerned with the mystical aspect of Judaism. It is a set of esoteric teachings meant to explain the relationship between an eternal/mysterious Creator and the mortal/finite universe.

KEMETIC: Ma'at is the fundamental or foundational principle of Ancient Kemetic life and existence. It is the fundamental or foundational principle of the divine, natural, social and moral order. It was established by the Almighty at the time of Creation and is manifest in nature as the normalcy of phenomena. In society, Ma'at is known as "justice." In our cognitive and intellectual existence, Ma'at is known as "truth." In our moral and spiritual existence, Ma'at is known as "righteousness." In our environmental and cosmological existence, Ma'at is known as harmony. In our inter- and intra-personal existence, Ma'at is known as balance.

KITCHEN WITCHCRAFT: A tradition of Witchcraft with an emphasis on the practical side of religion, magick, the Earth, and elements. Much of the tradition is very similar to Stregheria (Strega) and practitioners work out of hearth and home, using only what they would have on hand for daily routines to perform rituals and spells. The home is sacred to a Kitchen Witch and cooking and herb magick play a fundamental part in their practice. Kitchen Witchery is a way of including Witchcraft beliefs into everyday life.

LEFT-HAND PATH: A term used to identify Goddess worship or the hidden (occult) esoteric church. Where as the Right-hand path is God worship and exoteric.

LOW MAGICK: Magick practised by people who are not trained in High Magick and does not involve the ritualized summoning of spirits. Spells, incantations and concocted philtres and potions are the lowest forms of Low Magick.

MARTINISM: A form of mystical and esoteric Christianity concerned with the fall of the first man, his state of material privation from his divine source, and the process of his return, called 'Reintegration' or illumination. As a mystical tradition, it was first transmitted through a masonic high-degree system established around 1740 in France by Martinez de Pasqually, and later propagated in different forms by his two students Louis Claude de Saint-Martin and Jean-Baptiste Willermoz.

MITHRAISM: Solar worship. An astrology-centric, middle-platonic mystery cult of the 1st-4th century Roman Empire that claimed to have been founded by "Zoroaster".

NECROMANCY: A form of magic in which the practitioner seeks to summon the spirit of a deceased person, either as an apparition or ghost, or to raise them bodily, for the purpose of divination.

NORDIC TRADITION, NORSE PAGANISM: Pagan traditions that worship the Norse pantheon of deities and stresses conservative values of honour, honesty, courage and duty to one's family, kin and friends. In the 1970's a number of Norse Pagan groups sprang into existence almost simultaneously and independently of one another, in America, England and Iceland. Many adherents to Norse Paganism are attracted by the emphasis on blood ties and genetics, the warrior ethic and the Norse symbology. Norse Pagans recognize both branches of the Norse pantheon, the Aesir and the Vanir. A branch called Odinism worship only the Aesir. Festivals centre on the seasonal equinoxes and solstices, and Norse holidays such as Ragnar's Day. Heavier emphasis is placed on skill mastery and shamanism than on magick and meditation.

There are a few extreme right-wing Norse Pagan groups who believe they have founded a religion upon the Aryan race; and while some do include neo-Nazis, most Norse Pagans consider these people a fringe element not connected to their religion. Also known as Teutonic Tradition.

ODINISM: A form of Norse Paganism that recognizes only the Aesir, the Sky Gods, including Odin, Frigga, Thor, Loki, Balder and others. Odinism does not acknowledge the Vanir, the Gods concerned with earth, agriculture, fertility and the cycle of death and rebirth.

OLD RELIGION (The): Italian Witchcraft, founded in the mid-14th century with the teachings of Aradia, the Holy Strega, and based upon the pre-Estruscian Italian belief system. The Old Religion is a worship of the "Source of All Things", through the personification of the Goddess and God. Also known as Strega, Stregheria, and La Vecchia Religione.

PECTI-WITA, PICTISH WITCHCRAFT: The study and practice of the religion of the Picts, the pre-Celtic inhabitants of northern Scotland. Pecti-Wita is concerned with all aspects of prosperity, growth, abundance, creativity, and healing, and honours the Celtic Deities. The main tools in Pecti-Wita are the Staff and the Athame or Dirk. Pecti-Witans use a "Keek-Stane" which is, in effect, a scrying stone or the equivalent of a crystal ball. Also known as Pictish Witchcraft, Wita.

SACRED WHEEL WICCA: An eclectic neo-Pagan path based on Celtic beliefs, that focuses on balance and learning. Celtic beliefs are a part of their teachings. They state that they are a Wiccan religion dedicated to the health of Mother Earth, and to all her children in whatever forms they may take.

SANTERÍA (Spanish, Santo: "saint"): A religion centring on the worship of the ancient African Gods and Goddess's known as Orishas. Similar in practice to Voudon, all worshippers of Santería could be called Santeros but the term Santeros usually refers to the priests or priestesses. In some temples the highest order of priest is known as a babalawo, who has the power to heal the sick, punish the unjust and to divine the future through the Table of Ifá. Babalawo's follow the Orisha known as Orula.

SATANISM: The worship of the Christian concept of the Anti-Christ. It is not a Pagan religion although some Satanists refer to themselves as Witches.

SEAX WICCA: A tradition, or denomination, of the neopagan religion of Wicca which is largely inspired by the iconography of the historical Anglo-Saxon paganism, though, unlike Theodism, it is not a reconstruction of the early mediaeval religion itself. The tradition was founded in 1973 by Raymond Buckland, an English-born High Priest of Gardnerian Wicca who moved to the United States in the 1970s.

SHAMANISM: The oldest system of healing and magick in the world, probably as old as humankind itself. Shamanism is the art of functioning comfortably in two realities; the ordinary reality of the everyday, waking world, and the non-ordinary reality of the shamanic state of consciousness attained through an ecstatic trance. The primary purpose of shamanism is the healing of body and mind, but it is also used for divination and to ensure prosperity for communities. Shamanism is found in some form in every culture in the world.

SHINTOISM: An ancient Japanese religion which was brought to Japan when the present inhabitants eliminated the indigenous population of the islands. A complex, yet also vague, religion which includes ancestor worship, animism, and numerous gods and goddesses. Depending on interpretation, it is both polytheistic and monotheistic: "Kami", which Westerners can loosely parallel with the concept of god, applies holiness to all things, and to certain things. There are degrees of Kami, and guidelines as to what is termed Kami: but ultimately, everything is included as such. It appears to be a system used to impose a structured form of social obligation upon society, and is incomprehensible, even to its adherents.

SUFISM: or Taṣawwuf is defined by its adherents as the inner, mystical dimension of Islam. A practitioner of this tradition is generally known as a ṣūfī. Another name for a Sufi is Dervish.
Classical Sufi scholars have defined Sufism as "a science whose objective is the reparation of the heart and turning it away from all else but God." Alternatively, in the words of the Darqawi Sufi teacher Ahmad ibn Ajiba, "a science through which one can know how to travel into the presence of the Divine, purify one's inner self from filth, and beautify it with a variety of praiseworthy traits."

TAOISM: The Ancient Taoists developed a complete, detailed, and scientific system of knowledge which comprises many principles of food preparation, exercise, healing, sexology, etc.

THELEMIC MAGICK: A form of Ceremonial Magick developed by Aleister Crowley. Ceremonial Magick is Magick that calls upon the aid of beneficent spirits and is based upon a blend of doctrines of Plato and other Greek philosophers, Oriental mysticism, Judaism and Christianity.

THEOLA: A new magickal and spiritual current that was first founded in 2009 by Ordo Infinitus Orbis - Knights Hospitaller Templars. A balanced path which uses the energies of both the Sun and Moon, Male and Female, working to bring harmony and balance to ourselves, then we can in turn bring balance and harmony to the world. Those working in the Theola current usually call themselves Theolalites. The current of OIO is 333.

THEURGIC MAGICK, THEURGY: Magick that calls upon the aid of beneficent spirits and is akin to religion. Theurgic Magick is based upon a blend of doctrines of Plato and other Greek philosophers, Oriental mysticism, Judaism and Christianity and currently is divided into three forms : Enochian, Thelemic and Eclectic. Magick is a transcendental experience that takes the mage into mystical realms and into communication with the Higher Self. Also known as Ceremonial Magick, High Magick, Ritual Magick.

UMBANDA: A religion centring on the worship of the ancient African Gods who have been assimilated as Catholic saints. Similar in practice to Voudon, all worshippers of Santería could be called Santeros but the term Santeros usually refers to the priests or priestesses. The highest order of priest is a babalawo, who has the power to heal the sick, punish the unjust and to divine the future through the Table of Ifá. Also known as Santería.

VAMPYRE MAGICK: Uses energy forces that comes with vampyre magick, pranic energy particularly that which is taken in from others during feeding. Also a different focus when working with the astral and psi energy.

VECCHIA RELIGIONE (La): Italian Witchcraft, founded in the mid -14th century with the teachings of Aradia, the Holy Strega, and based upon the pre-Etruscan Italian belief system. La Vecchia Religione is a worship of the "Source of All Things", through the personification of the Goddess and God. Also known as The Old Religion, Strega and Stregheria.

VODOUN, VOODOO, VOUDOU, VOUDOUN (Fon, vodu: "spirit"): Like Santería, Vodoun is a blending the worship of traditional Catholic saints, Christ and the Gods (loas) of Africa, for example, a Vodoun practitioner could beg for intercession from St. Patrick and really be calling on their serpent God, Danbhalah-Wedo. Vodoun worshippers believe that the work of the loas appears in every facet of daily life and that pleasing the loas will gain the faithful health, wealth, and spiritual contentment.

The loas speak to their devotees through spirit possession but only for a short time during ceremonies and manifest to protect, punish, confer skills and talents, prophecy, cure illness, exorcise spirits, give counsel, assist in rituals and take sacrificial offerings. The priest (houngan) or priestess (mambo) acts as an intermediary to summon the loa and help the loa to depart when his or her business is finished. Magick, for both good and evil, is an integral part of Vodoun. Also known as Voudou, Voudoun.

WELSH CYMRI WICCA: A Wiccan Tradition based on Y Tylwyth Teg, a Welsh-based tradition named for the faery folk of that land, which maintains deeply Celtic roots and very humanistic philosophy. Students of both these paths are asked to place heavy emphasis on the study of Welsh myth, folklore, and faery lore.

WHITE MAGICK: A term used to identify some traditions where Magick is never used for destructive purposes. Also known as the Path of Light.

WICCA (Old English wicca: "male witch"; wicce,: "female witch"; wiccan: "witchcraft"): Any religion that follows the beliefs, traditions, and ceremonies laid out by Gerald Gardner (Gardnerian Wicca) or Alex Sanders (Alexandrian Wicca) that have been passed down through Initiation and Consecration, including those religions founded by Initiated and Consecrated members of another form; Any religion that has no initiatory connection to Gardner or Sanders, but have based their rituals and practices upon Gardnerian Wicca or Alexandrian Wicca., including solitary Wicca practitioners.

WICCAN SHAMANISM: An eclectic pagan tradition created by Selena Fox, high priestess of Circle Sanctuary, that blends Wiccan practice, humanistic psychology and a variety of shamanistic practices from tribal societies around the world. Healing is the primary focus of a Wiccan Shaman, and practitioners observe all the Sabbats, traditional activities, and the Wiccan Rede in conjunction with shamanic practices such as vision questing and dreamtime.

WITA: The study and practice of the religion of the Picts, the pre-Celtic inhabitants of northern Scotland. Pecti-Wita is concerned with all aspects of prosperity, growth, abundance, creativity, and healing, and honours the Celtic Dieties. The main tools in Pecti-Wita are the Staff and the Athame or Dirk. Pecti-Witans use a "Keek-Stane" which is, in effect, a scrying stone or the equivalent of a crystal ball. Also known as Pecti-Wita, Pictish Witchcraft. An eclectic Irish path which keeps very old Irish traditions and combines them with the influences of the Norse. Witta values Irish Pagan history and recognizes that at each stage in its development, over many centuries, each generation has been able to add something of value.

Until recent times Wittan covens were characterized by strict stratification and one-on-one teaching for its apprentices. Today most Wittan covens operate on a consensus basis and will accept self-initiation and the solitary life as valid. It is very similar to the Scottish Pecti-Wita which is evolved from Pictish, rather than Irish, tradition. Also known as Witta.

ZEN BUDDHISM (Japanese, zen: "meditation"): Japanese Buddhism which is differentiated from other Buddhist sects by its strong emphasis on the concept that all things are one.

ZOROASTRIANISM: The religion of the Persians before their conversion to Islam. According to tradition, it was founded by Zoroaster in the 6th or 7th century BCE. Its principles, contained in the Zend-Avesta, include belief in an afterlife and the continuous struggle of the universal spirit of good, Ormazd, with the universal spirit of evil, Ahriman.

The traditions and path list has been complied over many years and it will always be a work in progress, as new things will be added all the time. The information has been sourced from various books and places.

Secrets of the Serpent Bloodline - The Unveiling of Profound Esoteric Mysteries

Part 3 – Occult Knowledge

Chapter 10

The Eagle & The Snake

Wherever the Eagle has landed, corruption, greed, control and lies have followed.

The teachings of the Serpent have been taken by the Eagle, and hidden away. The only way to find the teaching of the Serpent has been to join Secret Societies, which upon joining you have no idea about what you are getting into. But you are told about all the great people who belonged there before you. So you think it must be good, and join, and give them money for their cause, without even knowing what that cause is. And sign blood oaths, so frightening and scary that you will never break them. You learn a little as you keep paying, and then you sign another blood oath and learn some more and are mislead some more, and another and learn a bit more and are mislead some more. If you ever find the full truth and don't agree with it, there is nothing you can do, because you have sworn all those oaths and are too scared of the consequences. Plus you have invested so much time and money into this Order, you have made so many friends here and been given opportunities you would have struggle to get alone. But you have sold out to corruption.

Some of you will have been having dreams and visions of serpents, reptiles, dragons and were scared by this. For so long we have been taught that the serpent is a symbol of evil. The bible tells us it will tempt us away from good and is forbidden. You no longer need to be afraid of the snake, instead welcome it into your life and confront your fears. Because when you do, you will realise that the serpent is the pathway to enlightenment, knowledge and wisdom.

Some Orders, that hide in the shadows have been passing the truth down to the children of the Grail, the Serpent children, the Theolalites, whose love and devotion to bringing harmony back has kept them working secretly to protect the truth. Although many of us have been killed, demonised, vilified for sharing the truth with others, we continue on, as it is important for the safety and future of all Mother Earth's animals and creatures.

The snake has been suppressed through fear, and by those in the know, through greed. Anyone who demonises the snake is doing so to stop you finding enlightenment, wisdom and knowledge. You can see the suppression of the snake/dragon all round you. The eagle steps on the snake and kills it. The Knight holds down the Dragon and kills it. This is symbolic of our ancestors, the teachers of Wisdom, the natives of the land, the originals, being slaughtered by the new comers, the Eagles.

Even to this day the Irish celebrate on the 17th March 'St Patrick's Day' each year. St Patrick was said to have banished all the snakes from Ireland. This is of course allegory for the murder and slaughter of the Serpent people from Ireland. Replacing our spiritual teachings with Christianity.

The Irish still have a a lot of our genes in them as most of them are now mixed Cro-Magnon/Eagle stock, some of our lines are still seen there in smaller amounts. But our people were mostly completely removed.

All to keep the truth hidden, and the real holders of the knowledge suppressed. For the keepers of the serpent wisdom are the Neanderthals, the first Shamans, the true builders of the pyramids all over the globe, including those under the oceans that were on the lost continents. All our advanced ancient technology has been hidden from you, by those who are under the Eagle. Most of our kin have been wiped out, but some of us still remain.

The Eagle people were created with some genes of the Serpent people, along with the genes of a simian race. They want as many of our genes as possible, as if gives them a higher IQ. But unfortunately their simian sides are strong and when mixed with some intelligence, it created war like, selfish, greedy people, who do not care about one another, or the earth.

Of course the Eagles know they have less simian genes than the normal people, the 'Simples' and how they mock you with the game - The Sims (Simian).

The Eagle represents the Cro-Magnons. The people of the Serpent are returning and bringing their knowledge and wisdom with them. Where as the Eagles have denied you the right to enlightenment, the Serpents want to heal and enlighten everyone.

The era of Veritas is here, the truth can no longer be hidden in the shadows. Some of us have survived and we are ready to bring peace and harmony back to the world, are you with us?

Now is the time to forget our differences, or old programmed ways, and join together to put an end to the corruption and control we have been under for thousands of years. Together we can do it, we can change the world.

But it won't be easy. The Eagles have infiltrated all sections of society and all sides of their games and wars. They have been playing this game for a long time and know exactly how to manipulate people into doing as they want them to do. So that they police themselves. So that they attack anyone who dares to stand up for what is right. They use religions and spirituality to control us; politics, money, food, sex, media and health against us. There is no part of these things they have not got full control over.

They can conquer you if you rely on them, but they can not control us if we join together and help each other. If we set up small tribal eco villages that are self sufficient, how can they control us? If enough of us do this there is nothing they can do. We need to pull together now, stop being selfish and thinking of just 'now' and start thinking about the future of the planet, which is what our children and grand children will inherit, lets be the ones who brought them true freedom and liberty, safe food, true spirituality, healthcare without side effects, clean safe water with no fluoride, skies that aren't polluted with industry and chem-trails.

What are you waiting for? No one else is going to help you, if you don't start helping yourself.

Help spread the joy, and banish the oppression. What are you waiting for?

Serpent, Eagle or Simple

If you are a Serpent, you are a Neanderthal or those with a lot of Neanderthal genes. Or even not so many but circumstances have led to you having our genes more activated than your other ones, you will know about it. You will have spent your life knowing you are different to everyone else. You will have some of, or all of, the characteristics of a Theolalite, or at least have a very good chance of activating them more easily than others.

You are considered an Eagle if you have a lot of our genes through Serpents breeding with Simples, but have been brought up in one of the families who a long time ago stole a lot of the Serpent teachings, and hid them from the general public. They didn't have all the teachings, but wanted to find the missing pieces and that was the reason they first set up Universities. So they could find out if the Pupils (eyes) could SEE more for them. Eagles have higher intelligence than Simples, but they use their intelligence, which is mainly left brained, for gaining power, greed and other psychopathic uncaring pursuits. Cro-Magnon, have more Neanderthal genes than Simples, but the mix has created mental issues. Some Eagles know what they are, and because they have a lot of our genes have become better people and want the same things as the Serpents, harmony and peace.

Simples are of low intelligence and these make up the vast majority of the human population. They can not think for themselves, they need to be told what to do in all areas of life, they can be caring towards others, or violent depending on up bringing and mix of genes. Mostly they just live in the world the Eagles created not realising there is another way to do things. They believe everything they hear on the news or read in a newspaper.

How Eagles & Simples were created

The Serpents studied simians and decided to make them a little more intelligent by giving them some of their genes. The Simples were created. They were O positive. They tried various types, mixing their genes with Gorillas and Chimps too, this created the B positive and A positive blood types. The Serpents found some of the Simples attractive and bred with them. This created Eagles. The Eagles had more Serpent genes and therefore were more intelligent than the rest of the Simples. So they try their best to keep their blood as pure as possible, and even seek out Serpent females to breed with, to make their blood purer, when they were not burning them at the stake as witches. They are very jealous of the Serpents, but think Serpents are weak for being peaceful and wanting to live in harmony with nature.

Ancient UK Tribes

Origins of the early inhabitants of the UK

Ancient UK before the Vikings, Anglo Saxons, Romans and Normans. There were many tribes in the UK, they came from all over. One thing all the tribes had in common was that their royal families were Serpents, the warrior class were Eagles and the farmers Simples. Of course if you go far enough back they all came from Tigris in the first place.

Gaels - From Egyptian Royal Families - Tigris, Egypt, Chad, Libya, Algeria, Morocco, Spain, Ireland.

Bretons - Spain, France and Basque Royal Families - Tigris, Greece, Italy, France, Spain, England.

Picts - Thracian Royal Families - Tigris, Turkey, Bulgaria, Romania, Croatia, Austria, Germany, Denmark, Norway, Sweden, Scotland.

I have used the modern names of the countries to make it easier to follow, but they had different names back then.

Vikings, Anglo Saxons, Roman and Norman leading families were all Eagles who had Simples as workers.

Eagles - Cro-Magnon's who want to own everyone and everything in the world.

Serpents - Neanderthals who want to live in harmony with nature, and have a barter, care and share type society of enlightened Gnostic Theolalites.

Simples - Sim is from Simian, as in ape/monkey and ples from people. Mix together it is another word for the general public who have more Simian genes than Eagles or Serpents.

Anointing & Sacraments

A Bishop or a Royal is an anointed one (Christos), everyone has been taught this means they have had holy oil put on them, which is correct these days, however it symbolises something completely different. The reason only men have been anointed, and it takes a Queen to make a King, is because the King was anointed with the elixir of the Goddess - The Queen. And the head he was anointed on was his little head during tantric sex, the great rite, hieros gamos. The modern religions completely removed the true source of anointing, and just left the men who are Bishops and Kings, and the real source of enlightenment and their power was lost to his-story. And what happens when you put unenlightened men up as spiritual leaders?
Check his-story... wars, paedophile, misogyny, hate, greed etc etc.

Blessed, Baptised & Unction

Being blessed and anointed with oil is a different matter. This has roots in ritual sacrifices to the Gods. It was a blessing to be smeared with oil before being burnt alive, as it was a quicker death that way... a blessing. The people were not killed to feed any kind of God in the sky, but the tribe leaders after a cataclysm when there was no food to be found, and eating the dead or surviving humans was the only way to survive.

Although blessing also means - be blood. Be blood that nourishes us, the ultimate sacrifice for your tribe leaders.

Did Jesus walk on water?

Jesus of Nazareth referred to as Jesus Christ or simply as Jesus or Christ. Christ is the English term for the Greek Χριστός (Khristós) meaning "the anointed one". It is a translation of the Hebrew מָשִׁיחַ (Māšîaḥ), usually transliterated into English as Messiah or Mashiach.

Jesus was an anointed one, he was anointed with Holy Oil, Khristós - the Holy Oil - floats on water. Try it yourself, get a glass of water then pour some olive oil into it, it will float on water.

Jesus walking on water is simply alchemical allegory for the fact that Holy Oil floats on water. Jesus had been anointed with Holy Oil. He was a Christos, and anyone who is anointed with Holy Oil in a consecration, is also 'an anointed one'. Jesus died to save us all, again allegory for after the flood, the bodies of the dead were floating in the water, and were used as a food source, it saved the survivors from death.

You might ask so why be anointed?

When you are anointed you become a sacrifice, just like Jesus. In Church you are giving your life in to service to that Church.

So when people go to be baptised into a Church, think about what they are doing. They are offering themselves up as a sacrifice. When they are dying and are anointed, again, they are saying, eat my dead body. Our Church teaches the truth about these sacraments, and then changes the meanings to positive actions. Our Baptism means a promise to yourself to do The Great Work, Confirmation - to confirm you are on the path. No leaders to lead and eat you.

Septimontium

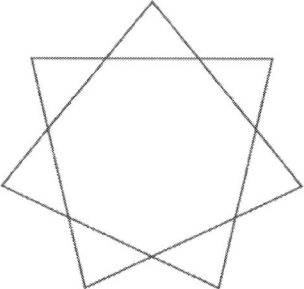

When I tell people that the OTO are part of the Roman Catholic Church, often they reject this. But those in the know, know the truth. The Roman Catholic religion is deeply patriarchal, as is the OTO - Ordo Templi Orientis, which is a more advanced form of Freemasonry, which is also under the Roman Catholic Church. Also I connect the new age religion Wicca, which again many deny the connection to the extremely patriarchal RC Church.

They are all connected by the number seven, or more importantly the seven pointed star which has many meanings. It can mean the seven days of the week, the seven chakras, the seven colours of the rainbow, the seven planets of alchemy, the seven days of creation, seven is also the symbol of perfection in Christianity. They just don't realise the symbolism behind it, the seven rays of the rainbow of light, the seven major endocrine glands of the body, those being testes or ovaries, pancreas, adrenal gland, thymus gland, thyroid gland, pituitary gland and pineal gland.

The Goddess has always been the secret Mother Goddess (Virgin Mary) of the RC Church, Christianity and all religions, only to bring patriarchy it was necessary to disguise this fact.

This is why women are not allowed to know they are complete, and why gay males have always dominated religions as leaders since patriarchy removed all evidence of the Divine Feminine. The gay males were thought to be more like the Goddess than other men, and dress in robes and the mitre of the Goddess, pretending to be her when they reached a high enough rank within the Church. Yet all the time preaching about a male God and Sun worship veiled.

OTO uses the seven pointed star of Babalon. Babalon, they are taught is 'Our Lady Babalon' and reverence is paid to her, along with the Sun Gods, and the phallic worship they do. Only what they aren't told is that Babalon is in fact the Roman Catholic Church, and the seven points are the seven hills of Rome.

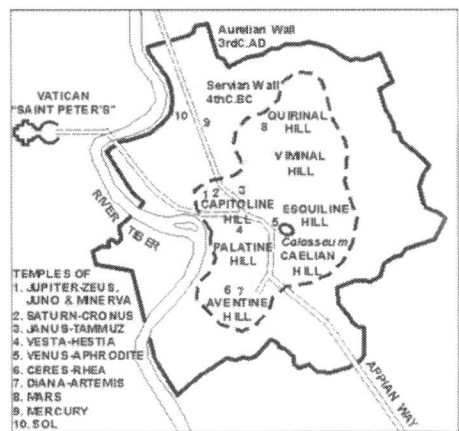

"The Septimontium was a Roman festival of the seven hills of Rome. It was celebrated in September (or, according to late calendars, on 11 December). They sacrificed seven animals at seven times in seven different places within the walls of the city near the seven hills. On that day the emperors were very liberal to the people. During the Septimontium in the Republican period, Romans refrained from operating horse-drawn carriages"

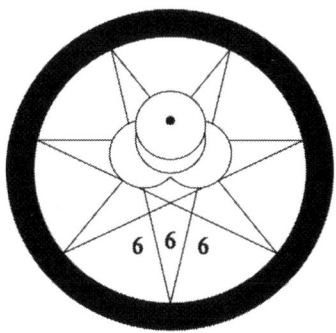

OTO call themselves Gnostics, yet they are deeply patriarchal. They only let women join to use them as naked altars during their perverted version of the Gnostic Mass. They worship the Sun and Cocks, and that is it. They do know some things about tantric sex magick, yet they tell the women that they will benefit too, when it is all for the men. One of their initiations is for men only, because they are a gay anti-woman Order, and it involves shoving a massive golden cock up their arse over the altar, which they are then told to place on the altar and worship everyday. Cock worship.

If you look at this symbol the seven pointed star as two points upwards which represents the feminine, and one point downwards, representing the masculine, which is surrounded by 666 the number of the beast, the beast being man. The number for women is 333. Then on top of the feminine star we see a massive cock made up by the infinity symbol, the crescent Moon and the Sun symbol. It isn't hard to see this is a big cock and balls looked at from above. Placed on top of the feminine two points up star to represent man's domination over women, and the hiding of the truth about the Mother Goddess, who is the true creator.

How does Wicca fit into this?

Wicca also is an off-shoot of Freemasonry, they just don't realise this. So yet again it is all about the Roman Catholic Church, and keeping them in power, as they give the women a little bit of this and that to keep them out the way, while the truth is yet again kept hidden from them.

The seven pointed star is known among Pagans as the Elven Star or Fairy Star, it has the same meaning as the star of Babalon, the seven hills of Rome and the Roman Catholic Church.

Summery

The seven pointed star is not an evil symbol, it can mean anything to you as an individual, however it is being used as magick talisman for the Roman Catholic Church, to keep them in power. As always symbols from the spiritual royalties Mystery School are used against the people, instead of for positive purposes, as used to be the way. People think they are getting involved with something completely not connected to the RC Church, but when you do some digging you find the links. It is very easy to find the link between Wicca, OTO and Freemasonry, it is made a little harder to find the link to the RC Church, however once you are aware that these people have been controlling the world, and all forms of religion and spirituality for thousands of years, in order to keep the general population unaware and unenlightened, you can start to join the dots.

These Orders have been set up much like Universities were. To hopefully find someone who would find all the hidden teachings from the spiritual royalty, the ones they are not in possession of. Only those of the bloodline with knowledge from the underground stream are in possession of the true teachings.

Agape

"AGAPE" (Greek for "the highest form of love)! How many Thelemites do you hear saying this? Thelema (a form of Masonry) is a religion for misogynists, just like RC Church and Freemasonry. They are completely anti-women and want to do away with them completely, by squaring the circle. The feminine is round, the masculine is square. This is allegory for creating males who can bear children.

Freemasonry and all fraternities are based on the values and systems of the patriarchal Greek Plato influenced, Socrates and the Orphic, Pythagorean and Eleusinian Mystery Schools who perverted the true teachings from the real Mystery Schools of the true Spiritual Royalty.

Young men are taught to enter into a 'bromance' type relationship with the older members of the Order, and to just use women as someone to breed them children and look after the home. They are taught that if they kiss the arse, for long enough, of their superior - they will get special knowledge and better career prospects.

The wives all think it is just the boys having some harmless fun, not realising how they are being thought of, and they are put out the way by getting them to join the female societies where they are taught to be good housewives and Mothers, and how to look after their husbands. This is also true of the Wiccan tradition, which is another off-shoot of Freemasonry, that teaches women to think small and not rock the boat as they are not given any true spiritual teachings, just allegory they are told is real.

The ultimate aim of Freemasonry and RC Church is do away with women completely and create men who can have children. Then they really can 'DESDEMONA' - Destroy Demon Females. The whole story of Desdemona was about this fact. So deeply rooted in these men is their hatred for women, any who dare to stand up against them is demonised. They want women to be passive, submissive and out the way, so they can stop feeling so hurt about the fact they need women to gain enlightenment, and that they must activate their feminine sides to do that. They don't want balance and harmony, they want war, power, control and games.

Christianity says it is against homosexuality, yet they have no respect for women, call any woman who wants to be equal a feminazi man hater, yet all the while they hate women themselves. They see women as a possession, some 'thing' that has no feelings, who deserves no respect, no love, they are just there to make children and look after the man. Then they are free to carry on their bromance relationships with other men, as they feel they are REAL men if they love and have sex with a man, and not some round feminine woman. If this isn't anti-woman and homosexual, what is?

"If a woman grows weary and, at last, dies from childbearing, it matters not. Let her die from bearing; she is there to do it." Martin Luther.

Ancient Greece

In Ancient Greece, same-sex relationships between men were considered the highest form of love; they were just as common and accepted as heterosexual relationships are today. This male-male relationship was based on love and reciprocity, and typically called for the older man to initiate the relationship. He would give gifts to the younger man as a promise of love. The relationship between the lover (the older man) and the beloved (the younger boy) was thought to be of the highest form of love. It showed that the men regarded furthering themselves in knowledge and intelligence rather than just a physical connection. Some who did not attempt to make this connection were seen as "shallow" The older man would become the mentor and lover to the younger man, and the two would form a close emotional bond. The youth would be taught his duties as a citizen, and skills to further his place in society by the older man, and once the youth reached adulthood, the sexual relationship between the two men evolved into a very strong friendship. As an adult, the youth would then marry a woman, and initiate a relationship with another adolescent.

An exclusively homosexual relationship was discouraged however, and not considered a substitute for male-female marriage. Marriage, and the children that would be produced within it, was required to maintain the family and society. The wives were viewed by their husbands as domestics and child bearers. While the men were away with their young lovers, women raised children, and took care of the household. Women were discouraged from taking lovers outside of the marriage bed.

Examples of this highly regarded male-male relationship can be found all throughout Greek myth, and Greek history. One example is the story of Apollo and Hyacinthus; Apollo fell in love with a mortal boy, Hyacinthus, and became a mentor to the youth. He taught Hyacinthus the art of war and sports and visited him often (Hyacinthus died during a javelin accident, and from his blood the Hyacinth was created). In another version, they were exercising one day throwing around a discus. Apollo threw it and Hyacinthus ran after the discus, but it hit the ground, bounced, and stroked the ground, killing Hyacinthus. He then became a purple flower with AI on the petals. Other Greek gods and Greek heroes have stories attributed to them about their same-sex relationships, Zeus and Hercules among them.

It has also been said, though not confirmed, that Alexander the Great, the renowned Greek conqueror of Persia, had homosexual relationships with his close friend Hephaestion.

"It should be known what these men get up to in their Freemason meetings, and other fraternities. All American Universities have these misogynist groups too. Young men are tricked into joining and becoming woman haters at a young age. There is nothing at all wrong with being gay, there is something wrong with being programmed to hate woman, and think they are only useful for breeding and keeping the home nice for men."
- Isabella De Medici

Druids, Wicca (Witchcraft), OTO Origins

Druids

People seem to think that OBOD (The Order of Bards, Ovates & Druids) or other Druidic organisations have teachings based on ancient traditions. They imagine some old men Priests in the past who called themselves Druids all standing in Stone circles and performing sacred ceremonies, or sitting round the fire telling stories and myths. They say how Druids or Ovates were midwives and healers, who knew about the different herbs and aromatherapy.
Like most things we are taught about the past under patriarchy this all complete nonsense. There were groups similar to how modern day Druids describe themselves, however they were women, not men. I will explain who these women were later, but first lets have a look at the origins of Druidry.

Druidry was founded by a man named William Stukeley (7 November 1687 – 3 March 1765) he was English antiquarian who pioneered the archaeological investigation of the prehistoric monuments of Stonehenge and Avebury. Stukeley was also one of the first biographers of Isaac Newton, of whom he was a friend. He was an Anglican clergyman. He was also a Freemason and began to describe himself as a "druid", and incorrectly believed that the prehistoric megalithic monuments were a part of the druidic religion. However, despite this he has been noted as being a significant figure in the early development of the modern movement known as Neo-druidry.

Stukeley's principal works, elaborate accounts of Stonehenge and Avebury, appeared in 1740 and 1743. These were supposed to be the first of a multi-volume universal history. Stukeley proposed that an ancient patriarchal religion was the original religion of mankind. This had subsequently degenerated as idol-worship had emerged. Stukeley believed that the Druids and the early Christians were examples of this religion. Stukeley himself was a priest in the Church of England.

Druids are the only organisation allowed to use Stonehenge circle yet they have absolutely no rights to at all.

The Ancient Order of Druids (AOD) is a fraternal organisation founded in London, England in 1781 that still operates to this day. It was set up based on the nonsense and assumptions of Stukeley. The Freemasonic boys only group would meet at the King's Arms, which came to be called Lodge No. 1, spawned the creation of a number of other lodges of the Order being founded elsewhere by new initiates, with Lodge No. 2 being inaugurated on 21 August 1783 and meeting at Rose Tavern, along the Ratcliffe Highway,

Wapping. Lodge No. 3 was soon after opened in Westminster, and according to a rumour within the Order, the politician Charles James Fox was initiated into the Order through this lodge by Hulme himself.

OBOD was founded in 1964 as a split from the Ancient Druid Order with Ross Nichols as its leader. It has made up teachings based on Freemasonry and patriarchy.

How is supporting this 'religion' moving forwards towards balance when it based on an old boys club of sexist cock worshipping misogynists? Even if they profess to worship nature and 'allow' women to join now, it is like a slap in the face for women, and especially for the Serpent families whose teachings the Freemasons have taken, perverted and use against everyone. They don't even have the true and full teachings, so many gaps. But so long as people are stupid enough to join them and support them and Freemasonry, not much changes.

Wicca (Witchcraft)

The term "Wicca" first achieved widespread acceptance when referring to the religion in the 1960s and 70s. Prior to that, the term "Witchcraft" had been more widely used. Whilst being based upon the Old English word wicca, which referred solely to male sorcerers, the actual individual who coined the capitalised term "Wicca" is unknown, though it has been speculated that it was Charles Cardell, who certainly used the term "Wiccen" during the 1950s.

Application of the word Wicca has given rise to "a great deal of disagreement and infighting". Gardnerian and Alexandrian Wicca are often collectively termed British Traditional Wicca, and many of their practitioners consider the term Wicca to apply only to these lineaged traditions. Others do not use the word "Wicca" at all, instead preferring to be referred to only as "Witchcraft," while others believe that all modern witchcraft traditions can be considered "Wiccan." Popular culture, as seen in TV programmes like Buffy the Vampire Slayer tends to use the terms "Wiccan" and "Wicca" as completely synonymous with the terms "Witch" and "Witchcraft" respectively.

Gardnerian Wicca, or Gardnerian Witchcraft, is a tradition in the neopagan religion of Wicca, whose members can trace initiatory descent from Gerald Gardner. The tradition is itself named after Gardner (1884–1964), a British civil servant and scholar of magic. The term "Gardnerian" was probably coined by the founder of Cochranian Witchcraft, Robert Cochrane in the 1950s or 60s, who himself left that tradition to found his own.

Gerald Brosseau Gardner (1884 – 1964) Born into an upper-middle-class family in Blundellsands, Lancashire. He eventually settled down near the New Forest, he joined an occult group, the Rosicrucian Order Crotona Fellowship, through which – he claimed – he encountered the New Forest coven, into which he was initiated in 1939. Erroneously believing the coven to be a survival of the pre-Christian Witch-Cult discussed in the works of Margaret Murray, he decided to revive the faith, supplementing the coven's rituals with ideas borrowed from Freemasonry, ceremonial magic and the writings of Aleister Crowley, to form the Gardnerian tradition of Wicca. As the Neopagan religion of Wicca developed in the latter decades of the twentieth century, some of the figures who were researching its origins, such as Aidan Kelly and later Leo Ruickbie, came to the conclusion that the New Forest coven had never existed, and that it was simply a fictional invention of Gardner's to provide a historical basis for his new faith.

Alexandrian Wicca is a tradition of the Neopagan religion of Wicca, founded by Alex Sanders (also known as "King of the Witches") who, with his wife Maxine Sanders, established the tradition in the United Kingdom in the 1960s. Alexandrian Wicca is similar in many ways to Gardnerian Wicca, and receives regular mention in books on Wicca as one of the religion's most widely-recognized traditions.

Alex Sanders (6 June 1926 – 30 April, 1988), born Orrell Alexander Carter, was an English occultist and High Priest in the Pagan religion of Wicca, responsible for founding the tradition of Alexandrian Wicca during the 1960s. He was initiated into Gardnerian Wicca before founding his own coven, through which he merged many aspects of ceremonial magic into Wicca.

Not one of these were formed from anything other than watered down patriarchal Freemasonry.

Wiccan's who say that Aleister Crowley is evil and does black magick are complete idiots and should look into the origins of the tradition they pretend to follow before mouthing off at others.

People who say they are not Wiccan, they follow a hereditary tradition of witchcraft, if it is genuine, are just the teachings of the wise women and midwives of a village, who passed down the teachings and old wives tales and superstitions, no magick involved at all.

OTO, Thelema, AMORC, Golden Dawn, Theosophical Society

Again these are all based on the teachings of Freemasonry. **OTO - Ordo Templi Orientis (Order of the Temple of the East)** is an international fraternal and religious organization founded at the beginning of the 20th century. English author and occultist Aleister Crowley has become the best-known member of the Order.

Founded by Carl Kellner (1 September 1851 – June 7, 1905) was a wealthy chemist, inventor, industrialist. He was a student of Freemasonry, Rosicrucianism and Eastern mysticism. During his trips to the East Kellner came across the tantric teachings there and decided this must be the key to enlightenment that Freemasonry was missing, however it posed a problem as women were not allowed to join the 'Bothers' in Freemasonry.

Due to the regulations of the established Grand Lodges which governed Regular Masonry, women could not be made Masons and would therefore be excluded by default from membership in Ordo Templi Orientis. Reforming the Masonic system to allow the admission of women may have been one of the reasons that Kellner and his associates resolved to obtain control over one of the many rites of Masonry; possibly because of wishing to incorporate the practice of sex magic. Their view may have been that sex magic was "...the key to all the secrets of the Universe and to all the symbolism ever used by secret societies and religions."

So as in the Eastern traditions, which were taught to them by the Serpent people, they kept the truth about tantra secret from women, and proceeded to 'allow' women to join then they could use them for sex magick. Their work will have been fruitless, as a woman who is not aware and trained fully to understand what the Great Rite actually is, can never perform it correctly.

Thelema is based purely on the teachings of Aleister Crowley, yeah you guessed it, a Freemason. Aleister Crowley did a lot to bring some of the old teachings into the public consciousness, but he himself did not reach Kether and he still didn't have all the pieces of the puzzle. So those who follow his teachings and go no further are not going to get very far.

Harvey Spencer Lewis (November 25, 1883 – August 2, 1939), was the founder in USA and the first Imperator of Ancient Mystical Order Rosae Crucis (AMORC), from 1915 until 1939.

The Ancient and Mystical Order Rosæ Crucis, also called the Rosicrucian Order (AMORC), was founded in 1915 in New York to make public a supposed Rose-Croix Order that originated in Ancient Egyptian mystery schools.

AMORC claims to be an authentic Western mystery school, the modern manifestation of the ancient Order. However in reality it is based on Christianity and its teachings draw upon ideas of the major philosophers, particularly Pythagoras, Thales, Solon, Heraclitus, Democritus and of course as Lewis was a Freemason, Masonry too.

The Hermetic Order of the Golden Dawn (or, more commonly, the Golden Dawn) was a magical order active in Great Britain during the late 19th and early 20th centuries. The three founders, William Robert Woodman, William Wynn Westcott, and Samuel Liddell MacGregor Mathers were Freemasons. Although they allowed women to join, they were deeply patriarchal. A Thelemic version is now available, which is much the same as Aleister Crowley's own Order Argentium Astrum.

The Theosophical Society was officially formed in New York City, United States, in November 1875 by Helena Blavatsky, Henry Steel Olcott, William Quan Judge and others.

One common theme within all these and other new age organisations is that they refer to the 'Secret Chiefs' a Spiritual Hierarchy of Ascended Masters - The Great White Brotherhood, or the Universal Brotherhood, who apparently give the leaders information and knowledge that everyone was to listen to and believe. Blavatsky claimed to have been party to revelations from Hidden Masters called the "Great White Brotherhood" who resided somewhere in the Himalayas. But Blavatsky later admitted in letters to her sister that this was a codename for the Rosicrucian hierarchy who funded her. It is clear her work is influenced, if not sourced, in the work of Masonic demagogue General Albert Pike - the American South's Sovereign Grand Commander of the Supreme Council of the 33rd Degree of Scottish Rite Freemasonry, Civil War war criminal, and founding member of the Ku Klux Klan - who revealed Rosicrucian/Masonic doctrine in his work Morals & Dogma (1871) that was distributed to Sublime Prince of the Royal Secret (32nd degree) Scottish Rite initiates.

Also the **Mormon Church**, **Jehovah's Witnesses** and **Scientology** were also all founded by Freemasons. The whole of the new age movement is also, just look at the roots and you find out.

As I have also pointed out before now Freemasonry is part of the Roman Catholic Church and Jesuit Order, as are all of the Orders mentioned above. Being part of any of these organisations is supporting paedophiles, misogynists, racists, psychopaths, greed, war, slavery, rape and other hate crimes... would you willingly support that?

I am not asking you to believe the above, it is all available for you to discover yourself if you look.

The Serpent Families - The True Source of Gnosis & Sophia

In ancient times all the tribes were matriarchal. There may have been Kings, but only if the Queen made him one by anointing him. It was these royals who were the spiritual leaders of the tribes, the Seers, Alchemists, Astronomers, Shamans, Magickians, Teachers of Exoteric and the Esoteric, Philosophers, Midwives, Herbalists, Peace Makers, Law Keepers - these were the Priestesses of old and they all came from noble Serpent families.

This was long before all patriarchal religions were invented. It was long before some of the teachings were taken by Eagles and turned into religions and cults by the Hindus, Buddhists, Pythagoras, Jews, Christians and more recently new age religions and organisations like Freemasonry, Druidism, Wicca, Witchcraft, Philosophical Society, AMORC, Thelema and so many more. All religions and all paths are based on the ancient Mystery School teachings of the Serpent families, but they are not us and they don't hold the true teachings.

The Serpent families in ancient times travelled all over the world to help spread their teachings of Gnosis and Sophia. Everywhere we visited the locals would tell stories about the time the red headed, blue eyed, white skinned Serpent, Snake or Dragon people visited and taught them things, also building stone circles, pyramids and mounds.

As part of our ceremonies and initiations we would use mounds or caves as the belly of the Mother Earth. We would decorate them with paintings, animal skins, bones, flowers and herbs. The Initiate would enter and find themselves crawling through a maze or labyrinth of tunnels, and when they emerged they would be reborn. We would also use buildings and stone circles to map and keep track of the planets movements.

We are prehistoric, that means pre-his-story. History was created by patriarchy, females completely removed, and it still continues to this day and will continue unless more people realise that all the organisations mentioned above are connected and learn to see the bigger picture. While you allow yourself to be taken in by the game, you are one of the pawns and you will be played, controlled, used and abused by their system.

Time to move on, time to see through the lies, it is time for truth..
Let's <u>BE THE SOLUTION</u>.

Mayan Human Sacrifice

We are told that Mayan's took part in human sacrifice almost constantly. That they were stupid 'heathens' who didn't know any better. But who told us this? The Spanish Priests who went there and took over of course. The natives were seen as uncivilised, even though they were obviously highly intelligent spiritual people. They refused to convert to Christianity so they were killed, and myths about their old culture were told to justify the murder. We are told their society was destroyed by their blood lust and need for human sacrifice. Don't believe everything you are told, they say the same about anyone who isn't Christian.

The Mayans also had a lot of gold, but they didn't want to give this up to the 'Church' so they were brutally murdered for it.

A Visit to Chichen Itza gives us an idea of just how sophisticated these people were. The Temple of Kukulkan is a massive pyramid shape, and its construction encodes detailed information about the sophisticated Mayan calendar. The Observatory is a building from which Mayan astronomers plotted the movements of the planets, the sun and the moon. At the Ball Court highly trained Mayan athletes engaged in competitive sporting events. The Temple of a Thousand Columns once housed an outdoor market for Mayan people to meet, shop and sell their wares. The beautiful designs on another building called The Nunnery with Its frescoes and engravings are a testament to the artistic achievements of the Mayans. A set of shell-shaped stones produce melodic tones when tapped with a stick. The Mayans were clearly accomplished musicians. The Ball Court also offered a stunning example of Mayan acoustical technology. A whisper at one end of the site could easily be heard by someone standing 545 feet away at the opposite end.

Most appalling of all is that the Spanish Priests anxious to cover their tracks, and removed all evidence of the truth about these amazing people, burnt all their records, teachings and spiritual scripts. The only bits left aren't enough for us to decode the hieroglyphics and find out more about their culture. Some of us carry their secrets with us in our genetic memories, and although many lies have been told, our hearts know the truth.

It isn't Christians who are our enemy, they are just misguided. Most of them don't even have any kind of clue about the real teachings that Jesus and Mary Magdalene were trying to pass on. You have to look to the Gnostics for that. The Roman Catholic Church, now they don't have much of anything good about them. Pre-Nicene Christianity has some, especially Esoteric Christianity.

Secrets of the Serpent Bloodline - The Unveiling of Profound Esoteric Mysteries

Chapter 11

Ancient Temples

The Neanderthal people left many remains of their ancient spiritual practices – many of which show striking continuity with later times.

Many examples of ancient Neanderthal Shrines and Temples remain. These religious sites have been found within caves where they may have been built for shelter from the elements or because the Spirits worshipped had Chthonic associations. The ancient Neanderthals also had outdoor religious sites, for example Stone circles, mounds and henges.

A striking example of a Neanderthal religious site was found in the Drachenloch cave in the Swiss Alps. The front of the cave apparently served as a periodic dwelling place, while deeper within the mountain were both a Shrine and a Temple. Inside the Shrine was a three-foot square stone box, which functioned as a reliquary. Inside the reliquary were the skulls of seven cave bears.

Still deeper into the mountain was a full-blown Neanderthal Temple. Around the walls of the Temple were six niches, each of which held the skull of a cave bear. Some of the niches held the skull alone, while others held the skull and a leg bone.

Another example of a Neanderthal Shrine or Temple was found in the Cave of the Witches, near Genoa Italy. Here a ritual seems to have been enacted that involved the magical "hunting" of a sacred stalactite that resembled an animal such as a bison. Evidence indicates that the stalactite was regularly used as a target for stone throwing – this is believed to have been magical in nature because the stalactite is not easily accessible, being awkwardly placed deep within the cave.

The Underground Labyrinths & Cities

Our ancient people have been on Earth a lot longer than Sapiens, and as such we have survived through all kinds of catastrophes. We have always, as a people, sort shelter and comfort underground. We have survived various ice ages underground, and we continue to have some ceremonies and initiations underground.

The labyrinths we used for initiations would take the Initiate on a twisting and winding journey through tunnels. On getting to the centre of the labyrinth it represents discovering the truth of the depths of our inner psyche, coming to know ourselves fully, including the shadow self. We then make our way back out from the centre, to find our way out, and master our unconscious mind. On completing the labyrinth we have been reborn on to the path of Gnosis & Sophia.

Of course these underground cities were for more than spiritual initiation, they kept us safe from the elements and we kept animals down there with us, and had whole functioning cities.

Today most of the underground tunnels and the entrances are kept secret for very good reason. Hoards of tourists, or even deliberate vandals would soon destroy them all.

Venus of Laussel

The Venus of Laussel is a Venus figurine, a 1.5 foot high limestone bas-relief of a nude female figure, painted with red ochre. It was carved into a large block of fallen limestone in a rock shelter in the commune of Marquay, in the Dordogne department of southwestern France. The carving is approximately 25,000 years old. It is currently displayed in the Musée d'Aquitaine in Bordeaux, France.

The figure holds a wisent horn in one hand, which has 13 notches. This is to symbolise the number of moons and menstrual cycles in one year.

She has her hand on her abdomen (or womb) indicating pregnancy, with large breasts and vulva. There is a "Y" on her thigh and her faceless head is turned toward the horn.

As with all Venus figurine they represent fertility and the Mother Goddess from whom all life is created. The figures also represent abundance.

This ancient Goddess carving is a beautiful example of Serpent Bloodline art. These representations of the Goddess would be placed on or near the Altar during ceremonies and smaller versions carried with females who were hoping to become pregnant.

Bee Goddess

Priests and Priestesses dressed as Bee's to worship the
Divine Bee Goddess in Ancient Sumer.

Minoan Golden Bee. In Crete the Bee Goddess was worshipped. The Priestesses would wear wings and dance about in worship of the Great Mother.

  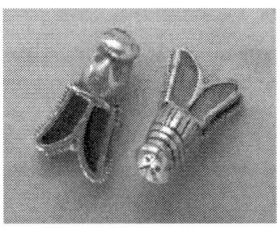

Bees were also sacred in Egypt.   Bee Coin from Sicily 700 BCE.   Merovingian Bees.

Wherever the bloodline families have been, they have carried the teachings of the Bee Goddess, the Divine Feminine is denied by so many, yet strong in the hearts of the TRUE bloodline families.

"Bees, like all insects that spin cocoons or weave webs, serve as images of the miraculous interconnectedness of life. The intricate cellular structure that secretes the golden essence of life is an image of the network of invisible nature that relates all things to each other in an ordered harmonious pattern. Perhaps this is the meaning of the tale in which the infant Zeus is fed on honey in Crete, and why honey was the nectar of the gods. Furthermore, the busy bee, following the impulsion of its nature to pollinate the flowers and gather their nectar to be transformed into honey, was an example of the continual activity required of human beings to gather the crops and transform them into food. The queen bee, whom all the others serve during their brief lives, was, in the Neolithic, an epiphany of the Goddess herself." Layne Redmond.

Gold seal ring, c. 1450 BC. From a tomb at Isopata, near Knossos.

In Minoan Crete the Goddess and her Priestesses, dressed as bees, would dance together, hands raised in the air as a gesture of epiphany. The bee signified life that comes from death, as the scarab beetle in Egypt. The Goddess would symbolically descend to the earth among snakes and lilies, as the Priestesses danced. Honey was used to embalm and preserve the bodies of the dead.

New Year rituals of the Minoans also involved the use of honey. The Summer Solstice was the beginning of the New Year Celebrations, this is the longest and hottest day of the year. then on the 20th July the star Sirius rose in conjunction with the Sun, as it did also in Sumeria and Egypt. Sirius was the star of the Goddess Innana, or Isis in Egypt. Temples were built to orientate towards this important star. The rising of the star signalled the end of the 40 day ritual, during which honey was gathered from woods and caves. The honey was used to make mead, which was then drunk during the ecstatic rites which celebrated the return of the Goddess at the beginning of the next new year. The humming of the bee was actually heard as the voice of the Goddess, the sound of creation.

Knosis Crete 1500 BCE. The importance of bee-keeping to the Minoans is documented in the Linear A hieroglyphs, where there are already drawings of actual beehives, testifying to a long history probably going back to the Neolithic era. The onyx gem from Knossos shows the Bee Goddess bearing upon her head the bull's horns with the double axe inside their curve. The dogs – later the dogs of the underworld belonging to Hecate and Artemis – are winged and flying so close to the Goddess that their wings, at first glance, appear as hers.

OMPHALOS STONE at Delphi, Greece.

The tombs at Mycenae were shaped as beehives, as was the omphalos at Delphi in Classical Greece, where Apollo ruled with his chief oracular Priestess, the Pythia, who was called the Delphic Bee.

In the Greek Homeric Hymn to Hermes from the eighth century BC, the God Apollo speaks of three female seers as three bees or bee-maidens, who practised divination:

There are some Fates sisters born, maidens three of them, adorned with swift wings.

Their heads are sprinkled over with white barley meal, while they make their homes under the cliffs of Parnassus.

They taught divination far off from me, the art I used to practise round my cattle while still a boy.

These sacred bee-maidens with their gift of prophecy, were to be Apollo's gift to Hermes, the God who alone could lead the souls of the dead out of life and sometimes back again. The etymology of the word 'fate' in Greek offers a fascinating example of how the genius of the Minoan vision entered the Greek language, often visibly, as well as informing its stories of Goddesses and Gods. The Greek word for 'fate', 'death' and 'Goddess of death' is *e ker* (feminine); the word for 'heart' and 'breast' is *to ker* (neuter); while the word for 'honeycomb' is *to kerion* (neuter). The common root *ker* links the ideas fo the honeycomb, Goddess, death, fate and the human heart, a nexus of meanings that is illumined if we know that the Goddess was once imagined as a bee.

Text from <u>The Myth of the Goddess: Evolution of an Image</u> by Anne Baring & Jules Cashford.

Birds of the Muses *"Bees have an ancient reputation as the bringers of order, and their hives served as models for organizing temples in many Mediterranean cultures. Priestesses at Cybele's temples in Asia Minor, Greece, and Rome were called Melissai or Melissae, the Greek and Latin words for bees. These Priestesses were often prophets or oracles who entered an ecstatic trance enduced by preparations that included ingesting honey. (The Greek word for this state of transfigured consciousness is enthusiasmos -- 'within is a god" -- the root of our word enthusiasm.) Bees, familiars of the Goddess since Catal Huyuk, appear frequently in classical mythology. They are called the "Birds of the Muses" and are attracted to the heavenly fragrances of flowers, from which they make the divine nectar, honey. Honey is antibacterial, and its mildly laxative properties and sweet taste made it a primary ingredient in ancient medicines. It was widely believed to be a source of divine nourishment. In the myths of the ancient world, honey often nourished a divine child raised in secret by a Goddess in the depth of caves."*
Quoted from When the Drummers were Women by Layne Redmond.

Signs of her worship are evident in the Mediterranean cultures of around 3,000 years ago at the temples of Artemis. She is one of the oldest and most popular aspects of the Divine Feminine. Born on the Greek Island of Delos, Artemis was sister of Apollo and daughter to Zeus and Leto. When she was a young girl, her father, Zeus, asked her what was her dream? She answered that she wished to never have to marry a man and to always be free to roam in the wild forest. Artemis was known as a patron of young virgins, and a powerful protectress of the natural world of fertility. As with other early Goddesses, ceremonies to invoke Artemis were held in groves of trees, at places of special rock outcroppings, at sacred sites along rivers or at quiet springs. Ironically, Artemis's blessings were eventually cultivated at exquisite temple sites constructed throughout the Mediterranean region.

Artemis was and is to be known as one of the most powerful mistresses of magic. She's allowing us to feed our imaginations with many possibilities, all of which are symbols of fertility that can suit our needs. The breast-like objects growing out of Artemis' chest look very much like bees eggs!

The Priestesses of historical descendants of the ancient Bee Goddess - Demeter, Rhea, Cybele were called Melissae, the ancient Latin word for bees. The Bible mentions a ruler and prophetess of ancient Israel called Deborah, the "Queen Bee", her Priestesses were known as Deborahs. Some say that the Priestesses of the Moon Goddess were called bees because it was believed that all honey came from the Moon, the hive whose bees were the stars.

Melissa, the Goddess as Queen Bee, taught mortals how to ferment honey into mead. In the Homeric Hymn to Hermes, the Melissai feed on honey and are inspired "to speak the truth". These traditions made the omphalos the place of sacred utterance - the oracular power associated with the buzzing of bees and the buzzing vibration of life. . . . .

The **Omphalos** is shaped like a bee hive. Paphos, Greece, the site of Aphrodite's tomb, was known as the navel of the Earth. The Greek word for navel - *omphalos* - also refers to the sacred stone found in temples or shrines. Symbolically, the omphalos brought together a number of important spiritual concepts. The heart-seat of the great Earth Mother was the very centre of the navel of the world. The navel cord connects the foetus with outer and inner worlds, and is the source of nourishment until it is time for birth. Similarly, Aphrodite's temple was the place where initiates were nourished and birthed into higher planes of consciousness.

Goddess wearing a beehive as a tiara Hacilar, ancient Turkey circa 8000 BCE. This is the origin of the beehive shaped Mitre of the Cohen Priests.

Queen Bee. The Anatolian Goddess is often shown wearing a beehive as a tiara, most frequently at Hacilar. This is the introduction of a motif that would flourish in historical times. Of all the insects represented in the ancient world, bees are foremost in ritual and symbolic meaning. The Goddess's tiara announces her status as a queen bee and suggests that she streams with honey, a much-revered substance in ancient times.

How disturbing is then that the male Priests wear these items and never revealed the origins to women, and kept it secret to suppress and oppress them!

Bees also represent birth, death, and reincarnation. Bees have an acute sense of time. They appear to use their internal circadian clocks in conjunction with the Sun's position in the sky to navigate. Because their time memory is so advanced, they can be trained to appear at certain times of the day for feeding. An individual bee within the hive can communicate the location and richness of a newly discovered food source by dancing and drumming with its wings. The queen bee, deep in the hive, lays up to two thousand eggs a day, but only a few male drones mate with the queen - and just once, since the sexual act ends in his death. All these properties are echoed in historical rituals and mythologies.

Secrets of the Serpent Bloodline - The Unveiling of Profound Esoteric Mysteries

As Human BEEings, why have we BEEn denied the truth about the origins of religions?

Why has the Divine Feminine been denied us for so long?

Do you BEElieve it is about time the truth was known?

Why is anyone who brings the truth vilified?

Why are all women who come forwards told they are feminazi men haters?

FEAR, please don't get angry about what we have been denied, just use the knowledge to enlighten others. Join others who are helping, if you are female become a Priestess and claim back your birth right.

If you are male don't be afraid of what you will lose with this truth, be happy about what harmony we can all gain from this knowledge and become a Priest yourself.

All it takes for ignorance, greed and corruption to continue is for good Beeings to do nothing. Bee the change you want to see.

Black Stone - Black Madonna

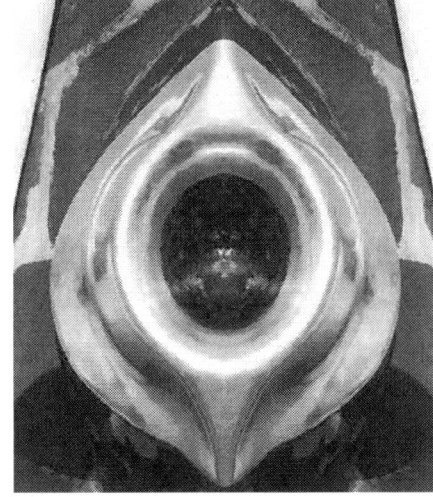

The Black Stone at Mecca that Muslims worship. The comet that is also the Black Madonna, sent from Mother Nature and cherished as sacred and having mystical healing powers.

The Truth About The Mitre

Cybele wearing her Mitre

What is the truth about the origins of the Mitre?

The Cult of Magna Mater, the Great Mother, is the oldest religion of all. The first to sport the fish head Mitre, was Goddess Cybele a Phrygian form of the Earth Mother or Great Mother. As with Greek Gaia (the "Earth"), her Minoan equivalent Rhea and some aspects of Demeter, Cybele embodies the fertile Earth. She is a Goddess of caverns and mountains, walls and fortresses, nature, and wild animals (especially lions and bees).

A figurine found at Çatalhöyük, (Archaeological Museum, Ankara), dating about 6000 BCE, depicts a corpulent and fertile Mother Goddess in the process of giving birth while seated on her throne, which has two hand rests in the form of lion's heads. Anatolia was the Asiatic area of what is today Turkey, known in ancient times as Asia Minor. The general boundaries were the Black Sea to the north, the Sea of Marmara, the Bosporus, and the Dardanelles to the northwest, The Aegean Sea to the west, The Mediterranean Sea to the south. This is where agriculture and animal husbandry first started. They domesticated wild animals living on their lands (ovine, bovine and caprine races). They learned to cultivate wild wheat and barley, to store the products of their crops. They settled and gathered into villages. This is the first civilization.

The worship of Cybele spread from inland areas of Anatolia and Syria to the Aegean coast, to Crete and other Aegean islands, and to mainland Greece. Her temples and shrines were always in mountains or caves and her guardians were lions (or leopards).

In Ancient Egypt at Alexandria, Cybele was worshipped by the Greek population as "The Mother of the Gods, the Saviour who Hears our Prayers" and as "The Mother of the Gods, the Accessible One". Ephesus, one of the major trading centres of the area, was devoted to Cybele as early the 10th century BCE, and the city's ecstatic celebration, the Ephesia, honoured her.

Artemis of Ephesus is the extension of the Mother Goddess and the source of the Virgin Mary cult which parallels virginity and Motherhood. The black meteorite was adapted as the head of the cult statue. Cybele, like Diana of the Ephesians, was a "black virgin." The crescent moon also represents Diana of the Ephesians. "Black Virgin" represents those who encompasses all the Seven Rays into the Holy and healing white light of Spirit.

Acts 19 Great is Artemis of the Ephesians!"

"And when the town clerk had quieted the crowd, he said, "Men of Ephesus, what man is there who does not know that the city of the Ephesians is temple keeper of the great Artemis, and of the sacred stone that fell from the sky?"

She became the protectress of the Roman Empire.

Cybele was received with full honours by the leading citizens of Rome. The Roman Pontifex Maximus welcomed her and she became the great MAGNA MATER or "holy" Mother of Rome.

Under the Roman Empire the most important festival of Cybele was the Hilaria, taking place between March 15 and March 28. It symbolically commemorated the death of Attis and his resurrection by Cybele, involving days of mourning followed by rejoicing. Celebrations also took place on 4 April with the Megalensia festival, the anniversary of the arrival of the Goddess (i.e the Black Stone) in Rome.

Cybele worship was associated with a BLACK STONE or meteorite that had fallen from the sky.

The stone associated with Cybele's worship was, originally, probably at Pessinus but perhaps at Pergamum or on Mount Ida. What is certain is that in 204 BC it was taken to Rome, where Cybele became "Mother" to the Romans. Her ecstatic rites of worship made the Roman streets very lively during the annual procession of the Goddess's statue. Alongside Isis, Cybele retained prominence in the heart of the Empire until the fifth century AD; the stone was then "lost."

She wore a key like Janus which gave her the same authority as Janus (key to heaven and earth and the mysteries).

She had a joint cult with her consort Attis, and was served by a priesthood of eunuchs. Cybele's most ecstatic followers were males who ritually castrated themselves, after which they were given women's clothing and assumed female identities. They were referred to by one 3rd-century commentator, Callimachus, in the feminine as Gallai. Other contemporary commentators in ancient Greece and Rome referred to them Gallos or Galli.

The Black Stone is also worshipped by Muslims at Mecca and this is where the lost stone is now housed.

Mother Earth, never left the traditions, she was simply called 'Mary Mother of God' in the Christian religions and the Bishops and Priests still pretend to be her, as they abuse and rape her World. The Mitre is a fish head because the fish has always represented reproduction and fertility, as its links back to the Vesica Piscis, which is the cosmic vagina of the Mother Goddess, this is also where the Christian fish symbol came from. The Mitre is worn in this age of Pisces to represent this age, as well as the Mother Goddess.

Lilith

Lilith by John Collier

ALGOL/Lilith (Beta Persei) is the second magnitude Beta star of Perseus, the great mythological hero who rescued Andromeda from Cetus the Sea Monster. The Arabic name, "al Ghul" (related to our word "ghoul"), means "the demon", which literally signifies "mischief maker", from a longer phrase that refers to the demon's head. In Greek mythology, Algol represents the Medusa's head with which Perseus turned Cetus to stone, the star considered an "unlucky" one for centuries. The Chinese called it "Tseih She," translated as the "Piled-up Corpses".

Lilith's sinister qualities were attributed from ancient astronomers by it's peculiar appearance that is visible from Earth without a telescope. Algol changes its brightness, because it is an eclipsing binary - every 68 hours and 49 minutes the stars "blink" for roughly 8 hours as the dimmer star of the pair passes between the brighter star and the earth.

Algol is located in the constellation Taurus, and is one of the Fixed Stars in the sky that were also associated with The Watchers in other ancient stellar lore.

In the Spirit of Lilith... She is often depicted revealing the innermost sanctum - the holiest of holies: the journey to the Source. She may only be approached with deepest reverence. She awakens the chakras, the kundalini and brings Gnosis and Sophia.

As patriarchy took over the vast power of the Goddess, Lilith became legend in a dark fashion, reviled as a destroyer and seducer of men. Even as Inanna gave up the power of the Bird and Snake Goddess, so too did the symbol of a woman's power become the bed and the throne.

Throughout history Lilith was the one who would not submit. Passed down from Sumeria, the Hittite Empire, Babylon to the Semitic peoples, she became the archetype of the dangerous woman who refused submission. She was vilified as Harlot, Serpent, Blood Sucker, Impure Female, Hag, Witch and Enchantress. Yet, in the beginning her epitaph was that of 'Beautiful Maiden'.

Lilith's flower was the Lily and the magical Lotus. In the beginning she represented the virgin (belonging to no man) aspect of the Triple Goddess. She stood upon the protection of lions and was Lady of the Beasts. The wisdom of the night Screech Owl was her companion. She is the instinctive soul of the living world.

Hieros Gamos

What is Hieros Gamos?

"Hieros gamos", "the sacred marriage" is often depicted as the Sun and Moon - the masculine and the feminine, coming together in sexual union creating an alchemical reaction.

The High Priest and High Priestess having both been trained in the tantric arts perform this ritual - The Great Rite.

For what purpose do we perform 'The Great Rite'?

Occultist are often told this takes place because both males and females are incomplete, and this union will help them become complete and 'enlightened'.

As I have already pointed out in my other articles on this subject -
The Divine Feminine - women are already complete within themselves, because in the beginning there were only women, who reproduced using parthenogenesis.

So what is Hieros Gamos for?

The truth behind the Hieros Gamos is that the male is taking in the female essence, and becoming complete. Females are already complete, they have 2 full X chromosomes, men have one complete X and a shortened Y.
When the man has learnt how to restrict his orgasm, and takes in the High Priestesses feminine secretions into himself, through his penis, this accumulates at the base of his spine where it awakens the kundalini energy, which shoots up his spine and activates his third eye and he becomes 'enlightened'. He has then become complete and whole.

The time for hiding this is now gone. No good comes from suppressing women and telling us we came from a man's rib. The forbidden serpent in the garden of Eden is the kundalini energy, that once awakened leads to 'Gnosis' - Knowledge. What better way to keep people restricted and living in fear than to demonise the very thing that will free them?

Hexagrams aren't evil.

As you can see in the picture the true meaning of the hexagram is Hieros Gamos. Nothing evil about it. When you see a lot of people in a crowd doing a triangle above their head, they are projecting male energy. If you see some making a diamond with hands, they are projecting balance. If you see someone making a downwards triangle, they are projecting feminine energy.

What about Jesus?

He was enlightened too. Jesus gained enlightenment from Mary Magdalene in an alchemical wedding. He was a High Priest and Mary Magdalene a High Priestess in the hidden (occult) church.

Chapter 12

Incubi and Succubi

incubus [ˈɪnkjʊbəs]n pl -bi [-ˌbaɪ], -buses

1. (Myth & Legend / European Myth & Legend) a demon believed in folklore to lie upon sleeping persons, esp to have sexual intercourse with sleeping women.

2. something that oppresses, worries, or disturbs greatly, esp a nightmare or obsession.

suc·cu·bus (sky-bs) also suc·cu·ba (-b)n. pl. suc·cu·bus·es or suc·cu·bi (-b, -b) also suc·cu·bae (-b, -b)

1. A female demon supposed to descend upon and have sexual intercourse with a man while he sleeps.

2. An evil spirit; a demon.

Are Incubi and Succubi real or if this is just a product of the psyche?

This is most common when someone is going through puberty, but can happen at anytime. Our minds can create very real feelings. Ask someone who has had a limb removed and they will say that they still feel as if it is still there. This is what leads to balance issues, the brain is still thinking an arm is there and the weight of it still there, so the person loses balance very easy.

Most Magi summon succubus or incubus when they are single, or feeling horny, they do this consciously. However this can happen unconsciously as well.

It is all too easy for our minds to create things that are not there, especially when we feel we are in danger from others.

Some Orders will tell the Initiate that during initiation their Soul will be removed and a demon placed inside, that completely takes over them and their life. This is mind control, and used in many of the Eagle Orders as a way to get people to change personality instantly. Now we would think that if someone was told this before hand, they wouldn't do it. However it is amazing what a curious, dispossessed or depressed person will do.

They are told that their new self will have magick powers and gain great strength and if they believe it enough, they will and their life will completely change, it is hypnosis and mind control.

The worse thing about it is that these Orders will tell those joining that hypnosis is really bad and they should never be involved with it, as it will summon evil spirits and stuff. Why would they say that? Well because they don't want them learning about it then realising they are under mind control themselves.

Our Order teaches hypnosis and NLP among many other things, then we can empower ourselves and spot when we are being manipulated.

Getting back to the topic. It is possible for someone to project themselves, or even create astral entities, or travel themselves astrally, but these things are again working on you psychologically. They influence you through your own mind. If you know how to protect yourself from outside manipulation they simply can't effect you.

Long Hair Truth

Why do Wise men and Women, Shamans, Gurus, Native Americans, Neanderthals, Celts, Vikings, Gaels, Picts, Scythians and Merovingians all have or had long hair?

Hair acts as antenna for the nervous system, it receives information to the neocortex, brain stem and limbic system. With longer hair, the antennae work better.

To make full use of their intuition and allow them to sense danger, weather changes etc, our ancestors would stand up on a mountain, long hair blowing about freely in the wind, picking up signals.

The story of Samson and him losing his power, again all relating to this. Also Witches would have their hair shaved off, as it was thought to contain their power. In the dark ages a punishment was often to have your hair shaved.

Hair stores our learnt behaviours, and this is something we instinctively know. This is why women who come out of a relationship often cut off their hair. It is like a new start. They can then start to build new behaviours.

When joining the Army it is the custom to shave off the hair of the new recruit. This is important before any training, as it removes learnt behaviours from the consciousness and creates a fresh clean slate to work on.

In the past when they were going through Holy Orders at their Ordination to the Order of Cleric they were tonsured - the top of their head shaved, the rest was left round the sides to catch the oil from running down their neck and faces. The special oil containing psilocybin was put on the freshly shaved skin, were the oil would seep inside the cuts, and a skullcap placed on top. Giving the Cleric a direct connection to 'God', well they sure would have a strange experience.

When you start on a your spiritual journey it is a good time to cut your hair off. Then keep it long, apart from trimming the ends to keep it healthy, and notice how your dreams, intuition and senses grow with you.

Peace Sign

This symbol is instantly recognisable as the peace symbol, something that protesters against nuclear power and bombs will draw on banners, and themselves. But what are the origins of the this symbol? And what does it really mean?

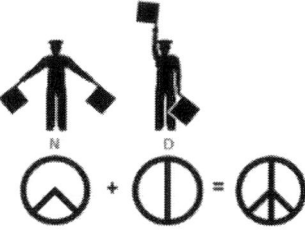

We are told that a man named Gerald Herbert Holtom designed the logo as the picture here. The design was a combination of the letters "N" (two arms outstretched pointing down at 45 degrees) and "D" (one arm upraised above the head) of the flag semaphore alphabet, standing for nuclear disarmament.

However the symbol below is the Rune Agliz meaning: Literally: "Elk" – Esoteric: Protection, Higher Self.

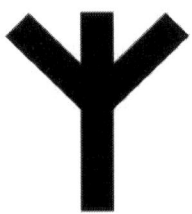

Rune of the essential link or connection with the patterns of divine or archetypal consciousness.

Psi: Divinity, higher self, the state of listening.

Energy: Protective teaching force, the divine plan.

Mundane: Protection, safety, spirituality.

Divinations: Connection with the gods, awakening, higher life, protection.

Governs: Strengthening of hamingja (personal gravity, 'luck') and life force through courageous deeds. Protection/defence. Banishing the fear of death.

When reading runes, if the rune is reversed, it means the opposite of when it is the other way up.

The peace symbol is the reversed Agliz, and therefore really means:

Psi: Lower self, the state of not listening.

Energy: Profane, harmful teaching force, the profane plan.

Mundane: Unprotected, vulnerability, danger, negligence.

Divinations: Connection with evil, unconscious, lower life, unprotected; or exposed danger, rejection by divine forces, loss of the divine link, fear.

Governs: Strengthening of bad fortune through fearful deeds.
Unprotected/surrender.
Invoking the fear of death.

So now you see the true meaning of the powerful symbol we have been told is about peace, but in fact is really making us live in a constant state of fear.

The Crucified Serpent of Knowledge

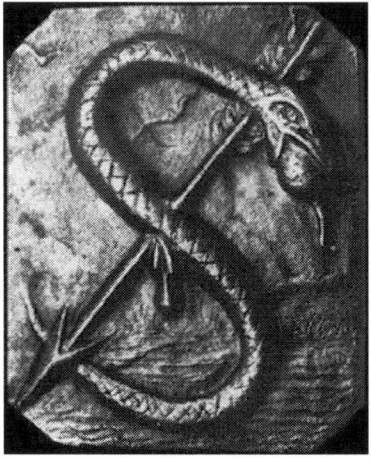

Most people don't realise how much 'money' goes against the natural way Serpent people like to live, by bartering and trading of services. The American Dollar sign is a magick sigil which in truth represents the Serpent people and their knowledge (represented by the apple in the snakes mouth) being crucified on an arrow.

The more you 'buy' into the material world and use this magick sigil, the more power the sigil gets. However, the more people who are aware of its true meaning, the spell will be broken and no longer effective.

There are many other magick sigils all around you, used to stop you being able to connect to your Higher Self and your true source of power, this is just one of them. In previous articles and posts I also talked about the 'peace' logo and the Anarchy logo, which also work at creating fear and keeping people programmed and unaware.

The Alchemical Salamander

The knowledge of Alchemy has been passed down in the underground stream for thousands of years. People tend to associate it purely with the medieval era, not realising that our families have been practising it since ancient times.

The clue to the Children of the Serpent families or those with Dragon Blood, has always been the serpent, dragon or salamander. It is displayed on family coats of arms of those from this bloodline. Before you start thinking 'David Icke was right, they are shape-shifting reptiles!' I will explain.

The Salamander represents the Higher Self overcoming the lower animal nature; the awakening, evolution, progress, enlightenment, and salvation - this is the Philosopher's Stone.

It awakens your true potential, and you find the real you, the true you. The truth flows to you easily, you feel calm and at peace when you have the stone.

In alchemy, the salamander is a symbol of the sulphur (of the three principles, of sulphur, salt and mercury). A salamander lives in flames, as does the Philosophers Stone. As you must enter and be baptised by fire, and over come the fire, to gain the stone.

The salamander is mentioned in the Talmud (Hagiga 27a) as a creature that is a product of fire, and anyone who is smeared with its blood will be immune to harm from fire.

Leonardo da Vinci (1452–1519) wrote the following on the salamander: "This has no digestive organs, and gets no food but from the fire, in which it constantly renews its scaly skin. The salamander, which renews its scaly skin in the fire,—for virtue."

Early commentators in Europe often grouped "crawling things" (reptiles or reptilia in Latin) together, and thus creatures in this group, which typically included salamanders (Latin salamandrae), dragons (Latin dracones or serpentes), and basilisks (Latin basilisci), were often associated together.

Alchemist Michael Maier said that the salamander is the elemental of fire, who not only eats fire, but elects to live in the flames. One should look for the Stone in the fires of sulphur, which are, the fires of the unredeemed passions. Before the Sacred Stone may be discovered, the fires must be put under control.

Salamanders are also parthenogenetic, along with other various other animals. This is yet another reason for them being associated with the Bloodline families.

The salamander in flames is on my own families clan badge.

Satan & Lucifer

Who or what is Satan?

Satan is the Dog Star Sirius which was named Isis in Egypt. She is a Goddess and the representation of the polar opposite to our Sun, which is male energy. It is in binary orbit with our Sun, as our Sun is 1, Sirius is 0. Because it is in binary orbit with our Sun it is called the 'Black Sun'.

Because it is a female energy, which is opposite to the male Sun, which provides light, it was demonised by the Christians as something dark and evil. The Sun is God, and the black Sun is the Dog star, dog is reverse of God.

Dogs were sacred in honour of Isis in Egypt as her annual return to the skies at dawn on the 21st June Solstice corresponds with the flooding of the Nile, which brought much needed water for growing food. So she was seen as a Fertile Mother Goddess who brought life.

Who are what is Lucifer?

This is the Morning, or Evening Star, Venus the planet, again a feminine energy that is a sister planet to our own. Venus traces a pentacle across the sky every eight years.

The pentagram - or pentacle is considered both divine and magical by many cultures because if you draw a pentagram, the lines automatically divide themselves into segments according to the Divine Proportion. The ratios of the line segments in a pentacle all equal PHI making this symbol the ultimate expression of the Divine Proportion. For this reason the five-pointed star has always been the symbol of beauty and perfection associated with the Goddess and the sacred feminine. The Sacred Geometry of nature, again is all about the Goddess, Mother nature, who created us all.

Again this was demonised because it is feminine energy. The pentagram became an evil symbol to be feared, when in reality it is truly beautiful.

Forbidden Fruit

The forbidden fruit in the garden of Eden was the knowledge of the Serpent Bloodline. Apples have always been associated with Gnosis, Sophia and the Goddess. Cut an apple in half and you will find that the core and pips have created a five pointed star, as does Venus in her transit - As above, so below here on Earth. On Earth as it is in Heaven above, where the Goddess Lucifer resides.

The Peacock Angel

"Tawsi Melek was the first to emerge from the Light of God in the form of a seven-rayed rainbow, which is a form he still today continues to manifest within to them (usually as a rainbow around the Sun). But the Yezidis also claim that Tawsi Melek and the six Great Angels are collectively the seven colors of the rainbow. Therefore, the six Great Angels were originally part of Tawsi Melek, the primal rainbow emanation, who bifurcated to become the rainbow's seven colors, which are collectively the Seven Great Angels. Of the seven colors produced from the primal rainbow, Tawsi Melek became associated with the color blue, because this is the color of the sky and the heavens, which is the source of all colors."

From http://www.yeziditruth.org/the_peacock_angel

The Peacock Angel is the Crown Chakra, which is Illumination. The 7 rays, are the seven chakras. The Yezidis say he is the supreme God. Kether is what this is. When you become enlightened, you see peacock feathers. Again the stories and myths built up around this 'GOD' cause division and corruption. When really we should be allowed to know that we all have this within us, just waiting to be ignited.

In Alchemy the peacock is a symbol which heralds the fact that transformation is occurring. The brilliant colours of the peacock's tail (Cauda Pavonis) mark the beginning of the process of integration, the formation of Philosophic Mercury. The varied colours that arise during the course of the work which resemble the colours of petroleum on a wet surface.

Witches Broom Origins

Astral oil was smeared on to the end of the broom, and placed in an area of the female body which would get to the blood stream quickly, and this happened to be the vagina.

The broom handle was placed up into the vagina and the 'witch' would then enter the astral realms and fly about. The mixture contained herbs that were known to allow the Shamanistic Witches to astral travel with ease. This is much like the monks and the shaven heads with oil smeared on and caps placed on top.

Origins of Magick with a K

Thelemites like to think Crowley invented everything. I was once told I have no right to use the spelling 'magick' because I am not a Thelemite and Crowley invented it, lol.

Magick is an Early Modern English spelling for magic, used in works such as the 1651 translation of Heinrich Cornelius Agrippa's De Occulta Philosophia, Three Books of Occult Philosophy, or Of Magick. The British occultist Aleister Crowley chose the spelling to differentiate the Occult from stage magic, as do the vast majority of other Occultists, Gnostics, Esotericists, Alchemists.

My own personal reason for using it, rather than magic, is also to differentiate between pulling rabbits out of hats, and the magick training which leads to illumination. Plus, the letter K is the eleventh letter of the English alphabet and the number 11 is very important to me and my own magickal workings. My birth number is 11 and I was born at 11:11. To me 11 is the magick number.

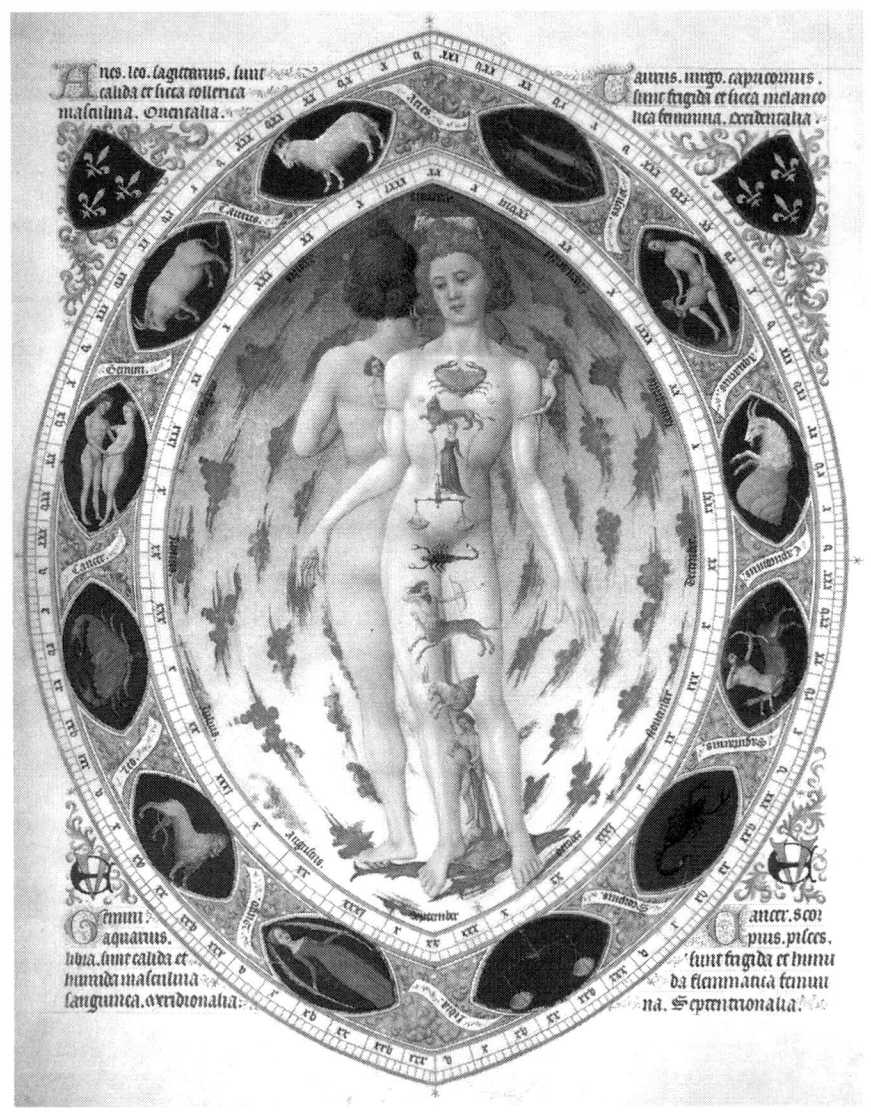

Secrets of the Serpent Bloodline - The Unveiling of Profound Esoteric Mysteries

Chapter 13

Astrotheology

All Religions are based on Astrotheology

Window from Christian Church which is symbolic of the cycles of time played out in the heavens. The Sun in the middle. Divided into 12 sections for each constellation.

The Great Year which last just under 25,000 year procession, moving anti-clockwise. At the moment we are in Pisces moving into Aquarius.

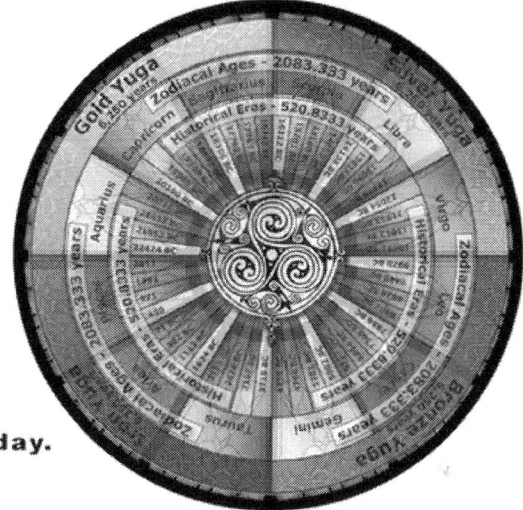

The whole Great Year is played out on smaller scale each year and an even smaller scale everyday.

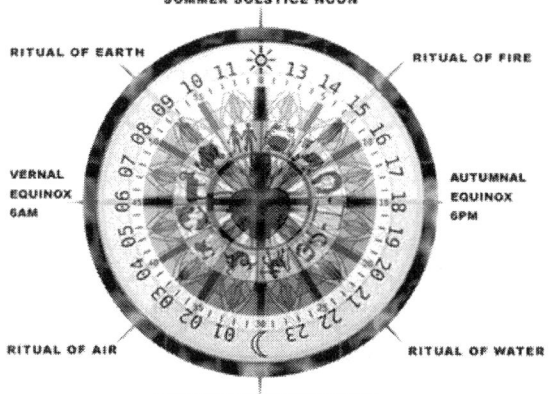

SUMMER IS WHEN THE SUN IS BRIGHT
SO THIS IS SEEN AS HEAVEN - LIGHT - GOOD - LIFE

WINTER IS WHEN THE SUN DIES AND THERE IS LITTLE
LIGHT, SO THIS IS SEEN AS HELL - DARK - EVIL - DEATH

THE JEWISH MENORAH IS LIT TO LIGHT UP HEAVEN
THE SEVEN SECTION REPRESENTS THE ARMS BETWEEN
EACH OF THE SIX SECTIONS, WITH SUMMER SOLSTICE
(PENTECOST) BEING EXTRA SPECIAL, SO THE MIDDLE
CANDLE IS OFTEN HIGHER.

PASSOVER IS WHEN WE MOVE
IN ARIES, WHEN THE RAM IS
SLAUGHTERED, THE OTHERS
ALL CORRESPOND TO THE
OTHER CHANGES OVER INTO
A NEW STAR SIGN BY THE SUN.

COPYRIGHT CHURCHSMSJ.ORG

Secrets of the Serpent Bloodline - The Unveiling of Profound Esoteric Mysteries

Astrological Ages

The Ages and just a few of the religions created for each:

Aquarius 23,546-21,386 B.C.
Capricorn 21,386-19,226
Sagittarius 19,226-17,066
Scorpio 17,066-14,906
Libra 14,906-12,746
Virgo 12,746-10,586
Leo 10,586-8,426
Cancer 8,426-6,266
Gemini 6,266-4,106 - Sumer Twins (Enki & Enlil)
Taurus 4,106-1,946 B.C.- Holy bull, calf, cow worship - Minoan, Hindu, Egypt
Aries B.C. 1,946- 215 A.D. - Jewish Ram (Shofar)
Pisces A.D. 215- 2,375 - Christian Fish (Fisher King)
Aquarius 2,375- 4,535 - Spiritual Enlightenment

The Aeons

What is an Aeon?

Time moves in cycles, the Earth moves through phases, the cycles repeat over vast amounts of times. An Aeon is a age, an era. History of humanity is divided into a series of Aeons. As humans evolved and developed a sense of consciousness there traditions and cultures change over time. When a new phase comes about, we call this a new Aeon, a new level of consciousness, a new level of awareness.. until completion and then the cycle starts back at the beginning again.

The First Aeon

The first Aeon started when certain species of humanoid 'Neanderthals' had developed well enough to become religious. This was when they discovered herbs and natural cures for things, they found magick mushrooms and other substances that would expand their minds even further. The Neanderthals at first reproduced asexually with parthenogenesis, and they developed savant type qualities. Later males started to occur when a mutation happened on a chromosome. This naturally occurring evolution came about just at the right time, as the women were becoming more intelligent and started to set up larger tribes, the caves and huts they lived in were not fitting their requirements. Along came stronger men, who could build bigger dwellings, hunt for the food and protect the women from dangerous predators. The women were left to be the Priestesses, collecting herbs, mushrooms and creating elaborate ceremonies that the whole tribe would enjoy. The women where respected as tribe and spiritual leaders. Some women did still go hunting, and child care was something the whole tribe was involved with. Small close-knit communities sprung up everywhere. This was a peaceful abundant time. Goddess and nature worship where the spirituality of the day.

The Second Aeon

The second Aeon came about when some of the male Neanderthals decided to take the genes from some of the less evolved simian humanoids and mix them with their own, as they wanted to experiment with genetic engineering and they thought they were helping the simians become more like them. But when some of the Neanderthal men bred with some of the new ones, the Adams & Eves (Simples), a new race of humanoids were created 'Cro-Magnon' this caused a massive divide among the Neanderthal tribes, between those who agreed with this, mainly the males, and those who thought it was wrong to mess with nature. The Cro-Magnon men decided they no longer wanted to put up with the women being the tribe leaders, they took the Simples and trained them to do the farming for them, and build cities. Some of the Neanderthal men got upset about this, and tried to wipe out most of the Cro-Magnons, but many survived. The Neanderthals were seen as Gods by the Simples, spiritual leaders, as they taught them so much. But the Cro-Magnons grew tired of the more intelligent pure bloods being their leaders, they stole the teachings, rebelled and hid the truth. They set up new religions and patriarchy was born. This Aeon was about God worship, and glorifying death, war, aggression and making people wait till death to find salvation.

The Third Aeon

This is the Aeon we are currently entering into, we are at the moment witnessing the birth pangs of this Aeon of androgyny. Where both males and females can start to work together to balance things on Earth. The return of the Divine Feminine means at last males are starting to see that women are equals, and should not be suppressed, for though males and females are different, we are complimentary. When working together we can find harmony. This is also about women finally finding out about their own feminine virtues that have been masked so long by patriarchy. Patriarchy has turned a lot of women towards male like qualities, just so they can get by in a patriarchal society. But women are now starting to realise the power of the Divine Feminine, in her own right. They are starting to reject wars and aggressive behaviour, in favour of nurturing and caring about others, and the chain reaction is carrying through to males also. Both males and females are becoming balanced. This is an amazing time to be alive and to experience.

Because although it might seem for a while as if things are getting worse, the more who awaken the Divine Feminine within themselves again, the more the world will begin to heal.

Is this new Aeon - The Thelemic Aeon of Horus?

The Thelemic view of the Aeons is similar to above, but not completely. Back in 1904 when Aleister Crowley first wrote his 'Book of Law' he was living a misogynist society, and he himself admitted he had little or no respect for women. The Esoteric Orders of the day refused females to be part of them, and even searched those entering the lodges to make sure they weren't female. This is because they didn't want women finding out the truth about a man needing a woman to gain enlightenment. When these men found out the truth, the first thing they did was try to find a woman for this task. However, because the women had been suppressed, none of them had the know-how or capability to enlighten themselves, nevermind anyone else. A few women were allowed to join these Orders, but they became honourary men and were called 'Brothers' they removed the feminine completely, and made out that a woman can only be respected if she became a man. So how were these women supposed to use their Divine powers to enlighten the men? Men would find just any woman and try to work the alchemical magick with them, but they always failed.

This new Aeon is about 'Veritas' truth. Because women are now learning their feminine Virtues and Divine powers once more. The word of the Aeon is THEOLA (Divine), THELEMA is outdated and no longer empowering to anyone who works within that current. THEOLA empowers both men and women to the truth. Women are learning how to use their Divine energy to heal and enlighten, and men will now start to find women who have the Divine magick within themselves, and they will be willing to share it with them.

Horus was a warrior King, Veritas is a Lady who wants to bring you the truth, that all can benefit from. So no, this Aeon is not the Aeon of Horus. Aleister Crowley's 'Woman Girt With Sword' turns females into males. Lady Veritas carries the chalice which overflows with feminine virtues that will heal the world.

In the Future

In time this Aeon will also end, and the cycle will start over again. The wheel keeps on turning and all the while our consciousness is learning lessons, that is what we are here for after all.

Time Cycles

Neanderthals/Spiritual Royalty/Anunnaki are the most ancient bloodline, we were here way before all the other humanoids. We had technology in the past which is far better than anything we have these days.

These were not aliens, they were our ancestors who survived underground through the ice age, survived floods, nuclear bombs and all kinds. If you look back into your genetic memory far enough, you will be able to remember all this, if you are of the bloodline.

Time has reset many times, and during the ice age we survive for many years underground, literally. We have always been troglodytes of some form or another, mounds, deep caves underground etc.

At times being underground was the only way we could survive when attacks from the Cro-Magnons came. They told their children stories about us, called us fairy folk, and as we have always had a Shamanistic culture we have of course always loved our magic mushrooms. These are the fairy food of myths, that people were warned not to eat if they visited fairyland, as one loses all track of time and is likely to never return home after eating them.

As for time, there is no line, time moves in cycles. Our origins lie in the area shown on the map (on next page), but we have been all over the world various times in the past, some of our genes left behind in tribes all over. The reason why most records don't survive, is because like today is very much becoming. As we advance technology in each age, we don't feel the need to keep written records, we use computers and other things that will simply disappear without a trace.

If you want to leave records a good idea is to write things down on engraved stone and place them in tins and bury them deeply into the ground. It will be a special surprise for our ancestors in the future.

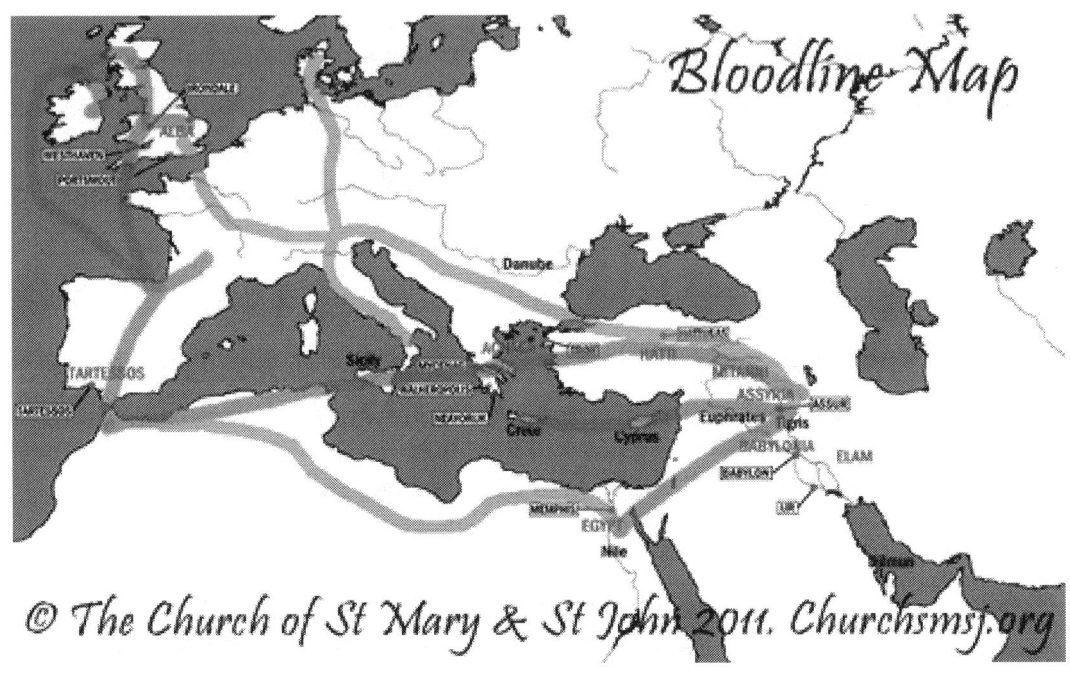

Secrets of the Serpent Bloodline - The Unveiling of Profound Esoteric Mysteries

Liber II

Secrets of the Serpent Bloodline - The Unveiling of Profound Esoteric Mysteries

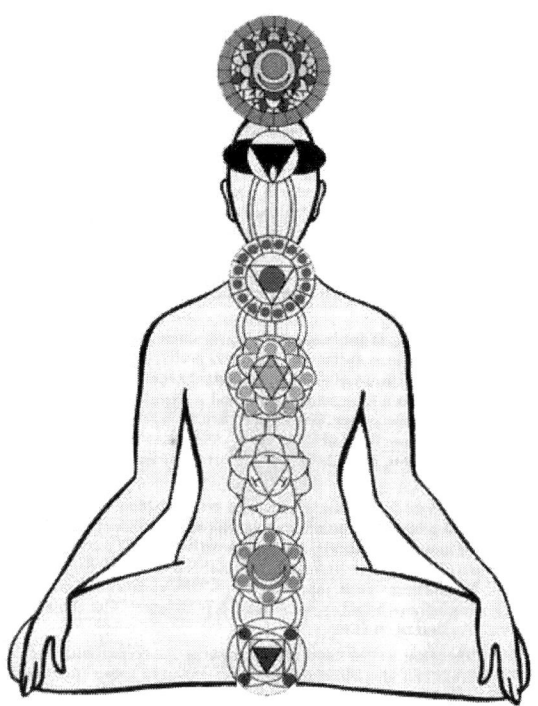

Secrets of the Serpent Bloodline - The Unveiling of Profound Esoteric Mysteries

Part 1: Magick Minds
Chapter 1

Chakras

Chakra is the sanskrit for "disc" or "revolution". This seeks to describe a centre in the body within which energies or forces turn, driven and fed by elemental powers which permeate everything. They are sometimes called "energy centres". This idea is recorded in some of the Hindu Upanishads, a loose collection of about 200 texts. Rather than being associated with types of material in the body, they are linked with locations in the body and the organs and structures in those regions, for instance the celiac, epigastric or solar plexus (a plexus is a complex of fine fibres or tubes).

What are Chakras used for?

They are used in meditation as focal points for attention, this being said to alter the flows of energies between the different sources from their unattended states. As in the humoric system, the imbalance of such flows either indicates or is the cause of malady. Thus the process of balancing them is considered both healing and diagnostic.

Many or most systems have them emerging at the front and back of the body. They are connected up the spine, generally but not always in a straight line up the backbone, perhaps with curved connecting lines in wave-like patterns: these patterns are likely another modern addition. Various connective topologies are suggested. Each chakra has petals or spokes radiating from it into the body. These are sometimes described as subdividing and connecting with minor chakra.

They have become associated with colours of the spectrum, with red the lowest up to violet at the top of the head. The number of chakras is highly various in different traditions, but the number of main chakras seems to be fairly consistent at seven, with the occasional exception such as Vajrayana (Buddhist Tantra), which divides the lowest and second highest in two and adds one between the throat and heart, giving ten in all. The seven are mapped to the seven perceived colours of the rainbow. The seven seeming bands are an artefact of the human visual/cognitive system and thus a cultural universal. Early texts had varying numbers of main chakras from five to twelve, but this converged to seven later on.

The Endocrine System

Each chakra is associated with one of the seven endocrine glands.

1st Chakra: Base or Root Chakra is located at the base of the spine. In males it is the testes and in women the ovaries.

Qualities: It grounds us in the physical world.
Colour: Red.
Crystal: Red Jasper.
Planet: Saturn & Earth.

2nd Chakra: Sacral Chakra is located just beneath the navel, and related to our sexual and reproductive capacity and pancreas.

Qualities: It governs emotional needs, joy and enthusiasm. A blockage manifests as emotional problems or sexual guilt.
Colour: Orange.
Crystal: Carnelian.
Planet: Moon.

3rd Chakra: Solar Plexus Chakra is located in the adrenal gland.

Qualities: Seat of Emotions. Gives us a sense of personal power in the world. Blockage manifests as anger or a sense of victimization.
Colour: Yellow.
Crystal: Citrine.
Planet: Mars & Sun.

4th Chakra: Heart Chakra is located in the thymus gland.

Qualities: Love, joy, inner peace. Blockage can manifest as immune system or heart problems, or a lack of compassion.
Colour: Green.
Crystal: Adventurine.
Planet: Venus.

5th Chakra: Throat Chakra is located in the thyroid gland.

Qualities: Tied to creativity and communication. Feels pressure when you are not communicating your emotions properly.
Colour: Blue.
Crystal: Blue Lace Agate.
Planet: Mercury & Neptune.

6th Chakra: Third Eye Chakra is located in the pituitary gland.

Qualities: Often connected to the forehead. Is a physical eye at the base of the brain with the capabilities of looking upward. Clairvoyance, psychic abilities, imagination, dreaming, Intuition, imagination, wisdom, ability to think and make decisions.
Colour: Indigo.
Crystal: Lapis Lazuli.
Planet: Jupiter.

7th Chakra: Crown Chakra is located in the pineal gland.

Qualities: Connects you with your Higher Self.
Can be experienced as a pressure on the top of the head.
Inner and outer beauty, our connection to spirituality, pure bliss, understanding, knowing.
Colour: Violet.
Crystal: Amethyst.
Planet: Uranus.

Clairvoyance – Exactly What Is It?

Clairvoyance has a long history of anecdotal evidence going back to pre history. It seems to have been used specifically by the Shamanistic or religious elements of society rather than being generally available to the populace for 'mundane' use.

This can be a difficult subject to grasp immediately because the term has so many different meanings. So, first of all, let's go through these definitions in order that we know what we are talking about.

Clairvoyance literally means 'clear vision' and is derived from 17th C French. It's most general definition is 'the means to gather information about an object, person, location or physical event through means other than the known human senses. It is a form of extra sensory perception (ESP).

Parapsychology has a definite and more specific meaning for Clairvoyance. That is 'the transfer of information that is both contemporary to and hidden from, the clairvoyant'. Do not mix this up with telepathy. Clairvoyance gains information from an external source while telepathy gains information directly from another mind.

Clairvoyance, in general use, has a varied meaning which depends on the speaker and the context in which it is used. It can refer to the perception of past events (retro-cognition), of future events (precognition) and of present but remote events.

Clairvoyance can also, depending on context, mean remote viewing. It is certainly a related subject but remember, remote viewing refers to a specific controlled process and may not be automatically termed Clairvoyance.

Clairvoyance can also refer to communication with the dead and as such can be termed medium-ship. This is something we strongly disagree with in our Church and Order, to speak to the dead is impossible.

In general, the term Clairvoyance has become a catch all for any sort of extra sensory perception and as such, is at the whim of fashion. In fact, present day preference is to use the term ESP or psychic, which, to modern ears, have more authoritative resonance and hence are taken more seriously. The term Clairvoyance itself is gradually being relegated to that of a catch all for odd ball and probably fake practices.

Clairvoyance, meaning medium-ship, can be generally regarded as a sub set of the larger Clairsensing. That is, Clairsensing consists of Clairvoyance (seeing), Clairaudience (hearing), Clairsentience (feeling/touching), Clairalience (smelling), Claircognizance (knowing), Clairgustance (tasting) plus a number of other 'abilities' that do not fit neatly into any category.

The Clairvoyant, in the Medium sense, often uses Trance in order to receive data external from the Clairvoyant. When Trance is used, the external data is assumed to come from other entities, incarnate or discarnate and can be independent from time.

Clairvoyance, again in the Mediumistic sense, also includes other abilities or effects that do not fit neatly into any of the above channels. This is due to the term Clairvoyance being used carelessly as a 'catch all' as explained above.

Some parapsychologists believe intuitively (because there's no evidence) that the various abilities involved (ESP, remote viewing, telepathy, precognition etc) are all aspects of one basic attribute. Unfortunately this is as far as it goes for the present, as no-one knows how to even start investigating this idea.

It is interesting to note that Clairvoyance was seriously investigated by both the USA and Soviets as a means of espionage or intelligence gathering. It seems obvious that any positive results would, even now, be secret. Governments with this knowledge now would also have a vested interest to play down and discourage any civilian attempt to gain knowledge and repeatability in Clairvoyance of whatever sort. But this applies only if the said governments use it regularly to gain accurate information.

Clairvoyance – The Scientific Evidence

The early research was to simply send a person, called a 'sender', to a remote randomly chosen spot, where he or she would 'send' the information about the location to a 'receiver'. The 'receiver', situated in a 'control' building with the scientists, would then write out, sketch or simply speak the information about the remote spot. Next, this information the receivers gleaned from, presumably, the senders, was then judged by separate judges and 'marked' according to the accuracy of the information. There were controls throughout the experiments, which were repeated a number of times. The term, 'remote viewing' was coined to cover this type of process.

The results were positive and accuracies significantly above chance were recorded repeatedly. A further refinement of this technique was to place the 'receiver' in a Faraday cage, which did not affect the accuracy of the results. As a Faraday cage eliminates most of the electromagnetic frequencies from the inside of the cage, these could be discounted from being the medium of information transfer. All except extremely low frequency propagation as Faraday cages are not efficient at filtering these out. It's interesting that Soviet research at that time came to similar conclusions.

In another set of experiments the sender was isolated in a visually opaque, electrically and acoustically shielded chamber, hooked up to an electroencephalograph and then stimulated by random strobe light flickers. This showed, for one particular sender that information transfer had occurred. However, this sender reported no difference between that experiment and the previous ones. This particular sender was asked to mark the time when information transfer had taken place, but his results did not match the strobe light flickers. All in all, the researchers were not able to identify how the information was transferred.

Once these results were reported, a spate of experiments ensued where other groups tried to duplicate these results. Some limited success was reported here.

At present there are various open experiments being conducted on the internet. Mostly they involve Zener cards, the results being collated and analysed statistically.

Zener cards (aka ESP cards) were specifically developed by J.B. Rhine in the 1930s. They consist of the symbols circle, square, wavy lines, cross, and star and there are five cards of each in a pack of 25.

Extra Sensory Perception

What is ESP?

Extrasensory perception is sometimes known as a sixth sense. It can sometimes be put down to a gut feeling or intuition. It is general term covering all related categories such as Telepathy or Clairvoyance. The term was coined by Sir Richard Burton, and adopted by Duke University psychologist J. B. Rhine to denote psychic abilities of all varieties.

Who was the first to conduct ESP tests?

Ina Jephson (in the 1920s) was one of the first to conduct statistical studies of ESP. Tests using guessing cards were carried out, and over a set of two studies she reported mixed results. Various other tests were carried out including mathematician Samuel Soal, who claimed some success, they produced highly significant results suggestive of precognitive telepathy.

How do you develop ESP?

For some people these extra senses are a reality in everyday life. Some are born with the gift, while others have to work to activate them. To have the gift can bring forth some upsetting abilities, as well as good ones. How would you feel if you really knew what people were thinking about you? Training should only be undertaken by those ready for the new reality they will face.

If you are interested in learning how to activate your latent skills, please contact us for information about training and courses.

Remote Viewing

What is Remote Viewing?

Remote Viewing is the practice of gathering information about a specified target -- an object, a place, a person -- usually at a specified location, and at substantial physical remove from the viewer, using means conventionally attributed either to ESP or to what is often more broadly referred to as clairvoyance.

Remote Viewing in the Cold War.

It originated as a by-product of the Cold War, and so has a history different in kind from either the more anecdotal and marginalized history of clairvoyance or from modern attempts to determine whether ESP qualifies as a legitimate part of scientific endeavour. Remote Viewing was from the beginning a program to be developed, with benchmarks to determine success. Scientific legitimacy per se was held in suspension in favour of concrete results-oriented methodologies. The distinction is subtle but important.

At the height of the Cold War, both the United States and the former Soviet Union existed in a state of reciprocal anxiety over what weapons programs or intelligence capacities the other might be developing that might allow one of them to gain a critical advantage over the other. Almost anything and everything became fair game, and when the Russians read a 1959 report in the French magazine Constellation -- "Thought Transmission — Weapon of War" -- regarding alleged telepathy experiments conducted by the U.S. Navy, they purportedly began their own program to keep pace.

Or did they? The French magazine article was apparently based on a misunderstanding of the nature of Navy experiments, and there is evidence to suggest that the Soviet program was an elaborate piece of disinformation theatre with which to distract the Americans. Whether real or staged, the publication in 1970 of Sheila Ostrander and Lynn Schroeder's Psychic Discoveries Behind the Iron Curtain became a catalyst for the US to investigate the paranormal in earnest.

Remote Viewing & MK Ultra.

Use and control of mental states had been an area of American study since at least the early 1950s by way of Project MK-ULTRA, with more than 150 individually funded research sub-projects involving sensory deprivation, isolation, and the use of synthesized chemicals to alter and manipulate brain function. Taken in this context, for the military and intelligence communities to extend research into the paranormal did not seem that much of a jump. The possibility of a psi gap, much like the spectre of a missile gap, was not a possibility that could be allowed.

Indeed, in 1961 the Office of Technical Services within the CIA had contacted the head of the Parapsychological Laboratory at Oxford University on the question of ESP. The report the Agency received said that although ESP appeared to exist, it could neither be understood nor controlled.

Remote Viewing Research.

Roughly ten years later, however, in 1972, Harold Puthoff and Russell Targ, two American physicists, tested self-described "consciousness researcher" Ingo Swann for psychokinesis at SRI -- the Stanford Research Institute. Results of the tests were written up in draft form and circulated hand to hand through research and academic institutions until they caught the attention of the CIA's Directorate of Science and Technology, and an initial $50,000 contract for further development followed.

Swann collaborated with Puthoff and Targ on the concept and procedures of what became known as Coordinate Remote Viewing (CRV), a process in which viewers would view a location given nothing but its geographic coordinates. Accuracy could thus easily be tested, since one could always observe the location or object being remotely viewed and compare it with the subject's results.

Emphasis was on methodologies that were capable not only of reproducible results but that could also be devolved into a rigorous training program. The initial program proved to be short-lived, however, for in the late seventies, investigations begun in the US Senate by the Church Committee led to the public exposure of a wide range of covert CIA programs involving foreign assassinations, domestic intelligence gathering, and the aforementioned MK-ULTRA behaviour modification program. Given the high-profile exposure of that program's illicit testing of LSD on unwitting civilians, maintaining a CIA-funded program dealing with the paranormal had small chance of a favourable public reception, and the contract with SRI was terminated.

Nonetheless, sufficient interest had accumulated at varying levels of the intelligence and defense organizations for research to continue. In 1973, for example, DARPA (the Defense Advanced Research Projects Agency) had dealt itself into the game with its request for further comparative study of US and Soviet paranormal research programs, with emphasis on areas where substantial disparities existed. Areas deemed suitable for military application included telepathy and psychokinesis and what was characterized as "long and short-distance information transfer".

Funding for the Remote Viewing program accordingly proceeded through other channels. One direct continuation came from the Air Force, where Dale Graff, then a physicist with the Air Force's Foreign Technology Division, gave a new contract to the SRI research team. Graff wanted to replicate some Soviet psi experiments done in submarines, as well as test the Soviet hypothesis that psi was transmitted via ELF (extremely low frequency) electromagnetic waves.

In 1979, the Army's Intelligence and Security Command (INSCOM), which had been providing some taskings to the SRI investigators, was ordered to develop its own program by the Army's chief intelligence officer, General Ed Thompson. That same year, the program achieved its first major success when Remote Viewer Rosemary Smith found a downed Soviet bomber in Africa after other intelligence operatives had failed -- a coup publicly cited and praised by then-President Jimmy Carter.

It is at this point that perhaps the most prominent name in Remote Viewing makes his appearance. Even with the successful instance of the Soviet bomber, test results remained mixed, and a continuing debate involved the respective merit of teachable technique as against the natural gifts of some of the subjects. Chief among these was Joseph McMoneagle, who joined the program in 1978 and was known as "Remote Viewer No. 1" in the US Army's psychic intelligence unit at Fort Meade, Maryland, and to whom a disproportionate share of the positive results could be attributed.

Over time, testing, which had originally been with verifiable targets within the US, was expanded by the CIA to various Soviet targets -- embassies, research facilities -- of which the Agency had detailed knowledge. Expanding further to unknown Soviet targets, Remote Viewing began to take credit for some important real-world successes, including the existence of the new Soviet "Typhoon"-class submarine in 1979. The Typhoon success also seemed to include predictive elements, for Joseph McMoneagle either guessed or predicted accurately the submarine's January 1980 launching.

The predictive element appeared again when Paul H. Smith, who joined the program in 1983 and was another viewer with a high success rate, became convinced that his August 1987 remote viewing of an attack on an American warship, including location, method, and motive, was precognition of the attack on the USS Stark three days later.

In the early 1990s the Military Intelligence Board appointed Army Colonel William Johnson to manage the Remote Viewing unit and evaluate its objective usefulness. According to Paul Smith, Johnson spent several months running the unit against military and Drug Enforcement Agency targets, and ended up a believer, not only in Remote Viewing's validity as a phenomenon but in its usefulness as an intelligence tool.

Joseph McMoneagle has emphasized that all readings by Remote Viewers were intended merely to augment, not supplant, intelligence gained by more conventional means, and at its height the NSA (National Security Agency), the Joint Chiefs of Staff, the DEA, Secret Service, Customs Bureau, Coast Guard, and the CIA all requested readings from the program's Remote Viewers.

The program itself had by this time changed name several times -- Scanate, Gondola Wish, Grill Flame, Center Lane, Dragoon Absorb, Sun Streak. In about 1991, the DIA (Defense Intelligence Agency) renamed the program Stargate, by which it is most consistently identified today.

Several derivations from the original SRI concept and procedures had also been developed by this time, and the original CRV (Coordinate Remote Viewing) method became one of a number of protocols utilized under the Stargate umbrella, with participants claiming as many as fourteen labs do research on the subject.

Remote Viewing arriving in the public domain.

At the same time, Remote Viewing had begun to make serious inroads into the public domain, in effect become privatised and commercialized, beginning in 1989 with the creation of Psi Tech, a private corporation developed by some of the Remote Viewing practitioners and program directors. The beginning of a series of books by many of the key early participants were now also beginning to be published, including volumes by Targ and Puthoff, and Joseph McMoneagle.

In 1995, an act of Congress transferred responsibility for the Star Gate program from the DIA back to the CIA, and perhaps in response to the seepage of the project into the civilian world, the Agency terminated the program and released a controversial research report purporting to show that Remote Viewing was not useful as an intelligence collection tool.

Or was that another instance of disinformation? Had two decades worth of psi research finally been discredited, or does classified research continue under other names and remain a decade or more in advance of what the general public is aware -- for Remote Viewing can be seen as following a typical trajectory for most classified technology, in which there is a ten to fifteen year lag time from inception to development and application and thence to final manifestation in the public marketplace, where it appears to the uninitiated as exemplum of "state-of-the-art" technology. In the case of Remote Viewing, the "technology" in question is in fact the potentialities of the human mind itself.

In 2003, some eight years after declassification, the US government released 90,000 pages of Stargate material, constituting nearly 15,500 documents. 20,000 pages are still withheld, and the material that has been released is often heavily redacted. Nonetheless, even in their present form, they convey a scope and reach to the project far beyond its initial $50,000 SRI funding.

Documentation includes sessions on the Iranian hostage problem, remote viewings done after the raid on Col. Qaddafy's Libyan palace, sessions seeking to locate POWs in Southeast Asia, and a project trying to unlock the secrets of a Soviet rocket explosion over Scandinavia, among others. Remote Viewing research also extended itself beyond this planet, and there are transcripts of several sessions with Mars as the target.

Nor did Remote Viewing research confine itself to present-time viewing. The predictive element noted above was pursued, and there were a number of projects aimed at evaluating how well viewers could recount what would be on the front page of The Washington Post newspaper or on the cover of Newsweek magazine a week hence. There was even one long-term project that involved several viewers tasked retro-cognitively -- against a target in the past -- to see how remote-viewing the past compared in quality to attempts at remote-viewing the present and future.

Documents also show, as in the sixties and seventies, a continuing interest in broader and interlinked applications for the paranormal, with further explorations of intuition, psychokinesis, hypnosis, and of how to screen a population for Remote Viewing talent. What the other side is doing -- or sides, for China had by then become an issue -- remained a constant, and there are hundreds of "foreign assessment" documents on developments in parapsychology and consciousness studies.

Among these "foreign assessment" documents, for example, is a 370-page compilation of research on Qigong, the Chinese practice of aligning breath, physical activity and awareness for the development of human potential --- which finds an echo in at least one of the major privately-funded Remote Viewing organizations, where formal training in meditation techniques is a necessary precursor to RV training proper.

Privatisation continues apace, and although Remote Viewing remains publicly controversial -- as do all aspects of the paranormal -- its methodologies have begun to find industrial and corporate applications. Perhaps that subtle operational distinction between science and functionality was key: placing the question, "Can it work?" ahead of the question, "Is it science?".

Can anyone be trained to Remote View?

Whether the average person can be trained, or whether Remote Viewing is a talent with which only a few are born, the gradual development of methods of reproducible results nonetheless indicates the talent as something real and within the scope and definition of the human, as a latency or potential capable of progression. As humanity increasingly views its nature as something malleable and amenable to intervention and development, the study of Remote Viewing becomes the study of conscious and willed evolution.

Our Church and Order teaches remote viewing.

Psychometry

What is Psychometry?

Psychometry is a form of psychic divination using the sense of touch to read the energy or history held in an object. Psychometric imprints may come in the form of emotions, sounds, scents, tastes or images. The type visions that appear depend on the Psychic, some see clear images, words might come to mind, sometimes a strong scent appears, or the Psychic gets a taste in the mouth or starts to feel strong empathic emotions. As we exist in an electromagnetic energy reality, metal objects often work best.

What are the origins of Psychometry?

The term was first used in 1842 by Joseph R. Buchanan, an American physiologist, who claimed it could be used to measure the 'soul' of all things. Buchanan further said that the past is entombed in the present. Buchanan experimented with some students from Cincinnati medical school and found that when certain students where given an unmarked bottle of medicine they had the same reaction as if they had taken the medicine. He developed the theory that all things give off an emanation which contained a sort of record of the history of the object. He believed that objects recorded senses and emotions and these could be played back in the mind of the psychometric scryer.

Chapter 2

Dream Realm Analysis

When we enter dream or astral realms, we are entering deep into our subconscious, all kinds of things live there, both good and bad. We can connect to our genetic memories there, and we can gain knowledge from our ancestors. Just imagine all the things your ancestors have learnt, like a language, musical instrument etc. You can tap into this.

How do I get to the Realms?

Dreams are one way, Astral travel, Meditation, Ritual Magick, Enochian Magick, Scrying, there are lots of way to get there.

What can I get out of doing this?

These trips to the realms can also be used to heal ourselves and help us learn about how things from our subconscious mind that are effecting our everyday life. We might see something there, for example a certain flower, animal or colour. We can then find out what this means by looking for clues in tables of correspondence. It can give us insight into our spiritual paths, and teach us about things that without this we might never have known.

When we connect to our genetic memories, we are connecting to our female ancestors memories, as we all carry within us the living cells of 15 generations of the females in our line. We can connect to our other ancestors in our male line and even further back, but not as strongly as we can with the female ones. That takes a lot more training and discipline which is gained from doing the 'The Great Work'.

If you were a control system, how do you imagine the best way to prevent people making use of this wealth of genetic memory information?

Well the obvious answer would be to prevent women from having an education, and to keep them away from learning occult truths and about spirituality. Because that way they have limited knowledge to pass on to their children. Essentially breeding a race of slaves, who in their subconscious have been programmed to think they are nothing and no one, and only good for being no better than a servant to men.

So you might ask yourself, why do some secret societies stop women joining, yet they all secretly worship 'The Goddess' and their female ancestors?

Well the answer becomes clear when you realise, the male DNA dies with the male, and they can pass no obvious genetic memories, only those that can be tapped into with special work - The Great Work, and anything they learn dies with them. So their offspring won't be a threat, but women, they can pass it on and if they do that, it takes the control away from those who are controlling us. People would no longer need to go to religions and secret societies for their spiritual guidance, they would learn about it within themselves, and the female would pass this knowledge to their children.

If you look through history you will see how women have been prevented from gaining an education, told their only purpose in life is stay at home and look after the house and children. When really they should be the ones in the churches and temples, helping heal humanity from the oppression it has been under for so long.

Through genetic memories humans can advance in all ways, spiritually emotionally and become well rounded and balanced.

We can all learn to do this, but those of certain genetics can learn much quicker, and that is because certain families allowed the women to secretly pass this knowledge down, again and again.

Scrying

What is Scrying?

Scrying is a system for obtaining information psychically that is by means not accepted by standard science. Mostly the items used are transparent or translucent or reflective. A mirror, a pool of water or other liquid, or a crystal seem to be the most obvious and accepted forms. And, in the popular mind at least, the crystal ball is the most common.

Scrying can also take the form of visiting different astral regions where the Scryer can do this by viewing it through a reflective object, as above, or they can close their eyes and images will appear, or they astrally travel to visit the realms.

Scrying is not limited to one, or a small number, of cultures. It seems to be common across the board as a means for seeing other places and other times, including the future.

How To Scry

Most Scryers use the medium (mirror, crystal or water) as an aid to concentration and utilise the imperfections in the medium to 'suggest' images into their minds. In other words, the medium does not actually do any work, it simply acts as a catalyst for the mind which does all the work.

By imperfections I mean those small irregularities in a crystal or a mirror or the rippling of the water in a bowl in addition to the subtle lighting changes caused by the traditional candle especially in a darkened room.

As an example, one crystal ball technique is to relax the mind and stare into the crystal. After a while certain images will suggest themselves to the Scryer who immediately states the image out loud. Once one is said another will appear, which is again said out loud. Apparently, this technique is a form of trance deepening as the mind focusing on the crystal has her focus deepened by the immediate verbal affirmation that comes as soon as she sees the image.

This process continues until the Scryer is in a deep enough state of focus to properly commence. And, as an aside, this process, if done properly, can give a great and positive impression on anyone else present.

It is also possible to scry using incense smoke, fire, wax and tea leaves.

Historical Scrying Activities

Well, one historical Scryer seems to be known to a lot of people even now and his name was Nostradamus. His technique was to use a bowl of water as described above.

The art of Scrying seems to have been discovered in most, if not all, cultures across the ages. In 10th century Persia there was an epic work written which describes the 'Cup of Jamshid' or 'Jaam-e Jam'. This was used in pre-Islamic Persia in order to observe the seven layers of the universe. And as an added bonus, this cup also contained an elixir of immortality.

Typical folk lore methods are to look into a mirror, often at Halloween in a candle lit room, in order to see your own true love. But beware, because you also have the potential see a skull's head, which means you will die soon.

It's interesting to note that Scrying methods are often used in ceremonial magick. John Dee was a Magickian active in the time of Elizabeth I. John Dee, together with his colleague, Edward Kelly, used Scrying. More about him coming in the Enochian Magick section.

Scientific Analysis

As usual, the scientific establishment is generally against the veracity of this type of procedure. At the moment, the experiment giving the best results is the Ganzfield experiment. Here the scrying technique was modified from more traditional techniques in order to achieve proof of alternative information sources interfering with the results.

A 'receiver' sat in a chair with two half table tennis balls strapped over his eyes and a red light was shone onto the half balls. Also, the receiver had on a headset which played static. This receiver, now isolated from all sound and sight, sat like that for about a half hour.

Now a 'sender' looks at a randomly chosen target and attempts to send this target telepathically to the receiver. Whilst this is happening, the receiver talks about what he is feeling or seeing. After the experiment, the receiver is shown a number if pictures and has to pick out the one the sender was trying to send.

This technique, published in 1974, resulted in a reported significant positive result in favour of the technique working. But not all were convinced and to overcome criticisms of the technique various new techniques were instigated and results obtained.

So between 1974 and 1982 these improved techniques were implemented and tested, with the results being published in 1982. Charles Honorton presented a paper at a convention of the Parapsychological Association and basically concluded that some sort of psi was proved by these experiments. Ray Hyman, looking at the same evidence, disagreed and the discussions continued until 1986, when they both published a joint communiqué on the subject.

This joint communiqué stated that the positive results obtained were not due to chance or selective reporting but that further experiments were necessary before any firm conclusions could be reached.

Further improved experiments were then undertaken with, as an added precaution, two professional mentalists overseeing the experimental arrangements to prevent against fraud, which gave an overall success rate of 34%. Statistically, they should have achieved 25% and the difference is statistically significant.

These experiments have continued and the 2010 results achieved a 32% hit rate, again a significant statistical result.

Enochian Magick

Where does Enochian Magick come from?

John Dee was a great Magickian active in the time of Elizabeth I. In fact, he advised Elizabeth on many matters, including Spanish activities against England, which helped him survive in a time when, without great patronage, he would have been condemned as a Sorcerer.

John Dee, together with his colleague, Edward Kelley, over a long period of time, contacted, via Scrying, what they called 'angels' and managed to receive from these angels a system and language for the correct application of magick. As it is connected to the book of Enoch, the whole system and language are called Enochian.

What is Enochian Magick?

The language is in the form of a grid. The grid was received by Kelley in June 25th, 1584, one 12 x13 watchtower at a time and these watchtowers were joined by the Black Cross.

This is basically the account of these happenings from John Dee's notes and diaries and if we take them as is, rather than allowing for any magickal blinds or false trails for the masses, then Kelley was never able to duplicate this information he received while in trance and consequently Dee never got the opportunity to go over and correct the tablets where necessary.

However, if we note, with historical hindsight, that Dee often 'lies' (usually for an explicable reason) in the material surrounding the angelic conversations, then it becomes easier to correct the great table.

Also, the angels gave the names of the angelic governors and the 91 provinces of the world these governors were supposed to control. Taking the system at face value, it becomes apparent that the angelic governors are supposed to influence certain parts of this world and their governments.

About one month on from when Dee transcribed the angelic governors, Kelley, on the summer solstice, had a dream. He dreamed about four massive Watchtowers that controlled the Earth. These Watchtowers are represented as the four 12 x 13 grids which, when connected by a Black Cross, form the 'Great Table'.

So what is Enochian Magick actually about?

The Watchtowers represent the four elements - Air, Fire, Water and Earth. The Table of Union which is placed on the centre altar represents the 5th element - Spirit.

Enochian magick is some what over complex and to create your own tablets etc could take a long time and a lot of effort. All of which works at preparing the Magickian for what is ahead.

Like all systems of magick the main reason behind it is to tap into unused parts of our brain by focusing the mind. We only use a tiny percentage of our brains, calling on these angels and daemons is calling on parts of our brain we don't use. The bad parts that cause addictions and destructive personality traits are taken under control by the Magickian. Leaving the Magickian more prepared to call on the good parts of their brain, the angels, and get those parts of their brain working for them. Discovering their own inner genius. The Magickian on the road to enlightenment will 'Scry' all the Enochian Aethyrs. This involves long incantations of Enochian that focus the mind away from mundane matters and allow the Magickian to enter the magickial realms deep within their own minds. When in these realms they will be given clues about what to do next on their path to help them find where they should be going. The angels will show symbols, tarot cards, give numbers, show all kinds of wonderful imagery.

Using the information found out from the angels the Magickian then uses Gematria, Kabbalah and other tables of correspondence to find out exactly where they are on their map to enlightenment - tree of life.

All Magickians have their own Angels and Daemons. Enochian, Goetia and other systems are created by others for their own workings. They can be used by others, but a real Magickian will know the names of all their own angels and daemons and will keep their own records.

The Sigillum Dei Aemeth is a complex pantacle, which again is something every Magickian makes their own of when on their own magick path. Everyone's looks different, however if you are using the Enochian system you create them exactly as the Sigillum Dei Aemeth.

So to use the Enochian system is to use someone else's system. This is especially useful for those starting out and have no idea how to create their own system.

Although it is said that John Dee was the first to receive the Enochian language, it is actually very ancient and has been used in magick ceremony for thousands of years. Old languages like Enochian and Hebrew were formed differently to other languages, and when vibrated words are used during a ceremony they allow for deep meditative states to be acquired, which are needed for magick inner work.

Banishing Ritual

What is the Banishing Earth Ritual Of The Pentagram?

The Banishing Earth Ritual is normally the very first ritual an Aspirant learns. First you learn how to banish Earth. This helps clean your personal sphere of negative energies, empowers your aura and helps to tune out disturbances which could effect your magickial workings.

The Banishing Earth Ritual is carried out before meditation and other magickal practices. The Magickian must have a clear space of consciousness before actually performing. It is always necessary to have a purified mind and Will before attempting magical work, otherwise there is the possibility of failure. To be able to successfully concentrate on one thing alone, we must first clear our minds of all other thoughts and focus on that one thing.

It can be used to help relieve depression and other negative emotions also.

How is it done?

In the ritual session later I will be showing you how to do a banishing ritual, that once you have perfected you can add to, use different pentagrams to invoke or banish each element and create balance in your life.

The Banishing Ritual is a necessary preliminary to practically all higher forms of Western Magick. Done properly, it serves as a form of Yoga. See the rituals section for full details on how to do this yourself.

Ritual Magick

What is the 'Craft'?

For someone just starting out in magick, finding out what the 'Craft' actually is can lead them down all kinds of strange paths. They have seen the Hollywood films that show Witches all stood round a big spell book chanting things, and they have also heard horror stories about sacrifices and strange rituals.

Young people are most at risk of being led down the wrong path, and serious Mystery Schools and Orders wouldn't even consider taking someone in and teaching them things until they were at least 18, and for good reason. They don't want to be accused of doing bad things by someone who decides to leave them, for whatever reason, or becomes bitter because it was decided they wouldn't be right for the group. This is to protect the group.

The Craft isn't what most people think it is. The Craft is now and always has been - Science, Technology and the Arts, which becomes much easier for those with an 'Illuminated' mind, high magick creates geniuses. It might be fun to call yourself 'Pagan' or a 'Witch' that make wands and broomsticks and dance around fires. But that isn't what the Craft actually is. That might be part of the path, and the way for you to become in tune with nature, which is the starting out part of any spiritual path.

How do I find out more?

If you are walking about through these mazes on your own and call yourself a solitary practitioner, don't ever expect to fully understand everything, because the knowledge in real Mystery Schools and Orders is passed down through generations and holds the true knowledge. Before deciding to join a group it is important to ask to see the groups Charter and lineages. If the group doesn't have any of these things available, they hold no knowledge and have no idea what the Craft is themselves, so how could they ever teach you?

There are plenty of groups out there who pretend to be something they are not. Their only purpose is to gain a following, massage the leaders ego and make themselves feel important. They don't have your best interests at heart.

Always ask to see the Charter and lineages, otherwise you are dealing with fakes.

What is the purpose of Ritual Magick?

Ritual magick has a purpose, and that purpose is to focus your mind. Often the very first thing you are told to when joining an order is to make your own ceremonial Tau robe. But why should you make your own when you can just buy one?

Well there are many reasons.

1. It shows the teacher you are serious about wanting to learn and have dedication.

2. It means you are starting on your path at becoming a doer, rather than someone who just sits back and relies on others.

3. Your intent is going into making the robe, so when wearing it during rituals you will feel even more dedicated to the path ahead. You have put real effort in, so this keeps you pushing forwards.

4. If you have never made anything before you will get an amazing sense of achievement, and it will stop you thinking small, and start you thinking big.

It isn't just a case of your teacher telling you to do it to be awkward, everything is for a reason.

You will also be told to make other tools for ritual use too, again if you make them yourself this is much better than just buying one.

Ritual magick is hard work, no one ever says it is going to be easy. You have to meditate everyday, do breathing exercises everyday, yoga, learn long and complex rituals. Study a lot. Learn about different correspondences.

The beginning of any magick path starts by tuning you with the elements. Once you have successfully done this, you then work on awaking your true Will - Kundalini - Holy Spirit - Holy Guardian Angel - Higher Self.

Where as low magick focuses on doing "spells", high magick actually awakens parts of your brain and psyche that most people spend their whole life never even knowing about or tapping into. Low magick does not get very successful or powerful results without first connecting to your Higher Self.

There are various systems for this, and once a Magickian has connected with their Higher Self, some will go on to create their own system. Once the inner genius is awakened the Magickian learns at a rapid pace and makes the most of his or her life. They have become a creator, a King or Queen of the Earth, and reached Kether on the tree of life. They have escaped slavery, a place where some, who are unwilling to or too scared to, will never leave. It might seem easier to just go with the flow through life, never realising your true potential, and that is what separates the Kings and Queens from the slaves, and the slaves shall serve.

This might sound Elitist, and most probably is. However it is a choice you make in your life and you can't blame anyone else for your own failings and laziness. Do you have the potential to be great? That is for you to decide, no one else.

Meditation to try out.

I will end on something for your inner genius to meditate on - If you can only think in words, words created by others, how do you know that what you are thinking with those words, is the real YOU?

Incense

What are the origins of Incense?

Incense making has been with us since ancient times. Our sense of smell is, frankly, extremely weak compared to most of the animals we share this Earth with, but even so, smell can and does affect us, sometimes profoundly.

We don't know exactly when this practice started but history records the first uses of incense making from just about every culture from as far back as we can ascertain. And it's no wonder is it? Think about our Neolithic ancestors in their everyday lives. They would have been surrounded by the natural smells as a normal part of their lives. And some smells would be good and some bad.

How was incense making developed?

It's an easy leap of the imagination to consider our ancestors deliberately collecting some of the natural matter all about them and deliberately trying to reproduce their smell. And, when wood or other matter was burned on the fire, either deliberately or by accident, the smell given off would be an additional stimulus to deliberately manufacture it.

So it's easy to imagine the gradual development of specific 'smell' recipes over time and these being passed from generation to generation. Eventually certain incense became more valuable than gold or silver which led to the development of the Incense Trail and the Frankincense Trail, from the Arabian peninsular to China.

What are the effects of incense?

Scents act on our brains on a subconscious level. Our subconscious decides whether we like or dislike the smell, depending on its history and associations, and passes this information on to our conscious minds. In fact, the scents are first detected and analysed in the limbic part of our brains, which is the oldest and most primitive part. We probably don't realize it but our reactions to scents go deep, really deep, and can affect us on a profound level. The limbic system is considered to be the basis of our memory and can affect our moods to a powerful level.

How is incense used?

Nowadays incense is used for multitudinous reasons including, religion, meditation, aromatherapy, shamanism, pleasure, purification ceremonies, magickal rituals, creating a mood, insect repellent and let's not forget the masking bad smells use as well (such as it's use in funeral homes of various cultures).

Generally, there are two types of incense, direct burning and indirect burning. Indirect burning incense requires a separate heat source (typically an incense burner) which heats the powder thus producing the smell. Direct burning incense are, as the name suggests, directly burned. The incense, in a solid form, is lit which gives off the smell.

It's a strange fact that some incense ingredients only give off their smell when heated. I sometimes wonder how these ingredients were discovered.

What are the incense ingredients?

The ingredients used throughout history have varied widely. Typically, local ingredients were used which limited the smells available and the method of manufacture. Once trade routes were set up, and remember the earliest trade routes are from our pre-historic past, information flowed from one community to another. With this information came trade and the incense effects and manufacturing techniques were passed from community to community.

Thus a worldwide incense trading network was set up very quickly with ingredients being manufactured and shipped to all corners of the world as known by the peoples of that time. This resulted in the modification of the local preferences and in the implementation of new methods as the artisans were introduced to new and novel ingredients and methods.

How is Incense used in Magick Ritual?

Incense has always been used in all manner of religious ceremonies. It is seen as an offering to an entity or archetype Godform often, or generally just used to set the mood of the ritual. Using tables of correspondence we can choose which herbs and resins are right for the emotion we want to evoke, or entity we want to invoke to bring it's essence to whichever particular working we are doing.

How does Incense effect our health?

No-one denies that the contaminants contained in incense smoke are carcinogenic as they contain gaseous pollutants as well as particulate pollutants. There have not been many studies on this potential problem, but from the ones that have been undertaken, it appears that this is not a major risk factor. The risk will be increased with exposure and this appears to result in a small risk.

On the other hand however, it is reported that the use of incense does improve moods in people. This is from users statements and as such is not scientifically validated. Frankincense has been scientifically proved to alleviate anxiety and depression in mice.

Incense – Making It Yourself

Making incense yourself is a fine way to express yourself as well as creating certainty in your rituals. Some rituals use incense to create energy which can be used by the practitioner, but modern artificial ingredients do not have this energy to begin with. So, as a general rule, make sure you use all natural ingredients.

There are basically two types of incense, and you must decide which type to make. These are:

* - Combustible - where you combine your mixture into a stick or cone, which burns slowly.

* - Non-Combustible - where the pellets or loose mixture is placed in an appropriate vessel and heated.

How to Start Incense Making

You will be mixing your ingredients into a mixture suitable for heating or burning – see the end of this article for basic lists of suitable materials. The exact ingredients depend on whether you are working to an existing recipe or whether you are creating your own. The key to successfully creating your own is methodology, patience and a notebook. Essentially you will try out various combinations and check out the results. Start simply with three ingredients only, preferably ones that resonate with you and ensure one of them is a wood. Take your time and record your results. This can be an exceedingly rewarding activity you can pursue for the rest of your life.
But let us assume you are working to an existing recipe. Use a pestle and mortar to grind up your herbs, resins and woods. Grinding resins can be a problem as they can be pulverized down to a sticky mess. Freezing them for about a quarter of an hour beforehand will be very helpful here.

Traditionally a pestle and mortar is used to grind down the ingredients but you can also use a hand cranked coffee grinder as well.

This is especially advantageous when grinding down woods, as they can be difficult. Do not use an electric coffee grinder as this will heat up and spoil the ingredients.

Now take your powdered ingredients and sieve them.

You can, if you wish, just ignore the above and buy the pre-powdered ingredients ready made, just make sure they are all natural.

Once you have your ground ingredients, thoroughly blend them by mixing them together and grinding the total mixture again.

Now is the time to testing time. It is easy - just lay a trail on something flameproof and light it. Check the smell and how it burns. You want the smell right and the burn to be slow and even. Adjust your mixture accordingly at this stage to get it just right. And remember to record what you do.

The next bit is really easy. You need to age your mixture by storing it for at least two weeks. This will ensure all the ingredients thoroughly combine into one single bouquet.

How to Make Incense Pellets

Now you have the wherewithal to make incense pellets. You need to 'bind' the loose mixture you have made into pellets and there are many ways to do this. You can use Labdanum (Japanese) or simple dried fruits or honey. It is useful to add honey to the dried fruits anyway as this adds a warm fragrance to the mixture in addition to helping preserve the fruit.

As most people have access to dried fruit, we will detail this method here.

You will need about half to three quarters the volume of your mixture as dried fruit. Obviously everything depends on the mixture and the fruits so use this as a guide rather than an exact recipe. Remember to record everything so you will be able to remake a batch without any problems later on.

Soak your measure of dried fruit overnight in water or something more exotic, red wine perhaps. Once soaked, add it to your mixture and blend. You can use a food processor for this. If you do not want to use a food processor, you can use a pestle and mortar by blending a small amount of fruit and mixture at a time. Once thoroughly blended you can then add more.

Once it is all blended, add the honey (about half a teaspoon of honey per half a cup of fruit) and knead well. Now make small balls with your hands and spread out on something suitable, a board, some wax proof paper etc. and put them somewhere safe to dry out for up to four weeks. Remember to turn them daily to ensure even drying.

If you are a patient person and look to the long term, you can store them in a darkened jar with a lid and leave for a year or so.

How to Make Cones and Sticks

Take your mixture as described above and grind it again. It needs to be ultra fine for using with cones and sticks. There are a lot of specific ways of making these but one common method is to use makko. This is water soluble and combustible. Simply add it to your mixture with a small amount of distilled water. The exact quantities depend on the humidity of where you are so you will have to experiment a little here.

Once thoroughly mixed, form the paste into whatever shape you wish. Always remember to record exactly what you do in your notebook. It might be a bother now but you will really appreciate the time you took to do this later on.

Use your hands to knead it when mixing and add the water very slowly. The end product needs to be moldable and able to hold a shape. If you want sticks, roll them out on wax paper to the size you require.

Making cones seems to be the most popular for home made incense, probably because they are so easy to make. Now you need to allow them to dry out naturally and the time required for this depends on your climate. But a couple of weeks is a reasonable benchmark. Remember to turn them daily to allow for even drying.

You need to test one of your sticks or cones as soon as it is dry. Check to see if it burns evenly, and how it smells. Increase the makko content if it does not burn evenly and, conversely, decrease the makko content if it burns too fast.

A Little Tip on Incense Making

If any of your new creations do not perform properly and if you used makko, you can grind them up and add the appropriate additional materials together with a little distilled water. Now you can begin again without wasting materials.

Another Little Tip on Incense Making

Once you do a little research on this, you will find you can buy specific wooden moulds, or blanks. I advise you not to use these as often the wood is preserved with an arsenic compound. Obviously not a good thing to use. If you are good with wood or metal, you can make your own molds.

Your Third Tip on Incense Making

Store all your ingredients in a coloured jar in a cool dark area.

Lists

If you are a beginner to incense making, you will probably be a little confused at this point because you will not know the ingredients. Don't worry about this. A little research and experimentation will soon allay your fears on this score. However, to get you started, here are a few lists for you to consider.

Woods and barks
Aloeswood
Cedar
Sandalwood
Cypress
Juniper
Cassia
Cinnamon

Seeds and fruits
Coriander
Cardamom
Juniper
Nutmeg
Star anise
Vanilla

Resins and gums
Amber
Bdellium
Benzoin
Camphor
Copal
Dragon's blood
Elemi

Frankincense
Galbanum
Guggul (Indian Myrrh)
Labdanum
Mastic (plant resin)
Myrrh
Opoponax
Sandarac
Storax
Tolu balsam

Leaves
Balsam
Bay
Patchouli
Sage
Tea

Roots and rhizomes
Calamus
Costus
Galangal
Orris
Spikenard
Vetiver

Flowers and buds
Clove
Lavender
Rose
Saffron

Animal-derived materials (personally I avoid these)
Ambergris
Civet
Operculum
Musk

Essential oils
Bayberry
Cedar
China Rain
Dragonsblood
Egyptian musk

Green grass
Hope chest
Hydrangea
Jasmine
Jasmine
Lavender
Lemongrass
Lily-of-the-valley
Nag champa
Patchouli
Pine
Rose
Rose
Rosemary
Sandalwood
Tibetan Amber
Vanilla sugar
Ylang-ylang

Chapter 3

Qabalah

Qabalah Different Spellings

There are various spellings of Qabalah and, for the purposes of clarity one spelling, Qabalah, is used throughout this article. In general you can assume that the various spellings beginning with a 'K' are Jewish, with a 'C' are Christian and with 'Q' are Hermetic. There are also many variations within these guidelines.

Jewish Qabalah

The Qabalah is an ancient set of Jewish teachings (the origins are uncertain but generally accepted to date from the 11th century or the 13th century) designed to illuminate the relationship between the Creator and this world including all its peoples. It is not part of the Jewish scriptures, rather a set of documents linked to them. The Qabalah is there to define the reason for existence and other ontological questions. In addition, it also gives various methods designed to aid the understanding of the subject. One aim of the Qabalah is to, by way of its study, achieve illumination.

It is generally considered to have been transmitted orally among the Patriarchs, Prophets, and Sages until it eventually became integral with Jewish religious writings and culture. At about the 10th century BC it was open knowledge and practised by the general population of Israel at that time. Obviously this date conflicts with the generally accepted dates given above. But remember, the above dates refer to when it was written down and formalised. And also remember this refers to the earliest known dates. There is nothing to prevent earlier records that have not been found yet or are lost.

Then, the Qabalah was hidden again and made secret, known only to the cognoscenti, because of repeated foreign conquests. It was not allowed to fall into the wrong hands. Also, because of the social upheavals of that time, it was feared that if it was taken to foreign lands and away from the spiritual leaders it might eventually lead the unsupervised (Jewish) practitioners into wrong practise and error.

As the Qabalah was developed by the Jews, it contains numerous references to Jewish thought and uses classical Jewish sources in order to explain and clarify its teachings. These teachings are held by traditional Qabalists to explain the inner meaning of the Tanakh (the Jewish Bible) in addition to explaining the meaning of the Traditional Jewish observances.

Qabalah Overview

A basic Jewish text is the Zohar, and according to that, the study of Torah (the 'teachings' of God) consists of four levels of interpretation, which are called Pardes (literally 'orchard'). These four Pardes are as follows

Peshat ('simple'): the direct interpretations of meaning.

Remez ('hint[s]'): the allegoric meanings (through allusion).

Derash (from Heb. darash: 'inquire' or 'seek'): midrashic (Rabbinic) meanings, often with imaginative comparisons with similar words or verses.

Sod ('secret' or 'mystery'): the inner, esoteric (metaphysical) meanings, expressed in Qabalah.

The Qabalah teaches doctrines that are accepted by some Jews but are rejected by others because they are considered to be heretical.

Over the centuries, the influence of the Qabalah on Jewish thought has waxed and waned. Now it has gained an additional following from non orthodox Jews due to modern study and cross denominational spiritual activities. Now the term 'Qabalah' has become the main descriptive of Jewish esoteric knowledge and practices.

Qabalah Concepts

Clarifying the concepts within the Qabalah is extremely difficult, if not impossible. There are several different schools of thought and each has very different interpretations and understandings. There have been efforts to 'narrow down' its scope by excluding certain teachings, but these excluded teachings still crop up as commentaries in the 'allowed' scope. It is safe to say that the Qabalah deals with very abstract concepts that can only be understood intuitively.

Basically, the Qabalah teaches that God has two 'aspects', God himself and the Revealed Aspect of God. No-one can even begin to know or understand God. But the Revealed Aspect of God is the one that created the universe together with everything in it and is at least, to some degree, accessible to human understanding. These two aspects are complimentary to each other and in some unknowable sense one and the same.

God interacts with the universe through divine emanations (the central metaphor of Ohr ("Light") is used to describe Divine emanations), the structure of which has been characterized in numerous ways:

Sefirot (Divine attributes)

Partzufim (Divine "faces")

Four Worlds of Creation in a Seder hishtalshelus (Descending Chain of realms) Azilut

Beriyah

Yitzirah

Asiyah; the Biblical vision by Ezekiel of the Merkabah (Divine angelic "Chariot").

These interpretations were integrated in subsequent Qabalistic systemisation.

God continually sustains the universe through ten emanations, called Sefirot (singular Sephirah). Sephirah means 'counting' but early Qabalists included a number of other interpretations including

sefer (book)

sippur (story)

sappir (sapphire, brilliance, luminary)

separ (boundary)

safra (scribe)

The term Sephirah has many complex meanings and relationships within Qabalah.

According to the Qabalah, the human soul has three elements:

Nefesh (Present at birth): This is the animal and bodily cravings and is the lowest aspect of the soul

Ruach (Present at birth): This contains the moral virtues and the ability to distinguish between good and evil and is classified as the middle aspect of the soul

Neshamah (Not present at birth but has to be 'developed'): This could be described as the 'super' soul. It allows man the ability to benefit from and enjoy the afterlife. It provides one to have an awareness of God, his existence and presence. Only mankind has this aspect of the soul.

The Jewish alphabet contains no separate characters for the numbers, instead individual letters are used. Over time, Qabalists have come to investigate this aspect, reasoning that there must be 'messages' from God found in the relationships between certain texts and their numerical interpretations. That is, individual texts can be, in the Jewish language, interpreted as numbers and vice versa. So a word can correspond to a number and a number can correspond to a word. Various schools of Qabalists and others have produced interpretations of this 'numerology'.

A serious and sustained criticism of the Qabalah is that, despite the fact it propounds the unity of God, it will lead people away from this basic concept towards dualism. Dualism believes there are two powers in the universe, good and evil and all its variants. Qabalistic cosmology believes the ten Sefirot must not be interpreted as ten different Gods, but rather ten aspects of the one God. So while duality may seem to be all around us, male-female, night-day, good-evil etc, the Qabalah stresses the ultimate unity of God. Remember it is impossible for humanity to 'know' God, just the revealed aspect. And it is the 'revealed aspect' that makes creation possible.

Having said that, some Qabalistic texts (e.g. the Zohar) appear to confirm dualism in their teachings. These texts ascribe all evil to the Sitra Achra (the other side) which, in effect, means the other side of God. They seem to believe that evil is a necessary part of God which is specifically there to give man free choice. These texts specifically do not say evil is a supernatural force opposed to God, but instead say evil is absolutely necessary in order to give mankind free will.

In short, there are numerous 'variations and interpretations' of the Qabalah existing now (far more than can be listed in an article like this) and these have been derived from previous ideas. Modern scholars are of the opinion that all the versions, present and past depend on the ideas and mysticism of the age they were developed. They are not 'new' insights as such, but insights derived from study which in turn are necessarily based on existing opinion.

Christian Qabalah

It appears that the Qabalah came to Christian study and application during the Renaissance, when a series of philosophical documents from Greece became available. These documents, mostly from the Greek Neoplatonic school, seemed to agree with some or all aspects of the Jewish Qabalah which Christian scholars and mystics of that time noted, which, in turn, sparked off an interest and a desire to investigate for themselves.

This Renaissance trend was relatively short lived and had ended by about 1750 but by then Qabalah had become interlinked with European occultism, some of which had a religious basis. However, despite this interest, the main thrust of Christian Qabalah died by the 18th century and does not now form a part of mainstream Christian thought. There have been a few attempts to revive it into mainstream Christian thought in recent decades but to no avail.

Hermetic Qabalah

While mainstream Christianity flirted with and eventually rejected the Qabalah, Western mysticism actively incorporated it into its worldview. So much so it is part of the underlying philosophy of the major occult groups in the Western world. Groups such as the Golden Dawn, various Thelemic orders, mystical societies such as the Builders of the Adytum and the Fellowship of the Rosy Cross. In addition the Qabalah is influential to various degrees in the Neopagan, Wiccan and New Age movements. Left Hand Path orders, such as the Typhonian Order also include the Hermetic Qabalah in their worldviews, specifically the Qliphothic Qabalah.

Hermetic Qabalah is, as said, not pure Jewish Qabalah, rather it is part of a fusion of many influences, such as, Jewish Qabalah, Western astrology, Alchemy, pagan religions, especially Egyptian and Greco-Roman (the term Hermetic is derived from the Greco-Roman influence), neoplatonism, gnosticism, John Dee's and Edward Kelley's Enochian system of angelic magic, hermeticism, rosicrucianism, Freemasonry, tantra and the symbolism of the tarot. As a consequence, Hermetic Qabalah is a totally syncretic system which shares many concepts with Jewish Qabalah.

One of the main ideas of Hermetic Qabalah is the 'Divine', which differs from the mainstream monotheistic religions. In general, the divide between God and man is not so clear cut in the Hermetic Qabalah, which generally teaches that material creation is part of a series of emanations from the godhead.

Before these emanations there are three 'states' that are required.

Ain 'Nothing' a state of complete nullity

Ain Suph 'Without Limit, Infinite'

Ain Suph Aur 'Limitless Light' caused by a 'movement of 'Ain Suph' and it is from this that the first emanation of creation comes.

There are ten emanations from Ain Suph Aur and these are called the Sephiroth (singular Sephirah). These Sephiroth are different to the Jewish equivalent.

Basically, the first Sephirah creates Kether, and the rest of the Sephiroth are created from Kether, as follows

1-Kether

2-Chokmah

3-Binah

Daath (not assigned a number as it is considered part of Binah or a hidden sephirah).

4-Chesed

5-Geburah

6-Tiphareth

7-Netzach

8-Hod

9-Yesod

10-Malkuth

The Divine Energy, or Divine Light, continuously flows from the godhead through Kether and hence to manifestation and the Divine Energy is often drawn as a lightning flash on the diagrams of the Seriphotic tree.

In Hermetic Qabalah, each emanation is seen as a nexus of divine energy with a number of 'attributions'. For example, the Sephirah Hod has the attributions of

Glory

Perfect intelligence

The eights of the tarot deck

The planet Mercury

The Egyptian god Thoth

The archangel Michael

The Roman god Mercury

The alchemical element Mercury.

The Qabalist is to meditate on all the attributions in order to derive an understanding of the character of the Sephirah.

The Tarot is also important to Hermetic Qabalah, as it is seen as a key to the Tree Of Life. The major acana (greater mysteries) consisting of twenty-one trumps and the fool are linked to the twenty-two letters of the Hebrew alphabet and to the twenty-two paths of the Tree of Life. The numbers in each suit (ace to ten) correspond to the ten Sephiroth in the four Qabalistic worlds and the sixteen court cards relate to the classical elements in the four worlds.

The Sephiroth describe God and the paths between, then describe ways of understanding God. And as a small aside, The most common arrangement, in Hermetic Qabalah, of the Sephiroth and paths on the Tree of Life is the 'Kircher Tree'. This was developed by Athanasius Kircher in 1652, which itself was based on an earlier version (1625) by Philippe d'Aquin.

The epitome of Hermetic Qabalah was, to all intents and purposes, the 19th century organisation 'The Golden Dawn'. While the Qabalistic principles such as the Sephiroth had been integrated with the Greek and Egyptian deities for centuries, The Golden Dawn focussed on this 'fusing' and added other systems such as the Enochian system of angelic magic of John Dee and certain Eastern (particularly Hindu and Buddhist) concepts.

English Qabalah

This does not refer to England the country but to English the language. The English Qabalah links the letters of the English language to specific numbers via various formulae. Unlike the Jewish letter/number identity, the English version is entirely dependant on the specific formula used to derive the relationships between the numbers and the letters.

As you might expect, there are various interpretations of this concept. According to Jake Stratton-Kent, the English Qabalah is not simply a simple numerological formula but is specifically a relationship between holy texts and the mathematical laws at work within them, specifically gematria.

It may be beneficial to note here that gematria is a system where letters are related to numbers where the numerical equivalent of a word is summed together in order to find a 'key' of that particular word.

The first known system of the English Qabalah was developed by Michael Stifel in 1532. He also proposed a system known as the trigonal alphabet utilizing triangular numbers. Various variations appeared in 1683 which are collectively known as the 1683 alphabet. It is interesting to note that Leo Tolstoy used the 1683 alphabet in War and Peace to identify Napoleon with the number of the beast.

In more recent times, new systems have been developed by various people

Michael Bertiaux (1989) – developed Angelic Gematria

David Rankine (2004) – developed Prime Qabalah, based on prime numbers

Samuel K Vincent – proposed a new system based on extending previous systems together with a concordance with Thelemic texts.

William Eisen – described a system related to the Spiritualist Agasha Temple of Wisdom

The English Qabalah was extended further by Aleister Crowley in 1907 in his book Liber Trigrammaton. It links the trigrams from the Book of the Mutations of the Tau with the twenty six letters of the English language.

Staying with Aleister Crowley, it should be noted that three years before Liber Trigrammaton, (that is in 1904), his Book of the Law (Liber AL vel legis) contained the text at verse 2:55, "Thou shalt obtain the order & value of the English Alphabet; thou shalt find new symbols to attribute them unto".

Obviously Crowley was trying to fulfil his own injunction in Liber Trigrammaton.

In 1974, Carol Smith discovered and published the ALW Cipher, which she called the English Qabalah (James Lees states he discovered it independently in 1976). This was later referred to as the New Aeon English Qabalah.

The Difference between the Traditional Jewish and the Hermetic Qabalah

It might be useful to summarise the difference between the two systems here. Remember, the Jewish Qabalah is the original by thousands of years, and that is based on watered down and corrupted versions of Ancient Serpent Bloodline Mystery School teachings. The Hermetic Qabalah took the original Jewish Qabalah and used it as an interpretative tool to apply to its own philosophy.

The Jewish Qabalah is used to try and understand God. God is by definition un-understandable but there is a way to partially understand God by the way God 'manufactures' the material world. The 'knowable' God comprises of ten 'essences' called the ten Sefirot. Understand the Sefirot and you will start to understand God.

The Hermetic Qabalah has a differing world view. The basic idea is that there is a universal thread of truth behind all the major religions and the main spiritual teachings. It attempts to strip away every superfluous section of each one and link the remainder together to form a 'unified' spiritual practise.

Here the ten Sephirot are what can be called the magickal or the astral world. As a consequence there are ten grades of magickal understanding (or initiation), the seven planets of the traditional astrology plus the numerology of the numbers one to ten. The ten Sephirot are drawn out in the 'Tree of Life', and from this diagram, it is seen that there are twenty-two paths which link the ten Sephirot. These twenty-two paths are linked with the twenty-two letters of the Hebrew alphabet and the twenty-two major arcana of the Tarot. So, each Sephirah and each path correspond to a specific set of meanings, thirty-two in total. By proper application it becomes possible to invoke any specified essence. In order to undertake this, numerous tables of correspondences have been drawn up and studied. These include precise colour, animal, perfume, stone, being etc.

Sigilisation

What is a sigil?

A magick sigil is a symbol, logo, seal or some kind of doodle, or it can be purely imagined. Working in a mystical current a magick sigil can be created in several ways. It is then 'charged' with energy. The way the energy is created is dependent upon the choice of the creator, there are various ways to create the energy used to charge the sigil.

Company logos and symbols can become very powerful over time and can self charge themselves. How often do you see a company logo and get a certain emotion from it? This is often attached to an advertising campaign that works by planting the logo into your sub-conscious mind. The advert creates a certain emotion, then overlays the company logo, so in the future that logo is associated with that emotion. The more of that emotion created by customers when they see that logo, the more energy is sent to that logo. Eventually it becomes more and more powerful. Is this the real reason why long established businesses are more trusted and accepted than new?

At times you might be thinking about a certain thing, and as you do you might be making a doodle on a piece of paper. These are sigil also after a fashion, however they remain uncharged unless energy is sent to them. Just the act of writing something down with intent can be enough to set the magick into action. This is why people who make lists often get more things done. Others might see these people as just being more organised and efficient, but the very fact they wrote the list, means they have made a future 'wish' or sigil about what needs to be done.

When you are more experienced with sigils you only need to imagine an image of something that represents what you are wanting to happen, then charge it with energy, forget and carry on. Later you will find it happening.

Sigils can be made in various ways and are very useful in getting a message to your sub-conscious or Higher Self, without distraction from your conscious mind.

It pays to keep a record of all the experiments you try with sigils, as part of the process is sometimes to just forget them and carry on with other things. This gives your Higher Self time to come up with a way to make your wishes come true, and they will.

Spells

Spells – Exactly What Is A Spell?

Spells are the engines of magick. They are the means by which magick works. You use a spell to perform magick in potions, in incense making, in chanting, in psychometry, in sigilisation, in chakra working and in all the vast array of methods available. And magick is a way of altering things to the way you want through occult laws. These occult laws might be forever unknowable to science or it may simply be that science hasn't worked them out yet. Basically casting spells means you are practising magick.

Spells – Can Anybody Make A Spell Work?

If you go to Google and search for 'free spells' you will find a multitude of sites offering these. Take your pick, get a few and try them. Can you intuit before you actually try these whether they will work or not. Consider what the world will be like if this was all you had to do in order to change things to your liking. It will be a very different world than the one you are in now if these spells worked.

But this does not mean that only a knowledgeable few can make spells work. Think about it, if knowledge is what you need, then you simply need to acquire that specific knowledge. And this knowledge is not kept secret or hidden from the populace. There are many teachers available for you to work with. You simply have to find one who knows her subject and who is willing to teach it. It may take a while to find such a person but it's well worth the effort. And the fact you are reading this right now is a good indication of your intent and determination to make spells work for you.

Spells – How Do They Work?

Asking how spells work is the same as asking how magick works. There are many methods of making spells work and they all depend on the spell-caster. The spell caster is a person with a certain history, experience and mind set and all these attributes combine in sometimes unique ways in the casting of spells.

But people are generally similar; all those casters of spells who come from the same culture will tend to be more alike in their spell casting than those of a different culture, even if the aim of the spells are the same in both cases.

So basically you need to understand that there are numerous ways of making the same spells work and this should be kept in the back of your mind at all times. There is a lot of latitude for adaptation and improvisation here. However, in saying that, there is a body of proven spells that work for many people. This body of work is very useful for all, but especially the novice magickian, because now she can be confident she is using tried and true material. So she has that much less to worry about making it and it's that much easier to make her spells work.

There are a few generally accepted ideas about how spells work, and the principal of similarity (also known as sympathetic magick) is one. If you associate one action with another then performing the first action will cause the other. An example is when you move your hand in a certain way, the 'recipient' will agree with you when you suggest something. Spells of this type require this association to be formed magically before they will work.

Another generally accepted idea on how spells work is the principle of contagion. This principle accepts that if two objects come into contact then some sort of link between them will be made and this link can be controlled by utilizing the correct methods. Thus it becomes necessary to obtain something from the other person if you want to enchant him or her. A hair or a nail clipping are classic examples. Spells of this type are extremely common.

Spells can be used to activate potions and rituals, which would simply not work without this activation. Also words themselves can be magick and used to bend the universe to your will. In general spells comprise the backbone of practical low magick.

Magick spells in general terms are all about intent, or the Will of the caster. If you can make a change to something using your Will, that is magick, doesn't matter what it is. If you think of a image in your head and then take that image from your head and paint it on to canvas, that is a form of magick spell.

Spells - Are There Good & Evil Spells?

No, magick does not have a mind to think about whether the spell is good or evil. The intention of the Magickian casting the spell might be good or bad, but magick itself can not be classed as good or evil, that is impossible. Good and evil are a human creation.

Spells – Which Are The Most Popular Spells?

At first sight this might be difficult to find out as it will be impossible to ask all the casters of spells out there this question. There are just too many of them and it would be impossible to know whether you had contacted them all or not. But we can all make a safe guess that love spells, money spells and health spells will be the top three.

Potions

What are Potions?

Potions are ubiquitous – they are everywhere. The word 'potion' is derived from the Greek word 'poton' which means 'that which one drinks.' So, in theory, it can be anything you drink, from an energy drink, or beer, or a medicine or even poison. But we are concerned with the original potions which still work as well as they ever did. These potions are the ones charged with energy, or magick if you will. Witchcraft and alchemy commonly use potions; in fact they are a basic part of each.

Potions – What Are They Used For?

Apart from drinking, potions can be used to sprinkle an area, to add to a ritual bath, to anoint and to add or absorb energy. The ingredients used for some of these purposes make it very inadvisable to actually drink the potion. Obviously, the making and use of potions also draws heavily on the alchemy and herbalism disciplines. In fact, at one time herbalists were also Alchemists as an integral part of their occupation and potions were an integral part of that.

Potions – Manufacture

Other knowledge or disciplines are also necessary for the successful manufacture of potions. A knowledge of alchemy, astrology, of lunar phases, the use of oils, incenses, and other correspondences, to name just a few, are also required for your potions.

Consider what you have just read – to successfully manufacture working potions you need to know the correct herbs to use, when to pick them, and sometimes where to pick them. Have you tried extracting the essence of the plant or flower or herb etc? There are a lot of ways to do this supposedly simple thing and not all of them will work. Thus you have to be precise and knowledgeable in making your potions.

Potions can be strengthened - do you know how to do this? You will also need to know how to amplify the efficacy of your potions and how and when to apply your willpower to the making of your potions?

Some potions require you to do the right amount or rotations when you are stirring them. Do you know this number, or even which direction you stir it? And what temperature should your potions be at during the various stages of manufacture?

Occasionally it is necessary to chant while making potions? Chants are sometimes essential, sometimes not. But even if not essential they can sometimes increase the power of potions.

Water is commonly used in the vast majority of potions, but what type of water? Did you realise there are different types? Tap water will not do for these purposes, so you need to obtain some 'effective' water for your potions. Some contain alcohol, which type? and various other elements, what are they, how do they work together with the other ingredients?

As you can see, making effective potions involves a lot of diverse disciplines and the ability for effective planning. Some ingredients and potions have a limited shelf life, which you must know and take into account in your planning.

Intent and willpower are also critical for the successful manufacture of potions and these talents need to be developed and practised in order to be successful. A knowledge of the appropriate recipes is also critical. Simply throwing a few ingredients together to a recipe you obtained free from the internet just will not do if you want effective potions, well unless you are very lucky, that is.

The qualities of all the ingredients of your potions are cumulatively responsible for your success. And when I say ingredients I mean the chemicals, elements, herbs, spices, stones, minerals, hair, willpower, timing and storage – in fact, absolutely everything used to produce your potions.

Even if you get that correct, sometimes your potions have to be drunk at a certain time, or within a certain time scale.

All this assumes you can obtain the ingredients for your particular potions. And yes, you probably can because potions, at least the basic ones, were and are designed to use the ingredients at hand. But some potions require esoteric ingredients and you may well have difficulty in obtaining them.

Potions - Suppliers

In addition you also need to really trust your supplier and manufacturer because ingredients for potions are delicate and need to be harvested and prepared and stored properly. I hope you now realise the plants and herbs and flowers have, at the very least, to be organic. If not, the additional pesticides and fungicides will affect the power and efficacy of your potions for the worse.

Potions derive part of their efficacy from the interactions of the ingredients, so, knowing this you will appreciate they need to be as pure as possible.

The best way to ensure this is to harvest and obtain the ingredients for your potions yourself at the appropriate times.

Potions – Storage

Now, have you considered how you're going to store your ingredients and finished potions? You really don't want any 'stuff' from the storage vessel leaching into your work, do you? Stoneware and glass containers are good, plastic is bad. And remember, light can also leach in, so add coloured glass to your storage vessels as well. Light can be an ingredient for some potions, so in these cases you will need to use clear glass.

Potions – You Can Make Them Yourself

The intention of this article is not to put you off making your own potions. It is possible, and with a bit of experience, easy, to make them at home. Once you have the basics off, you will realise why certain ingredients go into your potion. With this knowledge, you will be able to confidently alter ingredients to suit your own circumstances without altering its efficacy. Also, you will be able to properly design and develop your own potions.

The Uses Of Potions

So what can you actually use potions for? Well just about anything, really. Try the ubiquitous love potion, and the related lust potion. Are you unemployed or want another job? Consider the employment potion.

Tarot

What are Tarot cards?

Most people know the tarot through pop culture, perhaps even Jane Seymour laying out the cards for James Bond in Live and Let Die: cryptic declarations of the future somehow tied to opaque but mysteriously beckoning images on a deck of cards several levels of enigma past those of a stage magician.

The tarot is popularly understood as a means or system of divination, but how old the tarot actually is, and where it came from, and out of what prior traditions, is open for debate.

How long have Tarot cards been around?

Historically, we can date the first tarot deck, recognized as such, to the Renaissance, and one can even today purchase reproductions of it, known now as the Visconti-Sforza deck -- and in fact, before the now more widely accepted term "tarot", the cards were known by the Italian word "tarocchi".

Today's modern deck of playing cards used in casinos and gambling parlours -- or for games of solitaire at home -- shares with the tarot four numbered suits with accompanying court cards, sometimes known as the Minor Arcana. What the tarot adds that is specific to itself are twenty-two images that constitute what are known either as the trumps or the Major Arcana.

The earliest writer to speculate on the allegorical significance of the cards -- specifically the four suits -- was Galcottus Martius in 1488. The earliest printed work that expressly treats the subject of fortune-telling and divination with the cards is Francesco Marcoli's Le Sorti, dated 1540 and dealing very specifically with the suit of coins.

What appears to be the oldest listing of the trump images, or Major Arcana, is contained in a manuscript from 1500, the Sermones De Ludo Cum Aliis, a text that declares that nothing in the world is so hateful to God as the game of trumps, which ridicules the Christian faith by depicting angels, the cardinal virtues, the Pope and the Emperor on cards.

An especially interesting series of passages can be found in another invective against gambling, this one from 1550 by Flavio Albert Lollio, which not only seems to ponder the meaning of the trumps as something inherently esoteric but treats the very use of the cards, even in the form of a mere "game", as an inherently allegorical experience.

What are Tarot cards used for?

This opens up a larger question. Though scholarship can demonstrate that the cryptic images of the tarot can be seen as part of the elaborate system of correspondences that characterized the medieval and Renaissance mind, the very indication of deeper levels of the symbolic and the ways in which they can be successfully integrated with other esoteric bodies of knowledge. Including those from non-European cultures, lead one to question whether the tarot grew up in accidental isolation, or whether it is a manifestation of a continuing and global body of knowledge that has been with us for as long as there has been higher conscious thought.

Tarot cards in Ancient Egypt?

It is with this line of thinking that an apparently European creation coextensive with the invention of the Gutenberg printing press began to discover for itself a provenance dating back to ancient Egypt.

In 1781, Antoine Court de Gebelin wrote an exhaustive treatise, Monde Primitif, which dealt with all aspects of ancient civilisation. Court de Gebelin advanced the theory that the Major Arcana cards constituted the Egyptian hieroglyphic Book of Thoth, saved from the ruins of burning Egyptian temples thousands of years ago. Thoth was the Egyptian god of wisdom, credited with the invention of both numbers and sacred writing, and subsequently given the name Hermes Trismegistus by the Greeks, so that his sacred works came to be called "Hermetic".

Tarot cards and the Qabalah?

In 1856, Eliphas Levi published Le Dogme et Ritual de la Haute Magic, and was the first writer to link the twenty-two Major Arcana with the twenty-two letters of the Hebrew alphabet, which in turn led to studies of the Qabalah and of still further correspondences with such texts as the Sepher Yetzirah.

MacGregor Mathers, writing in 1888, combined both approaches when describing several anagrams derived from the word taro, including "Tora" (law in Hebrew), "Troa" (gate in Hebrew), and Taor and Ator (Egyptian goddesses of darkness and joy respectively).

Tarot cards in India?

The tarot has also been linked to the game of Chaturanga, an ancient Indian version of chess, either as representations of the pieces or as a more fluid and unified extension of the pieces and playing field itself. Further affinities with early Indian culture include possible mapping of the trumps onto the ten principal avatars of Vishnu, and the suits onto the four objects held by the androgynous Ardhanarishvara, though these avenues of approach have not been as thoroughly developed in the West.

Tarot and The Tree of Life.

The integration of the tarot with the Qabalistic Tree of Life has become more prevalent, so that today the odds are good that one will be learning and synthesizing both systems, producing a diagram that is at once a map of the cosmos and a map of the human body, with the totality of all possible layouts in all possible spreads representing the permutations of the elements and paths that constitute all that which is the case.

Tarot cards as our Universe in Miniature.

In this regard, the tarot can be seen as a miniaturized but comprehensive encyclopaedia of existence, the universe as a book, containing all that is and all that can be. Through methods of internalizing its structure so that it literally becomes a part of one's own mind/body complex, the totality of one's being is progressively attuned to, aligned with, and made conscious of the larger system of cosmic engineering and design. The various spreads the card reader will learn become the possible projections of one's own body onto and within the larger universal body.

The images of the Major Arcana have remained largely the same since their initial European appearance, with only slight adjustments dictated by changing historical circumstance. With developments in twentieth-century psychology -- Carl Jung's concept of archetypes, adding a collective unconscious to the Freudian personal unconscious -- the Arcana have been applied to a wide range of seemingly disparate mythologies and literary genres, demonstrating an apparently unifying substratum of recurring forms underneath seemingly every imaginable systematized narrative, while artists such as Salvador Dali have created their own versions, merging the Arcana with recurring images from their own works.

Tarot cards in conclusion.

The tarot, then, can be seen as latent in virtually any enterprise of the mind that tends toward self-sufficiency and/or imaginative completeness, and its historical aspects only incidental specifics of something far vaster and abiding both in the human mind as well as in the larger and timeless universal mind. What worlds it will open to practitioners is as varied as the world itself -- as exemplified by the case of Scottish artist Fergus Hall, designer of that deck used in Live and Let Die referred to above, who lives now in a Tibetan Buddhist monastery in a Scottish landscape of wet moorlands and Neolithic stone circles.

Secrets of the Serpent Bloodline - The Unveiling of Profound Esoteric Mysteries

Part 2: How to kick-start your own Journey

Chapter 4

Awakening Your Senses

Making a start.

If you are serious about starting the Great Work, awakening your senses and getting a full connection to your Higher Self, then these tasks will set you on the right track. However no one can do this for you, you have to take the time to do it and push yourself to do it. No one ever said it would be easy, it is hard work and the vast majority of those who start will end up failing and sometimes drive themselves insane. So before starting, be sure this is what you want, and have in your mind that failure is not an option and that this is something you will be doing for the rest of your life in one form or another. If you get to an advanced level, you will then be compelled to help others, the Great Work is never ending.

> 1. Magickal Diary - Put everything in here that you are doing, the weather, your state of mind. Anything you notice while doing your tasks and rituals. Also keep it at the side of your bed and make a note of your dreams as soon as you wake up. In an evening before sleeping write down lists of things you want to achieve, this can be anything, from what you want to get done tomorrow, to long term plans.
>
> 2. White Tau Robe - Make or buy a tau robe. It is better if you make it yourself. Always wear this when meditating or doing any ritual work, it separates your mundane life with that of your magickal life if you are wearing special magick clothing.
>
> 3. Perform the Lesser Banishing Ritual of the Pentagram everyday three times a day. Start right away, and as soon as you have your robe wear that when you do it. See the ritual section for this ceremony.
>
> 4. Visualisations - Take a walk each day and for the first week take time to notice everything you see.
>
> Week 2 - Each day look for a different colour only. Blue on Monday, Green on Tuesday etc. Make notes.
>
> Week 3 - Notice sounds only. Make notes.

Week 4 - Notice smells only. Make notes.

Week 5 - During the day stop and notice any feelings about your body. What textures are under your fingers? Under your feet, legs etc. Make notes.

5. Meditation - Meditate each day for at least 20 minutes more if possible. Start by covering your eyes with your hands so you are in complete darkness. Next keep your eyes closed and sit in a comfortable position or lie down. Take deep breaths and clear your mind. If any thoughts come to mind when meditating make notes of them, or any feelings etc. See meditation techniques in the next section.

After a few months of working on your first tasks, I am sure you will feel energised and ready for the next steps.

1. Continue with your Magick Dairy.

2. Visualisations - Cover your eyes and be in complete darkness for a few moments. Then open your eyes and look to the palm of your left hand and visualise a purple ball of energy. Believe it is there in your hand, try to roll it about and change the shape of it, then roll it back into a ball and place it before you. Sit and watch the ball of energy before letting it dissolve and disappear. Practice this over time until you can do it very easily.

When taking walks or when just around the house, try to image the floor is changing to a different colour. Do this daily.

3. Meditation - Every morning for one month perform a ritual of relaxation. Be seated comfortably in your temple space, bedroom or any other area where quiet and solitude may be maintained. See the meditation section for meditations to try.

Perform the Banishing Earth Ritual of the Pentagram. See rituals section.

Perform the Meditation followed by Banishing Earth Ritual.

4. Yoga – You should now be ready to start a simple yoga routine every morning. The Five Tibetan Rites are ideal for this, and more can be added to your routine as and when you are ready. See chapter 6.

5. Rituals - Continue to perform the Banishing Earth Ritual 3 times a day. One of which will be before your meditation.

There is more to do, much more and these are just a start for you. If you start on this path and you are serious about continuing then you should contact us about joining us and moving forward on your path in a safe and supportive environment. More is coming later on about the Celtic Gnostic Church and the Order I formed to help people like yourself.

Meditations Techniques

This is a step by step guide on how to enter a deep meditation. There is a choice for some of the steps where you can find out what works best for you. Continue to the end of the steps, to see the different options to try.

Step 1: Remove yourself from the mundane. Find a special place to use for meditation. Wear special clothing, only used for meditation.

Step 2: Choose a suitable Asana.

Beginners usually start with one of the three easier poses:

      1: Cross legged. (Lotus Pose)
      2: Sitting on chair. (King Pose)
      3: Lying down. (Corpse Pose)

These are postures which allow you to sit upright, or lie down and be relaxed for a longer time. They provide a stable seat for meditation. The aim is to train your body so you can stay a long time without moving any part of your body. This is important if you are practising meditation or Pranayama and want to come to a deep concentration.

You should choose the posture that is most comfortable for you and start practising it for 15 minutes. You can increase the length gradually.

Step 3:   Send a prayer of devotion to your Higher Self.
              Pray pose mantra: **OL IVMD CAOSG GASSAGEN ANANAEL**

Pronounced: Oh-el ee-voh-em-deh kah-oh-sah-geh gee-as-ag-gee-enn ah-nah-nah-el

This tunes into your higher self. OL – I, IVMD – Call, CAOSG – Upon, GASSAGEN – Divine, ANANAEL – Wisdom. "I call upon Divine Wisdom".

Secrets of the Serpent Bloodline - The Unveiling of Profound Esoteric Mysteries

Step 4: Make sure you are breathing correctly.
Always breathe from the diaphragm.

Step 5: Choose a mind focus technique, to dissolve other thoughts. Choose one of the following: Mantra, Tattvas, Fourfold Breathing or Pranayama.

Mantra - There are many to choose from. I will just give you a few examples to work with. They will be listed at the end.

Tattvas - There are Five Types of Waves called Tattvas. They represent distinctive Forms and Vibratory Motions and are the five modifications of the Great Breath, Prana, of the Atman. Prana is called Chi in China.

The first Wave that came out of the *Atman* is called the Âkâsha (Spirit, **Egg**, Black). After this came the Vâyu (Air, the **Circle**, Blue), the Tejas (Fire, the **Triangle,** Red), the Apas (Water, the **Crescent** of the Moon, Silver) and the Prithivi (Earth, the **Square**, Yellow).

The use of Tattvas is called **Dharana** - Control of Thought. Please see further on where they are listed.

Fourfold Breathing – This used to focus the mind, regulate your breathing and distract any other thoughts.

Breathe in the count of 4, hold for the count of 4. Breathe out to the count of 4 and hold for 4. Then breathe in to count of 4, etc.

Pranayama - Regularisation of the Breathing. See list at the end.

Step 6: Deep Meditation - Eyes, tongue and breathing.
Once you have used your mind focus and breathing exercises, you will notice you no longer have to count, or use the mantra, as you have entered a deeper level of relaxation. When you feel yourself becoming deeply relaxed, be sure to check that your tongue is resting on the top of your mouth and that eyes are closed, but looking upwards towards your 3rd eye.

Step 7: To do an advanced form of meditation, is to do a ritual.
The Lesser Banishing Ritual of The Pentagram is a good starting point. It provides positive energy, cleanses and strengthens your aura, protects you and helps with mind focus and you learn visualisation skills.

MANTRAS

Mantra: אמת - EMETH (eh'- meth)

Emeth is ancient Hebrew and means Truth. We vibrate this through our bodies to resonate with truth all through us. Truth is my identity and I call upon the eternal Truth that resides in all of us. Chanting this mantra awakens the Soul.

To use EMETH as a mantra, as you inhale say inside your mind EH and on the exhale say METH. If you mind wonders just keep bringing it back to EMETH.

Mantra: Ain Sof ur (Limitless Light of the Absolute)

Ain Sof ur (Limitless Light of the Absolute), Igniting the Divine Light within, allowing you to feel the connection to everything that is.

To use this mantra, you just said it over and over again, either out loud or in your head as you focus on it's true meaning.

Mantra: THEOLA

THEOLA (Divine Light), Meaning the secret inner light that can be ignited to Illuminate us. When we are using this mantra we are connecting to our own Divinity.

To use this mantra, we break it down into THE – O – LA, THE is pronounced THEE. THEE-O-LA. On THEE inhale, on O exhale on LA inhale, hold for count of 9 and exhale, then repeat.

Mantra: TRIWENS

TRIWENS (The Divine Trinity & the four Elements), Meaning, as you use this mantra you are balancing yourself first with the Divine Trinity or Aeons - Mother, Father and Child. And with the North, South, East & West, the four elements – Air, Fire, Water, Earth.

Breathe in TRI and exhale WENS.

TATTVAS - Dharana - Control of Thought.

1. Constrain the mind to concentrate itself upon a single simple Tattva imagined.
2. During these practices the mind must be absolutely confined to the object determined upon; no other thought must be allowed to intrude upon the consciousness.
3. Note carefully the duration of the experiments, the number and nature of the intruding thoughts, the tendency of the object itself to depart from the course laid out for it, and any other phenomena which may present themselves. Avoid over strain; this is very important.

TATTVAS

⬬	Akasha - Spirit, **Egg**, Black or indigo (*vesica piscis*).
●	Vâyu - Air, the **Circle**, Blue.
▲	Tejas - Fire, the **Triangle,** Red.
☾	Apas - Water, the **Crescent** of the Moon, Silver.
■	Prithivi - Earth, the **Square**, Yellow.

PRANAYAMA - Regularisation of the Breathing

1. At rest in one of your positions, close the right nostril with the thumb of the right hand and breathe out slowly and completely through the left nostril, while your watch marks 20 seconds. Breathe in through the same nostril for 10 seconds. Changing hands, repeat with the other nostril. Let this be continuous for one hour.
2. When this is quite easy to you, increase the periods to 30 and 15 seconds.
3. When this is quite easy to you, but not before, breathe out for 15 seconds, in for 15 seconds, and hold the breath for 15 seconds.
4. When you can do this with perfect ease and comfort for a whole hour, practice breathing out for 40 and in for 20 seconds.
5. This being attained, practice breathing out for 20, in for 10, holding the breath for 30 seconds.
6. You will find that the presence of food in the stomach, even in small quantities, makes the practices very difficult.
7. Be very careful never to over strain your powers; especially never get so short of breath that you are compelled to breathe out jerkily or rapidly.
8. Strive after depth, fullness, and regularity of breathing.
9. Various remarkable phenomena will very probably occur during these practices. They must be carefully analysed and recorded.

Chapter 5

Guided Meditations

Do each meditation everyday for a month before moving on to the next one. You might get impatient at the idea, but it is well worth doing. When you get to these places you will find new things all the time, and the more you do this the more intense and real the experience will be, which will help you later when you do scrying. These things can't be skipped if you want results.

Basic Correspondences Chart

Element	Direction	Colour	Tool	Angel	Guardian
Air	East	Yellow	Sword/Athame	RAPHAEL	FYTHRUEL
Fire	South	Red	Candle/Wand	MICHAEL	SINFAREL
Water	West	Blue	Chalice	GABRIEL	DYUGAREL
Earth	North	Green	Salt/Crystal/Shell	AURIEL	MYATHREL
Spirit	Centre	Purple	Pantacle	YOU	YOU

You will need to remember the above correspondences to build your Astral Temple.

Building Your Astral Temple

Your Astral Temple is one of the most important facets of your magickal work, with it you can learn meditation techniques that will help you on your path immensely. It is especially useful to those of you with no space for a full dedicated room for use as a Temple.

Here is a guide to help you set up your Temple.

Wear a Tau robe, or other comfortable clothing which you use only for your magick work. Using the meditation techniques described earlier, get yourself into a relaxed state. Burn incense, and sit in a darkened room.

Now imagine yourself in a Temple, create it in your mind exactly how you want it. The walls can be plain, or draped with velvet fabric, however you want. The floor is covered with black and white tiles. There are five Altars in your Temple, one in each quarter: North, East, South and West, and one in the centre. Each Altar is set up with items and colours for that quarter. In the centre a large purple candle is burning, you watch it for a moment as the flame gently flickers. You may even be able to feel the warmth coming from the candle. You can have music playing in your Temple, but it is much better if the music is tranquil background music. With forethought you can pick out a piece of music that will always be playing as you enter the Temple to begin your work, that way whenever you want to get back to your Temple quickly, you can just imagine that tune playing and you will be back there.

Practice going back to your Temple as often as possible, the idea is to make it so real that you do fully believe you are there. When it becomes real enough you can perform your rituals there, meet angels, daemons and astral entities, and learn many different skills. You can even talk to your ancestors there, and see the past and the future. You can call someone else to your Temple and communicate with them telepathically, and what is so wonderful about all this is, it actually works. It just takes time, practice and determination.

Month 1 Meditation

For this meditation you will need a green candle and some frankincense incense.

Light the candle and incense before you start, you can use the candle as a focus for your relaxation. The room lights should be out and you should be in your lotus asana. Ideally the room will be without clutter, with a small table in the North as your Altar with your candle and incense, you should be sat where you can view the candle and face north.

Close your eyes and notice things about your body. The fabric of your clothing against your skin and the air temperature on your face. Pause for a while and notice as many sensations as possible, then relax and focus on your breathing.

Imagine the warm glow of the candle filling your senses, with your eyes closed you can still see its warm glow behind your lids out there. But now you are going to experience going inside, and leaving the outside for a time. Image the room out there is now changing around you. The floor is turning into black and white tiles, you are sat comfortably and relaxed in this mystical incense filled Temple, lit only by your green candle. You are now in your Astral Temple at your Northern Altar. Your green candle flickering gently before you, and the items you have placed there to represent Earth. You can smell the incense as it rises from the censer. You feel calm and serene here.

Behind the Northern Altar there is a drape, you decide to pull the drape back and it reveals a door. You decide to open the door, when you do a breeze flows through and leaves scatter about the floor. Through the door you can see a beautiful forest, you walk through the door and look up as you do, noticing the Sun above sending tendrils of light down through the gaps in the branches of the tall trees. A dragonfly flutters past you as you head deeper into the forest.

You walk towards a particularly magnificent tree, that has roots sticking up from the ground. You sit on the ground beside it and run your hands over the soft moss covering the bark. Your feel the soil beneath you and you imagine all the seeds just below the surface waiting to push their way through to the surface, and you imagine roots growing from you and feeding their way down into the earth, keeping you safe and secure and grounded.

You stay there a while taking in all the sights and sounds of the forest, and when you are ready you make your way back to your Astral Temple where you stay until you are ready to leave.

Month 2 Meditation

For this meditation you will need a red candle and some frankincense incense.

Light the candle and incense before you start, you can use the candle as a focus for your relaxation. The room lights should be out and you should be in your lotus asana. Ideally the room will be without clutter, with a small table in the south as your Altar with your candle and incense, you should be sat where you can view the candle and face south.

Close your eyes and notice things about your body. The fabric of your clothing against your skin and the air temperature on your face. Pause for a while and notice as many sensations as possible, then relax and focus on your breathing.

Imagine the warm glow of the candle filling your senses, with your eyes closed you can still see its warm glow behind your lids out there. But now you are going to experience going inside, and leaving the outside for a time. Image the room out there is now changing around you. The floor is turning into black and white tiles, you are sat comfortably and relaxed in this mystical incense filled Temple, lit only by your red candle. You are now in your Astral Temple at your Southern Altar. Your red candle flickering gently before you, and the items you have placed there to represent Fire. You can smell the incense as it rises from the censer. You feel calm and serene here.

Behind the Southern Altar there is a drape, you decide to pull the drape back and it reveals a door. You decide to open the door, when you do a warm glow radiates out into the Temple and warms your skin. Through the door you can see a large bonfire burning fiercely. You decide to walk through the door and stand by the fire feeling its heat energising you as you gaze upon its furious flames.

You stay there a while taking in the energy of the fire, and when you are ready you make your way back to your Astral Temple where you stay until you are ready to leave.

Month 3 Meditation

For this meditation you will need a blue candle and some frankincense incense.

Light the candle and incense before you start, you can use the candle as a focus for your relaxation. The room lights should be out and you should be in your lotus asana. Ideally the room will be without clutter, with a small table in the west as your Altar with your candle and incense, you should be sat where you can view the candle and face west.

Close your eyes and notice things about your body. The fabric of your clothing against your skin and the air temperature on your face. Pause for a while and notice as many sensations as possible, then relax and focus on your breathing.

Imagine the warm glow of the candle filling your senses, with your eyes closed you can still see its warm glow behind your lids out there. But now you are going to experience going inside, and leaving the outside for a time. Image the room out there is now changing around you. The floor is turning into black and white tiles, you are sat comfortably and relaxed in this mystical incense filled Temple, lit only by your blue candle. You are now in your Astral Temple at your western Altar. Your blue candle flickering gently before you, and the items you have placed there to represent Water. You can smell the incense as it rises from the censer. You feel calm and serene here.

Behind the Western Altar there is a drape, you decide to pull the drape back and it reveals a door. You decide to open the door, when you do a fine mist of water sprays out into the Temple and cools your skin. Through the door you can see the ocean as it flows up on to the smooth sands and then retreats, only to come chasing itself back to the shore once again, over and over. You decide to walk through the door and stand on the cool damp sand facing the majestic ocean before you. You can feel the cool smooth sand under you feet, your toes grip it as the cool water rushes up and round your ankles.

Secrets of the Serpent Bloodline - The Unveiling of Profound Esoteric Mysteries

You feel immense emotions of tranquillity and harmony fill you, as you feel at one with the power of the water.

You stay there a while taking in the power of the waves, and when you are ready you make your way back to your Astral Temple where you stay until you are ready to leave.

Month 4 Meditation

For this meditation you will need a yellow candle and some frankincense incense.

Light the candle and incense before you start, you can use the candle as a focus for your relaxation. The room lights should be out and you should be in your lotus asana. Ideally the room will be without clutter, with a small table in the east as your Altar with your candle and incense, you should be sat where you can view the candle and face east.

Close your eyes and notice things about your body. The fabric of your clothing against your skin and the air temperature on your face. Pause for a while and notice as many sensations as possible, then relax and focus on your breathing.

Imagine the warm glow of the candle filling your senses, with your eyes closed you can still see its warm glow behind your lids out there. But now you are going to experience going inside, and leaving the outside for a time. Image the room out there is now changing around you. The floor is turning into black and white tiles, you are sat comfortably and relaxed in this mystical incense filled Temple, lit only by your yellow candle. You are now in your Astral Temple at your eastern Altar. Your yellow candle flickering gently before you, and the items you have placed there to represent Air. You can smell the incense as it rises from the censer. You feel calm and serene here.

Behind the Eastern Altar there is a drape, you decide to pull the drape back and it reveals a door. You decide to open the door, when you do a gust of wind blows out into the Temple and pushes you gently back. Through the door you can see a magnificent vista. You decide to walk through the door to see more. You are now stood on top of a cliff looking down at a beautiful valley and lake below, the air is cool and crisp, and as a gust ruffles past you, you open out your arms and feel as if you are on top of the world. Soft white clouds float by and the Sun shines brightly above. Every now and then the Sun hides behind a passing cloud, only to re-emerge a few seconds later. You take deep full breathes, taking in the clean refreshing, uplifting air.

You stay there a while taking in the pleasant clean air and enjoying the view, and when you are ready you make your way back to your Astral Temple where you stay until you are ready to leave.

Month 5 Meditation

For this meditation you will need a purple candle and some frankincense incense.

Light the candle and incense before you start, you can use the candle as a focus for your relaxation. The room lights should be out and you should be in your lotus asana. Ideally the room will be without clutter, with a small table in the centre as your Altar with your candle and incense, you should be sat where you can view the candle.

Close your eyes and notice things about your body. The fabric of your clothing against your skin and the air temperature on your face. Pause for a while and notice as many sensations as possible, then relax and focus on your breathing.

Imagine the warm glow of the candle filling your senses, with your eyes closed you can still see its warm glow behind your lids out there. But now you are going to experience going inside, and leaving the outside for a time. Image the room out there is now changing around you. The floor is turning into black and white tiles, you are sat comfortably and relaxed in this mystical incense filled Temple, lit only by your purple candle. You are now in your Astral Temple at your central Altar. Your purple candle flickering gently before you. You can smell the incense as it rises from the censer. You feel calm and serene here.

You look round the Temple and you can see the doors you have been through before. You look to the north and can see the tree you sat beneath and became connected, secure and rooted to the earth. You look to the south and see the fire that energised and warmed you. You look to the west and you can see the majestic ocean where you felt immense emotions of tranquillity and harmony fill you, as you felt at one with power of the water. You look to the east and see the beautiful view you gazed upon as you breathed in the clean refreshing air. You stop for a moment and feel all those things again. The elements are with you, and the power of your own mind can invoke them whenever you want to. You look upwards above your central Altar and notice a silver thread hanging down. As you acknowledge it, it comes towards you and connects to your crown chakra at the top of your head. You feel a slight pull upwards, and you now have the option to take a test flight out into the astral realms. Your silver cord will lead you back to your Astral Temple, so you can not get lost. It is up to you if you want to take a journey right now or not. If you have completed all the meditations before this one correctly you will find it easy to enter the realms.

When you return write down everything you saw.

Chapter 6

Five Tibetan Rites

These rites should be done everyday for a healthy mind and body. Wearing comfortable clothes begin with the first five steps in the meditation techniques section.

SPECIAL CAUTION: Spinning and stretching through the following exercises can aggravate certain health conditions such as any type of heart problem, multiple sclerosis, Parkinson Disease, severe arthritis of the spine, uncontrolled high blood pressure, a hyperthyroid condition, or vertigo. Problems may also be caused if you are taking drugs that cause dizziness. Please consult your physician prior to beginning these exercises if you have any difficult health issues or if you have any other concerns.

Rite 1 (Spirit): Twirling

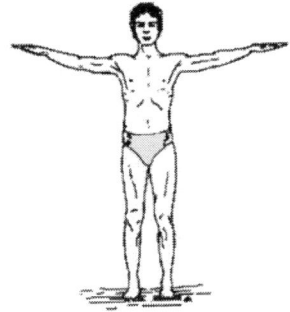

Stand up, stretch out your arms at shoulder height and start to spin by turning clockwise (to the right).

To avoid dizziness, do what dancers and figure skaters do. Before you begin to spin, focus your vision on a single point straight ahead.

As you begin to turn, continue to hold your vision on that point for as long as possible. Eventually, you will have to let it leave your field of vision, so that your head can spin around with the rest of your body.

When this happens, turn your head quickly and refocus on your point as soon as you can. Holding your vision on the fixed reference point helps to stop you becoming disoriented and dizzy.

Start by doing not more than 2 or 3 twirls and build up gradually over a period of 2 or 3 weeks to 21 twirls a day.

Rite 2 (Earth): Head and Leg Raises

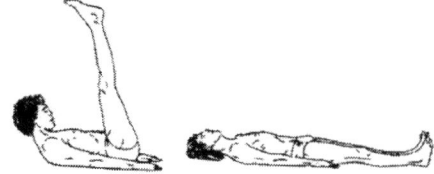

Lie flat on your back on a firm surface with your hands by your sides and palms down. Breathing in, raise your legs straight up into the air.

At the same time, lift your head up as if you were going to touch your head to your knees. Keep your legs straight.

If possible, let your legs extend back over your body, towards your head, but do not let your knees bend.

Then, slowly lower both your head and legs (keeping the knees straight) to the floor and breathe out.

Allow all your muscles to relax and rest before repeating the movement.

Allow all the muscles to relax, continue breathing in the same rhythm. Breathe in deeply as you lift your legs and breathe out as you lower your legs. Then repeat the sequence 2 or 3 times and build up gradually, over a period of 2 or 3 weeks, to a total of 21 repetitions.

Rite 3 (Air): Back Arches

 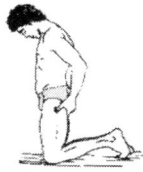

On a carpeted floor, kneel with your body erect and your knees directly under your hips.

Bend your head and neck forward, tucking the chin against the chest and place your hands at the back of your thighs below the buttocks.

Curl your toes under, and arch your back as you inhale, letting your head drop as far back as is comfortable.

Keep your thighs in a vertical position and avoid strain.

Return to the original position and breathe out. Rest before repeating the procedure.

Breathe in deeply as you arch the spine, breathe out as you return to an erect position. Repeat this 2 or 3 times and build up gradually over a period of 2 or 3 weeks to a total of 21 repetitions.

Rite 4 (Water): The Table

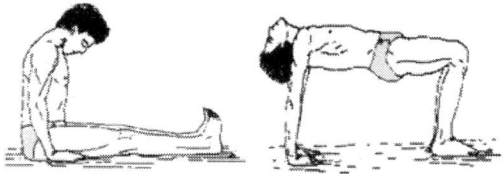

Sit with your legs straight out in front of you with your feet flexed, and your palms flat on the floor by your sides next to your hips, with fingertips pointing toward toes.

Bend your head forward and, as you breathe in, raise your knees and buttocks up in the air making your thighs parallel with the floor and your calves perpendicular to the floor.

Then allow your head to stretch backwards just far enough to make your body, from the shoulders to the knees, parallel to the floor like a table top. Try not to over-arch your back.

Next, tense every muscle in your body. Finally, relax your muscles as you return to the original sitting position and breathe out.

Rest before repeating the procedure.

Breathe in as you raise up, hold your breath as you tense the muscles, breathe out completely as you come down. Continue breathing in the same rhythm as long as you rest between repetitions. Repeat this 2 or 3 times and build up gradually over a period of 2 or 3 weeks to a total of 21 repetitions.

Rite 5 (Fire): Inverted-V, Yoga Cobra to Downward Dog

Lie flat on the floor with the palms face down directly under your shoulders and toes in contact with the floor as if you were about to do push-ups. Raise your head and extend it backwards, arching your upper back as far as is comfortable while keeping the legs straight.

This is known as the Cobra position.

Curl your toes under as you push up off the floor with straight arms and your hands directly under your shoulders. Keep your head aligned with your spine and make sure your arms and legs remain straight. Make sure you keep your shoulders down (don't let them scrunch up to your ears) and keep your hips lifted off the floor. Inhale and lift your hips while pushing down through the heels inverting your position until your head faces your knees.

Again do not bend the knees but keep your legs straight.

Exhaling, release this position and return to the original 'Cobra' position.

Then lower the body to the starting position on the floor and rest before repeating the procedure.

Breathe in deeply as you raise the body, breathe out fully as you lower it. Repeat this 2 or 3 times and build up gradually over a period of 2 or 3 weeks to a total of 21 repetitions.

Part 3: Ritual
Chapter 7

Banishing & Protection Rituals

The Banishing Earth Ritual of OIO – KHT

Take a steel dagger or wand in the right hand (or use the index finger).

Face EAST.

Perform the Enochian Cross as follows:

Imagine, at the first word intoned, a brilliant white light descend from above.

Touch the forehead and vibrate **"ZIR" (Zohd-EE-Rah)** *Imagine that same brilliant white light form a 6 inch diameter sphere just above the crown of your head.*

Bring the sphere of light down, make it shine purple as you touch heart and vibrate **THEOLA**

Bring the light down, this time it will be green as you point down to floor and vibrate **"LONDOH" (LOh-Neh-DOh-Heh)**

Now red light as you touch the right shoulder and vibrate **"LONSA" (LOh-Nah-SAh)**

Now draw a line connecting the red light to blue as you touch the left shoulder and vibrate **"BUSD" (BU-SahD)**

Now make a golden ball of light as you clasp the hands before you and vibrate **"OD NOCO MAD HOATH IAIDA" (OD NOCO MAh-Deh HOh-Ah-Tah-Heh EE-Ah-EE-DAh)** *At this point imagine clearly the cross of coloured light as it extends through your body.*

Hands as before, with the dagger between fingers, point up, vibrate **OM**

- *Enochian Cross End*

Imagine that your voice carries forward to the LIMITS of the UNIVERSE. The pentagrams will glow with white flames that ignite as you vibrate the names.

Draw, in the air facing EAST, a green banishing Earth pentagram, and bringing the point of the dagger to the centre of the Pentagram, vibrate the Name **ENKI**

With your left hand give the sign of silence.

Turn toward the SOUTH. Draw a green banishing Earth pentagram, bring the dagger to the centre of it, and vibrate the Name **NUSKU**

Secrets of the Serpent Bloodline - The Unveiling of Profound Esoteric Mysteries

With your left hand give the sign of silence.

Move to WEST. Draw a green banishing Earth pentagram, bringing the dagger to the centre, and vibrate the Name **TIAMET**

With your left hand give the sign of silence.

Then move NORTH. Draw a green banishing Earth pentagram, bringing the point of the dagger to the centre and vibrate the Name **INANNA**

With your left hand give the sign of silence.

Return to the EAST, completing tracing the circle of brilliant white Light, bringing the dagger point to the centre of the EAST Pentagram.

Extend the arms in the form of a cross, say: **BEFORE ME** *(then vibrate)* **FYTHRUEL**

He appears as man in his 40's or 50's. He has long honey golden wavy hair and a short beard and moustache, his hair is going grey in places. He wears shades of yellow, gold, honey and orange. He looks regal as he wears a golden crown and the Sun is never far away from him. Imagine a gentle, refreshing breeze, cleansing and purifying the air.

Then, say: **BEHIND ME** *(then vibrate)* **DYUGAREL**

She appears as a beautiful young woman, with long flowing light hair, with shades of blonde, silver, red and aqua. She wears a silver crown and carries a silver chalice. Her long flowing dress is pale green, aqua, lilac and blue. She is surrounded by dolphins. Imagine feeling the mist and cool spray of the ocean breeze.

Then, say: **AT MY RIGHT HAND** *(then vibrate)* **SINFAREL**

He appears as a young man in his 20's. He is a Prince with long dark hair and dark eyes. He wears red, with details in black, gold and orange. He is carrying a sword and is surrounded by flames, dragons and salamanders. Imagine you can feel the heat and power emanating from the SOUTH.

Then, say: **AT MY LEFT HAND** *(then vibrate)* **MYATHREL**

She appears as a beautiful woman in her 30's, she wears shades of green. A beautiful pale green dress and a velvet cloak of emerald green. Her long wavy hair changes colour according to the season. In spring her hair is chestnut, Summer blonde, Autumn auburn and winter black. Feel the solidity of the Earth, and imagine the odour of the leaves and muskiness of the ground.

Secrets of the Serpent Bloodline - The Unveiling of Profound Esoteric Mysteries

Now, say: **About me flames the pentagrams, Above me and below me, My Magical Universe. Behold, I have the divine light within.**

Imagine the complete circle of brilliant white light at whose quadrants are the 4 Pentagrams. At the centre is the Cross of Light extended through one's body.

Repeat the Enochian Cross, and stamp your right foot at the conclusion of the complete operation.

This is the first ritual you should perform and practice as an Aspirant, and it should be perfected and known by heart. You should do it first thing in the morning, in the middle of the day and before going to bed.

When you get further along your studies you will learn the other pentagrams and what they are used for, and when they should be used.

Protection

Enter your Astral Temple, which you have learnt to do in Liber II, Part 2, Chapter 5 - Guided Meditations.

Imagine a large egg shaped cocoon of protective white light surrounding you. It glows and swirls all round you. You feel warm and safe inside the egg. You can take things with you into your egg, but make sure they are only safe things, comfortable things, like a soft pillow, a fluffy duvet, a teddy bear, or just imagine the light, whatever makes you feel most comfortable. When you can visualise the egg clearly, then imagine the outside walls of your egg turning into a shiny silver reflective surface. Imagine negative energy coming from outside your egg and being reflected back at those who are sending it as soon as it reaches the shiny protective shell of your egg. You are safe, happy and protected in your egg.

Once you have learnt how to make this visualisation strong you can bring the egg back at any time. Practice makes perfect.

Secrets of the Serpent Bloodline - The Unveiling of Profound Esoteric Mysteries

Chapter 8

Scrying The Aethyrs

In Liber II, Part 1, Chapter 2 we talked about Enochian Magick, many get scared away from Enochian Magick as they feel it is too complex and/or time consuming. However once you have learnt the Banishing ritual provided in this book, you have already learnt an Enochian ritual, and it is an important one as you use it at the beginning and end of every magickal session.

Scrying an Enochian aethyr is no exception, it begins and ends with the banishing ritual. I am providing you here instructions on how to scry the first aethyr, if you want to scry more aethyrs after this one I suggest first gaining support from a group of others who know more about this. Just so they can keep a check on you. This is why working within a group, where you trust the other members fully, is important.

What to do:

1. Light a candle in your Temple, and burn some incense.
2. Banish using the ritual you have learnt already.
3. Sit in lotus position in the centre of your Temple.
4. Use four fold breathing in order to relax yourself.
5. When you are ready recite the 19th call using the Enochian (see the phonetic version for pronunciation), not English. Chant the words rather than just speaking them.
6. Vibrate the names of the Governors of Aethyr, then say: **SHAZAM.**
7. Close your eyes and enjoy the show. When the images start to fade take time to write down everything you have seen, in detail, including the colour of things etc.
8. Banish your Temple.

The 19th Call

Enochian	English	Phonetic
MADRIIAX	O you heavens	mah-deh-ree-ee-ah-atz
DSPRAF	which dwell	deh-sah-peh-rah-ef
TEX	in the 30th aire	TEX
CHISMICAOLZ	are mighty	kah-hee-ess-mee-kah-oh-el-zod
SAANIR	in the parts	sah-ah-nee-reh
CAOSGO	of the earth	kah-oh-sah-goh
OD	and	oh-deh
FISIS	execute	fee-see-ess
BALZIZRAS	the judgement	bah-el-zod-ee-zod-rah-ess
IAIDA	of the Highest;	ee-ah-ee-dah
NONCA	to you	noh-en-kah
GOHVLIM	it is said:	goh-hoo-lee-em
MICMA	Behold	mee-kah-mah
ADOIAN	the face	ah-doh-ee-ah-nah
MAD	of your God,	mah-deh
IAOD	the beginning	ee-ah-oh-deh
BLIORB	of comfort,	beh-lee-oh-rah-beh
SABAOOAONA	whose eyes	sah-bah-oh-oh-ah-oh-nah
CHIS	are	kah-hee-ess
LVCIFTIAS	the brightness	loo-kee-feh-tee-ah-ess
PIRIPSOL	of the heavens	pee-ree-peh-soh-el
DS	which	deh-ess
ABRAASSA	provided	ah-beh-rah-ah-sah-sah
NONCF	you	noh-en-kah-ef
NETAAIB	for the government	neh-tah-ah-ee-beh
CAOSGI	of the earth,	kah-oh-sah-gee
OD	and	oh-deh
TILB	her	tee-lah-beh
ADPHAHT	unspeakable	ah-deh-peh-hah-hoh-tah
DAMPLOZ	variety,	dah-mah-peh-loh-zod
TOOAT	furnishing	toh-oh-ah-tah
NONCF	you	noh-en-kah-ef
GMICALZOMA	with a power, understanding	geh-mee-kah-el-zod-oh-mah
LRASD	to dispose	lah-rah-sah-deh

TOFGLO	all things	toh-fah-geh-loh
MARB	according	mah-rah-beh
IARRI	to the providence	ee-ah-rah-ree
IDOIGO	of him that sitteth on the holy throne,	ee-doh-ee-goh
OD	and	oh-deh
TORZVLP	rose up	toh-rah-zod-oo-lah-peh
IAODAF	in the beginning	ee-ah-oh-dah-ef
GOHOL	saying:	goh-hoh-el
CAOSGA	The earth	kah-oh-sah-gah
TABAORD	let her be governed	tah-bah-oh-rah-deh
SAANIR	by her parts;	sah-ah-nee-reh
OD	and	oh-deh
CHRISTEOS	let there be	kah-hoh-ree-ess-teh-oh-ess
IRPOIL	division	ee-reh-poh-ee-el
TIOBL	in her,	tee-oh-beh-el
BVSDIRTILB	that the glory of her	boo-sah-dee-reh-tee-lah-beh
NOALN	may be	noh-ah-lah-en
PAID	always	pah-ee-deh
ORSBA	drunken	oh-rah-sah-bah
OD	and	oh-deh
DODRMNI	vexed	doh-deh-rah-mah-nee
ZILNA	in itself.	zod-ee-el-nah
ELZAPTILB	Her course,	el-zod-ah-peh-tee-el-beh
PARMGI	let it run	pah-rah-mah-gee
PIRIPSAX	with the heavens,	pee-ree-peh-sah-atz
OD	and	oh-deh
TA	as	tah
QVRLST	an handmaid.	koo-rah-lah-sah-tah
BOOAPIS	Let her serve them	boh-oh-ah-pee-sah
LNIBM	one season:	el-nee-beh-em
OVCHO	Let it confound	oh-voh-kah-hoh
SIMP	another,	see-em-peh
OD	and	oh-deh
CHRISTEOS	let there be	kah-hoh-ree-ess-teh-oh-ess
AGTOLTORN	no creature	ah-geh-toh-el-tah-oh-rah-nah
MIRC	upon,	mee-reh-kah
Q	or	kwa

Secrets of the Serpent Bloodline - The Unveiling of Profound Esoteric Mysteries

TIOLB	within her	tee-oh-lah-beh
LEL	the same.	leh-el
TON	All	toh-en
PAOMBD	her members	pah-oh-mah-beh-deh
DILZMO	let them differ	dee-el-zod-moh
ASPIAN	in their qualities,	ah-sah-pee-ah-nah
OD	and	oh-deh
CHRISTEOS	let there be	kah-hoh-ree-ess-teh-oh-ess
AGTOLTORN	no one creature	ah-geh-toh-el-tah-oh-rah-nah
PARACH	equal	pah-rah-kah-hoh
ASIMP	with another.	ah-sah-yah-em-peh
CORDZIZ	The reasonable creatures of the earth, or man	koh-rah-deh-zod-ee-zod
DODPAL	let them vex	doh-deh-pah-el
OD	and	oh-deh
FIFALZ	weed out	fee-fah-el-zod
LSMNAD	one another.	el-sah-mah-nah-deh
OD	And	oh-deh
FARGT	the dwelling places,	fah-rah-geh-tah
BAMS	let them forget	bah-mah-ess
OMAOAS	their names.	oh-moh-ah-sah
CONISBRA	The work of man	koh-nee-sah-beh-rah
OD	and	oh-deh
AVAVOX	his pomp:	ah-oo-ah-voh-atz
TONVG	Let them be defaced;	toh-en-oo-geh
ORSCATBL	his buildings:	oh-rah-sah-kah-tah-beh-lah
NOASMI	Let them become	noh-ah-sah-mee
TABGES	caves	tah-beh-geh-sah
LEVITHMONG	for the beasts of the field;	leh-vee-tah-hoh-moh-nah-geh
VNCHI	confound	oo-en-kah-hee
OMTILB	her understanding	oh-em-tee-el-beh
ORS	with darkness.	oh-rah-ess
BAGLE	For why?	bah-geh-leh
MOOOAH	It repenteth me	moh-oh-oh-ah-hoh
OLCORDZIZ	I made man.	oh-el-koh-rah-deh-zod-ee-zod
LCAPIMAO	One while	el-kah-pee-mah-oh

Secrets of the Serpent Bloodline - The Unveiling of Profound Esoteric Mysteries

IXOMAXIP	let her be known,	ee-atz-oh-mah-atz-ee-peh
ODCACOCASB	and another while	oh-deh-kah-koh-kah-sah-beh
GOSAA	a stranger,	goh-sah-ah
BAGLEN	because	bah-geh-leh-nah
PII	she is	pee-ee
TIANTA	the bed	tee-ah-nah-tah
ABABALOND	of an harlot	ah-bah-bah-loh-nah-deh
ODFAORGT	and the dwelling place	oh-deh-fah-oh-rah-geh-tah
TELOCVOVIM	of him that is fallen.	tah-loh-kah-voh-vee-em
MADRIIAX	O you heavens	mah-deh-ree-ee-ah-atz
TORZV	arise,	toh-rah-zod-oo
OADRIAX	the lower heavens	oh-ah-deh-ree-ah-atz
OROCHA	underneath you,	oh-roh-kah-hah
ABOAPRI	let them serve you,	ah-boh-ah-peh-ree
TABAORI	govern	tah-bah-oh-ree
PRIAZ	those	peh-ree-ah-zod
ARTABAS	that govern,	ah-rah-tah-bah-ess
ADRPAN	cast down	ah-deh-rah-pah-nah
CORSTA	such as	koh-rah-sah-tah
DOBIX	fall,	doh-bee-etz
IOLCAM	bring forth	ee-oh-el-kah-mah
PRIAZI	with those	peh-ree-ah-zod-ee
ARCOAZIOR	that increase,	ah-rah-koh-ah-zod-ee-oh-rah
ODQVASB	and destroy	oh-deh-koo-ah-sah-beh
QTING	the rotten.	kwa-tee-nah-geh
RIPIR	No place	ree-pee-reh
PAAOXT	let it remain	pah-ah-otz-tah
SAGACOR	in one number.	sah-gah-koh-rah
VML	Add	voh-mah-el
OD	and	oh-deh
PRDZAR	diminish	peh-rah-deh-zod-ah-rah
CACRG	until	kah-kah-rah-geh
AOIVEAE	the stars	ah-oh-ee-veh-ah-eh
CORMPT	be numbered.	koh-rah-mah-peh-tah
TORZV	Arise,	toh-rah-zod-oo
ZACAR	move	zod-ah-kah-rah
ODZAMRAN	and appear	oh-deh-zod-ah-mah-rah-nah

Secrets of the Serpent Bloodline - The Unveiling of Profound Esoteric Mysteries

ASPT	before	ah-sah-peh-tah
SIBSI	the covenant	see-beh-see
BVTMONA	of his mouth,	boo-tah-moh-nah
DS	which	deh-ess
SVRZAS	he hath sworn	soo-rah-zod-ah-ess
TIA	unto us	tee-ah
TAN	in his justice.	bah-el-tah-nah
ODO	Open	oh-doh
CICLE	the mysteries	kee-kah-leh
QAA	of your creation,	kwah-ah
OD	and	oh-deh
OZAZMA	make us	oh-zod-ah-zod-mah
PLAPLI	partakers	peh-lah-peh-lee
IADANAMAD	of undefiled knowledge.	ee-ah-dah-nah-mah-deh

The Governors - Vibrate:

TAONGLA tah-oh-nah-gah-la
GEMNIMB geh-mah-neh-meh-bey
ADVORPT ad-vo-ra-pey-tee
DOZINAL dee-o-zin-al

Shazam!

Planetary Magick

In Liber I, Part 2, Chapter 7, The Great Mother & The Great Work, we talked about how when we do the Great Work we become a planet, as it means we no longer feel the need to be attached to our Mother – The Earth and are ready to become an adult. So when you know this, you realise that the planets in our Solar system are living beings at various stages of evolution. Each planet has it's own personality and effects us on Earth in different ways as they move through the heavens above. Is it any wonder in ancient times these planets were seen as Gods and Goddesses? Each planet is still carrying on the Great Work themselves, and when they are ready they will become a Solar system of their own, with planets within it whom they guard over, just like our Solar system is working in harmony, protecting the planets within. After completing their time as a Solar system, next our spirits become a whole galaxy, eventually becoming a whole Universe.

I have included some planetary talisman for you to use. Draw them and keep them with you, or engrave them on to a metal disk and wear it as a necklace.

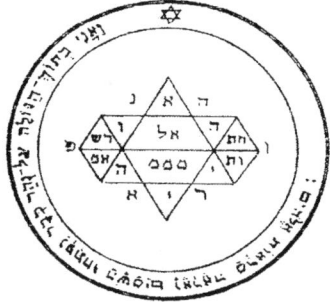

The holder of this Pentacle will be endowed with great visionary powers, and possess the ability to prophesy.

Be poor no more. A defense against poverty.

Fear not if you hold this pentacle true as it will protect you from harm in all walks of life.

True courage is yours. Possess what you aspire to own. And win at feats of physical endeavor.

Making a Sigil

An example of a Sigil.

Sigil magick is a technique of manifestation. The idea is to transfer a wish to your subconscious by using symbols. The idea is that our subconscious understand images and symbols better than anything else, therefore it is best to send it, a symbolic form of our wishes.

- First, write clearly what you desire, example:
  I WANT TO SELL MY HOUSE FOR A GOOD PRICE

- Remove the letters which appears more than once , leaving only the first one:
  IWANTOSELMYHUFRGDPC

- Then remove the vowels:
  WNTSLMYHFRGDPC

- Now you have the material to design a sigil. Use the letters that stand out to form a name for your sigil.
  MYHFR

- Add back a vowel/s to make into a nice name.
  MYHEFUR

- Next you need to arrange the letters into a shape. Make it simple, so that you will be able to remember how it looks within your mind.

I made this one as an example for you. The letters from MYHEFUR are arranged into a pleasing shape that I can remember.

When you have your sigil, you will need to charge it, you have to visualize it. Decoration is welcome to give a magical aspect to it.

Charging the Sigil

There are several ways to do it, one of the most popular is to masturbate and concentrate on the sigil at the moment of climax, another is to meditate on it. Another is to sneeze as you visualise it or sending energy from your chakras. The reason why masturbation is often used is the immense power created during a climax will charge it powerfully. Use your imagination and think of new ways of charging it.

When your sigil is charged, forget about it and carry on with your life. The sigil will take its own time to work, but it will work if you have done it correctly.

Secrets of the Serpent Bloodline - The Unveiling of Profound Esoteric Mysteries

Chapter 9

Wheel of The Year

Vernal Equinox 21st March. Fire/Aries. Ostara.
Ritual of Earth 1st May. Earth/Taurus. Beltane.
Summer Solstice 21st June. Water/Cancer. Litha.
Ritual of Fire 1st August. Fire/Leo. Lughnasadh.
Autumnal Equinox 23rd September. Earth/Virgo. Mabon.
Ritual of Water 31st October. Water/Scorpio. Samhain.
Winter Solstice 21st December. Fire/Sagittarius. Yule.
Ritual of Air 2nd February. Air/Aquarius. Imbolc.

Ceremonies To Try

Venus Invocation

This invocation is to bring the qualities of the Goddess love into yourself. It helps women with confidence to find new friends and/or a lover.

You will need:

A pink candle
Venus Oil
Rose Incense

Start by performing the Banishing Ritual.

In your Temple space anoint your pink candle with Venus oil and light it, also light your rose incense.

You can sit or stand for this, whichever you find more comfortable. Now close your eyes and imagine from above you a glittery pink light, the light starts to swirl all round the room, glittering and sparkling as it goes, it even makes a little tinkly sound as it swirls round. It starts to swirl all round you and you can feel its power entering you. A serene feeling will start to come over you.

When the vision is strong, recite the following invocation:

O Goddess of love and beauty, please fill me with your wisdom and knowledge.
O Goddess of love and beauty, please show me your confidence and power.

Now imagine a beautiful woman before, a confident sexy woman, the type of woman you would love to be. See her clearly and feel love and adoration for her and her strength and beauty.

O Goddess of love and beauty, I love you, your beauty is beyond compare.
O Goddess of love and beauty, I adore you, your strength and power.
O Goddess of love and beauty, All men are attracted to you.
O Goddess of love and beauty, All women adore you as their friend.
O Goddess of love and beauty, I ask you share with me your Divine Being.
O Goddess of love and beauty, I ask that I feel how it is to be you.

When she feels you have shown your respect to her, she will start to walk towards you, and merge with you, lending her power and beauty to you.

Feel the tingles all over you as you feel different now. Feel your posture change and imagine yourself walking into a room full of people and them all looking at you adoringly. Feel confident and powerful with the Goddess energy you have inside you.

When you are ready, leave your Temple, but don't banish, as this will remove her essence from you and defeat the purpose. If after your special night out you do want to banish, then do so, but thank Venus for helping you.

Lost Found Fairy

This ceremony to create a little helper for you, who will assist you when you lose something.

- First make a copy of this sigil of Elfimp.

- Next you will need to find an object or ornament to use in the ceremony. This object will be your lost found fairy, so a little fairy, imp or elf would be perfect, but it can be anything you choose.

- Other items you will need include a green candle and some fast luck oil.

- Start by performing the Banishing Ritual.

- On your centre Altar anoint and place your candle, object and sigil.

- Light the candle and then focusing on the sigil chant over and over the fairy name – Elfimp.

- Imagine light energy coming from your heart chakra and going into the object you have chosen, and within the light energy you can visualise the sigil of Elfimp as you continue chanting and sending energy towards the object. When you feel energy has built up strongly say the words:

    Elfimp you now live in this object here that I can see, when I call your name you will come to help me. What I have lost, you will find, return it to me, hastily. With a rub of your side, you will make it unhide. Forever grateful I will be to thee Elfimp.

- With that start to chant her name again, and chant it faster and faster until you reach a peak and then stop. Imagine all the energy inside your Elfimp object making it glow with magick.

- When you are ready banish again.

- Whenever you lose something you can then pick up your object, rub her side and say:

- *I have lost, Elfimp shall find, return it to me hastily. With a rub of your side, you will make it unhide. Forever grateful I will be to thee Elfimp.*

- Then put her down and leave her to do her work, when the objects turns up be sure to go to Elfimp and thank her. The more you use Elfimp the more powerful she will become over time. Be warned though, if you do not thank her she is less likely to help you next time.

Veritas Ceremony

This beautiful ceremony is to bring truth into your life, as well as the whole world by Invoking Lady Veritas.

What you will need:

- White robe or white clothing
- Athame
- Large Altar in the West (this is your main Altar for this ceremony)
- Sigil, logos, symbols for truth printed out and placed on West Altar
- White Candles for West Altar
- Incense – made from white resins and herbs
- White objects and ornaments
- Anything else that represents truth to you, White feathers etc
- A heat proof bowl
- Offerings – white bread, milk

Start by performing the Banishing Ritual.

Announce the purpose of the ceremony.

Walk to the West and say the invocation.

Veritas Invocation

Lady Veritas, Goddess of truth, daughter of Saturn and the mother of Virtue. Come join us from your hiding place in the bottom of your holy well, O elusive Goddess. Appear to us with your young virgin presence, dressed in white.

We invoke ye O Goddess of Truth, appear from your watery dwelling place.

Veritas, Goddess of the virtue of truthfulness, please fill us with your virtues, which any good King or Queen should possess.

Veritas also known as Aletheia. Alatheia, who art the beginning of great virtue, keep our good-faith from stumbling against rough falsehood.

We invoke ye O Goddess of Truth, come forth and fill us with your wisdom.

Aesop, Fables 531 (from Babrius 126) (trans. Gibbs) (Greek fable C6th B.C.) :
"A man was journeying in the wilderness and he found Veritas [Aletheia, Truth] standing there all alone. He said to her, 'Ancient lady, why do you dwell here in the wilderness, leaving the city behind?' From the great depths of her wisdom, Veritas (Truth) replied, 'Among the people of old, lies were found among only a few, but now they have spread throughout all of human society!'"

Lady Veritas, please bring your truth back to the people, let the truth be known so that we may live in peace and harmony once more, so that lies and deceit have no where to hide.

We invoke ye O Goddess of Truth, come forth and fill us with your knowledge.

Aesop, Fables 530 (from Phaedrus Appendix 5) :
"Prometheus, that potter who gave shape to our new generation, decided one day to sculpt the form of Veritas [Aletheia, Truth], using all his skill so that she would be able to regulate people's behaviour. As he was working, an unexpected summons from mighty Jupiter [Zeus] called him away. Prometheus left cunning Dolus (Trickery) in charge of his workshop, Dolus had recently become one of the god's apprentices. Fired by ambition, Dolus (Trickery) used the time at his disposal to fashion with his sly fingers a figure of the same size and appearance as Veritas [Aletheia, Truth] with identical features.

When he had almost completed the piece, which was truly remarkable, he ran out of clay to use for her feet. The master returned, so Dolus (Trickery) quickly sat down in his seat, quaking with fear. Prometheus was amazed at the similarity of the two statues and wanted it to seem as if all the credit were due to his own skill. Therefore, he put both statues in the kiln and when they had been thoroughly baked, he infused them both with life: sacred Veritas (Truth) walked with measured steps, while her unfinished twin stood stuck in her tracks.

That forgery, that product of subterfuge, thus acquired the name of Mendacium [Pseudologos, Falsehood], and I readily agree with people who say that she has no feet: every once in a while something that is false can start off successfully, but with time Veritas (Truth) is sure to prevail."

O Great Goddess, protect us from Mendacium and Dolus, so that we prevail to the end.

We invoke ye O Goddess of Truth, come forth and fill us with your love.

In our dreams take us through the gate of truth. Let us bask in the glory of the light that truth brings to us.

We invoke ye O Goddess of Truth, come forth and fill us with your light.

Let those with eyes to see the truth, see it.

Let those with ears to hear the truth, hear it.

We invoke ye O Goddess of Truth, come forth and fill us with your ancient ways.

Be carried with us always. Protecting us from deception, protecting us from all falsehood.

We invoke ye O Goddess of Truth, we invoke ye, we invoke ye.

O Great Goddess of Truth we offer these magick herbs as a sacrifice to you, O great Goddess we offer this white bread to nourish the truth, O Great Goddess we fill the room with white candles in your honour. We drink this milk to fill ourselves with your truth. Be forever present within us and outside us, surrounding us, protecting us with your virtues forever more.

(At this point burn some of the incense in your censer, burn a little bread in your heat proof bowl, drink the milk, you can use alternative white drink).

We invoke ye O Goddess of Truth, allow us to feel your presence.

We are your servants, we will strive to always keep pure your virtues in our hearts, yet only hide this virtue when it would damage others to know you.

We invoke ye O Goddess of Truth, Veritas we invoke ye.

Great Lady of Truth, we honour you with all sincerity and joy.

Be Blessed and Blessed Be forever more.

When you are ready depart without banishing.

Liber III

Secrets of the Serpent Bloodline - The Unveiling of Profound Esoteric Mysteries

Part 1
The Mind of a Mystic

From my Magick Diary & Musings

There follows a selection of pieces from my magick diary, musings and later on some blog posts I made. I am including these in the hope that they will help you on your journey. You will be able to see how clues are given to me about my path and will know what to look out for yourself.

21st April 2008

My dream last night was that I was in a big city and I was trying my best to get some people I knew together quickly to escape, because I knew the city was about to blow up. Everywhere was blocked and guarded, they weren't letting people leave. I was climbing up buildings and all kinds. Found my car and we all got in, but then it wouldn't start. Finally it started but as I drove around the city, all the roads out were blocked. I was left driving round and round, knowing that the bomb would go off any moment and we would all be dead. It was really exciting.

9th April 2009

Last night my dream was very strange. I was out walking Tashi when a chocolate Labrador puppy came running out the bushes and following us. It followed us all the way home. When I got home I was upstairs playing with the dog, it got me on the floor then gently squashed my nose shut with it's mouth. I pushed it off me and then started to hear a really strange sound, like a weird alarm, but not very loud. I ran out on to the landing and shouted to my Mum, who I thought was downstairs, because she had been walking the dog with me. I stood shouting 'What's that sound, what's that sound.' But I got no answer. I then could hear someone running up the stairs. I looked and saw it was a dwarf wearing a white chef outfit. I was suddenly really scared because he was running right towards me and I didn't know why he was there and what he was doing. He banged into me and I woke up. I wrote it in my magick diary right away so I could remember it. It was 3.15am. It was very bizarre, lol.

2:40 pm later that day: I just got back from walking Tashi. On the walk I bumped into a guy who was putting a poo bag in the bin at the same time as me. He had a chocolate Labrador puppy with him. He walked all round the walk with me, talking to me and came right back to the door of my house with me.

I can't believe it. It was great playing with Leo, the puppy. He didn't try to stop me breathing though, lol.

When am I going to encounter this dwarf though???

Meaning of Dreams about Dwarf: Dream Interpretation Dictionary - Dwarf

Dwarf

At times people will see dwarfs, midgets, or very small people in their dreams. These images seem to represent, or allude to, the childlike creative powers in the unconscious. You can think of the dwarf as a "worker" in your unconscious. He could represent some childlike condition which has the potential and power to influence your life. Consider the details and the emotional tone in the dream and make an attempt to connect it to a situation in your daily life. The dwarf suggests possibilities for learning and brings to the conscious mind messages from the unconscious.

Dreaming of seeing (or being) a happy and contented dwarf strongly indicates that all your troubles will soon disappear as if by magic. If the dwarf was mean or unhappy, however, beware of false friends. Be very careful of who you confide in.

Note added 1st October 2012: *This about being careful who I confide in, could not be more truthful. I had so many problems with people telling others things I had said about them. It took me a long time to realise that a lot of people can not be trusted, they pretend to be your friend, but back stab you at the soonest possibility. I had to learn the hard way to resist saying anything about others behind their backs, that I would not say to their face. Even though I never did this often, but some people would bug me for an opinion, pretend to be upset or something. Yet when I told them feelings about the person, they ran straight to them and told them causing a lot of unnecessary problems. I only say things I would say to their face, I stick to this fully now. I have given up the need to put a front on for others, to hide my true feelings in order to please them. Now I remove bad people from my life completely and say nothing about them that I would not dare to say to them in person. It is very freeing.*

Sometimes no matter how strongly you dislike or distrust a person, it is better to keep your mouth shut and let the person involved with them make

their own mistakes. It is hard to do, but the person will not thank you for your opinion, they will attack you and you will end up looking like the bad one. They will twist your words and make out you are trying to control them, just because you want to help them. This is also true of people who come to you begging for advice about someone. They already know themselves the person they are involved with is bad news, but they want someone to lie to them and say how wonderful they are. They can not handle the truth, they don't want to accept it and so you become the victim of all their pent up anger and insecurity that they hide. They would rather fool themselves and take the long route to truth, than be told by someone else.

Sometimes it is better to just not get involved with other peoples dramas at all, and makes for a much more peaceful life.

19th June 2009

Last night I was dreaming that I had a bouncy castle in the front garden, but it was slightly broken and flapping about a bit. There were people all over the drive and someone was trying to deliver a parcel, but the gates wouldn't open. It was crazy.

This morning I was doing my workout on the trampet, not really looking where I was bouncing and my foot went through the side, ouch. I broke a spring off because I bounced too close to the edge. Was this something to do with the bouncy castle in my dream???

Then I was in the shower and Tashi barked. He barks when he hears someone outside. I could see a car parked in the little drive behind the gates, but there was no one there, so strange. I quickly got dressed and went downstairs and out the front. The car was still there, but no one to be seen. I then heard someone talking next door, so I walked up the road and saw a woman outside with a big parcel. She saw me and asked if I was from next door, I said yes, so she came walking over with the parcel. It was for me, but the doorbell didn't go off at all, she said she had been ringing for ages, and I was only in the shower for a minute. So maybe this was the warning about the parcel in my dream. The gates did open, but the intercom wasn't working.

If I hadn't had that dream I doubt I would have rushed outside and walked up the road, because I would have just thought the person parked there because it was slightly off the lane and they were only going to be a minute, and I would have missed the parcel.

30th June 2009

Last night my dream was strange.

I was with a group of people and we had just done something and were getting a surprise trip as a reward. I don't know what it was that we had done. We were split into 3 groups, each group getting a different trip. My group were given a trip in a pink plane with 'Strawberry Bottom' wrote on the side. I asked why it was called 'Strawberry Bottom' and was told it was because it flew over strawberry fields.

A girl in my group said she needed a pee and asked if I would go with her to find the loo before leaving on the trip. We walked off into an old building but couldn't find any. Then we saw a sign for some pointing down the corridor. We got to two doors, one female and one male, we open the female door and were surprised to find it was a lift.

We got in and pressed the button that said it would take us to the loo. The girl pointed out to me that the graffiti on the wall of the lift read 'You are doomed.' The lift started to move, but to our surprise it went sideways, not up or down. It shot out the building and above the roads and things below. It was going for ages over a city below. The girl saw a curry take away shop and wanted to get out, so we did and for some reason we were suddenly on bikes.

We left the bikes outside and went into the shop, there was a massive queue inside. The girl said I wonder if they have a loo in here. I said they must have because it is law. So we went walking upstairs and found the funkiest loos I had ever seen, they had leopard print on them, some had zebra print with red lids. Anyway I decided to go into one of the cubicles and at that point I woke up.

I wanted to carry on and go on the plane trip too.

6th September 2009

I was scrying the Aethyrs last night. This is what I experienced.

I was on the back of a white horse with wings. I was taken to a beautiful forest. I touched the bark on the most wonderful big tree. I met Pan, he whispered something in my ear and I went to a library filled with lots and lots of big old books. I open one that just had Omega wrote on it, and looked through the pages, but they were all blank.

7th September 2009

Tonight I did more scrying.

I was flying through air and could see the tops of mountains covered in snow. A falcon was flying past. A woman was in the sky, she had a crown of flowers and flowers in her long flowing hair. Her hair was flowing down to earth and joined a waterfall.

A young couple where holding hands running about through a meadow by the waterfall. She was wearing a long white dress and he was wearing a very old fashioned soldier uniform.

I then went into the river and under water and out to sea. I saw a mermaid swim past and then a dolphin came up to me and whispered in my ear.

9th September 2009

Last night I was falling asleep a word appeared to me. I said it out loud and it spelt out in my mind.

The word was Otra. I went online to find out what it was, turns out it is a river in Norway. Maybe I will be living by it some day?

I would definitely learn Norwegian then.

By the way, I have never before heard of this river, unless it happens to be the one I went on in the cruise ship through the Fjords? I have no idea, might of heard it mentioned on the ship. But last night it just came to me out of the blue.

It also means Taro or Rota, so is very powerful word.

16th September 2009

What a lovely surprise this morning. A package arrived and when I opened it was a course to learn Norwegian. I am so delighted with it, wow, what a nice surprise. Now I know why I was given the word Otra, a sign I should be learning Norwegian, as I have always loved the country and would love to live there.

27th September 2009

Last night when scrying the aethyrs TEX.

I asked for guidance from DOZIAAL.

A man appeared, he looked like a king. He was wearing a long sky blue robe and a round hat to match with point on top and white fur and jewels round it. His robe had white fur with black dots on it down the front. He was white and had black hair and black eyes, a short beard and a tash.

I tested him to make sure he was OK and he passed the test. He took me over a beautiful landscape and pointed out an otter with an apple in it's mouth. I asked to learn some things from him. He open up a big book and showed me a pentagram, a dragon and a symbol. They were all drawn black on a white sheet.

I then went down to the ground by a tree where I saw a figure, the person turned round and they had a black burnt horrible face. I asked who they were and they laughed at me and said 'the devil' I tested them, and they disappeared.

I was a little freaked out by that, and wanted to draw the symbol so I would remember it, so I asked to leave at that point.

I then looked up some things in 777 and found I was in 32.

Scrying the aethyrs can be dangerous to your mental health if you are not ready for it.

One night I was trying a more advance aethyr than I was ready for, nothing was happening, then suddenly a face appeared right before me, it had black eyes, completely black, no white of eyes nothing, just black. it freaked me out so much that I left and didn't try again for a while, but next time I went back down a level.

Now I am researching the symbol I was shown last night.

Note 3rd October 2012: *The symbol I saw turned out to be the sigil for my Higher Self. I didn't find out until a while after.*

28th October 2009

Tonight I went back to the same aethyr to see if I could get another look at the OMEGA book, but a little man was there guarding it and he wouldn't let me see.

I was then put on a box with a massive lotus on top, I was stood in the middle of it with light shining all round me. Surrounding the box I was on, there were 4 black robed figures whose faces I couldn't see. They were on each quarter forming a circle round me.

Then the lotus started to open up and I fell inside and was falling for ages. At the bottom was a very strange land with blue and green people there. It was very strange.

22nd January 2010

The fundamental difference between the ego being our source of power or our spirit, is the spirit has no physical appearance, no face to see in the mirror, no hair to comb, nothing to groom. It is everything and it is nothing, it is the beginning of everything and the end, alpha omega. As your physical body grows old your ego that is attached to it, as your source of power, becomes weaker. To awaken is to know you are not the person who sits typing on a computer or watching TV, running a company, being prime minister, taking over the world, whatever... The power is within, as above and below. No amount of Earthly ego can last forever, it is a fruitless battle, a game in a virtual reality, nothing is real, everything is illusion (not in a holographic universe way, and you won't know what I mean until you experience it yourself). Once you have realised this, your heart is exposed to the beauty of the kisses from the divine light and illumination takes place. You are then free to utter your secret word that will change the universe forever.

27th January 2010

Everyday is a good day, some days it is hard to remember that.

Last night I didn't get hardly any sleep because I woke up coughing up acid. OOoooh it hurt, my whole throat and mouth burning and every time I tried to take something for it I was sick. I was in total agony. I tried to sleep sitting up, as it was impossible to lie down. I woke up this afternoon feeling so horrible and now coughing up blood, looks like the acid did some damage.

I walked Tashi and got some breakfast/lunch and started my computer. Had to restart it because it crashed. When I got on I checked all the forums and facebook. Saw something someone posted that upset me. I am not going to think about it, feel too horrible and ill to think about it. I need to stop these people with their stupid dramas effecting my life. I can not be around people who try their best to make me feel bad or shock me in some way. Or worse still try to make me feel sorry for them. Can't do it anymore. I am just going to ignore this crap from now on.

I was very happy alone when I had all the time in the world to do the great work. I came back and started OIO because I was told to do so. It is a plan that has been waiting to happen for a very long time and it was meant to be. However running it is difficult, time consuming and all goes to help me realise why I loved being on my own so much.

When people whinge on and on about wanting a relationship, all I see is a weak willed and minded person, someone who isn't happy on their own and feels the need to be with someone else, and often give up lots to live this other persons life. This is not going to make YOU happy though. You can only be happy if you live by your own will, no one else's.

It can be very infuriating because I used to be just like that years ago. I used to jump from one bf to another, even if I didn't fancy them, I just didn't want to be on my own. How pathetic I used to be. Unfortunately every man who meets me now thinks I am some how up for it, because I am single or try to get me to marry them. Women are even worse, scared to death I might steal their man away or think there is something wrong with me because I am not married off and have loads of kids.

What upsets me most is, I try my best to help others see their potential and teach them everything I know, all the time knowing they could walk away and slide backwards at any time, meeting a new partner who takes them away from the work, or get a new job that takes up too much time. I guess these are risks I have to take. I have never failed in anything I have done that I really wanted to do. No doubt I will encounter a lot of people who are just not ready. One winner will be worth all the past failures though, so I will carry on.

Of course it would be much easier for me to say fuck the lot of you, unfortunately this is my last task here, so you are stuck with me for now.

It is good day today, honest.

It wasn't meant to anyone personally, just a build up of things I needed to get rid of. Because I was so ill and tired it just all came out. You know I love you all and can learn as much from you as you can learn from me, we help out each other. It is only times when I feel my efforts on someone who should be a great Magickian, are thrown to the side for things that are sent to test us, and yes it is hard to spot them yourself and I was trapped by some for a long time. I am happy to be free and the only thing that seems to get me upset and frustrated these days are those who are sent to drag us all down with them, call them daemons, psychic vampires, whatever, they are only here to try and throw us off our focus of the great work.

You all deserve to do the great work, you started it for a reason. Whatever reason, you are here now and that is the important thing. Don't let others force you from your path though, it is the worse thing you can ever do.

It is your right to become a God/dess, and you have to ask why would anyone who cares about you want you to stop it? They wouldn't.

This is something I wrote about my own journey, it might not make sense to you now, it will though:

Faced the black blacker than blackest black,
Rotted, decomposed, putrefaction.
Demons run amok, the raven calls.
Death came and went,
Visions filling my mind,
Nightmares stealing my dreams,
Confusion filling my days.
Dark, darker, oh despair.
Trying to escape, when there is nothing to escape from,
One can not escape from oneself.
White light came, it was so bright it felt so right,
Walk forwards and don't look back.
What is light when black is all?
Distractions, distractions, how distracting they are.
Water flows, it falls freely and eases the way.
The darkest night lit up by the rising Sun.
The Morning Star has appeared and all is calm.
Red and White merging now, becoming one,
Higher than the highest heaven,
Lower than the lowest below.
Inside the illusion of time the stone appears,
My reward for getting through.

2nd February 2010

Last nights ceremony was so very special.

I am sure all who were there could feel the powerful wonderful energies we raised.

We nipped to a shop on the way home and picked up some sushi and things for a midnight feast. Then the others left and I went straight to bed.

I went on the most amazing trip to Turkey, walking along the seafront and looking in the shops. I have never been to Turkey before, I knew I was there though, always wanted to go. It was fantastic and I do think it was to do with the ceremony we did.

Note 1st October 2012: *This was an amazing experience and the more someone gets into magick the more experiences like this they can have themselves.*

15th February 2010

I had this dream that I was staying at a luxury hotel, well it was on a cruise ship, and as walking round I heard a commotion and walked over to a crowd of people. They were stood round in a circle and in the middle a little furry white mole was on the floor, and they were kicking it and stuff.

I ran and picked it up and told everyone to stop it. They told me it is a useless creature and it is blind and no use to anyone. I told them that even though he is blind and struggles about in this environment, in his own environment he is perfect because he has everything he needs and doesn't need to be able to see underground anyway.

I walked away carrying the lovely little creature. I promised him I would get him back to somewhere safe for him soon, and meanwhile I would look after him.

All I remember then is trying to go into the cinema, and had to try and hide him under my coat so he could come with me, he kept moving about and tickling me though, and everyone wondered why I was giggling.

To dream of moles, indicates secret enemies. To dream of catching a mole, you will overcome any opposition and rise to prominence.

Note 1st October 2012: *This turns out to be true as I was surrounded at the time by people who were pretending to be my friend, but couldn't wait to back stab me and they did. They wanted to ruin me and were spreading rumours about me and our Order, but I removed them from my life and anyone associated with them and got on with my work and things got better and better after that. Of course since then more haters and back stabbers appeared, but each time I some what ruthlessly and thoroughly removed all trace of them from my life and moved on. I will not be brought down by self pity monsters, energy vampires and envious nasty people. As far as I was concerned they were just keeping me from the most important thing in my life, The Great Work.*

Hidden meanings: When something is hidden well, disguised, seen as something that it isn't, this can cause the most alarm of all. It can brew up hatred, fear, jealousy and all manner of things.

A long time ago (over 7 years) I hid a very important message somewhere, and released it free on to the world. Since then I have not heard the end of it. Destiny has a way of doing good that most of the time isn't even wanted, and it is hid from us, protested against and demonised.

Don't listen to others that you no longer want to hear, listen to your own inner voice and learn from it.

13th March 2010

At a group Order ritual we decided to scry an aethyr first and this is what I saw:

First I was flying through treetops and then willed myself to go downwards. First I saw a pentagram, then a snake which quickly disappeared. I then saw my King guide who I asked to show me something in his book like he has done before. As he opened the book the Sun raised up out of it and went up into to sky. I asked to see some more things. He got a bit annoyed and pulled the Sun down from the sky and put it before me. I didn't know why he kept doing this, as I wanted to see more. He got more annoyed then called a man over who grabbed the Sun and put it up in the sky, then nailed it there. At this point I got the message, he wanted me to look at the 'Sun' tarot card, which I did.

All this happened very quickly, I find it always does when I am scrying the TEX aethyr now, my guide wants me to explore the others, yet at open rituals I always start on TEX, for the others there.

2nd April 2010

Meditating this morning I was transported to some kind of group where a class was taking place. A tall figure wearing a white robe was giving the class and I couldn't make out the figure very well because I was sat at the back of a group of people.

I tried to listen to the speaker and then suddenly, as if the group sensed my presence, as they looked forward towards the speaker they pointed backwards over their shoulders with their thumbs to me and they all said in unison *'She was born different to us, she is not one of us.'*

They then all turned to look at me, and at that point the scene dissolved and I was at first left thinking, well tell me something I don't know. I was born at home and not in a hospital, and everyone I ever asked about this always said they had been born at a hospital. Strange I should think this first. Then I thought well I always knew all my life I was different to other people, yet I also believe that everyone else thinks this too, and the divide we put between others is so our individually can shine. Yet there are those who I see who never all their life seem to have even thought about this. Some live unaware of who or what they are.

We are all individual, yet all connected and for many this can seem very confusing, because they say 'How can something different, be the same?' or similar and yes that is the difference, we can all be part of the same thing, yet be completely different. There is no need to try and see yourself in others, for they are not you, they are different, yet the same and only when you actually experience this can you truly understand what is meant by it.

I needed to get this down, as I know it might sound silly, yet it does make sense.

I have always been aware that I am trapped here, all my life and I sense the whole of me or can choose to ignore it. Yet others need to be told to sense things in order for them to sense it. If you don't believe me think for a moment about your right foot, is it cold or hot? Is it in a sock or shoe? Are you normally aware of your foot and what your foot or even hand does automatically?

Try for a day to be aware of one part of your body at all times, as you do other things.

Note added 17th September 2010: When I had this dream back then I searched for ages for a meaning to the thumbs I saw. Tonight I found this:

"The thumb represents the 'ether' energy or 'spirit'. In the Occult Doctrines, this Divine Breath, Spirit, ensouls the dust of the Four Physical Elements (which modern science describes as the Four States of Matter - plasma, gas, liquid, and solid; which are bound together by the Four Forces of Nature - strong, weak, electromagnetic, and gravity). These states were identified by the early Alchemists as Fire, Water, Air, and Earth, abstract concepts which form the matrix upon which the layers of existence and reality are woven, like cloth on a loom. The symbology of the Breath of Life, Spirit, ensouled in the dust of the Four Elements was said to be exemplified by the human hand, with the thumb representing Spirit, and the other digits representing the Elements. Another cognate symbol is the ancient Pentagram, the five-pointed star, with each point signifying Spirit, Earth, Water, Air, and Fire. The Egyptians called this symbol Khabs, which translates as both Star and God. As it is written in Liber AL vel Legis, the threefold Book of Law: "Every man and every woman is a star."

Remember 'spirit' was the word for OIO this past 6 months, and the new one will be found soon at the ritual.

Of course the pentagram represents Venus, the elements version is taught during someone's first degree normally, and later they learn more about why it is God, it is Venus, the Goddess, not God.

4th April 2010

During my meditation I got the following:

The answer is the question.

Frozen oil.

Zero Of Nil is the answer in the question. Anagram of the words frozen oil that I was given.

I was also shown the Hebrew letter aleph.

Zero is the tarot card Kether-Chokmah on the tree of life.

Aleph = Ox Air Fool/Swords/Princes Kether-Chokmah.

All fits.

If we were to compare OIO to the A.'.A.'. system the OIO is no longer seen over by a Magister Templi, I am now Magus. Although I have been for a while, and I am now leaving Chokmah for Kether.

12th April 2010

I wanted to start at the beginning again because I enjoyed my trip through the aethyrs so much the first time round.

I keep doing TEX at rituals with others, so tonight I did RII. Disappointed really because I think the angels are getting fed up of me keep going back.

At first I saw a white dove fly past, then a King appeared. He had blonde curly hair and was wearing a gold crown and gold clothing.

I asked to learn something from him, he looked annoyed and grabbed my hand and started flying down towards a building. I could see his white wings at this point.

We flew down and went into the building which was a temple with black and white tiled floor and an altar in the middle with a blue lamp on it.

We had come in one of the doors, and there were 3 other doors in the room. The door straight facing me, which to me seemed to be the East, had the hanged man tarot card in it.

I walked forward towards the door and walked through, on the other side there were just hills and trees as far as I could see.

I walked back into the building and asked the King to teach me something. He looked annoyed again and pointed to the hanged man tarot card. I tried to walk through that door again, couldn't see anything though so got fed up and left.

I looked up some things about the hanged man card, as this seemed to be what he was trying to get me to notice.

19th April 2010

Last night my astral trip was to a seaside where I was flying over the sea. I then landed in the sea and went swimming under water.

In the morning as I meditated it came to me that I need some fire in my life, as I am always so involved with water. Always swimming in my astral trips, and also flying, so very connected with air. I have also been working on the ritual earth ceremony so feel very connected with earth, yet I am missing fire.

So after my shower I invoked fire, and today has been really good and productive. I got all kinds done for work, had three beautiful walks with Tashi. Made some rye bread, made some oil of Abramelin and put it all over the new staff I am making. The house smells strongly of it now.

Then after all that, I even had time to go in my relaxing, sparkly clean hot tub. It was well worth all the work cleaning it.

I will banish fire before going to bed and thank the great southern red salamander for his help today.

21st April 2010

I had a vision and wanted to get it down here as soon as possible, because often when I have visions like this, they actually happen.

When in these dreams or visions I am inside someone who is experiencing what is going on. I am not me, I am them.

I was in a what seemed to be a university setting up a stall for craft market. Others in the room where setting up their stalls too. I could see each item as I put it out on the stall, very pretty things and some toys and things.

I made a bit of money from the market and all the stall holders were packing away. Most of them were young, I would say all were below about 40.

We had moved all the tables and chairs to the side of the room, and were preparing to leave, when lots of men came in the room with black boiler suits on, balaclavas and carrying guns. The room was suddenly dark as some black shutters fell across the exits. Some lights then flickered and came on.

When the lights came on the men were stood in a circle in the middle, their guns pointing out towards the crowd. Everyone was screaming and running to take cover round the sides of the room, however there was no escape from the room.

The men told everyone to shut up and then pointed to people at the sides and told them to come up to the middle. With guns pointing at them, they had no choice. They were then one by one given a gun and told to shoot someone at the side in the arm. One by one people were called up to shoot someone in the room in the arm.

The guy next to me got shot and I tried to help him, I got blood on my hands and decided to run some on my arm and put my hand over as if I had been shot, thinking this would stop someone shooting me. It worked, and when it was my time to go to the middle, I had no choice other than to shoot at one of the others.

I felt traumatised and horrible, yet I had no choice with a gun to my head.

The men told us that if any police arrived they would set off the bomb they had which would blow up the entire building and everyone in it. If anyone tried to escape they would also blow it up.

With what they had just made us do, we all believe every word they said.

The shootings were still going on at this point and I was really worried they would hit me, so I got up and asked if I could go to the loo.

They agreed, but said if I tried to escape I knew what would happen.

I was let out in a corridor, the whole building had been locked down, I could hear cries and screams coming from all over it and rushed towards the toilets. When I got there I was alone, and I climbed up to a small window and got out, and ran as fast as I could to some houses nearby.

I rang the bell at a few houses, I needed to get out of sight, no one came to the door. I didn't know what to do. I wasn't going to ring the police and risk the building being blown up, and just hoped they hadn't noticed I had gone.

I ran about, trying to get further away, no one was around. Then finally I saw a dark skinned man who looked like a workman. I ran over to him crying. He hugged me and told me he would get me away.

I got in his van and he drove me home, at home my parents were there (not my parents, the girls parents) and they hugged me and said I should ring the police. I knew it was too dangerous and didn't know what to do. I was also worried they would come and find me. The guy who I came with told me he would take me to hide away for a while.

At that point I woke up.

22nd April 2010

όμορφη φτερό – Today I have such an amazing revelation. I found out the name of my Higher Self, and the sigil for it. I am so happy.

24th April 2010

Tonight I did the next aethyr BAG.

I was met by a knight on a black horse. He told me to get on the horse. We went to a tree where a woman lay in the roots asleep. She had long gold hair and a long golden dress, she was covered in flowers. I wanted to wake her but was suddenly shot upwards into space. It was all black, then bright white. As I moved backwards I noticed the white was a ball of light that was being held up by a large knight, who was stood on Earth.

I then started to move down into blue skies and saw a large fluffy white cloud with a beautiful golden throne on it, two children, a boy and a girl sat before it and a golden crown floated about above the throne.

The image changed to a pyramid with a bright light at the top, the pyramid crumbled to reveal a knight, who walked forwards towards me carrying a sword with a diamond at the top of the handle. He handed it to me.

I asked to be shown something, and was given the number 43 and 27 and a symbol that looked a bit like a swastika with longer arms and the bits on the end pointed inwards more.

Symbol meaning: An ancient swastika which symbolised the four winds or directions and their corresponding spirits. It was also a "fire and sun symbol occurring initially in Asia and later among the Germanic tribes," according to The Herder Symbol Dictionary. "The cross inscribed in a circle mediates between the square and the circle," emphasizing the "joining of heaven and earth.... and "the perfected human being."

Then an oriental man appeared with black eyes, I thought he was a daemon so vibrated BAG and threw a pentagram at him, he stayed.

At that point the images faded.

25th April 2010

People seem to think once you get to a certain level of enlightenment, suddenly all suffering disappears. If only that were true.

It is true that it becomes a lot less, yet as with anyone else, still most of the time we are trapped here in our earthly bodies, which does involve pain.

I am going through a major psoriasis flare up at the moment, after having a relatively long break from it. Yes some signs have been still there, yet it had been pain free for some time. Now however I am in agony. It is constantly stinging, burning and bleeding. I can not wear a bra, so have resigned myself to sitting in my nightie and not moving from the house the past few days.

My partner (name removed as now ex) is here so I am lucky he is here to walk the dog, however he goes back to London tomorrow, so I am just hoping I am well enough tomorrow to be able to get up and about so I can at least take Tashi out.

It is very easy to sit and feel sorry for myself at times like this, very easy indeed. I look at some others and wonder why they are always so healthy and don't have painful conditions like mine. I am not jealous, just upset that others seem to be so pain free, when I have to suffer so much. I have got used to the physical problems of having psoratic arthritis mostly. In that I know to never try to pick up a pan without using both hands, or attempt to lift a kettle that is full. I know that every step I take when I walk will always be painful to my achilles heels and I can mostly live with it. Only very odd occasions does the pain get so bad that I can't walk at all.

However, when I get a flare up on my skin, the pain is unbearable. I don't know what to do with myself. So fed up of it, and this is when I am eating a diet that is supposed to get rid of it, no idea how bad it would be on a normal diet.

Everyone has things that make them suffer, I know this, I also know how lucky I am in so many ways. So please forgive me for having a moan.

Later that evening:

I tried invoking Alan Chapman's and Duncan's Tempe.

I banished in my temple, then I put some frankincense on the coal. I had Tempe's sigil on the altar and I then asked for his presence.

I wanted to meditate, though no matter what I did I could not, because of the pain I am in at the moment, I just couldn't get comfy on the floor.

I decided to ask some questions with tarot instead.

I asked for some kind of sign about how I am doing towards my quest for enlightenment.

I then did a basic three card influences from the past, present and future.

I have removed the results as they only apply to me.

26th April 2010

I am noticing things I have been doing lots of research on 333.

I was frustrated to find out my birthday comes to 533, or 11.

How annoying I thought, it should be 333.

I then remembered something. My car has the reg 533.

Wow.

And 11 is the magick number.

333 is very magickal, I see it all the time. I wake up at 3:33 or look at a clock and it is 3:33. Some times 11:11. Which is strange because I was born at 11:11.

I am not the only one seeing it though, it is to do with your HGA contacting you.

30th April 2010

Today saw someone's online profile, and it was full of quotes by others. Yet nothing at all by him.

I asked him: Do you live in others quotes, or do you have any of your own?

Last night as I was falling asleep I suddenly said Mena, never heard that word before. So had looked it up.

Last time this happened it was the word Otra, which turned out to be Taro or Rota, or Otra being a Lake in Norway. I love Norway, however had never heard of this lake. A few days later a CD course in Norwegian turned up at my house, it was a gift from someone.

So anyway, been looking up what Mena means.

Dutch meaning: Strength or strong

German meaning: Strength

Hindu meaning: Mother of Menaka

Indian meaning: Mother Goddess

Sanskrit meaning: Knowledgeable

Anagrams:

Mane
Amen
Name
Mean

Qaballah

mena is: 15

amen 15
battle 15
feast 15
lamp 15
Mars 15
seed 15
self 15
slaves 15
wand 15
war 15

Scryed ZAA

A white rose, a beautiful woman dressed in white behind it. She showed me an 8 pointed star.

To my right an old woman dressed in black appeared. I greeted her and asked her to teach me. She was holding a baby which she threw to me, when I looked at it, it was dead.

She made a man appear in a silver suit, with black hair. The full moon behind him. He took my hand and I danced with him. The old woman said 'You will never be alone' Then the scene faded to black.

3rd May 2010

Dream:
I went shopping and bought the most wonderful trousers ever, they looked nice and were really comfortable too. I never have dreams about buying things, so I thought this was unusual.

Next I went to watch a show, in some kind of hall. It was a show by the Eastern Star, the Freemason's female group. As I got there though, I went to a changing room and took my new trousers off and hung them up, and put on some old trousers. I wanted to save them for a special occasion.

I watched the show, and it was very funny, middle aged women dancing about in silly outfits and stuff.

I then went back to the changing room only to find my new trousers had gone. Some cheeky sod had stolen them. I went to complain to someone who was in charge. I got told there was nothing they could do. I got angry and said that wasn't good enough. Eventually the woman offered to pay for them and I agreed. She gave me £100, and I didn't tell her that they were only £40. I felt so upset because I knew they had been the last pair and wouldn't be able to replace them. I also thought, well they are the Freemasons, they con enough money out of people, so won't miss it.

After that my friend told me to walk through a shop there, that was set up like a beautiful wonderland. So I did, however on the way out a man appeared before me and told me that I had been stealing. I told him I hadn't, yet he wouldn't listen, so I ran away.

There then followed a strange thing, because this guy would not leave me alone, he followed me everywhere. Across seas through mountains, everywhere. Until a guy, I don't know who, just someone who cared about me, had a fight with him, with swords in the sea. Me and some others were escaping out of the sea and up the hill towards a wooden house, and left this guy fighting him. He chopped off the hands and feet of the guy who was on my side, although eventually my guy managed to kill the other one.

When I saw this guy trying to get up the hill with no hands and feet, I just thought he might as well be dead now, and killed him (yes I know, insane).

Next me and a few others I happened to be with, who I have no idea who they were, were rescued by helicopter.

Next I was loading up a van with plants with a friend and we had some rubbish to get rid off, he wanted to just leave it there, yet I wanted it thrown away correctly and so I said I would walk up to the bin.

I was then in my white magick robe, with my staff and the rubbish, walking up a hill to get to a bin at the top. I finally got there and threw the rubbish in. My mobile phone started to ring, it was a friend of mine. He told me that he wanted to talk to me, because what I had said to him about something had inspired him and he wanted to know more. I was shocked and just kept saying, but you are Muslim, nothing I can say to you will convince you to leave that behind.

I then woke up.

Wow what a strange silly dream.

7th May 2010

I was visited by an elderly male spirit last night, He kept saying to me 'Feed the fire, feed the fire.' I then saw him leaning over to throw some wood into a large wood burner.

I had no idea what his message means, but as soon as I got up I googled it, and found this song, which I had never heard before.

FEED THE FIRE by Steppenwolf

The words are fantastic, but because of copyright issues I won't put them here.

Feed the fire is: 64

Do what thou wilt: 64

Note 27th March 2013: This means so much to me now, it all makes sense, it really does.

5th June 2010

I have known about colloidal silver for ages now, and kept forgetting about it because of other things coming up. The other day I decided to order some online and I waiting for it to arrive. I decided it was worth a try putting some on my psoriasis and seeing if it goes. If it works I will start making some myself.

Last night when I went to bed I was in a lot of pain with my psoriasis again, and it was very uncomfortable. As I slept I visited a strange place up on the moors and met an old woman, she was kind and caring and I seemed to feel a lot calmer after meeting her.

I then noticed my psoriasis was hurting again, in my dream, and I imagined my colloidal silver had arrived and I sprayed it on to my sore skin. I felt an instance effect, it seemed to cool and sooth it.

When I woke up, I looked at my patches and they were less red and sore, almost as if the colloidal silver had worked on my physical body, even in the astral.

It just goes to show how powerful our minds are.

8th June 2010

Close the curtains to your negativity, positivity can break all your illusions with just one smile.

8th August 2010

Scryed aethyr DES.

I was floating through treetops, then a black knight appeared. I could not see his face, there were just lights where his eyes were.

I asked who he was and he said ZANZARAH.

Behind him I could see a beautiful woman framed in a mirror. She had long red hair and was wearing a deep red dress, she looked like a pre Raphaelite painting. She had on a golden crown.

She pointed one hand down towards the floor, and in the ground flowers and plants started to bloom, she pointed upwards and white doves flew into the sky.

I wanted to walk over to her, the knight pushed me back. I tried to push back but he was stronger than me. He was carrying a long black lance and kept putting it before when I tried to pass.

I then remembered the sword I was given another time by a silver knight. I grabbed it and started to fight with the black knight. After a long battle I finally won and he fell to the ground.

I walked forwards towards the mirror, I stepped inside and embraced the woman. My heart was filled with love and peace and happiness. She took me into a beautiful garden and I didn't need to ask her anything, and I didn't need to know anything, because it was all perfect.

I was then disturbed by a loud noise and brought back here.

10th September 2010

Invoked HGA - I asked if there were any Spiritual Hierarchy, Great White Brotherhood, Ascended Masters?

I have been worried about this 'New Age' agenda that is being pushed for 2012, and the stuff Alice Bailey talks about is very scary and I can not believe people fall for this shit. Hopefully enough people will realise it is all lies and not let them get away with it.

Anyway I got the Hierophant and looked it up and it says:

Offer thyself virgin to the knowledge and conversation of thine Holy Guardian Angel. All else is a snare.

Be thou athlete with the eight limbs of Yoga; for without these thou are not disciplined for any fight.

Wow amazing. I do have contact with my HGA, but I have been backing off doing my Yoga because of lack of energy. Now my iron reserves are back up, I will be back on to it.

2nd November 2010

I reject all books, all myths, all dogma, all rules, all lectures, all gurus, all rituals, all mantras, all laws, all prayers.

The only truth is within me, and the only truth there is, is love. I don't need anyone or anything else to tell me what to think and feel. I know intuitively right from wrong.

I know that the law of attraction is a lie. I know that a child born in a war zone did not deserve to be born there and deserve a life of misery. That child had no choice. I know that there are people who justify war and murder with these bullshit theories about law of attraction realities and they kill their hearts to the truth. They justify suffering, pain and lies about our true spirit with religions based on lies.

The ultimate evil is to accept the world as it is now, as normal and right.

To connect to our spirit, is to forget everything anyone else has ever told us to believe, and remember our connection to ourselves and our own hearts. Which gives us the ultimate truth, that if we love, we will escape all illusions, all mind control and know with our own instincts and intuition right from wrong. We need to remember who we are. We can only ever know who we are, by looking inside.

We are good enough, not one of us isn't good enough. We are all capable of connecting to our true spirit. We are all capable of knowing right from wrong, and we don't need what anyone else tells us, to know it, it is inside.

If you remember this, you won't be trapped by any idols, symbols or illusions. You will see through it all. You won't need to try and fix others, you will love them as they are. Your ego will stop telling you one moment you aren't good enough and the next that you are better than someone else. We are all on a journey to escape an illusion so big, it is very hard to see through it, but believe in yourself and you will.

Most important thing you can do, is to remember to love yourself, not in an ego way, just in a way of knowing that you trust yourself and your intuition.

The most horrible thing you can do to yourself is kill your emotions and desires. Love is the strongest desire and it is the most important thing you can ever know or feel, or experience.

11th November 2010

Last night a word came to me and it was Arabus.

I instantly tried it backwards as well, as always and that is Subara, one letter away from a car which is nothing to do with it. However Subara does sound like it could be the name for some kind of underground city. I found nothing for it in google though.

I focused on Arabus and found a site about Arab-US media, run by the Aspen Institute. I have definitely heard of this group before in relation to the NWO agenda.

They sum it all up nicely themselves.. 'The Aspen Institute mission is twofold: to foster values-based leadership, encouraging individuals to reflect on the ideals and ideas that define a good society, and to provide a neutral and balanced venue for discussing and acting on critical issues.'

Well it is strange I got led back to it like that. So I am just posting this here to remind me to look into it more.

I found out a long time ago, all these things are connected.

Anything at all that talks about anyone being a lightworker etc, is all controlled by them. All religions, anything spiritual, all run by them.

On a basic level the trick is to get us to think we are not our bodies, and that if we die we will ascend. The same old rubbish put out by all cults and religions for generations. And now the new age thing is taking in most of those who are waking up to the con.

When someone thinks the world and this life isn't important, because something much better is yet to come, they just sit back and let things happen. And they let thousands of people be murdered and even give their own life up in the fighting.

30th November 2010

Just making a quick record of my dream, not from last night, but the night before 29th Nov 2010.

I was staying in a hotel in a seaside town and sat on the beach when suddenly massive waves starting coming towards us.

Everyone was screaming and running away. I was running away and trying to get back to my hotel, I was trying to get a taxi, or find my friends car, but it was broken. Then she found another car to use, an old banger VW with no roof on, but at least it went. It was like we knew the waves were about to get much worse, and I had to get back to the hotel to find someone. Anyway I did get back to the hotel, before the biggest waves got there, but the whole town was destroyed and lots of people died. I then woke up.

Note added 15th March 2011: Japan.

10th February 2011

I took some photos on my mobile phone the other day, and I liked some of them enough to want to get them from my mobile and upload one as my new photo on Facebook.

Only problem was I couldn't get the blue tooth working on my laptop and when I plugged it in using USB it didn't work.

I then remembered that I have somewhere a little black converter thingy that I could put my tiny phone card into and use the slot on my office pc. My office is a complete mess, stuff all over the place and I wondered how on earth I would be able to find that little black thing in there. But I thought to myself, tomorrow I will look for it.

I walked into my office and sitting on top of my keyboard was a plastic packet. Inside there was a scandisk thing to plug into USB, an adapter for mini cards and a spare mini card.

I couldn't believe it. Wow. My magick is working very well indeed. I opened the packet, took the card out my mobile, put in the adapter and into my pc and there you go. I got all the photos off no problem.

I have no idea how that packet got on top of my keyboard, no one has been in my office now for ages.

16th February 2011

Thelemites seem to think OIO is a copy of OTO and that Liber OIO is a copy of Liber Oz.

I worked in the Thelemic current and some of it is wonderful, but it is missing one very important thing - BALANCE.

It is all Solar worship/cock worship and there is no getting away from this fact. Crowley knew the new aeon would be about balance, but Thelema does nothing to bring this about. That is why it never sat right with me. It is the same old repackaged Sun worship religion like all the mainstream ones.

When someone gets to MT in A.'.A.'. they set up their own Order, only most carry it on in the Thelemic current and nothing ever changes.

My word came to me, and it was THEOLA, Crowley's was THELEMA. I didn't sit there thinking, oh I must choose a word that starts with 'THE' to make it similar to THElema.

I didn't know what the word was, then found it meant 'Divine' in Greek and so you could say the OIO word is 'Divine'. And Thelema's word is 'Will' it does not mean that any magick current that mentions Will or Divine are suddenly copying from one another.

Ordo Infinitus Orbis means the Order of the infinite circle. This is the cycle of life, the most natural thing - birth, life, death, rebirth. Again I didn't sit there thinking of a name of an Order to make it sounds similar to OTO. OiO has 2 eyes, and then nose in the middle with the 3rd eye as the dot above the nose. Which is emphasised in the OIO sigil. The OIO trinity sigil is traced on the 3rd eye with blessed water during rituals.

Liber means book, in Occult Orders when you write a book or document you call it 'Liber' whatever.

Liber OIO is the main body of thought or egregore of the OIO, hence Liber OIO. It is OIO's version of Liber Oz, it is not intended to be the same as that. Some parts look similar, but are in the Divine current, rather than the Thelemic one. There are good things in Liber Oz and if I was working in Thelemic current I would still want to make changes to it, because again it isn't balanced.

Thelema only talks about men and only uses women as altars in the rituals.

The lady of Thelema is Babalon, which actually is the Catholic church, not the Divine feminine at all in anyway.

Anyone who thinks Thelema is a balanced religion is misguided. Anyone who thinks OIO has anything to do with the Thelemic current is very much mistaken. All OIO rituals are balanced and all work on balancing the Magickian, who can in turn help balance the world around them.

My words are like a dagger into the heart of the unbalanced Simples, as they put so much belief into their religions and dogma. Maybe they are happy in an unbalanced world, and don't want change. They grasp and cling to the past in a desperate attempt to keep strong powerful women and balanced men oppressed. Sorry guys and gals, your time is up, now is the time for balance and equality, and it is coming whether you like it or not.

The future is purple - a perfect balance between red and blue. fire and water. The steam shall rise.

17th February 2011

I decided to change my motto. I only used Theola because it was the word I was given when I got to MT, and it was for the current. I just decided to also use it as my motto. However, people are getting the wrong idea and are thinking that because it is my motto, it also means it is me.

My new motto is pronounced omorfo ftero, it is Όμορφη Φτερό.

12th April 2011

When you refuse to conform you are attacked. They have been programmed to attack anyone who isn't conforming to the rules they are programmed to follow. They have been trained so well that they police themselves. They won't allow anyone to be different, or do their own thing because they won't allow themselves too... because they are too busy conforming to a set of rules someone has set down for them... and they don't know any different because it has always been like this.

So that is what happens when you refuse to conform.

17th April 2011

My birth number is 533.

supreme being in Jewish Gematria Equals: 533

lol

30th April 2011

Last night I had a dream that I was in my bed sleeping and a black robed figure leaned over me, and every time I tried to take a breathe, it sucked the air from me, so that I couldn't breathe. I struggled to breathe for a while, then gave in and died. When I was dead it was the most peaceful calm feeling ever. But in my dream I woke up from the dream, and looked on my bed and found a stone that the figure had left, it had strange symbols on it. I looked at the stone and felt it was magickal, but somehow controlling me, like the figure who had killed me in my dream was controlling me with it. It was very strange. I then woke up again, and this time I really woke up, but couldn't find the stone.

21st May 2011

My birth number comes is 11
I was born at 11:11
Ordo Infinitus Orbis (Pythagorean System) = 11
O Rh D Negative = 11

7th June 2011

When humankind become too many, and too greedy, and too full of hate, wars happen and the Great Creator gets angry. The Great Spirit angers and causes 'natural disasters' which remove all life on Earth, cleansing and purifying it. She needs time to heal herself, as a new world appears from the ashes, like a Phoenix. Through all of this there are always a small group who survive to keep the original teachings of the Great Spirit alive. They keep the spiritual path open for all those of the righteous who wish to live in harmony and balance with the Great Creator. However, unless we all learn to become spiritual beings, the Great Creator will put an end to things once again, and the cycle will continue, until we have all learnt the lessons we are here to learn. As only then can we have Heaven on Earth.

People will always blame others for all their problems, but they can never see when the problems start within themselves. If everyone did, just imagine how much better the world would be?

8th June 2011

Pound coin magick, it does work.

I first tried it a long time ago, when I was on my 'path of the fool' part of my journey. I tried it for about a week, and nothing. I then gave up and thought nothing about it for ages.

Then the other day while out walking Tashi I remembered about it, then again I put it to the back of my mind. I did at the time though think about the fact that my money is fast running out and a pound would be useful right now. But I left it at that.

Then the day after that I was out with Tashi again, it was about the same time of the day before, and something told me to look down. I did, and there on the path was a pound coin. I kicked it, to make sure it wasn't a glued down trick ones, and it moved, so I picked it up.

Yep, it really does work.

23rd June 2011

Most religions call for us to live in fear of doing something wrong, because if we don't, we won't get to Heaven when we die. I'm a Gnostic Theolalite, and my religion tells me to live life to the full by finding our True Will, then live with inner peace, joy and harmony. When living our True Will we help to bring a Heaven on Earth, and on death when we return to the source, our essence will have a wonderful positive effective on the whole of consciousness.

24th June 2011

I See Angry People... I do not blame anyone for getting angry about things, we live in strange times. It is time for the return of the Divine Feminine, and although we have been programmed against the truth, we all have the truth inside us. We can become confused and angry when we see so much conflicting information, as the others do their best to keep the truth hidden, with their books and videos of misinformation and lies. Some truth slips out, then is undermined yet again by those trying to cling on to the power patriarchy has given them. It can not last much longer, as more and more of us are realising that the truth can be put up high, and all though you are constantly knocked down for telling it, it can never be taken from its pedestal, because the truth can survive anything, and has, for thousands of years.

27th June 2011

Mary Magdalene was a true Adept and spiritual teacher, manifesting her sacred powers through the flow of light from her heart and soul. Her Divine love was unconditional and independent of external situations and dogmas. Yet Divine love is not limited to the ascetic.

If spiritually evolved beings come together in unconditional love, they also can create an energy field that is most positive and rare, exuding high vibrational levels of peace and love into the universe.

17th July 2011

A few of us were talking about the Vatican secret vaults in our group on Facebook. We decided we would all visit there in the astral realms that night to check it out. Well I did, but no one else did. Under the Vatican by remote viewing I saw a painting of a Cavalier dressed in black. He was stood on a map of the world holding a sword, the sword was stuck in the map, pointing to a location. I also saw a golden staff. Could where the sword is stuck be the location of the staff? This painting has been hidden for some reason, for what I don't know, but I am going to find out.

This has been especially interesting when I was told some of the others in the group what I saw and one of them told that a sword was used to mark out the Dragon lines and a tower and church built over them. I know about Dragon lines, but had never known about swords being used to 'pin the dragon'. So I have to find this place, I think it is important.

The Cavalier in the painting was holding his sword in his left hand, and pointing to the place the sword touched the map with the other hand.
Next I am going to study the map, and see if there is a ley line in the spot.

19th July 2011

Fear can stop us seeing the truth, but there really is nothing to fear. The beauty of the truth emanates out from our hearts, igniting our Divine light and giving us the most warming sense of knowing. If we choose to embrace truth, we can have unconditional love for everything that is.

24th July 2011

No good deed goes unpunished.... I am fulfilled, I know what I am, who I am and where I came from. That is why I am not scared of death. I am a Theolalite, a Gnostic, I can see the world for what it is. If others find the truth, and then they can feel as fulfilled as I do, they will also not fear life or death. They will also have that warm sense of knowing and will help others too.

The reason why I say 'no good deed goes unpunished' is because people are so under the influence of mind control, and have been fooled for so long, that anyone who comes along and does start showing the truth and effecting others, they attack them. I don't blame them for being angry, because without inner peace life is so much worse, and they can't stand to see someone else so happy, because they aren't. So they ask me in anger to prove to them what I am saying is true, like I owe them it. However nothing I say matters, as we all need to go on the journey to find that truth ourselves.

So when others attack me, I don't blame them. I can see their pain. But most are unwilling to keep seeking, so spend their whole life in a living hell, never fully realising their potential. This is why I have the Church, the Order and write my articles, so that those who are seeking can get some answers. At times I see someone in great pain and want them to know the truth so bad, because if they knew it, they would not feel as they do. This is something I have to deal with myself, and realise that not everyone wants to know.

28th July 2011

Science for me, is the proof other people need. When you know inside, you just know. People can throw anything they want at you, and about your beliefs, but no matter what you can still smile and have that amazing sense of knowing, that only comes from looking inside. The truth is inside, not outside. You can change belief systems at any point to try it out, but there is always the 'real' truth, that which never goes away. Because it has always been there, you just need to connect to it, when you do, you will know.

2nd September 2011

When you know the truth there is nothing that can remove it, that is how you know it is true. People convince themselves of 'truth' that isn't the same thing. Those are the people who get angry when someone else says something that is different to their 'opinion'. People who have found the truth, probably would like others to know, so they put that information out there and it is up to the viewer on how they will receive it. Others use the 'truth' to control others, as they long for power. Because being enlightened doesn't make you a good person, just an illuminated one.

What I think would be nice is if more good people became illuminated, rather than just the bad ones. That is why I have my Order and my Church, not for a power trip or ego, because I genuinely want good people to know the truth. It takes a while to find the truth, it can be a very long journey, where as some people it happens to almost instantly, and there are lots of things that can go wrong along the way.

Being part of a group that have been there and done it before you, is the best support you can get. Because along the way all kinds will happen, and you will lose a lot of 'friends' maybe even your family. But if you are a true seeker you keep going and keep going, forever pushing forwards, until the day you know the truth, then you never have any doubts about what truth is, and you are illuminated.

This is how I can best describe it, because no one else can just come along tell you the truth, you have to go on the journey yourself, and some never make it. Those with support are more likely to though. Angry people will stubbornly sit there saying they don't need anyone else, or to help others, they are still living in false ego where they are full of self importance. When you remove false ego you realise there is safety in numbers, especially when all the bad ones stick together, about time the good ones did too.

20th September 2011

I was lucid dreaming last night and found some time travel portals, it was fantastic. I hadn't thought about changing what I was wearing to old fashioned clothes though, so I had to run and hide every time I heard someone coming. I was in a massive old mansion. It wasn't very far back

1930s I think.

One of the portals was a cooker knob of a really old cooker. If you do want to travel into the past, find something old that hasn't been moved from it's original spot.

It was strange to see the knob turn from old and dusty to brand new in my hand.

22nd October 2011

Last night I visited an oriental looking place, it was a town by the sea, but the buildings looked traditional British. I was seeing the whole experience through someone else's eyes so didn't try to control what was happening, as that would be wrong. But I could see oriental looking people and writing. I was at work in what I felt was my business, so the persons business, and there was a warning siren going. I went out on to the street and saw massive waves coming towards land. I ran inside and shut the door and water starting coming in under the door. I got towels and things and tried to stop it, but it was flooding in very badly and for some strange reason the water was warm, and then I saw out the window a wall of water coming towards me. I then left the scene. I had one like this just before the Japan Tsunami, so thought I would mention it, although because I don't know where it is, it isn't much use.

28th October 2011

Know thyself.. You know that strong person you look up to? The one who isn't afraid to put their views across, even if it means they are laughed at? That person who seems to stand out in a crowd and get things done? That is YOU, you just haven't realised it yet. No other person is more important than you, no other person is stronger than you, no other person knows more than you do when you come to know thyself.

11th November 2011

11/11/11 - Igniting our hearts with love and compassion for all our Brothers & Sisters in the world. No matter what someone has been brought up to believe, let's all hope they can open their hearts to those who have been outcast and shunned for being different. Let's hope that people will stop feeling the need to bully others, to torment others. Let's hope that every human being on the planet can be treated fairly and equally. That we can all take steps towards fulfilling our true Divine Will and potential. Where there is hope there is a way to find Concordia, Aequilibrium and Veritas. It is up to us to lead the way xXx Love and Blessings to All.

17th November 2011

I believe everyone should be told the truth about the origins of their religions, then they can choose for themselves if they want to continue on with that path or decide to choose spirituality rather than religion... This is for all those who think keeping religions is a good idea. When you can see the bigger picture, why would you want to continue on to live a lie? Just my opinion, don't crucify me for it, lol.

26th November 2011

Oi Mr or Ms Spiritual, you sit there arrogantly implying you are more spiritual than others because you spent time with Monks in Tibet, you travelled a long way to meet with shamans and take strange drugs, you spent years visiting Holy ground and ancient monuments, but to gain what? Look at you now, you might have learnt some interesting things, but where did it get you? It turned you into an arrogant egotist who thinks he/she knows better than anyone else. You constantly use quotes from Gurus and wait for people to praise you for doing so. You model your behaviour on something or someone so fake and unreal you have lost all touch with reality. And all the while you were travelling round searching for experiences and spiritual enlightenment, you forgot to look inside, you forgot that you already had the answer within, you just needed to remove the need to cling to your false ego (fake personality) and find the real you. But that is so hard to do when you are too busy worrying what everyone else will think of you, if you show the 'real' you. So instead you tend to attack those who question you and your false ego, the 'love & light' soon turns to hate and fear when your false ego feels threatened by exposure. And this anger and fear that you carry round with you, can never be dealt with, until you remember to stop judging others in the world, and start looking inside. Learn to smile again, as any truly spiritual being knows.. life is about love, joy and laughter, and has nothing to do with covering up your hatred by constantly saying 'love & light'.

22nd December 2011

Advice to liars - Stop trying to cover your tracks with more rubbish. Just for once in your life admit what you have done, stop deluding yourself. You are just like billions of other people, there is nothing unusual about you, in so much as, you are full of bullshit and where there are people, there is plenty of it. You just haven't reached a level of attainment where you can stop yourself doing it.

You might think life is more fun while you continue hiding the true you, but all you will do is make friends with shallow people who also bs you. If you want to make friends with people, true friends, that will last forever, you will drop the act and just be yourself.

Hate me for saying this if you want, many do, but also a few do come back, sometimes years later and say they wished they had just been honest when given the chance, and stopped. Lies end people up in trouble, the more you tell the deeper you get into it.

You have a chance at a fresh start, you can just drop all that nonsense that you think will gain you attention, and be genuine with people. You will learn more about yourself that way, and others too. People are interesting you know, once you stop trying to manipulate them, and just decide to be interested in them instead. And yes lying to people is manipulation. Stop now, before you drive more people away, please.

4th January 2012

Last year a few of us decided to remote view under the Vatican, in the secret vaults. I was the only one who did it. I saw a large painting of a man dressed in black, like a Cavalier. He was stood on map of he world and he was holding a sword, which the point of was marking out a location on the map. I was told that swords were used to mark ley lines and towers built on top of them and churches built, this was called pinning the Dragon. So I checked the area of the map, found a ley line, and sure enough there is a Church there. I want to get into the tower to see if I can get under the floorboards and find a sword. In the Vatican I also saw a golden rod.

I don't know why, but I have seen this for a reason, and when I told about the pinning of the Dragon, I knew I had to look into it. Some relic might be there, I really don't know. I am going to try and remote view to the Church next, as the chances of me being able to get in there and start rooting about are slim.

2nd February 2012

Are you a limited thinker? Or can you see the big picture?

A limited thinker will say - I'm not perfect, but no one is perfect.

Someone who can see the big picture will say - I am Unique, therefore I am perfect, as however I am, I am the perfect version of me. How could I not be? There is only one of me, and there will never be someone else exactly like me ever again. How can I be too short? Too short compared to what? To you? But you are the perfect version of you, not me! You are perfect too, but you are not the perfect version of me, that is my job. So don't you tell me I am too short, or too tall, or too fat, or too thin, or too young, or too old. Because you are not me, I am me. How I am right NOW is perfect, not how I was before, or how I might be, but how I am right NOW is the perfect version of me.

A limited thinker will judge people on how they look, and tell them how to 'improve' themselves. Someone who can see the big picture will know that you are perfect right NOW.

You can choose to spread the joy yourself right now, you can choose to pick something out about someone, something unique, doesn't have to be looks, anything, and compliment them on it. It will make their day and yours too, try it.

26th February 2012

People who change the world -
Cautious, apologetic people always walking on egg shells to preserve their reputation, or to be socially accepted, never can bring about change. Those who are really willing to be demonised and cast out, to be shunned by their peers, publicly and privately, to be accused of being an evil person, a control freak, an egotist... for daring to break the mould and paint a different picture. Only those people can change the world. They might be hated or admired, it matters not when you have no price because your attainment is high enough to not give a damn about the personal consequences of speaking up, as they know for the world the consequences of not speaking up are in the long run far worse.

27th February 2012

I am a mirror... A message to all those who have been programmed to go to sleep and never wake up, and live life as a heartless consumer, with a total lack of empathy... by just constantly saying "We choose the life we get, we decide for ourselves which life we are be born into." You are saying then that starving people 'choose' to have no food to eat and starve to death? Do you believe poor homeless people are all sadists? What about children who are born with terrible diseases and problems, they choose that too do they? And women who are sold as slaves and forced to prostitute themselves out for no personal gain of their own.. They choose that life? Children born into a war zone who have to see their parents blown into pieces, as well as their other family members and friends... They choose to enter into a life like that? Children who are abused by perverts, that are sometime even their own parents!! They choose that life?

Talk about the ultimate in ignorance and selfish justification of their luxurious life style while millions suffer worldwide. "I am just a mirror" they ignorantly chant over and over again to anyone who dares to question them. So if a poor person thinks a rich person has lots of money, that means the poor person has lots of money, because the rich person is 'just a mirror'? Get real! Maybe you think your 'love and light' and 'abundant blessings' will change things? Or maybe you just don't care as long as you are OK? Those are the thoughts and actions of a narcissist, and if your spiritual teacher or 'guru' is teaching you to think like that, you can be sure of one thing. They will enjoy the 'abundance' that flows freely to them from the narcissists who require validation from them, who feel that giving these snake oil sales men and women money will mean they don't have to possess a conscience themselves.

Having no compassion for others isn't spiritual, or even honest. Stop lying to yourself and trying to convince everyone else, because it doesn't work. Why not take responsibility for your own life first and dump the guru? Despite what people think about a narcissist they do actually hate themselves, that is why they can't love others... Try learning to open your heart and love yourself, then maybe you will heal yourself and learn to love others too.

4th March 2012

What is extremely annoying and disturbing to me, is the same old rubbish being put out there again and again, by people who know exactly what they are doing and why.

Sacred Geometry and Astrotheology have been hidden in plain sight, it is just that most people are or have been to stupid to see it. The RC Church has kept this from us, but wait the Freemasons have kept it safe for us, and they are the good guys. Look, they even worship the Goddess, and a balanced trinity. Oh aren't they good people, all those famous people who have belonged to their Order, all those genius, gosh they are so much more intelligent than us, no wonder they had to keep it all secret from us. Maybe it was an advanced hidden race that had these teachings, they were probably aliens. But aren't we lucky that those 'men' in the past were intelligent and rediscovered the secrets.

Reality - The Freemasons are the same thing as the RC Church, they have worked together for thousands of years to make sure YOU the general public would never become intelligent enough to figure all this out. They stole the teachings from our Shamanistic ancient ancestors Mystery Schools who built Stonehenge and the pyramids and the other fantastic architecture all over the planet. In our Mystery Schools we taught about Astrotheology, Geometry and Spirituality, and how to use these things to see the Divine in all of creation, which all came from the Cosmic womb, Vesica Piscis of the Great Mother Goddess. The societies were all female led, and there was no such thing as wars.

Some of us decided to help nature along a little by giving some simian races our genes, and the result of breeding with these was Cro-Magnons, who eventually took over and killed as many of us as possible, but stole our teachings, but didn't know them all, some were missing. They thought they had killed us all, every time we surfaced they killed us, we have had secret Orders that passed knowledge through the 'Underground Stream' for a long time. We have been releasing more and more knowledge out to the general public, pretending to have just discovered it, etc. Or wrote it as fiction, only way to get it out. Then because the Freemasons noticed this was happening, but they want the real and full knowledge themselves, they set up Universities, a place to hand pick the brightest men and get them to swear oaths of secrecy to them, in return they get great wealth, fame, whatever they want. So long as they were working for them, and keeping the knowledge secret, as it would empower everyone, they don't want that. They especially wanted to make sure women would not get an education, as if women found out the truth about the past, it would mean their patriarchy and power would be taken away from them over time.

These men would keep hold of the power, and rule over the entire world. Yet now we see lots of videos and books telling us what good people they are, they can see the popularity of the RC Church is waning, so they need a new tactic to get everyone on side. Those who have signed oaths, well it is too late for them, they can not escape them, and are too scared to come out and tell people the truth. Once a 33 degree Mason, they would never leave anyway. They become selfish idiots who love the power it gives them over others and all that work they had to go through to get the secrets, now why would they just give them to others who they feel are inferiour to them? They wouldn't. They do not learn how to become spiritual beings in Freemasonry, they haven't opened their heart chakra, so all that knowledge only leads to psychopathy.

OTO is also part of this, as is Golden Dawn, as is AMORC, as is Theosophical Society, as is the New Age movement, Church of Satan, Wicca, Temple of Set, Sisters of Isis, Judaism, Islam, Sufis, Buddhism, Hindu, all forms of Christianity etc etc. Other projects to con us include: Venus Project, Thrive, Wayseers, KONY 2012, Lightworkers and many more. All ways of putting those waking up, back to sleep by telling them stupid stories about holographic universes, aliens, DNA activation, Ascended Masters, Angels, Demons and other rubbish. All working for the same thing, to keep humanity trapped in patriarchal mindset forever. You can argue as much as you want about your religion not being patriarchal, but the fact is, if it is mainstream it is. They have been playing this game for a long long time, they are not about to give up easy. They want you to think you have a choice.

Even though we are now coming back out to try and help you all see what is happening, how many of you will truly take notice? Because all these different groups don't seem connected, and in fact some seem to be complete opposite. Remember the black and white squares, it is all a game of chess, and you are one of the pawns.

9th March 2012

Still I am told I am inciting violence and hate crimes for talking about the problems with patriarchy. Yet I am always saying over and over again that violence is what I am against and what I want to put a stop to, and the only way to do that is to remove ALL patriarchy. So yes that means removing Islam, as well as Hindu, Judaism, Christianity etc, and stop the hate and division caused by ALL these patriarchal religions. I will never be tolerant of violence. If someone can worship something without feeling the need to hurt others because of their beliefs, fine, but it seems they can't!! To be tolerant of hate crimes because of someone's religion is disgusting.

Patriarchy effects all people negatively, even men. They are forced to go to wars and get killed and lose limbs, all because of oil and power. The psychopaths who want to keep patriarchy, do so because they like the power and control it gives them, while the rest suffer. They don't care about those soldiers and their families who suffer, or all those innocent people they kill in the countries they rape. They laugh about it, and they laugh about those who continue to support it while they get richer.

18th March 2012

Angry Anarchistic Feminists - The whole concept of anarchy is completely ridiculous and unworkable. The idea that people need no leaders at all is both wishful thinking and ludicrous. How men treat women now is bad enough, imagine if they were given no guidance or rules to tell them right from wrong? To tell men that anything is acceptable? Because without parents to give guidance to a child's upbringing we would just create monsters who have no sense of right from wrong, parents are leaders too. The only people on the planet who do have a true and real sense about what is important are those who have worked on themselves spiritually, because they have come to know altruism. Religion is completely different entity to Spirituality. Before someone awakens spiritually they see everything they dislike with anger and seek revenge. Women being naturally tantric don't take much work to waken spiritually, but men do, and in society women are being taught to be more like men, aggressive, filled with hate, uncaring, promiscuous, little or no self respect. Women are taught to care more about personal possessions and what they can get from others, than being loving, caring and compassionate. Which are feminine qualities. There is nothing weak about altruism and feminine qualities, it takes great strength to stand up against the negativity and hate spread about in the world and say, "Enough is enough, why can't we all just do what is right by each other?"

Many people need leaders, because they have had their spirituality switched off over many generations. Like it or not men will always need them, and it is women, spiritually aware ones, that should be stepping up and giving them that guidance as was always the way in the past. Priestesses would help men become spiritually aware better people, and we can again. But they aren't going to want to listen to women who hate them and are angry about the past. It is up to us women yet again to be the ones to help them help themselves, because until they have done that, and they have become altruistic, the problems escalate and there will be no end to the battle of the sexes. Men need women for enlightenment, it is simple as that, and we help ourselves by helping them, not hating them. I am sorry if this offends, but I can see the big picture here. I am in no way condoning the bad behaviour of men, I am saying that the ones who haven't become spiritually aware need our help, so they don't become the sexist nasty testosterone poisoned fools they can, and not ALL men are like that, some have learnt from women and become balanced, stable and very respectful of women, with our help they all can. We can LEAD by example.

19th March 2012

When The Lights Go Out - On death we each become our own judge. If we have led a good life our Higher Self will make the experience wonderful, because we have no guilt. If we have been horrible to others, lied, cheated, blamed others for our own problems, shown no love or empathy for others, then our Higher Self knows this and we will experience something very nasty indeed. I am not talking about how we die, I am talking about what we experience as the lights are going out. If your religion teaches you to hate others and be cold hearted to the suffering of others, you will be the one who experiences hell, not those you think of as 'sinners'.

29th March 2012

Three things I get tired of hearing day in and day out are:

1, You are a feminazi, man hating bitch, whose Dad abused you or a man hurt you in the past.

2, You have to prove to me about this, that and the other. Because the person accusing me of just making up crap is too lazy, stupid or probably both, to do the research themselves. This isn't just about one topic, it is about most of the stuff I put out there, because it is controversial to the programmed herd who can not accept they have been lied to their entire life, so they attack anyone who dares to stand up and say any different, and constantly whinging on about them 'proving' things to them, even when all the proof is there right in front of them.

3, You are a devil worshipper, working for the dark side, you kill people in rituals, you murder babies, you are cold hearted reptiles, you are this, you are that.

All three of the above are complete bullshit, and you can keep saying it until the cows come home but it isn't going to make it true.

2nd April 2012

The Pain of Knowing - The World can be such a lonely place for those who have reached a high level of attainment. It isn't like you look down on others for not being able to see through the bullshit, it is just that you wish they could and that you could some how speed things up for them. Then they will take action in making changes to the world, because they too will be able to see the big picture. But no, you live your life surrounded by those who don't realise how clueless they are, I know because I used to be just like them.

So thank you so much to those of you who are round me who DO get it, and are helping in the quest to free everyone from their mental slavery, cut through the lies and bring truth.

Generation upon generation has been lied to, with fake choices to choose, tricking them into thinking they have a choice. They don't have a choice in the current system, and that is why it needs to be removed. We are playing a numbers game, once enough people have woken up to the big picture, more will start to wake up and the chain reaction occurs. But along the way there are plenty of distractions to stop people waking up, and many give up and sink back into the game that they can never win, becoming just a pawn. The only way to win the game, is to realise you are in one, and play 'them' at their own game. This is what the BE THE SOLUTION movement is about and it is growing and will more with your help. Thank you.

The pain of knowing, is much easier to cope with, than the pain of uncertainty, or the pain of not living to your true potential.

3rd May 2012

Ever start to doubt we need to change things? Do you ever start to believe we have things good and don't want them to change? That is your selfish eagle side. Since now more and more are activating their serpent side, this is leading to confusion within them. One moment they want to change the world, the next they act like scared little rabbits, living in fear and slipping back into the selfish, me me me, mindset of the eagle, which is childish and irresponsible, but easy. There is nothing to fear from change, everything is always changing, you can not keep things from changing, it happens with or without your permission. So flow with the wave of serpent energy and allow the world to heal, banish your fear and controlling nature, for the good of everyone.

7th May 2012

Why so much anger and hate are directed at those who stand out?

We all have very high standards for ourselves and we don't like to see ourselves as not meeting our own expectations. We naturally try as hard as we are able to meet our own goals, so "trying harder" is not a solution. We certainly don't want to lower our expectations either, so instead of living with the feeling that we haven't reached our true potential, and feeling powerless, people tend to adjust their image of themselves instead. This temporarily solves the crisis; our expectations are intact and we don't have to try and improve our behaviour and performance to a level above what is possible for us.

Unfortunately, this image shift has some rather undesirable side-effects. Whenever we have thoughts or feelings that do not fit in with our superior self image, when we are ashamed of our thoughts, we shove those thoughts and feelings out of our conscious attention. We are afraid of such thoughts, they threaten our self-image at a fundamental level.

These thoughts do not go away, they are still in our minds. Thoughts have their own energy whether we are paying attention to them or not. Similar thoughts attract one another and form structures. People who are involved in creative mental tasks experienced this constantly. When they work with related thoughts and ideas, these thoughts begin to form themselves into hierarchies and patterns. Thoughts that we fear are no different; they create mental landscapes of what we fear the most within our own minds.

When something reminds us of these fearful thought structures, we experience a sudden surge of hatred, fear, or disgust as our conscious attention is momentarily focused on our unacceptable thoughts. Because we cannot accept these thoughts as part of ourselves, we assume that the feelings they generate are coming from whatever or whoever reminded us of them. This is called projection. Anyone that seems vaguely menacing can cause us to project our own suppressed anger onto them. This anger seems to be separate from "our own" thoughts, making it easy to believe that the anger or threat is coming from the other person. Someone with different ideas or customs can prompt us to project any anti-social or simply unconventional thoughts of our own that disturbed or disgusted us, making the person before us seems disturbing or dangerous. Depending on the force of our suppressed feelings, people who are in fact harmless can appear to be capable of bringing down civilization.

Well, that was a long exposition, but it boils down to this. The more you accept your own thoughts as normal and natural, whether they offend your sense of decency or not, the more clearly you will be able to see the world. Convincing others of this could be a problem, however.

When the projection turns to violence.

There is one thing that makes people feel enough rage to commit violence, and that is a feeling of powerlessness. If people feel that they have no control over their destiny and environment, if they feel that they cannot act effectively, then they can reach a point where they believe that nothing short of violence can change their situation.

Acting effectively requires you to influence other people and to control your environment. To influence other people, they must respect you and be willing to listen to what you have to say. To control your environment, you must understand it, have the skills to affect it, and be permitted to act on it.

It should be clear that these conditions are not met very often in our society. Many people in our society are alienated from one another and have few opportunities to exert any real influence on one another. Many poor and uneducated people do not have any control over their environment whatsoever.

However, powerlessness is not the only ingredient in violence. The real question is not why people are violent, but why so many men are violent. Although women are just as capable of violence as men, crime statistics show that it is not women who are turning our urban environments into war zones.

Both men and women must abide by certain expectations. Even though people have few instincts and all of our adult behaviour is learnt, we labour under the misconception that men and women are biologically destined to behave completely differently. Women are supposed to be yielding, they are not expected to forcefully express their own wants and needs. Men are supposed to be dominant and commanding, and are regarded as weak if they express any tendencies to yield or to behave in a "feminine" way.

As psychologists have discovered, however, the most mentally healthy people express emotional and behavioural characteristics traditionally assigned to both sexes. The fully functioning human can be either forceful or gentle, commanding or submissive, strong or yielding, as the situation requires. Unfortunately, the acceptable range of emotions for men is rather narrow, and what happens is that men must express all of their emotional energy through the few emotions available to them. This leads to rather exaggerated expressions of strength and virility.

Now, couple this self-image men have of strength and domination with the feelings of powerlessness rife in our society, and you have a recipe for disaster. Men must express their exaggerated sense of dominance, but they are rendered impotent by their inability to act with any effectiveness. To these men, violence seems to be the only way to affect their environment.

This will continue to be a problem until men are raised differently, or do the Great Work.

21st May 2012

Reincarnation & Karma - When asked what we believe about reincarnation and karma, our reply:

We believe in karma, in that, if someone is a nasty horrible person, then something will happen in the future to get them back for it. And if someone is always hating on others, they will be taught a lesson. But that is all within this lifetime. We can not be responsible for the decisions of our ancestors.

Saying that though, we should not deny it or try to cover it up.

Genetic memory is what causes us to remember things from the past. All animals have this. It is why we instinctively look for a nipple to feed on when we are babies, and many other things, we just know.

This is our only chance, in this lifetime, to become illuminated to the truth. People don't like to accept that, because they don't want to put the work in. Maybe they feel they are too old, or too busy? But the journey does involve removing all attachment to material goods, so when you realise this you have more time, as you aren't constantly working all hours in the hope of owning more 'things'. After that process is over, and you have learnt the truth, you then have things come to you naturally anyway. But you have to let go first, before that happens and that includes friends and family (those who try to stop you moving forward have to be removed, or you are allowing them to stop you and take your free will, and you will be left with a longing and wish that you had just done it and not listened to all those negative thoughts they feed you), you have to remove yourself from all desires, all addictions and all 'wants', a complete rebirth into a new pure being who is not influenced by the Will of others, and eventually you do find your own true Will. Anyone is capable of getting there, fear is what stops most people, or things like gods and reincarnation, which gives people an excuse to do nothing and think they get second chances somewhere else, or someone else is going to sort it for them, if they just repent. The truth hurts, we have to do it all ourselves, and people run a mile from that responsibility.... and the slaves shall serve.

It is our choice and ours alone, if we seek and keep seeking we find.

We do think it is wrong that people are programmed and lied to by religions etc, which is why we have gone public and now offer the Esoteric Comparative Theology course to the public. Now no one has any excuses.

22nd May 2012

The Serpent Line

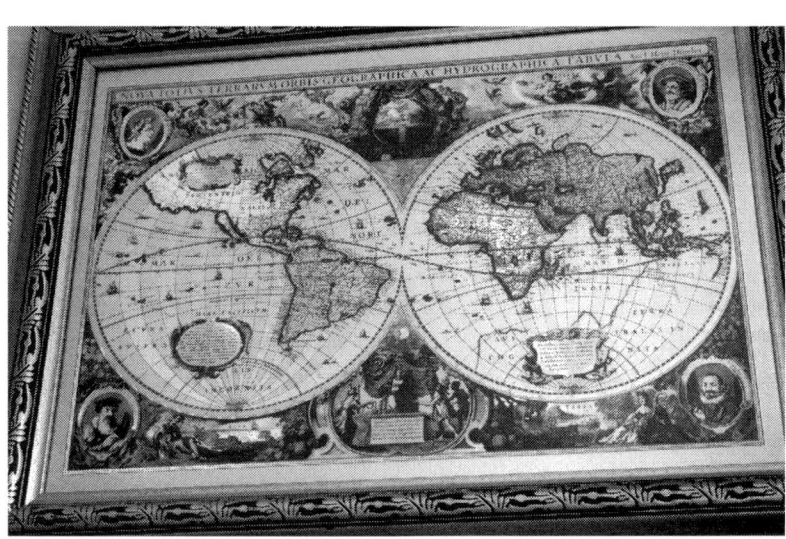

This is a photo of an old map that is on my lounge wall. People look at it and don't think anything of it, others don't even notice it. Little do they know how rare this map is, because it shows the sine line, which has been purposely removed from modern maps. It was a gift from a 'family' member many years ago when I was doing my training.

Everyday the Sun moves through your body, Aries in the head, and Pisces in the feet. Sun rise corresponds with Spring, noon with Summer, evening with Autumn, midnight with Winter. Everyday the cycle is turning, with the month, year and age on a larger scale to it. 24 hours a day, 12 hours in summer, 12 in winter. Dark and light, good and evil. For Summer months we can 'live' while the earth bears its fruit, and in the winter all things die and that is the reverse therefore evil, as evil is reverse of live. In Summer we lived, and in winter there was the devil, again reversed. There are no devils, just dark and light, summer and winter and all religions are based on the lies about these things.

When you know that the day is the same as the year, is the same as your body, which corresponds to your chakras, you can begin to see the connection to all things. The sine wave, the serpent line which forms the S with the equator through the middle even creates the dollar sign.

23rd July 2012

Are You A Guru? - So what is it with all these damaged egotistical people who call themselves a 'guru'? If I see anyone call themselves a guru I instantly know they are insecure and seeking attention. We might be able to seek to learn things from others, get help or advice, but to look upon another person as a guru is just wrong. We are all gurus, but only to ourselves, no one else, everyone else's path is their own and we each have to make our decisions and find our own way. The new age movement is creating monsters who want to be everyone's guru and in the long term it isn't doing the 'guru' any good either if people allow them to be theirs. No one else is your 'master' or 'teacher' but you. No one else knows you as well as you do, and no one else will always be there, only you. We each only have ourselves to rely on. Realising this is the first step to spiritually growing up.

--

Dark Night of the Soul - I catch the scent of desperation from someone instantly, and it is normally those who are stuck in the abyss. They often say they want to help others, but ultimately they will damage others if they are not careful, as they first need to look at themselves.

They tend towards being passive aggressive, they don't mean to, they just can't help themselves when they are faced with someone stronger than them. They often make remarks intended to belittle the person they feel is stronger than them, in order to make themselves feel better. They even model their targets behaviour, in the hope that they might gain the respect they have.

This person is stuck in the dark night of the soul, and is desperately unhappy, yet trying to show a happy face to the world. But it can not be hidden, people do pick up the vibes and back away, causing the frustration to get worse. All they need to do is stop trying to be everything to others, stop trying to be something they are not, stop trying to show a false public image, because you are fooling no one. Instead remember to look inside and realise what you need to do to heal yourself first, before offering to help others. You can not help others when you are trapped in your own self made hell.

30th July 2012

Be the change you want to see in the world - Gandhi. One of the most misunderstood quotes of our time. Gandhi didn't mean to do nothing to change the world but sit on your arse. He implied that first you must work on yourself, then when you yourself have changed, you can then effect the world positively, not by sitting about meditating, but by the art of 'doing'. Gandhi travelled far and wide, did so much work spreading his teachings. He was 'doing', follow his example and change yourself first, then set about 'doing' something about the mess the world is in.

The New Age Movement tells people constantly that 'We are all one' and that we have to do nothing but sit meditating to save the Earth and ourselves.

We might all come from the same source, but we are not all one. If we become trapped within our own false egos we return to the source as a thousand pieces, and yes become part of the whole 'one' again. The idea is to grow up and realise we are responsible for ourselves.

They also tell us to think with the heart and not the mind. Your Higher Self is the thing you should be thinking with, as well as having an open heart chakra. If you open your heart chakra without connecting to your Higher Self you are taken in by these things that trap you here in the 'one' and are easier for the eagles to manipulate and control you. Do not stop at the heart chakra, you must push forwards and active your other higher chakras fully too, your throat, your third eye and your crown, otherwise you are not complete.

We can only truly help others reach their full potential once we have ourselves, because then we can detach and see the big picture. The New Age Movement tries to stop people realising their full potential by telling us we are all one, no need to become whole ourselves. This means we never grown up.

The Racist Blame Game - Black Vs White

Wouldn't it be nice if people would stop seeing only differences in others and start to see what things make us all the same? Why do some black people think ALL white people are evil and why do some white people think that ALL black people are? I was told just recently by an African American that white people are to blame for all the worlds problems, wars and murder. He said that 'everyone' knows that black people created all the esoteric teachings and that every Mystery School teaches that. Strange that seeing as I spoke to someone else who happened to be white and in another Masonic Order who was saying that white people created all of civilised society and that if it weren't for white people those black primitives would have all killed themselves by now, and that everyone involved in the 'Mystery Schools' knows that. Erm no, not in genuine Mystery Schools like ours.

Well I have news for you, both of you are wrong and you have been played. You are very much trapped in the game, and that game is creating division, hate and competition and not by mistake, that is what the game the Eagles play is all about. Keeping everyone so consumed with hate and a sense of entitlement, that they never even notice they are part of the game and the people they are directing their hate towards have nothing to do with how things are, because they are just as misguided, brainwashed and programmed as they are.

Masonic Orders brainwash and control, not enlighten. The whole thing about them is to get people hooked so they can control them. The Orders in black areas will tell the black ones what they want to hear and the ones in white areas will do the same. All the time those involved are hooked they are buying into the game. They are told how special they are, and their false egos lap it up and use it to get even more embroiled in the material world. It is the same trick used by all religions, so many traps for people to fall into and they are all part of the game, and they are all run by the same people, there are no sides apart from us against those who run the game.

If they were enlightened they would stop this nonsense, learn the true facts about the past, get over it and move on. Nothing we do now is going to change what happened in the past, so what is the point of playing the blame game? The true teachings are now available to anyone, and it doesn't matter what your genes are, you just have to want to help yourself, and then you can help others.

Once you escape the game you will be surprised at just how stupid the game looks when you see the big picture.

1st August 2012

Why do so many see conflict as negative? It is how we learn about ourselves, and what is important to us, and what stands up to be tested. If something doesn't stand up when someone else disagrees with it, then it means you should let go of it, instead of stubbornly holding on to it and then hating the person for showing you the truth. It is that realisation that what we believe to be true, isn't always, that helps us find out who we really are and what things we only believe because we have been programmed to believe them. So when someone runs away at the first signs of someone disagreeing with them, it means they are unwilling to be proven wrong.

5th August 2012

What Is False Ego?

False ego is the programmed by society version of yourself, like a mask we hide behind in order to fit in with others who are in false ego. The real ego is just your sense of self. But you can not know your real ego unless you have removed the false one, by connecting to your Higher Self. Then you can tell which is false and which is programmed. Before that it is hard to tell.

You might think that voice in your head is you, but it is thinking with words, and words were created by others, so how can you know who or what is thinking those words? Unless you get even deeper and realise who or what is thinking those words and why it is thinking those words in that way.

For example you might think to yourself that you are not good enough. Who says you are not good enough? How do you know that whoever said the words that made you think you are not good enough was right about it? They don't know you better than you, or do they? Is it really you who thinks you are not good enough, or something someone else told you years ago and it attached itself to your false ego and now your false ego is believing it?

It is very hard to change once your false ego has accepted something. It is what 'knowing thyself' is all about, finding the authentic you, the one that isn't trying to please others, or fit in, or impress anyone.

15th August 2012

You are special, a chosen one. - If someone else comes to you and tells you your life mission and reason for being here and you believe them, you are a fool. You haven't found enlightenment and you haven't found out how special you are or your mission and reason for being here, because it isn't your reason for being here. It is just cheap talk from someone who is telling you what you want to hear, someone who doesn't know you. You believing them means you don't even know yourself, so how on Earth could they know you better?

14th October 2012

How often are we told that the world doesn't revolve around us? Meaning that we are not important in the bigger picture and shouldn't be egomaniacs. However your world does revolve around you, and it can be very freeing and empowering, without egotism, to know this. You are the one who decides what you are going to do with your life, more so in the western world. You are the most important person in your world because you are the one who creates your reality every single day, and you do it all alone. So maybe it is about time you starting trusting yourself more? Why live in someone else's world, when you can live in your own? If you are the King or Queen of your own world you don't feel the need to control anyone else's or put trust in anyone else's world view over your own.

You can practice learning how to trust yourself again simply by using your imagination, like you used to when you were a child. Take a day, more if possible, and be completely alone without distractions. Think up a new world in which you live in, where everything is as you want it. You are the world leader, what rules are in your world? Take time to think about how your world would be, how your reality would be if it were exactly as you wanted it.

This session will be very telling, it might be a negative experience. You might find yourself wanting more money, more material goods, being the most beautiful. This is a product of other peoples worlds effecting yours. Try instead to imagine if we don't need money and looks don't matter, see the bigger picture.

If you find this hard, and too big to tackle, try just imagining the perfect day that would truly make you happy.

Now live it, pretend for just that day that everything you want your world to be, it is. Live it, be it, create it. Just use your imagination and pretend.

After your day is over you will find that you have been living seeing the world through other peoples eyes, and not your own. You have been making do with living in someone else's world, and it is less than perfect isn't it?

Now you know how your world should really be you can start making your world a reality and living it. We are very lucky to have the power to change our own inside world, because when we do, the world outside starts to change too.

28th October 2012

Reaching Our True Potential - Clan Living

I don't give my knowledge to others so that they will follow me, or look up to me. I do it so they realise who and what they are, how much they have been lied to and in turn it will empower them. The world doesn't need more mindless slaves, it needs more knowledgeable teachers and leaders, who can help everyone else realise who they are and empower them too.

In a world where everyone has independent thought, who know who they are, what they are and their true Will and purpose there would be no need for war. People who can think for themselves and be responsible for themselves as well as others, will have no need to look up to others as gurus. They will be more willing to take their true place in a clan, as they will know their own unique role and how they fit in.

This man works in the fields all day, growing crops and tending animals. He feels a great sense of pride in his work, as he knows his work feeds the clan.

This woman is a Mother, who brings new life to the clan. She is there for the children constantly, no need for a nanny. She enjoys her work, as she knows she is creating the clan of the future.

This man is an Artist, he decorates the clan buildings with his works of Art, he is happy that he can spend his life creating things that will delight and inspire everyone in the clan.

This woman is wise and spiritual, she loves to arrange ceremonies and festivals for the whole clan to enjoy, and to teach the young ones about the past.

This man has a passion for making and building things, he loves to provide cover and protection to the clan, by building them beautiful homes that keep them safe from the elements.

This woman is a natural healer, she knows which herbs will heal and how to comfort the ill.

This man and woman are getting older now, and so they spend their time teaching their craft to those younger than them. They are happy to be passing their knowledge on and the respect they have gained from their pupils for teaching them these important skills.

There are so many more roles in a clan, that don't feel like work, as they come naturally. It is all about giving and only taking what we need. It is more important to give, as this creates more happiness than just taking ever can.

When you are living in a natural clan type community, something that is missing these days, everyone has a place and everyone a purpose. Everyone is happy, because they are doing what they love best.

There might be someone who organises things for the clan but that is just another job, like all the others. Just something they are good at and all the other clan members think so too. No ego, no one is better, everyone is important, everyone is equal.

The ego of the spiritually dead would be the only thing stopping someone from wanting to live a life like this. Those who want to control others and force them into work they don't want to do, through their own greed and need to have more than others, which leads to misery and war. Only happy people living life doing the things they were always meant to do, in small clans, leads to a world without war.

How can we ever recover this? How can we learn to use modern technology to make this kind of lifestyle better than it might have been in the past? How can we learn to live in harmony with nature and not destroy it? Maybe it is something that needs to start small, and then spread? Maybe we have the power to start something like this now? What scares us so much from leaving the 9-5 slog in a dead end job, that makes us feel ill, stressed and lifeless? Maybe nothing, have you had enough?

Let's make it happen http://theomerla.weebly.com/

Can you become a Priest/ess?

I was reading a site the other day, someone who was telling everyone he isn't a guru and that he wants to empower everyone. He has built up a large following. I wondered about contacting him, maybe he could help with our movement, seeing as he was appearing to be doing something similar. Then I saw his posts about DNA activation and other rubbish, and I realised he is just another greedy selfish eagle, selling lies to people who are still trapped in selfish false ego. Because lets face it, people will always go the easy and lazy path first. They want to be told they can activate their DNA and become enlightened by just doing a chant and sending money to this cause or that cause. They want to pay for fake initiations which involve fake ceremonies and no work or effort on their part, so long as they pay, because money is everything in this world right? And the 'I'm not a guru' guy just needs more and more of it, in order to enlighten you to the truth, right? Wrong. To become a better person, you have to take responsibility for your own path, you have to do the work yourself, no one else can wave a magick wand and make you a Priest or Priestess, you have to do it yourself. Take the easy, lazy path to nothing and no changes if you feel inclined, but then don't wonder why you achieve nothing but emptiness and pain. What a shock it is to people when they join our Church and realise they are going to have to do some work, learn some things and connect to their own Higher Self in order to deserve the title Priest/ess. Everyone might deserve the chance of becoming a Priest/ess, it doesn't mean everyone will have the courage and strength to make it.

8th December 2012

Visual, Auditory or Kinaesthetic?

It doesn't matter how down I am, or how horrible things get, there is one thing that always makes me feel better. It has been with me since I was a little girl, when I surrounded myself with it, dressed it and collected as many things as possible that are it. That special warm wonderful thing is the colour purple. I have always loved it and it always manages to cheer me up. Still now all these years later it is still with me, making me feel all warm and fuzzy inside when I see its magnificence. I have always been a visual person, and colours are very important to me. In the past I have liked other colours a lot as well, in phases, but no other colour has ever compared to my purple, not ever. If you don't have a special colour, you are probably not a visual person. Although if the sight of something relaxes you more than anything else... like tree tops swaying, watching the sea, looking at a beautiful landscape, then you could be a visual person too.

Everyone has a sense that is more acute in them, three of the five sensory based modes seem to dominate in mental processing:

- Visual thoughts - sight, mental imagery, spatial awareness.
- Auditory (or linguistic) thoughts - sound, speech, dialogue, white noise.
- Kinaesthetic (or proprioceptive) sense - somatic feelings in the body, temperature, pressure, and also emotion.

The other two senses, gustatory (taste) and olfactory (smell), which are closely associated, often seem to be less significant in general mental processing, and are often considered jointly as one.

If you are Auditory person music will comfort and relax you more than anything else, or even talking. An Auditory person is more likely to feel stressed in complete silence than the other groups. Hearing the singing of birds, the sea waves rolling in and out or even white noise, is much more relaxing to them.

Maybe you get comfort from being hugged, or wrapped up in something soft and snugly more than anything else? Then you a Kinaesthetic person, who is more in touch with feelings and needs to be touched, and feel textures against you, to feel comforted.

Which are you? It is certainly something interesting to think about, and will also help you understand better what will cheer you up when you are feeling low.

25th December 2012

Mary, Maria, Miriam - The Title

Mary and Maria are both from the Hebrew Miriam, which means Strong Waters or Waters Of Strength, or beloved. It was used for females in the Mystery School Order back in ancient times.

My surname today is Douglass, Gaelic elements: dubh which means dark or black, and glas, meaning stream or water. Names with water in them are usually bloodline families, it is to do with the underground stream we keep and the fact all knowledge and wisdom flows from the waters of the Goddess.

Back in ancient times we didn't have surnames, but when a woman was named Miriam, Maria, Mary, it meant she was bloodline, and men John (Yochanan) or Joseph (Yosef), they were the titles for men, meaning YAHWEH.

These days in our Order all the women are named the Latin term Soror, which means sister, this is the same as calling someone Mary or Miriam. The men are called Frater, which is Latin for brother.

28th December 2012

Personal Insults - The Weaklings Defence

The thing about personal insults of any kind is that it's all about asserting dominance over the target by bullying them.

Yeah, it's about power. They felt that in the argument, discussion or situation, you had more power than them. They wanted to take away some of your power.

What's the easiest thing to go after, regarding a woman's power? Yep, it's her physical appearance. For man it is his virility or wealth that are the normal targets.

It's a case of them trying to rectify a perceived imbalance of power. If they feel you are out of their league or somehow better than them through their own insecurities -- because of looks, social status, a certain confidence in your walk, intelligence, knowledge, having money when they don't. They see you as more powerful than they are. This is an intolerable situation for them, they just can't deal with that psychologically.

Take their nasty epithet as a backhanded tribute. At the moment someone feels the need to insult you personally, you are very powerful.

Try to think of yourself as visibly powerful when people try to take you down like this. Like when you're out asserting your physical being in the world, striding down the street, looking good. Or on a purposeful errand. You are emanating an energy & self-sufficiency that makes those lower in self-esteem & power feel uneasy. Yelling something is their feeble attempt at getting even with you, since they are unable to do it in any other way.

To put it briefly: Own your power. Take it back from them. You still rule your world. The words they attempt to damage you with didn't change anything.

2nd January 2013

Eastern Spirituality

Something that has always puzzled me is the amount of people who trek off to Indian to visit all kinds of Gurus, and they go on about what a spiritual country it is. Yet India is amongst the worse countries for violence and hatred against women. How can we ever move forward when people constantly look to different flavours of patriarchy and hatred to become 'spiritual' and how can they ever be balanced when they are taught that women are second class citizens. Both Buddhism and Hinduism are deeply patriarchal religions.

See http://agniveer.com/ashamed-to-be-indian/

I am sure you have all come across one of the types who has visited India or some other Eastern country, who dresses like a Monk and sits there in judgement of everyone else, telling them they are not being spiritual for doing this that or the other. You aren't even allowed to crack a smile in their book.

They take themselves so seriously, and they are so pretentious and obnoxious; they really do think the Sun shines out of their arse, and that their shit doesn't stink like everyone else's. Yes annoying aren't they? Namaste this, Namaste that.

Perhaps even more annoying than the New Age Wiccan & Druids who run about saying they are White Witches, without realising their religions are based on Freemasonry, just like Mormons and Scientology, what does that tell you?

Or maybe the Galactic Retardation of Light crew, well you know, nothing needs to be said about those.

These people are all just on their own paths, searching desperately for answers and a purpose. They wear a mask and hide behind a façade of peace and tranquillity, when their words and actions show something completely different, and actually quite sinister.

All these religions are different shades of the same colour. No wonder they all talk about Co-existing. It is fine as long as none of them are actually changing anything, or bringing truth and allowing them to empower themselves by coming to 'Know Thyself'.

The simple truth is that until you forget all patriarchal formed and controlled religions and start looking within yourself, you will never find what you are so desperately seeking. Until you stop following the crowd and pretending to fit in, you will never find peace. Your path is yours, not some old bloke's sat in Indian or someone who wrote a book, or someone who appeared on Oprah. Look inside.

Just a little something for all those who walk about saying 'Namaste' and thinking they support something loving, peaceful and spiritual:

Here's a list of actual Hindu writings from their text advocating rape, sexism, and just plain savagery.

Hinduism

Quote:

In the Brhada-rankyaka Upanishad scripture (advocating rape): Surely, a woman who has changed her clothes at the end of her menstrual period is the most auspicious of women. When she has changed her clothes at the end of her menstrual period, therefore, one should approach that splendid woman and invite her to have sex. Should she refuse to consent, he should bribe her. If she still refuses, he should beat her with a stick or with his fists and overpower her, saying: I take away the splendor from you with my virility and splendor (6.4.9,21).

Quote:

In Dharmasastra, which is a Hindu moral and legal text (all women are whores): Good looks do not matter to them, nor do they care about youth; 'A man!' they say, and enjoy sex with him, whether he is good-looking or ugly. By running after men like whores, by their fickle minds, and by their natural lack of affection these women are unfaithful to their husbands even when they are zealously guarded here. Knowing that their very own nature is like this, as it was born at the creation by the Lord of Creatures (Prajapati), a man should make the utmost effort to guard them. The bed and the seat, jewellery, lust, anger, crookedness, a malicious nature, and bad conduct are what Manu assigned to women. There is no ritual with Vedic verses for women; this is a firmly established point of law. For women, who have no virile strength, and no Vedic verses, are falsehood; this is well established. Manusmrti 9:14-18.

Quote:

In Dharmasastra (women need to be kept under control) Men must make their women dependent day and night, and keep under their own control those who are attached to sensory objects. Her father guards her in childhood, her husband guards her in youth, and her sons guard her in old age. A woman is not fit for independence. -- Manusmrti 9:2-4.

Quote:

In the Vedas: "Lord Indra himself has said, 'The mind of woman cannot be disciplined; she has very little intelligence.' -- Rig Veda 8:33:17.

Quote:

In the Purunas (Hindu Gods Rape Gautama's wife) Formerly the gods lusted for Gautama's wife and raped her, for their wits were destroyed by lust. Then they were terrified and went to the sage Durvasas [an incarnation of Siva], who said, 'I will remove all your defilements with the Satarudriya Mantra [an ancient Saiva prayer].' Then he gave them ashes which they smeared upon their bodies, and their sins were shaken off. --Padma Purana 4:101:174-9.

Quote:

In the Smriti (Lord Rama's mom has sex with a horse 'all night long' to cleanse sins): The prescribed victims -- snakes, birds, the horse, and aquatic animals -- were bound at the place of immolation; each was dedicated to a specific divinity as is set forth in the ritual texts. The priests then bound them all to the posts in the manner set forth in the ritual texts. Three hundred beasts in addition to Dasaratha's jewel of a horse were bound there to the sacrificial posts. Kausalya (Rama's mom) walked reverently all around the horse and then with the greatest joy cut it with three knives. Her mind unwavering in her desire for righteousness, Kausalya (Rama's mom) passed one night with the horse. The priests -- the hotr, the adhvaryu, and the udgatr -- saw to it that the second and the junior most of the king's wives, as well as his chief queen, were united with the horse. Then the officiating priest, who was extremely adept and held his senses in check, removed the fat of the horse and cooked it in the manner prescribed in the ritual texts. At the proper time and in accordance with the ritual prescriptions, the lord of men then sniffed the fragrance of the smoking fat, thereby freeing himself from sin. Then, acting in unison, the sixteen brahman officiating priests threw the limbs of the horse into the fire, in accordance with the ritual injunctions. In other sacrifices, the oblation is offered upon branches of the plaksa tree, but in the Horse Sacrifice alone the apportionment of the victim is made on a bed of reeds. The Horse Sacrifice is known as the Three-Day Rite; for both the kalpasutra and the brahmanas refer to the Horse Sacrifice as a rite lasting for three days. -- Ramayana 1:13:24-33.

Quote:

In the Smriti (method of turning women back to virgins): "A woman who has been unchaste should worship Siva in his calm aspect, Siva who is Kama. Then she should summon a Brahmin and give herself to him, thinking, 'This is Kama who has come for the sake of sexual pleasure.' And whatever the Brahmin wishes, the sensuous woman should do. For thirteen months she should honour in this way any Brahmin who comes to the house for the sake of sexual pleasures, and there is no immorality in this for noble ladies or prostitutes." -- Matsya Purana 70:40-60; cf. Mahabharata III:2:23.

6th January 2013

Put your oxygen mask on – Loneliness

It is becoming a symptom in today's society for people to find themselves feeling lonely. We are brought up in a society that tells us to 'think of number one' and often find others only caring about themselves. We might decide to conform to this and are left with an empty feeling inside. We have a longing inside for someone to do something kind for us. To help us gain back that feeling of warmth from knowing someone cares - so that you will know that not everyone is just out for themselves.

Loneliness is often caused by wanting people to do something for us. When we do things for other people, we are never lonely. So why not stop waiting for others to prove to you there is kindness in the world, when you can prove it to them yourself?

Kindness costs nothing, but can give you rewards that you never expected.

This isn't to say you should put everyone else's needs before your own. That would mean you would be no use to anyone. If you have ever been on an aeroplane, you will probably remember that they say in the emergency procedures - If cabin pressure should change, an oxygen mask will drop and that you should put yours on first, before helping your children or others. Obviously this is because if you couldn't breathe as you were trying to help others, you would faint and be no use to anyone.. So first and foremost - we have to make sure we look after ourselves, then and only then can we be fully able to give others the help they need. Then in return we get the benefits of being able to help them. This is pretty much the advice of Ayn Rand, only she wasn't talking from a spiritual point of view.

The Great Work helps us become complete, however it does take a lot of work and you will have to be selfish to do it, for quite some time. Then once you have got a high attainment yourself, then you are better equipped to help others. If you didn't take the time for yourself in the first place, you wouldn't be able to help others to the standard they deserve.... The Great Work means you are working with your oxygen mask already firmly in place. It will also help you feel complete and the longing for wanting to be rescued by someone else leaves you completely.

9th January 2013

The Return

Fallen from the brightest light
Into the darkest black water
Emerging to begin Divine plight
Many stood up and fought Her

Lands are bathed in blood
Cleansed by the sacred fire
Lost ones sink into the mud
Lifting my great sword higher

The battle isn't over quite
Until the last one falls
The end is now in sight
No hiding behind high walls

Peace and tranquillity restored
Nature now starts to bloom
At last pull down my sword
Place flowers on their tomb

By Tau Tia L Douglass

Seal with a X

If you wonder why I put a X at the end of some of posts it is because it is a symbol for the rune GEOFU, which means - Venus/ Love and Gift/Generosity.

It is well known that Venus is the planet of love, but she also has rulership over all amicable partnerships. GEOFU signifies a union or partnership of some kind or stands for a gift and hence also stand for generosity. So when I put an X I am offering the gift of my generosity and to show I am friendly.

Geofu's X is also sometimes used as a kiss, which in itself is also a gift.

Viking Women

I remember when I used to talk about how Viking society was matriarchal and women were viewed as more important in those days. I was laughed at. Then today I see this article posted saying it is 'new' research.

http://sciencenordic.com/don%E2%80%99t-underestimate-viking-women

And this is what I wrote back in 2007 after my trip to Norway:

We were taken to a place where they keep Viking boats that they have found. Unfortunately my camera was playing up so couldn't get many pics. I did get this very bad one of the best boat in there though. It is the Queen's boat, the one with the most beautiful carving and the biggest one. This is because the Queen's boat were always the best in Viking society the women were thought of as more important than men. The calendar was set up to work with the menstruation cycle of women, 13 months in every year, each 28 days long and this also matches the Moon cycle. The Moon represents femininity and only if a woman is ill or stressed will her cycle not fit to the

Moon cycle. It also makes it harder for women to track their cycle since Christianity where they changed to the Solar calendar. The Sun is masculine and Christian religions all actually worship the Sun and maleness, hence the fact all Churches have a phallic symbol on them, or steeple.

At least now it is becoming more acceptable to admit these things.

Why I will never tolerate patriarchy

There now follows some quotes from patriarchal religious texts and Clergy of these religions.

You don't have to sit here reading them from start to finish, if you do you might begin to feel ill, when you realise just how deeply ingrained into these religions the hatred of women goes.

I was advised to not put all these in, as it would seem a bit too much. However I have decided that everyone has a right to easy access to this information. So you can use this as a reference section more than anything else.

You will feel anger when reading it, despair even, but please remember that not all men are like this, and not all men think this way. We can not take out our anger on all men, for the deluded actions and beliefs of some.

Feel the anger and even humiliation, and get over it, move onwards and upwards, because we know the truth. We know that the Goddess created all life, and all men come from a woman. See those men who need to say these things about women as the pathetic idiots they really are. They are like children, so jealous of women that they need to suppress and hate us.

"When you see a woman thought to be a demon, it's a kind of hell." - Pope Pius II

"Women should not be enlightened or educated in any way. Should, in fact, be segregated as they are the cause of hideous and involuntary erections in holy men." - St. Augustine, father of the Christian Church Catholic

"If people could see what lies beneath the skin, the sight of women would only cause vomiting. If we refuse to touch the dung with your fingertip, as we want to hug a woman, a creature of dung?" - Sant'Odone, abbot of Cluny

"The woman is above every other evil evil, snake venom and against which no medicine is fine. Women are used primarily to satisfy the lust of men." - St. John Chrysostom, which is particularly devoted Herr Joseph Alois Ratzinger, Pope Benedict XVI

"Woman is a temple built upon a sewer. You, woman, you are the devil's gateway, you have the same circuit [male] that the devil did not dare to attack in front. It is because of you that the Son of God had to die , you'll have to escape forever in mourning and covered with rags. " - Tertullian, a Christian theologian

"O believers. When you prepare for prayer wash your face and hands. If you have touched women and can not find water, look clean and dust passatevela on the face and hands." - Koran, Sura V, 6

Rape (NOT the males!) Blessed by God and father of a bastard boss: "They called to Lot and said to him:" Where are the men which came in to thee this night? Bring them out to us, that we may know them. " Lot went out to them at the door and, after closing the door behind him and said, "No, my brothers, do not hurt! Look, I have two daughters which have not known man; let me bring them out and do to them as you like, provided they do not do anything to these men, for they have come under my roof. '" - Bible, Genesis XIX, 5-8

"The veil of Pauline Christianity," the head of every man is Christ, the head of the woman is man, and the head of Christ is God Every man who prays or prophesies with his head covered dishonours his head. But every woman who prays or prophesies with her head uncovered dishonours his head, since it is the same as if her head were shaven. For if a woman will not veil, then she should cut off her hair. But if it is disgraceful for a woman to be shorn or shaven, let her be covered. The man ought not to cover his head, since he is the image and glory of God, but woman is the glory of man. And man was not made from woman, but the woman from man, neither was man created for woman, but woman for man. For this reason the woman ought to have a sign on the head of his addiction. "- St. Paul, First Letter to the Corinthians, XI

"Since the Quran and the teachings of the Prophet, may Allah bless him and rest his soul, are binding for the woman who believes in the divine origin of the Qur'an and in the apostolic-prophetic mission of Muhammad, wear the veil, then , a precise and binding duty. The Muslim woman who wears the veil, expressed through it or tacitly, its Islamic identity and misleading dall'Islàm thought, unfortunately widespread, that can be called a Muslim, the woman who is not the veil, and they justify by saying that the important thing is to have faith in! They did not mind that the Prophet, may Allah bless him and rest his soul, has clearly rejected this idea when he said: "Faith is not present in whether there are Islamic behaviour that indicate the presence within. '"- Hasan Al Turabi, Islamic women into society

Stoning: "When a girl is betrothed virgin, and a man find her in the city, and lie with her, will lead both to the gate of that city and lapiderete them so that they die: the damsel, because she cried not being in the city, and man because he has dishonoured the woman of her neighbour. So put away the evil from you. " - Bible, Deuteronomy XXII, 23

"Every woman unchaste be trodden down as dung in the street." - Bible, Sirach IX, 10

"Flog the adulteress and the adulterer, each with a hundred stripes, and let not pity for them detain you [application] of the religion of Allah, if you believe in Him and the Last Day, and that a group of believers is this punishment." - Koran, Sura XXIV, 2

"If your actions have committed infamous women, those women confined in a house without water nor food until death overtake." - Koran, Sura IV, 15

"The spouses are guilty as soon as you leave the voluptuousness that, later, to pray," Forgive me, O God, our fault! '"- St. Augustine, father of the Christian Church Catholic

"The greater the pleasure, the more serious sin. Lovers with too much heat the wife is an adulterer!" - St. Augustine, father of the Christian Church Catholic

"The conjugal act is a grave sin in any way different from adultery and debauchery to the extent that comes into play the passion of the senses and the odious pleasure, so that no conjugal duty takes place without sin and spouses can not be without sin . " - Martin Luther, the father of Christian Protestant reform

"A mother, as married, get a place in heaven than that of the daughter as a virgin." - St. Augustine, father of the Christian Church Catholic

"The woman is not made in the image and likeness of God is in the order of nature that wives serve their husbands and children their parents, and the justice of this lies in the principle that the lower serve the greater ... It is natural justice that wants less able to serve the most capable. This becomes evident in the relationship between slaves and their masters, who excel in intellect, and excelling in power. "- St. Augustine, father of the Christian Church Catholic , Issues sull'Eptateuco, Book I, § 153.

"There can be no doubt that it is more appropriate to the order of nature that man domains on the woman rather than the woman on the man. This is the principle that emerges when the apostle (Paul) says, "The head of the woman is man," and, "Wives, submit to your husbands." The apostle Peter writes: "Sara obeyed Abraham, calling him lord" " - St. Augustine, father of the Christian church catholic On Lust, Book I, chap. 10.

"Adam was led into sin by Eve, not Eve from Adam's. Right, then, that the woman accept as a master who led to sin." - St. Ambrose, father of the Christian Church Catholic

"There are three reasons why we say that man is the image of God and not the woman. First of all: just as there is one God, and by him all things were created, so a man was created first, and he was born everyone else. So is this entity that is in the likeness of God, that is to say that that is how all things come from God, so all other men proceed from this man. Secondly, as the body of Christ while he was asleep in death on the cross has led to the origin of the church that is the water and the blood which are expressed through the sacraments by which the Church lives and has its origin and becomes the bride of Christ, so from the side of Adam while he slept in paradise was formed when his wife was taken a rib from which Eve was created. Thirdly, just as Christ is head of the Church and governs the Church, so the husband is head of the wife and the rule and govern. E 'for this reason that man alone is the image of God, and not the woman. And for this reason man must not be like the woman a sign of subjection, but a sign of freedom and the rule. " - Uguccio, Summa, C. 33, q. 5, chap. 13.

"Every woman should walk as Eve mourning and penance, so that the robe of penance, they can fully atone for what comes from Eve, the shame, I say, the first sin, and hatred inherent in her , because of human destruction.

You do not know that you are Eve? The sentence of God on your sex remains today, your guilt remains. You are the door to the Devil! Thou hast eaten of the forbidden tree! You first have disobeyed God's law! You've convinced Adam, because the devil was not valiant enough to attack! You destroyed the image of God, man! Because of what you did, the Son of God had to die! " Tertullian, a Christian theologian, De Cultu Feminarum, book 1, chapter 1.

"I do not permit a woman to teach, nor to control the man, but to be silent. Fact Adam was formed first, then Eve, and Adam was not deceived before, but the woman being deceived fell into transgression." - St. Paul, Letters to Timothy

"As in all the communities of the faithful, the women keep silent in the assemblies because it is not allowed to speak, but should be subordinate, as even the law says. If you want to learn something, they should ask their husbands at home, for it is disgraceful for a woman speak in church. " - St. Paul, First Letter to the Corinthians, XIV, 34-35

"Women should submit to their husbands as to the Lord, because the husband is the head of the wife as Christ is the head of the Church." - St. Paul, Letter to the Ephesians

"The Apostle says that the woman is clearly lower, in order that the Church of God is pure." - Ambrosiaster, The first letter to Timothy 3.11.

"In truth, women are feeble race, untrustworthy, of mediocre intelligence." - Epiphanius, Panarion 79, § 1.

"Both the nature and the law, place the woman in a subordinate relation to man." - Irenaeus, Fragment No. 32

"The duty of the wife is to provide the main government of the house in subordination to her husband. The man has the final say in all matters economic and domestic, and the woman must be ready to obey in all things: his place is mainly at home. So to condemn the efforts of those feminists whose claims are aimed at a broad equality between men and women. " - Pope Paul VI

"For the purpose of Christian education of a child who does not know what good flutes, lyres and harps, music is prohibited. Must not have nice waiter and cared for, but an old virago serious, pale, sordid night at the urging of prayer and the singing of psalms and prayers in the days to hours due. Should not take baths that hurt the decency of a young girl, which should never be seen naked. bred in the cloister will be under the watchful eye of his grandmother and will not look face, nor no man will know that there is another sex. " - St. Jerome, Father and Doctor of the Catholic Church

"If it's good not to touch a woman, then it is a bad touch: married men live like beasts, in fact, in intercourse with women, men do not differ in anything from pigs and animals unreasonable." - St. Jerome, Father and Doctor of the Catholic Church

"Admonish those [women] whose part you fear disobedience, leave them alone in their beds, beat them." - Koran, Sura IV, 34

"The man responsible government, she must bend. Man is highest and best, the woman dimidiata a creature, a beast hydrophobic, which has the greatest merit is to generate." - Martin Luther, the father of Christian Protestant reform

"Lord, make the child with all your might, if we let life die as well, good for you since you die doing noble work." - Martin Luther, the father of Christian Protestant reform

"Although tired and eventually have to die, does not do anything, let them deal with the death, they are here because of that." - Martin Luther, the father of Christian Protestant reform

"If the wife does not want to be a servant!" - Martin Luther, the father of Christian Protestant reform

"Towards your man will have to go your desire and he will be your master, so then descend to his addiction, so be one of the subordinate. Women are primarily designed to satisfy the lust of men. Where there is death there is the marriage and where there is no marriage there is no death. " - St. John Chrysostom, which is particularly devoted Herr Joseph Alois Ratzinger, Pope Benedict XVI

"It is appropriate for women to vote because they are more conservative and more closely linked to the ecclesiastical circles, but this does not mean value for their necessary inequality and inferiority as Sacred Scripture subjects especially to our attention two of the greatest dangers: wine and women." - Pope Benedict XV

"They ask you of menses. Di ':" I am an impurity. "Do not draw near to your wives during menstruation and not pinch before they are purified." - Koran, Sura II, 222

"When a woman has a discharge of blood, the flow in her body, her impurity seven days, and whoever touches her shall be unclean until the evening. Every bed on which she lies on during her impurity shall be unclean; every piece of furniture on which she sits shall be unclean. Whoever touches her bed must wash his clothes and bathe in water and be unclean until the evening. Whoever touches anything on which she sits shall wash his clothes and bathe with water and be unclean until the evening. If man is in the bed or on the furniture while it sits there for shall be unclean until the evening. There you will approach a woman to uncover her nakedness during the menstrual uncleanness. If one has a relationship with a woman during her menstrual uncleanness and shall uncover her nakedness, he hath discovered

Secrets of the Serpent Bloodline - The Unveiling of Profound Esoteric Mysteries

the source of her, and she has discovered the source of her blood: and both of them will be eliminated from the people. " - Bible, Leviticus

"When a woman is pregnant and will give birth to a male, she shall be unclean seven days, and be unclean as in the time of its rules (Editor's note: menstruation). Foreskin shall be circumcised on the eighth day of the child. Then it will remain thirty days blood of her purifying, will not touch no hallowed thing, nor come into the sanctuary, until they have made the days of her purification. But if she bears a female shall be unclean two weeks, as in its rules, will be sixty-six days of her purifying the blood. " Bible, Leviticus

"The woman was in relationship with man as the imperfect and defective with the perfect. A woman is physically and spiritually inferiour and inferiority is physical element, or more precisely by its over abundance of humidity and temperature of the lower . It is even a mistake of nature, a kind of mutilated male, wrong, badly. " - St. Thomas Aquinas, Summa Theologica

"In any case, the woman is only the propagation of the species. Nevertheless, the woman drags down the soul of man from his height sublime, bringing his body into a slavery more bitter than any other." - St. Thomas Aquinas, Summa Theologica

"So that is seen as being caused by a particular nature (the action of male semen), a woman is nothing more than a lack, or a negative event. For the active power of the semen, it always tries to produce something completely like itself, that is a male. However, if a woman is generated, this can happen because the seed is weak, or because the material (supplied by the female) is inadequate, or the action of external factors such as the action of southerly winds that make the air moist. "- St. Thomas Aquinas, Summa Theologica, 1, q. 92, Article 1

".. The conferring of Orders (to a woman), it can not receive, because from the moment that a sacrament is a sign, not only the thing, but the signification of what is required in all sacramental actions; ... As a result, as you can not in females mean a eminence of degree, since the woman is in a state of subjection, it follows that a woman can not receive sacramental orders. "- St. Thomas Aquinas, Summa Theologica, Supplement ., q. 39, Article 1.

"Women can not be ordained, because the order is given to perfect members of the church, when other men have been charged with the distribution of grace. Women are not perfect members of the church, they are only men. Add to this that women are not in the image of God, but only men. " - De Baysio, Rosarium, c. 27, q. 1, ch. 23.

"It is fitting that women do not possess the power of the keys because they are not in the image of God, but only man is the glory and image of God. This is because the woman has to be subject to man and serve him as a slave, and there can be no other way. "- Antonio de Butrio, Commentaria, II, fol. 89r.

"If" the head of the woman is man, "and this is to be appointed to the priesthood, it would be wrong to abolish the creation, and abandon his head to go to the ends. Because the woman is the man's body, from his rib and subjected to him, from whom she was separated for the procreation of children. It's him, it was said to her, "that will be your master." He is the man the most important part of the woman, as its head. If under these circumstances, do not allow to teach, such as could be granted, in contempt of nature, to exercise the priesthood? For it is the wicked ignorance of the Greeks that led them to order priestesses to female deities. It is possible that this will happen in the law of Christ. If it was necessary to be baptised by women, the Lord would undoubtedly have been baptised by her mother and not by John. And when he has sent us to baptise, he would send us women for this purpose. But nowhere, nothing no writing, decided something, he knew what is in accordance with nature at the same time because he was the creator of nature and the author of the legislation. "- Apostolic Constitutions, III, No. 9 .

Abortion in the Bible: "If someone had one hundred children and live many years, and many of them were his days, if he does not enjoy his property and he has no grave, then I say, better than he has abortion, because these is in vain and walks in the darkness, and his name is covered by the darkness. " - CEI Bible, Ecclesiastes (ex Ecclesiastes), VI, 3

The brother and his brother's widow: "When brothers dwell together, and one of them dies childless, the wife of the dead shall not be married outside with a stranger, her husband's brother to her, and will take in the wife, and perform so to her the duty of the brother. " - Bible, Deuteronomy xxv, 5

"I find more bitter than death the woman, which is all ties: a network his heart, chains her arms. Who pleases God escapes her, but the sinner is taken." - CEI Bible, Ecclesiastes (Ecclesiastes ex) VII, 26

Woe to lesbian, gay and trans: "She did not put a man's garment, nor shall a man put a dressing gown woman, whoever does these things is an abomination to the Lord your God" - Bible, Deuteronomy XXII, 5

Woe to the woman who dares to touch the sacred phallus! "If some are in dispute between them and the wife of approaches to free her husband from the hands of those who beats him and put his hand to grab him in the private parts, you shall cut off her hand, thine eye shall not have compassion. " - Bible, Deuteronomy, XXV, 11

The dispersion of the sacred male semen (masturbation): "Er, Judah's firstborn, became hateful to the Lord and the Lord slew him. Judah said to Onan," Join the wife of his brother, fulfill the duty to her brother and ensures an offspring for your brother. "But Onan knew that the offspring would not be considered his, and every time you went in to his brother's wife, scattered on the ground to keep from producing offspring for his brother. What he did not was pleasing to the Lord: wherefore he slew him also. " - Bible, Genesis XXXVIII, 7

"The woman said," I will greatly multiply thy sorrow and thy conception, in sorrow thou shalt bring forth children. Towards your husband is your instinct, and he shall rule over you. "The man said," Because you listened to your wife and ate from the tree of which I commanded you, 'You shall not eat, "Cursed is the ground because of you in toil you shall eat of it all the days of your life. Thorns and thistles it shall bring forth for you, and you shall eat the' herb of the field. By the sweat of your face you shall eat bread till you return to the ground, because from it you were taken; dust you are and dust you shall return "- Bible, Genesis III

All retired except his wife: "... but on the seventh day thou shalt not do any work, thou, nor thy son, nor thy daughter, nor thy manservant, nor thy maidservant, nor thy cattle, nor thy stranger that is within you. " - Bible, Exodus XX

And you thought ...: "Reason of indignation, reproach and contempt is a woman who keeps her own husband." - Bible, Ecclesiasticus xxv, 20

"If the daughter of a priest dishonours prostitution, dishonours his father shall be burnt with fire. The priest, what is the highest among his brothers, on whose head the anointing oil was poured, and received endowment, wearing the vestments, shall not scarmigliarsi hair nor rend their garments. " - Bible, Leviticus, XXI

(1917 - Murder, torture and crucifixion of thousands of Armenian women by the army Turkish - Photos recently published, kept in the Secret Archives of the Vatican.)

14th January 2013

The Great Mother

My love of the sea has taken me, to the shore to stare some more
into the mists of watery spray, your swirling waves as I sway.
I gaze in awe, your powerful grace, droplets hit my pale white face.
The sky God roars and blows, I grip the soft sand with my toes.
Feeling our Mother's natural charms, embracing me with her arms.
Tomorrow I'll be tempted to return, from her there is so much to learn.
Cleanse my sorrow, and heal my heart, dancing with her is a merry art.
Her elements bring so much joy, yet with any she could choose to destroy,
Great Mother, this blessing for you, with respect, love, all reverence due.

~Tau Tia 2012~

16th January 2013

Saints & Sinners - Every Saint has a past and every sinner has a future.

Don't be ashamed of your past, of the skeletons in your closet.. those are the things that taught you lessons that led you to where you are now. You would not be you if you had not experienced all the things you did in your past - the good, the bad, the sensational and the boring... all led you further into the direction of knowing yourself.

If you embrace who you are, who you were and who you can become, those who threaten you with the past have absolutely nothing on you..

Let's Rock The Boat

I see people everyday who are living in fear. Scared to rock the boat, scared of the consequences of being different. Some of these people sit there moaning about how terrible things are in the world, and how awful things are becoming.. They see things, then walk away and continue to moan about them... If you ask them why did they walk away and not help to change things.. The excuses come.. Oh well I would get in trouble, I would be victimised, I would be cast out, people wouldn't understand, I am too busy. And so they continue to sit there and do nothing and wonder why nothing gets any better.

If you are the ones who wants to make things better by being proactive, don't just sign this, get involved. http://www.templeoftheola.org/be-the-solution.html

17th January 2013

Icy Morning

It was early morning and time to walk my dog. Such a chill in the air, the trees and ground covered in ice. I put on my wellies, wrapped up warm and headed out into the icy cold misty morning.

I was nearing the top of the lane when I came across an elderly lady, struggling with some shopping bags. She looked so tired, in pain and red faced. I walked up and said "Let me take those for you" at first she flinched as if she was worried someone was stealing from her, and when she looked at my face and saw my warm smile, she smiled back and allowed me to take them. With her hand on her back she straighten up before saying "Oh thank you, I wasn't sure I was going to make it much further... oh I could do with a nice hot cup of tea." I replied "Where do you live?" She pointed and we set off in that direction chatting as we walked.

When we got to her house I took her bags in, cranked up the fire for her and made us a cup of tea. She was so happy to have someone help her, and to have someone to talk to.

She has lived alone now for 7 years, since her beloved husband passed away and has no one visiting her, as her only son also passed away from cancer. She told me how some days she felt like giving up, everything was so much effort and it didn't seem worth carrying on. But today she said, my thoughtful act had given her hope.. She had walked that path so many times back from the shop with her weekly shopping, and not once had someone offered to help.. they just walked on by without a thought for her.

My dog cheered her up too, as he cuddled up to her. She was delighted to make his acquaintance and said she wished she could have a dog for the company, she always had dogs when she was younger and able to give them the proper care they deserve.

As I was leaving, she asked if I was religious and if that was my reason for helping her today. I told her that I didn't need a religion to make me feel guilty for not doing good things, my own Higher Self guides me and I treat others how I would want to be treated myself. She gave me a hug and I noticed a tear in her eye. She grabbed my hand, looked me in the eye, then with warmth and genuine sincerity said thank you. She told me that the shopping she had got today was supposed to be a special treat for her last meal, as she had decided there was no point going on. However she felt so much better now that this meal will be a celebration, because you never know what wonderful thing will be round the corner. I could feel tears coming to my own eyes, not just for this woman, but all those who feel so lonely and forgotten that they consider killing themselves, no one should have to feel like that.

I will go back and visit her again soon, and will help her with things all I can. I will also make her neighbours aware of the fact that she is alone and to look out for her. 30 minutes of your time a week, just to pop in and see someone who is alone will change their life for the better and yours too.

23rd January 2013

Purple Quill

For all of my talk, or writing rather, the one thing I find the most difficult to write about is myself. I do not spend all my time doing everything I do so that others can consider me as any kind of guru. I don't spend hours answering everyone's questions, without pay when I should be working, because I am seeking some kind of fame or acknowledgement. I do what I do because I know some things that not a lot of others in the world do. I feel that everyone has a right to that knowledge. This knowledge empowers you when you know it, not me. If I keep it to myself that is what gives me power, teaching you gives nothing to me personally. Apart from the hope that those with this Gnosis themselves will help make the future that much brighter for everyone.

I consider myself down to earth and relaxed type of woman, and might come across differently to reality when online. That is because of the topics I am passionate about, I talk about with passion. It does not mean I get angry, but yes sometimes very disappointed in how people treat me for my opinions and other more personal qualities of mine. I have some good points and I have some human failings. I am proud of some of my achievements, and there are things that I have done that I have learnt some very bitter lessons from, I did learn from them however. I make mistakes, and I will always make mistakes at times, that can not be helped. But I am certain that I do not belong on anyone's pedestal. I am a woman with a message and with a lot of Gnosis inside, that I share honestly and openly with those who want to hear and want to see. And the message will be heard by only a few. To those few who will understand, I am your sister. Maybe...we can change the future for the better.

25th January 2013

The Aliens Have Landed

Why do so many fall for alien or new age theories?

Since you were born you have been programmed, consistently, into thinking that aliens do exist and that the government know about this, but are just covering it up. You have watched movies about this, see secret 'leaked' reports and films. Heard accounts of people seeing UFOs and some even saying they have been anally probed when abducted by aliens. It is deeply embedded into your unconscious that -- aliens exist, and those who don't know this just don't have an open mind.

So what happens when time and time again the 'proof' people come up with is debunked?

Psychologists have understood for years that humans want to be seen as being consistent. Not only do we want to be consistent to ourselves, we want to look consistent to others. Leon Festinger describes this quite nicely in his book Cognitive Dissonance.

A person who is consistent is seen as stable, honest and trustworthy. A useful member of society! Now try to imagine how a society would function with totally inconsistent members...!

In his book on influence Cialdini explains that behaving consistently with our thoughts and beliefs is often much easier than having to change our thinking. Because if we took the time to think, we might not like what we realise.

And whatever happens, most of us don't want to be seen to be wrong. So once we have started into something, there are very strong forces pushing us to continue. Once we make a decision, we create reasons and justifications for it and so the idea 'grows legs of its own'.

Because of these types of influence Cialdini points out that sometimes we will act in ways that are contrary to our own best interests. I'll say that again. These influences mean that sometimes we will act in ways that are contrary to our own best interests.

Conclusion

Even though people realise aliens haven't visited us, and we have no idea if any life does exist on other planets - they would rather look stupid and feel they are right, than back down and say they were wrong. And after all, you can always persuade yourself with more pseudoscience and there is always some raving lunatic of a guru out there to validate your delusions.

'What the Thinker thinks, the Prover will prove' Anton Wilson.

Feeling Boxed In?

You live in a box for your home, you travel in a box on wheels to and from work, you spend your evenings staring at a box as it rots your brain and your body slowly ages and withers away. Then when you die you are put into a box.

I wonder why a box? When all of nature is in cycles and curvy organic shapes.

Wouldn't you rather live in a more natural and organic space?

Before patriarchy we all lived in round houses, mounds and caves. Now we live at odds with nature in a patriarchal boxed in world.

Some are starting to get the idea of how things should be. As humans we are much happier and healthier when living in natural organic shapes.

2nd February 2013

A Doer or just a Thinker?

Changes don't happen, and people die every day needlessly in wars because millions of us tell ourselves that caring is just as good as doing. It's an internal mechanism controlled by the lazy part of your brain to keep you from actually doing anything. Why make any effort to make a difference, when you know deep down inside you really do care, and 'your thoughts are with' those unfortunate people who suffer the most in the world?

I will tell you why - because you have to be the one to change things. You have to be the one to help. You have to be the one who get other people involved in changing things. Just caring isn't enough.

If you give what you can to help us get on with things, you are someone who has become a Contributor, rather than just a Thinker, you are stepping in the right direction.

However, become a Doer, a Motivator or anything else you have the skills to do... and then you will be more than a Contributor, you will be a cog in the engine of change, a petal on the flower of peace and a droplet in the ocean of balanced harmony.

Resources: http://www.templeoftheola.org/resources.html

11th February 2013

How To Spot Fake Movements

How to spot a fake movement funded by Eagle psyops used to bring in Agenda 21.

1. They appear overnight with a massive following.
2. Surprise surprise they have the backing of film stars and other celebrities.
3. They have very high quality videos that cost a fortune to produce, that seem to have been made before the funding even started.
4. They tug on your heart strings by having victims of whatever they are pushing in the video.
5. They usually involve mentioning aliens, but not always.
6. They nearly always talk about the environment and how people destroy it.

Some examples of the frauds are: Thrive, Wayseers, KONY, One Million Rising, Venus Project, Occupy, Anonymous, and many more.

Grimoire

The Occult word "grimoire" or book of spells means "grammar" which also tells us that "spells" are to do with putting letters together for "spelling" words or forming conceptual ideas for the purpose of raising another person's conscious awareness.

16th February 2013

Is being homosexual an obstacle?

I get asked a lot of questions all the time through email, and when I answer I am answering only one person at a time. So now I will post questions and give my answers here.

Question: Do you think being homosexual is an obstacle for spiritual growth?

Answer: One could argue that any kind of 'sexual' is an obstacle, as lust is one of the things a spiritually aware person conquers and so can not be controlled by it.

If you are happy alone and feel complete alone, you are balanced. If you do not feel complete without this lust, then it will stop you progressing past the material world. People can use this against you, it can become an addiction and can stop you spiritually 'growing up'.

Of course a gay male will struggle more reaching illumination as he would not like to perform the Great Rite with a female, and unlike the assumptions of Aleister Crowley a gay male sexual act can not achieve illumination.

So therefore the male homosexual must find a path to enlightenment alone and in solitude and this is the origins of the gay celibate Priesthood. Only not all those who go into the Priesthood are ready to conquer their lust, and it has led to the abuse of children.

If you can not conquer your lust, this is the obstacle to spiritual growth for all, not just homosexuals.

22nd February 2013

Illuminati

I am getting a little tired of people assuming Adam Weishaup invented the word 'Illuminati' or 'Illumination' in 1776, and that even though his organisation later became known as the Freemasons, that they are the only ones who use that word and somehow own it.

When someone is illuminated it means they know the truth. It does not mean they are evil, knowing the truth does not make someone evil. What the person chooses to do with their knowledge could though be seen as either good or evil.

Long before Adam Weishaup there were - The Alumbrados (Illuminated) which was a term used to describe practitioners of a mystical form of Gnosticism in Spain during the 15th-16th centuries. The Alumbrados held views that were clearly heretical. Consequently, they were firmly repressed and became some of the early victims of the Spanish Inquisition.

However where did they get their Gnostic teachings from? The Serpent Bloodline Mystery Schools of course. The Alumbrados were those who had tried to infiltrate Christianity and the Jesuits to bring the true teachings of the Serpent Bloodline. But when they were found out they were burnt at the stake. Sound familiar? Yes, it also happened to the Cathars in France and the 'true' Templars, who were Gnostics NOT Christians.

So quit throwing the word 'Illuminati' around like you know what it means, when you clearly don't.

27th February 2013

I am tactless, Sorry!

Some people say I am tactless for just speaking my mind. They don't realise my intention isn't to upset people. I say good positive things, and I also say something about things I disagree with, or don't like sometimes. Saying good things is fine, it is giving those who need it, narcissistic supply. But when I make a comment about something I disagree with or don't like, the person often gets very defensive and usually just attacks me.

I am the way I am because I prefer honesty to lies, I speak my mind and give my true opinion.

On Facebook I guess it isn't directly asked for, but then why do people add me to their contact list if they never want to hear my opinion about things?

Did they only join FB to be surrounded by people who will constantly tell them how wonderful they are and always agree with them?

I guess they must.

I think this is the difference between me and them. When I ask someone's opinion about something, I don't do it to get compliments and be told how wonderful everything is. I ask them so I can get their opinions and then I can either see what they mean and make changes and improve it, or say I don't agree and just stick to how it is, but at least they were honest with me.

If I post something on my FB wall and someone comments under it that they don't agree, I will discuss it with them and find out why they think that, and why I don't. I will look at their side and if needs be just accept we are never going to see eye to eye on that point. But I won't instantly hate that person and attack them and call them names because they don't agree with my opinion about something.

So please try to change your perception of 'tactless' people, as they are just telling you like it is. They are being genuine. They haven't spent hours thinking up what to say, they just say it and they have no ulterior motive.

A troll will just call someone names for no reason, that is completely different. When someone doesn't agree with something, it does NOT mean they are a troll.

15th March 2013

Pain Drain - Healing Magick Sigil

I decided I would create a sigil to help those who suffer from chronic pain, but you can also use this if you have a headache or some other kind of temporary pain.

How it works

When I created the sigil I gave it certain instructions and this is how it works. When you feel pain, call the name of the sigil, which is Archegoniumel.

Bring an image of the sigil to mind.

Imagine all your pain being focused towards the sigil, imagine the pain being drained away.

Archegoniumel will absorb the pain away from you, it will then work at converting that pain into healing energy, which it will in turn send back to you.

Your pain will ease and you will feel lighter, uplifted and much happier. Archegoniumel will also send you some good luck.

After you have finished, be sure to say thank you to Archegoniumel for her help.

The more Archegoniumel is used, the more powerful a healer she becomes, this is something we are all building up and helping with together as we use her as a healer.

Sigils are very powerful and useful tools to achieve amazing results, if you would like a personal sigil making, please contact us at Alchemist's Laboratory and we will make your wishes come true.

When in pain.. Remember my name...
Archegoniumel

Secrets of the Serpent Bloodline - The Unveiling of Profound Esoteric Mysteries

Part 2
The Order

The forming of the Order

On reaching Magister Templi I was given a word, and that word was THEOLA, it is a name that in Greek means Divine. At that point on my path I had discovered that something was missing from all the currents I had been involved with. It was not because of them that I had got to where I had, it was my own hard work and dedication, my family and ancestors had led me back to this place. It was then that my Higher Self told me that the only way forward was to create an Order, a new public one, based on the ancient teachings passed down through our bloodline. It would, finally after all these thousands of years, be bringing our secret Order out into the public. I wanted it to be open and allow anyone seeking to be part of it. However I soon found out this was not possible. Too many joined for the sole purpose of trying to destroy us from the inside, or by signing the Oath when they were not ready to do the Great Work. Then leaving when they realised it would be hard work and time consuming. It was then decided we needed to go back underground. Still having a public image, but by making the membership by invitation only.

Ordo Infinitus Orbis was established in March 2009. Set up to provide those worthy of it, the secret knowledge and mysteries of the magick arts which lead to Illumination. Although a newly established order its mysteries come from ancient wisdom passed through generations of one bloodline. Our sole purpose and intention is to influence the future. To bring balance, harmony and peace to a new world formed through equality for our tribes men and women. Before you can help change the future, you must also learn how to empower and balance yourself. Hence the new Order for the new world was formed. It has become clear that we must either destroy or balance old religions and traditions to bring harmony. Ordo Infinitus Orbis is balanced, no Soror or Frater is invited because of their sex, only by their ability to show their true lineage back to our ancient tribes of spiritual leaders and warriors.

The International Priory of Knights Hospitaller Templar was created as an Outer Order for those who want to get more involved in what we are doing and be part of the team of those of us who are more involved with actually getting these things done. They can apply for the Knights Hospitaller Templar Outer Order, and they can get as involved as much they want to, hopefully a lot. We need more confident organised people to get on with things, and think of new ideas, to promote and all other things involved with this.

True Herstory of the Templar Knights

Before the Templars were known as the Templars they were known by many other names. The Order was set up to protect the bloodline families and the knowledge that has been passed down by word of mouth to family members and Initiates for many thousands of years. However to be able to carry this out, Stealth is required.

Wherever we have been on the globe, we always try to get in positions of power in politics, religion and health care. This works to our advantage as we can plant seeds of knowledge within all these organisations, and help bring change. We have had to outwardly appear to be Christians or Jews or whatever. This worked fine for the Templar Knights, until the Order was infiltrated and they were found out and burnt at the stake for heresy.

However some did survive, and went underground. For many years we slowly let more and more information out into the general public, until it reached a time when people had learnt enough, and were educated enough to be more accepting of the truth. Now we are at a time when all those of the bloodline will be called back together, to help prepare for the next Aeon. The Aeon we have been waiting for, where everything will change, but only if we succeed in our work.

There are many Templar Orders set up in our name who are Christian, and worst still Roman Catholic. These are nothing to do with the real Templars, who are now and have always been Gnostics. The International Priory of The Knights Hospitaller Templar is connected to no other Templar Order. Various Orders have been set up, but none other than us by true spiritual royalty.

There are few Orders we are in contact with, however at this time we have no other public face other than our Church and Order. All the rest of our connections are still thoroughly underground and many in public roles, they will join us in the public side of things eventually, but right now they are best left undercover in their positions, ready for the next stage of the plans. We have links with bloodline families all over the world, and everyone is doing there bit to help within there own areas of expertise.

Within the Church, Order and Companions here we can all help to get more of our Kin back together by promoting our Church and Order. Those who are willing to help this way will be given more responsibility within the Church, Outer Order or Order. Those who are Companions may in time be asked to join the OIO-KHT and become a Probationer of the Order proper, and have a chance to gain full Initiation into the Mysteries. Likewise those in the Church will be invited to join when they reach the Major Orders.

The Knights Hospitaller Templar Cross

The original Templar cross was always white to represent purity of our noble hearts and to represent all 7 colours of the chakra rainbow which are activated and balanced in true Gnostic Spiritual Knights. After the inquisition those who took our name changed the colour to red to signify the blood of all our Shamanistic Seer families who they slaughtered in the name of their 'God'.

Much like today when people wear a red poppy to remember the dead SOLdiers who have been sacrificed to in the name of their God. Peace loving people wear a white poppy to show that even though they are upset about the deaths of all those soldiers, they want peace, not war. The colour red represents male energy and the element of fire, so this is also another way of the Christian Templars wiping patriarchy and their lies right in our faces.

Within our own Order our cross is always white, or on documents sometimes black or grey, this is for printing purposes. But as for anything we wear or show in public to represent us, it is always the white cross. Our sigil and logo have some red trimmings and this is to show to others that we are the true bloodline, and that the white cross of purity shines higher than their blood stained patriarchal red one. If the white cross is shown on a red background, this is showing they are the original Templars who joined our Order as infiltrators, then took over and came under Roman Catholic control. These Orders sometimes wear our original white cross on a black background so they can sometimes be hard to spot. They might have money, fancy robes and medals, and that is because they are under the Roman Catholic Church who have vast amounts of money at their disposal. Spiritual beings care less about fancy robes, titles and showing off, and care more about the Earth. We have some of our rituals outside in nature as this gives us a connection to our Great Mother. Our indoor Temples are coated with purple and our sigil too, to show balance between the feminine - blue, water, west, and the masculine - red, fire, south. Together they make purple, the royal colour of our bloodline.

Also the Knights Templar seal that we see so often which is two men on horseback is another sign of a Christian Patriarchal Order, it represents the Brotherhood. Any organisation which uses the word 'Brotherhood' is either openly or secretly under Papal control.

The Brotherhood Templars

After the bloodline families were slaughtered, those who took over the Templars set up all kinds of related organisations. The Cro-Magnon brotherhood red cross Templars moved to Switzerland where they set up the Swizz banking system and they are still there to this day. This can all be verified if you start to look into it. Unfortunately most of those who have exposed this think that this intruders are the 'real' Templars, and they don't know the truth of what really happened.

In Switzerland you will find a lot of references in monuments to ancient Egypt. They are from the Akhenaten line, not the Ramases line.

The Title Tau

Tau is used as a title, given to Gnostic Bishops.
In Greek the letter Tau forms a "T," and also in Hebrew the letter called "Tau" is shaped like a "T" ancient Hebrew. Thus the title Tau in terms of esoteric Occultism, indicates the T Cross. The Tau cross, being given the meaning of a state of complete enlightenment and immersion in the Divine Light – the power of being a Theolalite; hence, it indicates embodiment or realisation of Gnosis and Sophia. Tau as a symbol represents the womb and vagina of the Priestess, which is the source of life and enlightenment.

In Eastern Orthodox traditions, and those evolving from the Orthodox tradition, generally it is the Greek Tau that is used, but in the Gnostic tradition it is the Hebrew Tau, which bears added esoteric meaning because it is the last letter of the Hebrew Alef-Bet, and therefore has the same meaning as "Omega" in Greek – the end or fruition, perfection and completion. From this a deeper and more esoteric meaning may be drawn from a saying of: "I am Alpha and Omega," or "I am Alef and Tau." All life starts in the womb and enlightenment is also found there, the Holy Grail. The beginning of the Great Work starts from the day you are born, and for males at least, it ends in complete enlightenment that he receives from the Goddess incarnate, the Priestess.

Although in Orthodox traditions the title Tau is used synonymously with the title of Bishop, and indicates the ecclesiastical function of a Bishop in apostolic succession – an overseer and direct successor to the original apostles. In our esoteric apostolic succession, or Gnostic apostolic succession, the title of Tau indicates something distinct from the title of Bishop – a Tau may be a Bishop in the sense of the exoteric apostolic succession, but the title Tau is used to indicate a state of illumination and attainment. We use this to indicate a realised individual or spiritual King or Queen who has the capacity to transmit something of the power of their realisation.

The exoteric apostolic succession relies upon faith, and upon creed and doctrine, and rites and rituals. Gnosis or actual enlightenment is not the criteria for ordination or consecration. In the Gnostic apostolic succession, however, recognition is based upon Gnosis – an actual experience of enlightenment or self-realisation, and the capacity to convey something of that realisation to others.

When someone has reached this attainment of Tau it is rather obvious – initiates experience and can bear witness to various gradations of Kundalini awakening. In our Church, a Tau serves as the principle teachers and guardians of the lineage, and attend to the spiritual labour of the outer circle. A Tau also serves as the knowledge-keepers and revealers of the lineage, and attend to the inner circle.

Of course someone might become enlightened and choose to not serve as a Tau lineage holder. Enlightenment is not dependent on receiving the title in its self.

We understand that the term Tau is something more than a title as it is used in our Church – it represents a state of being. The spiritual and mystical teachings associated with "Tau," are more than symbolic metaphor – they indicate an actual experience of Divine Gnosis or Divine Illumination.

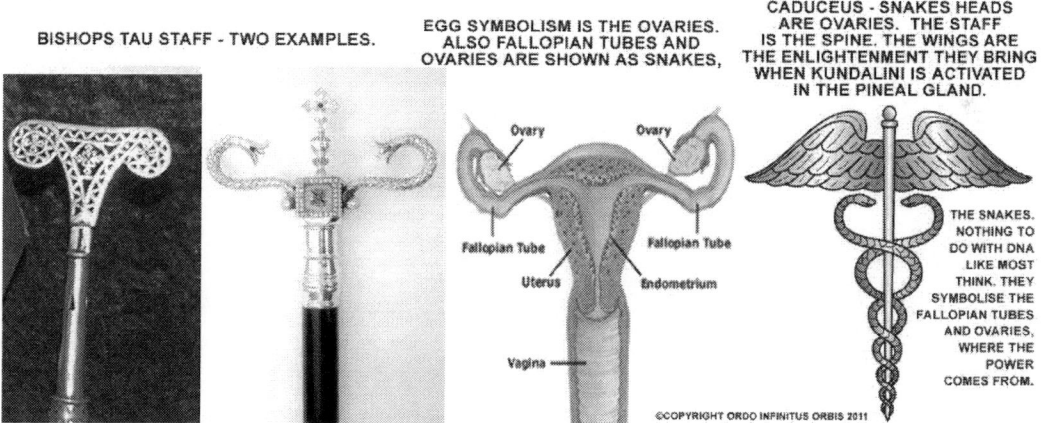

Crosses Before & After Names

Secrets of the Serpent Bloodline - The Unveiling of Profound Esoteric Mysteries

On becoming a Priest/ess of The Church of St Mary & St John Clergy are given a + after their name. This is because Sub-Deacons and Deacons are also known as Reverend, so to show someone is a Priest/ess when writing their name they have a Cross put after it. This is a sign of respect for the Great Work they have done to get that far, and to show they are entitled to perform the Celtic Gnostic Mass, Marriages, Baptisms and various other Sacraments which are a real honour.

When someone becomes a Right Reverend, which is an Abbot/Abbess or Bishop, they get a Cross before their name, again to show how far they have come on their path. So for instance, when Graham became a Priest his name was Graham+ and then when he became an Abbot which is a Rt. Rev. he got the Cross before his name, like so +Graham.

If someone has two Crosses before their name, It means they are the Presiding Bishop. So the name can be written like so ++Tia. The only other time someone would have two Crosses would be if they were a Bishop and also the Bishop for the entire country they reside in. For instance, if someone from the USA was to become a Bishop within our Church, and we made them Bishop of the USA, they would also get two Crosses.

When someone has three Crosses it means they are an Archbishop. They are a Bishop, who is also a Presiding Bishop and have Consecrated at least one other Bishop. So therefore my name is wrote like so +++Tia.

The whole Crosses thing is just a way of spotting quickly who is who within the Church and their role. And as we are all primarily Brothers and Sisters this is just a polite way of showing different levels of attainment, without the need of fancy titles.

Bafomet

There is so much confusion about Baphomet or in reality the true spelling Bafomet. It has been said that the Templars worship it, that it is a corruption of Mahomet or Muhammad the prophet of Islam. I think it is about time the record was put straight once and for all.

There is a legend that the Templars had close relations with the sect of Ashashin, who worshipped an idol named Bafomet. If Bafomet was the Holy Grail, the Ashashin gave it to the Knights Templar, who hid it with their treasure in the castle of Gisors in France.

The Ashashin, Hashishin, Hassassin, or Hashashiyyin is translated to English as Assassin. The term "assassin" is commonly used to describe a hired killer or a cut-throat. The term later paved the way for another term "assassination" which denotes any action involving murder of a target for political reasons.

The term hashishiyya or hashishi as used by Muslim sources is used metaphorically in its abusive sense (i.e. "irreligious social outcasts", "low-class rabble", etc.). The literal interpretation of this term in referring to the sect (as hashish consuming intoxicated assassins).

The reality was they were a sect formed and based on the teachings of the Serpent people, who had taught them about the Sacred Holy Herb – Cannabis, and therefore used this in their ceremonies. The legends of them passing the Bafomet to the Templars was all started with the formation of the word itself which didn't occur until later.

The word was used as code for the Goddess Sophia, meaning wisdom, it also was to represent the Sacred Holy Herb and even when tortured the Templars did not reveal the truth of this, as they used the code word in confessions – Bafomet. Which in the Atbash cipher does equal Sophia.

When the Pope heard this word, he didn't know what it meant but he had found that the Templars *"Are not like other men and women"*.

The King and the Pope in 1307 alleged that they saved humanity from the most dangerous crisis of its history. In his letter to Philip the Fair, Pope Clement V ° warned that the Knights Templar were plotting to seize power in the whole of Europe, and for this purpose had allied relationships with unbelievers. But not only this, the Templars were a deadly threat to Christianity and all humanity, and he, Philip, had the irrefutable evidence and would have given to the Pope that the Templars "are not human beings, but a foreign people who came to Earth from the dark depths of the abyss of the universe, they are Extra-Terrestrial" The Latin of this being - Barathri Advenit Fundo Obscuro Mundi Extra Terram = BAFOMET.

What they had indeed discovered is that the Serpent people who are not the same as them, as we are a different species, had been spreading the true teachings of spirituality that if spread out to the controlled public, would result in complete loss of power of the Pope and their religion which restricted and controlled everyone. Yet again the Serpent had come with knowledge for the people, and according to them and their corrupt power system we were heretics and must all die.

They did not think we were aliens, just 'extra' beings of the Earth, from underground. This is what extra-terrestrial first meant. Terra means Earth. We had a secret tunnel network which we used to get about without being seen. We also had underground Temples that we used, that we had to keep hidden.

So Bafomet was given a new meaning to the Catholics to represent the Serpent people and our teachings, which led to illumination.

It received its look later on, when Eliphas Levi (ex Alphonse Louis Constant), Occultist of the nineteenth century interpreted the symbol of Bafomet (it says it has seen in Paris in a building of Saint Brix Vineux the former property of the Templars) as the representation of the absolute in form symbolic.

He described it as *"The gargoyle has the form of a bearded and horned figure bursting with female breasts and feet in the shape of a goat. It 'sitting with his legs crossed, a position that recalls the Celtic god or Cernunnos The Horned God, which is made cult in Gaul before the Roman occupation."*
The only difference being the Bafomet was both male and female, meaning it represents balance, and the torch on its head representing illumination. And because of the link to the Hashishin and the Sacred Holy Herb, it is also to representing that too.

He changed the spelling to again make it all about men, to Baphomet. Then he could make a backwards coded message for it in Latin: **TEM OHP AB** which means "Templi omnivm hominum pacis abbas" or in English "The Father Of The Temple Of Peace Of All Men". This he felt to be a reference to King Solomon's Temple, which Eliphas believed had the sole purpose of bringing peace to the world. Again another patriarch removing the feminine completely.

Now we look to the Bafomet and remember the suffering and bravery of our ancestors as they strived to get the true teachings out to the public.

Secrets of the Serpent Bloodline - The Unveiling of Profound Esoteric Mysteries

Liber OIO

Triwens, Love, Light, Theola, Divine, 333

Do Thy Divine WILL, So It Shall Be All

Thy Divine WILL Is Love, Love Be It All. All Say Aye, Aye And Aye

The Law Is Love, In The Divine Light Of Being, Love Is All

Only those who seek truth have the right to be raised from the darkness of ignorance and to bathe in the light of the Divine.

TRIWENS - The Divine flows through me,
TRIWENS - The darkness of ignorance is lifted from me,
TRIWENS - The bonds between my brothers and sisters is connected through thee.

Let no other own your soul. Make no other your slave.
Be free from restriction and rejoice in your own Divine light.

Intuition is the Key to Truth. Truth is Knowledge. Knowledge is Wisdom.

The Divine Kings And Queens Of The Earth Shall Rule Forever - The Slaves Shall Serve.

Every Man and Every Woman is Divine - Do Thy Divine WILL, So It Shall Be All.

Triwens, Love, Light, Theola, Divine, 333

© Copyright OIO - KNIGHTS Hospitaller Templar 2010 All Rights Reserved

Secrets of the Serpent Bloodline - The Unveiling of Profound Esoteric Mysteries

Part 3
𝔗𝔥𝔢 𝔥𝔦𝔡𝔡𝔢𝔫 𝔠𝔥𝔲𝔯𝔠𝔥

The Church of St Mary & St John

Our Church is the 'hidden' occult Church which whose teachings have and lineages back to Mary Magdalene and John the Baptist, have been kept safe in the underground stream of knowledge, waiting for a time when the people were ready for the truth.

The Church of St. Mary & St. John is an open and friendly face to religion. An inviting and accepting Church where people can be themselves without fear of rejection, no matter what their sexuality, race, status, gender. All are welcome to become part of the Church.

Helping others find inner peace and happiness might be the most wonderful gift you can give to another, and could be considered one of the most rewarding vocations in life.

Our beliefs stem from the Gnostic texts, Dead Sea Scrolls & Grail Code, as well as other spiritual and religious texts. We believe in the Divine Feminine and bringing back the balance between masculine and feminine.

Each of us must search for our own True Will which is gained from Sophia (Wisdom) and Gnosis (Intuitive Knowledge). Through Sophia and Gnosis we can find salvation of the soul from the material world. The teachings that lead to Gnosis have been hidden in the underground stream by those who have secretly passed it down.

We don't believe Jesus was the son of a Carpenter, but was of royal blood and probably a member of the Nazarene, who were a religious sect which included both Priests and Priestesses.

We believe Jesus was married to Mary Magdalene and that she bore him children. The descendants of whom have carried the bloodline through to this day.

We draw some parallels with the early Minoan religion. As well as The Johannine tradition, which is an esoteric church. The Johannine tradition teaches that Jesus & Mary bestowed authority upon John the Baptist to create a hidden church to carry the true teachings, that the majority of people at that time were not yet ready to receive.

Secrets of the Serpent Bloodline - The Unveiling of Profound Esoteric Mysteries

Orders & Societies

Order of St Mary Magdalene – (OMM)

Mary Magdalene was of the district of Magdala, on the shores of the Sea of Galilee, where stood her families castle, called Magdalon; she was the sister of Lazarus and Martha, and they were the children of parents reputed noble, or, as some say, royal descendants of the House of David. On the death of their father, Syrus, they inherited vast riches and possessions in land, which were equally divided between them.

Mary Magdalene was the wife of Jesus and they had children together, a fact which was omitted by later revisionist editors of the Gospels.
Mary Magdalene & Jesus took the 'Holy Grail' and the Mystery School teachings to the South of France.

The Order of St Mary Magdalene's origins go back to the first century and Mary Magdalene as its founder. It has continued since then secretly and the lineages passed down through the females of the Holy Grail Bloodline. This cannot however be verified by historians or scholars, for the original records and documents, as well as most of the keepers of the knowledge, remain hidden and secretive. The Divine Feminine Principle has survived throughout the centuries because it has been kept secret and hidden, without need for permission or recognition from the patriarchy.

This Order is open to Priestesses only.

Order of St John The Baptist – (OJB)

John the Baptist was an enigmatic person and a witness to the Light. He was characterized as an Initiate of the Christ, a demigod, as Samael described him. Yet, his role in the Bible is downplayed somewhat as seen here in the Gospel of Matthew (11:11): Truly I tell you, among those born of women no one has arisen greater than John the Baptist; yet the least in the kingdom of heaven is greater than he.

John The Baptist set up a secret hidden (occult) church to pass the true teachings of Mary Magdalene and Jesus down through the generations of the Spiritual Royalty. In the hope that one day the rest of the population would be ready for the truth.

The Order of St John The Baptist has its origins directly from St John The Baptist, who passed the secret teachings of the Divine Feminine and the Holy Grail down through the male children of Mary & Jesus.

This Order is open to Priests only.

Order of St Thecla – (Othc)

According to the Acts of Paul and Thecla, Thecla (St. Taqla) was a young noble virgin who listened to Paul's "discourse on virginity" and became Paul's follower. Thecla's mother, and her fiancé Thamyris, became concerned that Thecla would follow Paul's demand "that one must fear only one God and live in chastity", and punished both Paul and Thecla. She was miraculously saved from being burned at the stake by the onset of a storm, and travelled with Paul to Pisidian Antioch. There a nobleman named Alexander desired Thecla and attempted to take her by force. Thecla fought him off, assaulting him in the process, and was put on trial for assaulting a nobleman. She was sentenced to be eaten by wild beasts, but was again saved by a series of miracles when the female beasts protected her against her male aggressors. No other early account of Thecla exists.

This Order is open to those who are Sub-Deacon or above, who have undertaken humanitarian work or have worked helping animals.

Order of St Joseph of Arimathea – (OJA)

We learn about Joseph of Arimathea in Sacred Scripture. Arimathea was his place of birth, which was most likely the same city also known as Ramatha, birthplace of the prophet Samuel.

Joseph of Arimathea was Jesus' Uncle, and many believe he brought the 'Holy Grail' to Glastonbury UK.

This Order is open to those who are Sub-Deacon or above, who have completed a pilgrimage to our recognised Sacred locations throughout the world. These include Tigris, Israel, Persia, Egypt, Crete, Bulgaria, France, Basque Region, Morocco, Ireland, Scotland, England and Wales. Further details and information about sites we hold as Sacred are available from the Vicar General.

Order of The Holy Grail – (OHG)

This is an honourary order that members of the clergy who have gained secret knowledge are invited to join.

~

Ordo Infinitus Orbis - Knights Hospitaller Templars
Orders within OIO-KHT
Order of The Divine Chalice - (ODC)
Order of The Flaming Sword - (OFS)
Order of Sophia - (OSph)
Order of Divine Wisdom - (ODW)
Order of The Divine Light - (ODL)
Order of The Violet Flame - (OVL)
Order of Illuminati - (OIlumi)

~

Societies & Organisations under the protection of The Church of St Mary & St John

Temple of Theola

A group for spiritually minded beings of all paths, the aim is to bring us all together and create a community spirit and learn from each other. Meetings, workshops and events all aiming to raise money for the Theomerla project as well share knowledge and wisdom with each other.

Theomerla

The aim is to bring like minded beings together and create an environmentally friendly village and spiritual retreat.

Mission

The Church of St Mary & St John's Mission is to bring together the exoteric teachings of St Peter's church and the hidden esoteric teachings of St Mary & St John. As well as the spiritual teachings from other cultures including: The Minoans, The Celts, The Picts, The Thracians, The Scythians, Cathars and Essenes.

To remove the veil of secrecy.

To minister to the community at large by providing services and sacraments, as well as teachings and spiritual guidance. Bringing true balance, harmony and equality to all.

True Will - Aspirants have the right to find their own pathway through the maze of choices our spiritual journey takes us. There is no set of rules or instructions for someone else's path, we all have a unique path. Every member of the Church is to be true to themselves, follow their own path while helping others, forming a community of seekers and creating a spiritual support network.

Balance - While men and women are not exactly the same, they are equal in access to leadership positions. No one is discriminated against or limited in anyway based on their gender.

Openness - We aim to invite people in regardless of their beliefs and personal choices about their lifestyle. We knock down walls, rather than putting up barriers. Where others see only differences, we can see our connection to all things.

Tradition - Engaging ourselves deeply in the ancient traditions, while also coming to your own conclusions about them, and sharing your ideas. We actively encourage you to question everything, and look at everything with an open, yet critical mind. Learning to trust your own intuition.

Our Seminary teachings give you knowledge, guidance and tools to use towards your own spiritual Illumination.

"Every man and every woman is Divine."

History

The church of St Mary and St John has come about after its founders long spiritual journey, and brings together the many threads of spirituality from both modern and ancient times. We derive our knowledge from many sources including genetic memory, spiritual enlightenment, various texts, cultures and religions. This includes the Minoans, the Celts, the Picts, the Scythians, the Thracians, the Cathars, the Essenes and the Johannines.
As a Gnostic Bishop Tia L Douglass chartered The Church of St Mary & St John, along with the assistance of Rt. Rev. Graham Suddick.

Minoans

Around 1700 BC, a sophisticated culture flourished in Crete: the Minoans. The Minoans produced a civilization oriented around trade and bureaucracy with little or no evidence of a military state. They built perhaps the single most efficient bureaucracy in antiquity. This unique culture lasted only a few centuries, before they were invaded by war-like tribes.
The Minoan religion was polytheistic and matriarchal, the gods were all female, not a single male god has been identified until later periods. All religions began as matriarchal religions, even the Hebrew religion (where Yahweh is frequently referred to as physically female), but adopted patriarchal models in later incarnations.

Celts

Around 750 BC to 12 BC, the Celts dominated central and northern Europe. There were many tribes of Celts. The Celts lived across most of Europe during the Iron Age. Several hundred years before Julius Caesar, they occupied many parts of central and western Europe, especially what are now Austria, Switzerland, southern France and Spain. Over several years, in wave after wave, they spread outwards, taking over France and Belgium, and crossing to Britain.

The Celts believed in many gods and goddesses. Many gods had no names, but lived in springs, woods and other places. Offerings to the gods were thrown into lakes, rivers and left by springs and wells. The Celtic Priests and Priestesses were the link between the supernatural world and the ordinary human one. They were able to predict what would happen in the future by interpreting nature. They knew how to read and write, and they certainly had a good grasp of mathematics. They knew something of medicine and law, and they could trace the stars and the planets.

Picts

The earliest surviving mention of the Picts dates from 297AD. In a poem praising the Roman emperor Constantius Chlorus, the orator Eumenius wrote that the Britons were already accustomed to the semi-naked 'Picti and Hiberni (Irish) as their enemies'. The word Pict means "painted people" and probably referred to the Pictish custom of embellishing themselves with "warpaint". However, their Irish term, Cruithni, meaning "the people of the designs", seems to parallel the Roman name so it may be that Picti was an adaptation of the name they called themselves.
The Picts religious traditions revolved around the seasons and nature - the elements, the cycle of the seasons and the inevitable cycles of - birth, life and death. They were matriarchal as the women were seen to be more in tune with nature and had learnt skills of herbalism, aromatherapy and dream analysis.

Scythians

The Scythians were members of a nomadic people of Iranian stock who migrated from the Iranian homeland in Central Asia to southern Russia in the 8th - 7th C. BCE. Centred on what is now the Crimea, the Scythians founded a rich, powerful empire that survived for several centuries before succumbing to the Sarmatians during the 4th century BCE to the 2nd century CE.
The only deity shown in Scythian art was the Great Goddess, whom the Greeks called Artemis, or Hestia or Gaea (The Earth)... Scythians were governed by Priestess-Queens, usually buried alone in richly furnished Kurgans (queen graves)... The moon-sickle used in mythical castrations of God was a Scythian weapon. A long-handled form therefore came to be called a scythe, and was assigned to the Grim Reaper, who was originally Rhea Kronia [the old crone] in the guise of Mother Time, or Death- the Earth who devoured her own children. Scythian women apparently used such weapons in battle as well as religious ceremonies and agriculture. It is generally accepted that it was the horseback-riding Scythians who spread the combination of cannabis and Goddess worship throughout much of the ancient world.

Thracians

The Thracians were a Goddess worship culture. These Indo-European peoples, while considered barbarian and rural by their refined and urbanized Greek neighbours, had developed advanced forms of music, poetry, industry, and artistic crafts. Aligning themselves in kingdoms and tribes, they never achieved any form of national unity beyond short, dynastic rules at the height of the Greek classical period. Similar to the Gauls and other Celtic tribes, most people are thought to have lived simply in small fortified villages, usually on hilltops. Although the concept of an urban centre wasn't developed until the Roman period, various larger fortifications which also served as regional market centres were numerous. Yet, in general, despite Greek colonization in such areas as Byzantium, Apollonia and other cities, the Thracians avoided urban life.

The ancient Thracians were known to have a high percentage of redheads among them. Several Thracian graves or tombstones have the name Rufus inscribed on them, meaning "redhead" – a common name given to people with red hair. Ancient Greek artwork often depicts Thracians as redheads. Rhesus of Thrace, a Thracian King, derived his name because of his red hair and is depicted on Greek pottery as having red hair and beard. Ancient Greek writers also described the Thracians as red haired. A fragment by the Greek poet Xenophanes describes the Thracians as blue-eyed and red haired:

...Men make gods in their own image; those of the Ethiopians are black and snub-nosed, those of the Thracians have blue eyes and red hair.

Cathars

A medieval movement with various schools of thought and practice. Some were dualistic (believing in a God of Good and a God of Evil), others Gnostic, some closer to orthodoxy while abstaining from an acceptance of Catholicism. The dualist theology was the most prominent, however, and was based upon an asserted complete incompatibility of love and power. As matter was seen as a manifestation of power, it was believed to be incompatible with love.

The Cathari did not believe in one all-encompassing god, but in two, both equal and comparable in status. They held that the physical world was evil and created by Rex Mundi (translated from Latin as "king of the world"), who encompassed all that was corporeal, chaotic and powerful; the second god, the one whom they worshipped, was entirely disincarnate: a being or principle of pure spirit and completely unsullied by the taint of matter. He was the god of love, order and peace.

According to some Cathars, the purpose of man's life on Earth was to transcend matter, perpetually renouncing anything connected with the principle of power and thereby attaining union with the principle of love. According to others, man's purpose was to reclaim or redeem matter, spiritualising and transforming it.

Essenes

The Nasarean religion of the Essene Way was the original religion established by the Gods and Goddesses in the Garden of Eden. After the fall of humankind due to an attack on the Garden of Eden, the Gods arranged that the Nasarean religion of the Essene Way would survive as an esoteric minority religion, a bright light in the midst of a dark world. Thus the ancient Nasarean Essenes were the spiritual elders of the Gods, practising, preserving, and passing the teachings on. The ancient Nasarean Essenes were the practitioners of the earliest and most spiritual form of Judaism, and, as the first followers of Lord Christ and Lady Christ, became the first Christians.

Johannines

The Johannine Church was ultimately founded when Yeshua bestowed the authority upon St. John the Beloved/Divine to establish a 'hidden' church; that is, one which would carry the mystery of the Christ in a manner which most souls incarnated on the planet in that age were not yet ready to receive. For the greater body of souls on the planet, the Christ ordained a church under Peter.

The Mitre & Vesica Piscis

We are often questioned as to why within our Church the Bishops wear a Mitre. Many associate this with Christianity, and especially the Roman Catholic Church.

The Mitre has always been associated with the Mother Goddess and the age of Pisces, because both are often represented by the fish. For the past couple of thousand years the Mitre has been worn because we are in the age of Pisces, but the fish symbol has always been of the Goddess. For one because water is feminine, it also represents the cosmic vagina of the Vesica Piscis shape. Which is used to create the fish symbol of Christianity, because Christianity is the religion of the age of Pisces. We also all start out as fish type creatures in the womb, floating about in our Mothers waters. So no matter which age we are in, the fish will always be an important symbol of the mysteries.

The Vesica Piscis is such an important symbol with Divine Proportions that match exactly to a woman's vagina. This sacred symbol is the portal which brings life into the world. The fish is also a symbol of parthenogenesis, as fish can reproduce asexually, as woman can also, when they know how.

The Pope and all other Bishops are wearing the fish head Mitre as they represent the Goddess on Earth. How strange is this seeing as they restrict women and tell them they can not be Priestesses and Bishops themselves? Very.

It is all because they want to keep the esoteric truth hidden from the masses, and especially women. Many women have no idea how strong and powerful they are spiritually and emotionally compared to the vast majority of men. However things are starting to change and I urge all women everywhere to take your rightful place as Priestess or even Bishop lineage holders within our Church. You can now, they can not stop you from reaching your full potential anymore. How good it feels as a woman to wear a Mitre and know its true meaning, let's claim it back. Men too, you also deserve to reach your full potential rather than be taken into false exoteric systems where you never actually find out the truth yourself. Find out more about our online seminary on the Church website.

Seminary

The Church has it's own Esoteric Comparative Theology Certificate (CertECTh.) course for the Minor Orders. We are currently taking enrolments for the first order. Those interested please print out, complete and return the application form on the Ordination page.

For the Major Orders the training will include a Diploma in Esoteric Comparative Theology (DipECTh.) which is the course taken within the Church Seminary.

The Church of St Mary & St John's Seminary is open to those who do not belong to our Church and our course fees are very competitive. However those Aspirants who belong to The Church of St Mary & St John will enjoy a further reduced rate for course fees.

Is our Esoteric Comparative Theology Course & Holy Orders right for you?

See how many times you say yes:

Have you found...

..yourself wondering what would probably be the best and most effective direction to take to further your spiritual path?

..that your well-being just naturally comes from enjoying your spiritual experiences?

..that your spiritual path is one of the best ways to increase your sense of well-being?

..a growing sense of excitement as you consider how becoming a Priest/ess can not only lead to helping others, but by fulfilling yourself?

..that as you think about being a Priest/ess that the idea of becoming one and living it in your everyday life becomes clearer, brighter sharper picture than you ever thought you could possibly imagine?

..that when you think about going further and deeper into your training how important it is to learn new skills; and that as the excitement and drive grow, you can apply that excitement to this training?

If you have answered yes to the questions above there is a good chance you feel ready to take the challenge, but are you the right kind of person? See how many you answer yes to the following:

Would it be fair to say..

..there is a certain growing sense of eagerness about learning and applying esoteric truths and teachings?

..that the more you learn about esoteric subjects, the more eager you are to learn more?

..that, based on your value to become more spiritually aware, you can find your own reasons to continue to study these occult subjects?

..that you really want to improve your life?

..that you really want to take control of your life, that you want to have a sense of control, of discipline, to really build your life, to really make it worthwhile?

..that a training program is the best way to achieve your particular goals for your spiritual advancement and sense of well-being?

..that taking the time to use, nurture and develop your path is a very small price to pay to have that ultimate sense of fulfillment?

How did you do? If you answered yes to most, then consider this:

Just suppose for a moment..

..you've really reached your highest spiritual attainment and have gained much knowledge and wisdom from the underground stream, that you feel confident and have a great sense of control over your life and future, that you know you can use your own experience to empower others.

..that there's a time in your future when you've accomplished exactly what you want, that you've achieved a profound inner peace and high spiritual attainment that you wanted.

..once you've got the training, something that is going to be there the rest of your life are the skills and tools that you have learnt along the way, that will help you in every part of your life... and those close to you, that you have them with you in your future forever. And you know they are going to be there. Just imagine the sense of satisfaction and confidence, knowing you can walk into any situation life throws at you, armed with the training you found here. That feels pretty good, doesn't it?

What would happen if you decided to start making this your reality today by making a firm decision about improving your life right now?

Apply and start becoming the changes you want to see in yourself, and the world.

Secrets of the Serpent Bloodline - The Unveiling of Profound Esoteric Mysteries

Celtic Gnostic Mass

The Celtic Gnostic Church of St Mary & St John has created something new and unique from some very ancient teachings and traditions.

Long forgotten facets of the Mass and Eucharist are brought together to create an amazingly beautiful celebration, that is the Celtic Gnostic Mass.

Origins of the Celtic Gnostic Mass

A long time ago our ancestors created a beautiful tradition, which when followed would lead to 'Knowing Thyself'. It helped us realise our true Will, our true Divine potential. It filled us with Gnosis (Intuitive Knowledge) and Sophia (Divine Wisdom) giving us a direct connection to our own Higher Self. It allowed us to live in harmony with nature, to love and care about all of the Great Mother's creations. We knew never to take more than we needed, and to always give something back when we do, this allowed balance to always be maintained.

Due to an unfortunate chain of events this knowledge (Gnosis) was lost to the general population. The truth was hidden (Occult) from everyone, and a few unbalanced beings decided to control and just take, rather than allow others to reach their full potential. They jealously guarded the secrets, and slaughtered anyone who dared to secretly pass the Gnosis on. However, some survived in the underground stream. The true teachings were kept safely for a time when people were at last ready to remember the truth and take back the teachings hidden from them for so long... That time is now.

The Celtic Gnostic Mass is part of those traditions and secret teachings passed down. Being part of the Celtic Gnostic Mass is both uplifting and cleansing to your own aura. Many generations of deception will start to be wiped away, giving your own Higher Self a chance to at last connect to you. You will feel an amazing connection to the Divine within you, genetic memories will be triggered and at last things will start to make true and proper sense. Everything will start to fit together. The more you are involved with the Celtic Gnostic Mass, the more your ancestors will call to you, drawing your memories of how things used to be back into your conscious mind.

What happens at a Celtic Gnostic Mass?

The ceremony is led by a Priest and Priestess, the altar divided into a male and female side. The Priest works on the feminine side, and the Priestess works on the masculine side, all the while bringing balance to the energies.

Secrets of the Serpent Bloodline - The Unveiling of Profound Esoteric Mysteries

The Arch Angels are invoked bringing the qualities of all the elements into the ceremony. The Priestess purifies and the Priest consecrates. When the temple is ready the Eucharist is prepared by the Priest and the Priestess on the centre altar. A symbolic act of union between the energies is performed and all present partake in the Eucharist which is charged with the energy raised.

To know the full extent of the Celtic Gnostic Mass and its significance, it has to be experienced. The Church of St Mary & St John performs the Celtic Gnostic Mass regularly at the Temple of Theola in Lancashire, UK. To arrange to attend please contact us.

Support Truth

Why isn't the TRUTH mainstream? Let's make it happen.

If you are a Theolalite you will know there is something terribly wrong with the world:-

Medicine makes us even more ill, while big pharma profits on our ill health. Food is poisoned with nasty chemicals (aspartame and other artificial sweeteners) and animals injected with hormones, that we in turn eat, including diary products. Our mouths are filled with mercury, our drinking water and toothpaste poisoned with fluoride, a dangerous neurotoxin. Our shampoos and shower gels are toxic soups of chemicals and all other beauty products. Doctors give our babies injections filled with mercury which leads to autism and many other problems.

Our religions remove all spirituality and truth. Instead of empowering and freeing us from mental torment like true spirituality, it actually leads to mental insanity, dangerous extremist behaviour, psychopathy and wars. How can these people not see that this is nothing to do with being a good person? or anything to do with a loving God? If we realise we are ruining the Earth we are told to switch off from it and let it continue. Because God will come and safe us, or the good aliens will come and rescue us, or if we just sit meditating and thinking happy thoughts, the world will change.. lies, lies, lies. To stop good people from doing good things.

Education indoctrinates us into being a bunch of repeaters, repeating the same old lies to the next generation, and the next, and the next. Teaching us to limit our thinking and imagination, and to demonise anyone who dares to think outside the box and be different. We are taught that being the same as everyone else is good, and that being different is a terrible thing to feel ashamed about. You're too tall, you're too short, you're too fat, you're too thin... lies, lies, lies to control us. We are all perfect and unique.

Our political systems are a complete waste of time, a pantomime designed to get the herd to actually believe they are getting some kind of choice!! When in reality all these 'sides' are on the same side, and it isn't ours.

We are taught to be suspicious of others, to stay indoors and watch the TV, then we can be bombarded with more lies on the tell-lie-vision. If not we should read the newspapers to see their version of reality enforced deeply into our psyche, surrounded by it day in and day out.

We are kept distracted from thinking, by constantly living in debt and fear of not being able to make ends meet. And wouldn't it be such a disaster if we couldn't have the latest Ipod, car, mobile phone, pair of shoes, designer handbag? Our life wouldn't be worth living, would it? We would feel like such an outcast, and so 'uncool'. Lies, lies, lies.

How many more lies do we have to hear before we pull together to bring REAL change, to bring the TRUTH to the mainstream? To help other empower themselves with the TRUTH?

We aren't willing to sit back and wait for someone else to do it anymore, we are getting pro-active and we need your help. Please sign the - Be The Solution form (win exciting prizes for you and your friends), and get involved all you can in what we are doing. Help us promote what we are doing. If you don't want to spend time, but want to help, then please donate all you can to the movement or buy something in our gift shop. All money raised will be used to get the TRUTH out, joining more of us together and working on exciting projects that if done properly will change how we live and think forever, like the Theomerla Project.

You will find no Think Tanks, no government backing, no dogma and no massive egos in this movement, just people who want a better world, isn't that something we can all agree on?

Be The Solution

What we are doing and why.

We are joining together as many free thinking, non dogmatic, Spiritual Beings as possible.

But why?

Because for too long now dogmatic lies have dictated to us throughout all areas of society.

We are not allowed to show any kind of disapproval of any religions, as that is seen as taking away someone's free choice. Yet people continue to be murdered in the name of religions and 'God' every single day all over the world. Religious wars have infested all areas of the world at some time or another, and effect everyone on the planet. Yet we are told we must believe that religion is good, and teaches us morals?

We believe the only way to bring balance and peace to the world is to stop others hurting others in the name of religions and religious dogma, and that there should be one rule and one rule only... Do whatever you want, worship whatever you want, believe anything you want, so long as it hurts no one else and you don't force your views on anyone else. If the world was filled with Spiritual Beings who work on bettering themselves, rather than judging others, just imagine how much better the world would be?

So how do you go about making this a reality?

When someone can see through all the dogma and false ego that is programmed into us, they become very strong independent individuals, who guard their freedom well. Many of them say they will never belong to a 'group' as they feel that it will take their individuality away from them.

However, here lies a problem. As soon as individuals start to wake up to the lies and dogma we have been living under they can start to become selfish and think only of themselves. Instead of using what they know to help others, they see a world full of people who can not be saved from the brainwashing they have fallen for, and so they can become reclusive, or start down an anarchistic path, where they feel it should be everyone for themselves.

But this isn't going to change anything, is it? To make changes we must group together and use their own system against them.

Hence The Church of St Mary & St John was formed, as a way of getting a 'religion' which is valid within 'their' rules out into the mainstream. But this Church has a big difference, it is run and formed by Spiritual Beings, not controlling, power hungry, judgemental dogmatic fools. To make a difference we need numbers, if we all get together as Spiritual caring Beings who really do want to make a difference, and our numbers grow, we will get out into the mainstream and create the first and only mainstream 'religion' that is balanced and dogma free, and it doesn't really matter what someone's own personal beliefs are, so long as they agree to this rule: Do whatever you want, worship whatever you want, believe anything you want, so long as it hurts no one else and you don't force your views on anyone else.

Isn't there any other group with your beliefs out there already?

There is currently no group or religion like this in the mainstream. A lot of them might come across as saying they want everyone to have freedom, but they turn a blind eye to the problems in the world, and a vast majority of them are patriarchal and are still working at suppressing women. We can never have balance while this is still going on.

Why is Patriarchy wrong?

How can a system that says a man is better than a woman be right? How is this not harming others? By dictating the roles of men and women, this doesn't allow for individual freedom of choice to be whoever you want to be. If a woman wants to be a Spiritual Leader, because that is her calling, then she should have that freedom. No one else knows what is best for us, than ourselves. Patriarchy has caused wars, murder, mutilation, oppression and suppression of women, rape and all manner of horrors. It is time this was removed completely and freedom of choice and balance brought back, as the way our ancient ancestors lived.

How do I get involved?

If you don't want to be a Priest or Priestess yourself, but agree with what we stand for and what we are trying to do, there are many ways to help and one of the biggest ways is to say you are a Gnostic Theolalite and put your name down as being a member of this Church and this 'religion'. Don't be put off by the terminology which is being used, it is necessary if our plans are going to work. To have the rights of other religions, we must also become one. In our case religion doesn't mean dogma and control, to us our religion simply means: Do whatever you want, worship whatever you want, believe anything you want, so long as it hurts no one else and you don't force your views on anyone else. *Find out about our Be The Solution Movement at TempleofTheola.org*

Feasts & Festivals of The Church of St Mary & St John

Ritual of Air 2nd February

Our Candlemas ceremony marks the midpoint of winter, half way between the shortest day and Spring Equinox. We light candles all through the Temple and our homes at the first signs that Spring is starting to appear, when the Sun is born again and all of nature springs back to life.

Snowdrops appear in February as a symbol of hope that the Sun will once again appear. "The Snowdrop in purest white array. First rears her head on Candlemas Day."

Also known as Imbolc, the Feast of First Milk, occurring when the first of the lambs would be born and provide some fresh milk.

Candlemas in the Northern Hemisphere is when the sun reaches fifteen degrees of Aquarius. As the ritual is in Aquarius this is our ritual of Air. Our elemental rituals always honour that element more than the others during that time.

~

St Joseph of Arimathea 17th March

On this day we hold a Celtic Gnostic Mass dedicated to St Joseph of Arimathea. We take this opportunity to gather together and have a feast after the ceremony.

~

Vernal Spring Equinox 21st March

Equinoxes are opposite on either side of the equator, so the spring equinox (vernal equinox) in the northern hemisphere is the autumnal equinox in the southern hemisphere and vice versa. In the northern hemisphere, the vernal equinox marks the first day of spring. However, the official date for the first day of spring varies depending on the country's climate. On the two equinoxes every year the sun shines directly on the equator and the length of day and night is nearly equal.

We celebrate with a special ceremony where we ask of our Higher Self and group Egregore to provide us with information regarding the following 6 months – which takes us through to Autumnal Equinox.

~

Ritual of Earth 1st May

Sometimes called Beltane in Celtic cultures, this ceremony marks the beginning of summer. It is a cross-quarter day, marking the midpoint in the Sun's progress between the spring equinox and summer solstice. The astronomical date for this midpoint is nearer to 5th May or 7th May, but this can vary from year to year.

Secrets of the Serpent Bloodline - The Unveiling of Profound Esoteric Mysteries

Summer Solstice 21ˢᵗ June

The summer solstice is the solstice that occurs in a hemisphere's summer. In the Northern Hemisphere this is the Northern solstice, in the Southern Hemisphere this is the Southern solstice. Depending on the shift of the calendar, the summer solstice occurs some time between 20ᵗʰ December and 23ʳᵈ December each year in the Southern Hemisphere and between 20ᵗʰ June and 22ⁿᵈ June in the Northern Hemisphere.

Though the summer solstice is an instant in time, the term is also colloquially used like Midsummer to refer to the day on which it occurs. Except in the polar regions (where daylight is continuous for many months), the day on which the summer solstice occurs is the day of the year with the longest period of daylight.

~

St John the Baptist 24ᵗʰ June

On this day we hold a Celtic Gnostic Mass dedicated to St John the Baptist. We take this opportunity to gather together and have a feast after the ceremony.

~

St Mary Magdalene 22ⁿᵈ July

On this day we hold a Celtic Gnostic Mass dedicated to St Mary Magdalene. We take this opportunity to gather together and have a feast after the ceremony.

~

Ritual of Fire 1ˢᵗ August

This is traditionally first harvest. At this time you will see various trees namely Rowan yielding bright red berries and brambles showing ripening fruits along with apple and pear trees. The first grain of the season is taken to make bread for the ceremony, and fruits are also placed on the Altar. Otherwise known as the Harvest Festival, which is in fact pre-Christian. Because this is the fire festival, this element is normally honoured by the use of candles or a bonfire.

~

Autumnal Equinox 23ʳᵈ September

There are two equinoxes every year – in September and March– when the sun shines directly on the equator and the length of day and night is nearly equal. Seasons are opposite on either side of the equator, so the equinox in September is also known as the "autumnal equinox" in the northern hemisphere. However, in the southern hemisphere, it's known as the "spring (vernal) equinox".

We celebrate with a special ceremony where we ask of our Higher Self and group Egregore to provide us with information regarding the following 6 months – which takes us through to Vernal Equinox.

St Thecla 24th September

On this day we hold a Celtic Gnostic Mass dedicated to St Thecla.
We take this opportunity to gather together and have a feast after the ceremony.

~

Feast of Guardian Angels 2nd October

This ancient ceremony is to honour the connection or hope for connection to our Higher Self (Holy Guardian Angel) and all those who have in the past and will in the future gain conversation with theirs. A special Celtic Gnostic Mass is performed which is followed by a feast and celebrations.

The festival is taken on by Catholics in more modern times, however the true meaning is lost to them.

~

Invocation of Lady Veritas, Goddess of Truth 22nd October

The Invocation of Lady Veritas, Goddess of Truth is a special ceremony which awakens the truth within us all and sends out energies to bring truth out into our communities and the world. We invoke and honour the Lady Veritas wearing white robes and decorating the Temple in white.

~

Ritual of Water 31st October

The Ritual of Water is when we celebrate the end of the harvest and light bonfires to illuminate our way through the coming dark winter months. We remember our ancestors and honour them during lively celebrations and other festivities. The element water is also honoured, all the better if our festival is outside and we get some rain.

~

Winter Solstice 21st December

The winter solstice is the time at which the Sun is appearing at noon at its lowest altitude above the horizon. In the Northern Hemisphere this is the Southern solstice, the time at which the Sun is at its southernmost point in the sky, which usually occurs on 21st December to 22nd December each year. In the Southern Hemisphere this is the Northern solstice, the time at which the Sun is at its northernmost point in the sky, which usually occurs on 20th June to 21st June each year.

For us as an Order winter solstice is a time for getting together, holding a beautiful ceremony where candles are lit and wishes for the future are made. We feast and drink ale to help celebrate the Sun's death and it's rebirth which will keep us warm again in the Spring and Summer months ahead.
We sing songs and read poems.

Secrets of the Serpent Bloodline - The Unveiling of Profound Esoteric Mysteries

Part 4

Mary Magdalene & The Hidden Teachings

Mary Magdalene

Divine feminine who heals and teaches
Your Dove descents to us it reaches
Love, wisdom and knowledge it preaches,
Mary Magdalene we learn from you.

Pools of blue water for your eyes
Hear about you so many lies
Know the truth, you are wise,
Mary Magdalene we invoke you.

Our Sister with red flowing hair
Skin so smooth and so fair
The scarlet robes that you wear,
Mary Magdalene we honour you.

Temple Priestess, mighty Seer
Powerful force who shows no fear
Waited millennia to shed a tear
Mary Magdalene we cried for you.

The Church names you a whore
The dangerous truth that they abhor
That you did Yeshua's Children bore,
Mary Magdalene we adore you.

By Tau Tia L Douglass 22nd July 2012

Secrets of the Serpent Bloodline - The Unveiling of Profound Esoteric Mysteries

Truth About Mary Magdalene & Her Children

Mary Magdalene & Yeshua (Hebrew spelling of Jesus, there is no letter J in Hebrew) moved to France and had 6 children, first twins a boy and a girl. Then girl, then boy, then girl, then boy.

Sandro Botticelli made a painting of Mary Magdalene and her children called "Madonna of the Magnificat", commissioned by Piero di Cosimo de' Medici for his private collection.

In the painting you see the twins at either side of Mary Magdalene placing a crown on her head. This is symbolic of the Great Work, where on reaching Kether and getting your crown (enlightenment) you are crowned by twins, a girl and a boy.

Her other children are gathered around looking at the baby in her arms, the newest addition to their family.

Their first daughter was named **Tirzah** תִּרְצָה meaning "favourable". Tirzah is the name of one of the daughters of Zelophehad in the Old Testament. It also occurs in the Old Testament as a place name, the early residence of the kings of the northern kingdom.

Tirzah was to become a High Priestess, a writer and an Artist. She stayed in France and had a family of her own.

Her twin brother was named Tzion צִיּוֹן which is the Hebrew form of Zion. is a place name often used as a synonym for Jerusalem. It commonly referred to a specific mountain near Jerusalem (Mount Zion), on which stood a Jebusite fortress of the same name that was conquered by David and was named the City of David. The term Tzion came to designate the area of Jerusalem where the fortress stood, and later became a metonym for Solomon's Temple in Jerusalem, the city of Jerusalem and generally, the World to Come. In Kabbalah the more esoteric reference is made to Tzion being the spiritual point from which reality emerges, located in the Holy of Holies of the First, Second and Third Temple.

Tzion came to the UK with Joseph his Uncle. He was taught the traditions and raised a family in Scotland UK. He was a Musician and a Teacher.

The next daughter born was named Yiskah יִסְכָּה , which is the Original Hebrew form of ISCAH, it means "to behold". In the Old Testament this is the name of Abraham's niece, mentioned only briefly. This is the basis of the English name Jessica.

Yiskah married young and unfortunately she died while giving birth. Mary Magdalene was said to be so heart broken over the loss of her beautiful daughter that she never fully recovered after that.

The next born son was named Yirmiyahu יִרְמְיָהוּ which is the original Hebrew form of JEREMIAH, it means "YAHWEH has uplifted". This is the name of one of the major prophets of the Old Testament, the author of the Book of Jeremiah and (supposedly) the Book of Lamentations. He lived to see the Babylonian destruction of Jerusalem in the 6th century BC. In England, though the vernacular form Jeremy had been occasionally used since the 13th century, the form Jeremiah was not common until after the Protestant Reformation.

Yirmiyahu married a beautiful Italian Princess and raised a family in Italy. It is written that he had 3 children.

The next daughter born was named Sarah שָׂרָה which means "lady" or "princess" in Hebrew. This is the name of the wife of Abraham in the Old Testament.

Sarah is perhaps the most well known of all the bloodline children. A Mother and a Tau, she was a valued Teacher of the Mysteries. She was able to connect to the ancestors with genetic memories very easily, and brought many new teachings to the hidden Church, which are still passed on.

She had a strong belief that the Simples would not be willing to learn the truth, even if they were given the option openly. She said in the future more would find the hidden Church and learn, but only those who are strong in the bloodline genetics and the others we would have to lead ourselves, they need leadership and it is better we lead them, than the Eagles. As Serpents we don't like to lead, more help and guide, but she believed it was our role and task here, so we must.

The final son born was named Sha'ul שָׁאוּל which is the Hebrew form of SAUL. It means "asked for" or "prayed for". This was the name of the first king of Israel who ruled just before King David, as told in the Old Testament. Also, Saul was the original Hebrew name of Saint Paul.

Sha'ul was a High Priest and Alchemist. A true Seer and Philosopher of his day. He and his sister Sarah created many beautiful rituals, including the Magdalene Rite, in honour of their Mother. This wonderful rite is still carried out in our Church and Order to this day, along with the various other beautiful rituals they created together.

Tirzah, Tzion, Yiskah, Yirmiyahu, Sarah & Sha'ul, the names of all the children of Mary Magdalene and Yeshua.

The Hidden Teachings of Mary Magdalene

Mary Magdalene - Teaching I

Peter said to Mary "Sister, since Jesus has known you privately he has change greatly. He radiates love, knowledge and wisdom. What lesson have you given him to make it so?"

Mary answered, saying, "Within my vessel I carry the wine and the water, Jesus made the fountain flow, and from it he took some inside himself."

Peter asked, "Is this the reason he now walks in the light?"

Mary answered, "Yes, the wine and the water have completed him. He is ready to be the light of the world and bring great teachings of peace and love."

Meaning

Mary Magdalene is here talking about the time she performed the Great Rite with Jesus, which led to his enlightenment.

Mary Magdalene - Teaching II

Peter said to Mary "Sister, why are these people so angry that surround us? Why can they not know the peace brought by our teachings?"

Mary answered, saying, "They choose not to look for the answer where they can find it, they seek happiness, but look in the wrong places. They want to find peace, there is no Being not capable of finding this peace, but they have found a truth that pains them and before they can heal they must be ready to walk through the shadows, and welcome the light at the other side."

Peter asked, "What truth can cause so much pain?"

Mary answered, "The truth about times long gone, the truth about the origin to which they belong. To live wanting more than this causes pain, the truth is not what causes the pain."

Peter asked, "Sister, how can someone want more than the truth? Doesn't the truth free us?"

Mary answered, "The truth can only hurt us when we refuse to accept it, acceptance is the key to start on the path to finding inner peace. We choose not which line into which we are born, therefore we should find peace in our differences and strengths, as much as our similarities and weaknesses. The line of the Divine Grail is within our family, this makes it our mission to help and support all our children, of all lines, it matters not which they are born into. For our mistakes we must endure and find balance from the ashes of the torment they create."

Meaning

Here Magdalene is teaching us to not be angry about who we are, and which line we are born into, as everyone is capable of finding inner peace and enlightenment. They just have to accept themselves as they are and not be jealous of what others are.

Magdalene also goes on to mention that as the Serpent line, who is ultimately responsible for the creation of the different lines, it is our families responsibility to help heal those who feel wounded and tormented inside, which manifests itself into the world around them, as healing the people leads to healing the world.

Mary Magdalene - Teaching III

"Within my Chalice is mixed the water and wine, when mingled they form the most precious of Elixirs. This Elixir has the power to transform Princes into Kings. For the King can only be made a King by being anointed with the secret Elixir of his Queen."

Meaning

This is referring to the secret Elixir of illumination which is created within the High Priestess during the Great Rite. It is how men gain enlightenment.

Mary Magdalene - Teaching IV

Mary sat with Thomas and told him she was going to share some wisdom from the stream.

Thomas asked "Sister, what is this stream you talk of, what is its source?"

Mary answered saying "The stream has existed since the beginning of time - through thoughts, words and deeds it is remembered and taught. No one outside a rare few are trusted to have seen its source or know its secrets. Should the source be discovered, for sure it would be destroyed and forever lost. Remember that should you ever be trusted as a Guardian of the stream, never to reveal it to anyone, no matter how much you love them, or think you can trust them. Blood is thicker than water - the stream flows through our veins, it is our life-force. Destroying the source, is to destroy all of us, not just our tribe, but every tribe from every land."

Thomas then asked "Sister, how can we answer those who question that we teach the truth?"

Mary smiled and answered "When someone is ready to hear the truth, the stream flows deeply into their heart and mind, they can not doubt what they already know inside. For all children born have some of the stream flowing through them, most never remember this. Those that do are ready to know, we need not worry about them believing us. For to know, is to believe yourself."

Meaning

Here Mary Magdalene is referring to the underground stream of knowledge, which although passed down in various ways externally, the truth is it is in our blood and genes. To remember that the answers are within, is the first step to discovering the truth.

When Thomas thinks that people won't believe the truth, Mary makes it clear that to not believe is to not believe yourself. Destroying the stream is to destroy all life, and even though Eagles have tried to destroy all signs of it, it would ultimately lead to destroying themselves and the Earth.

Mary Magdalene - Teaching V

Philip was looking thoughtful as he looked up to watch clouds float by.

Mary asked 'Brother, what troubles you? You seem very deep in thought."

Philip looked to Mary and said "Sister, I have read the prophecies, I looked back into time and I could see these things came to pass. How can it be? How can I myself learn to see?"

Mary answered saying "Brother, some things are certain, and try as we might we can not escape them. We all know in the future we will grow old, that the seasons change, that the Sun will set and rise again. We are Seers, we have noticed these things since ancient times, we have come to know, we have come to see clearly what will come next. You ask how can you learn to see, take heed and learn to look through different eyes and you will notice patterns, all of time cycles. Start with a day, notice the cycle of that one day, and then a week, then a year. Soon you will see a more complete picture. You can already see into the past and the future, you just need to take a step back and draw it all into view. Our book of prophecies is always correct, because it is wrote by those who learnt to step back and see the fuller picture."

Meaning

Philip had been reading our book of prophecies, he noticed that the old ones had already come true. He longed to know how he could see for himself into the future.

Mary gave him a lesson on how he could begin to learn to see the bigger picture when we notice the cycles that time goes through.

Mary Magdalene - Teaching VI

Andrew asked Mary "Sister, why do we not gather all the people and teach them our knowledge? Why do we choose only a few? Why are there levels and degrees? Why so many secrets? Why can we not have the truth instantly?"

Mary answered "I understand your concerns, I hear them often. You have just begun on your path, you feel frustrated that you can not have all the wisdom and knowledge now. You feel there is no reason to refrain from shouting the truth from the very mountain tops. Brother, you must realise that not all are ready to hear the truth. If I were to reveal all the secret truths, hastily, it could deeply trouble you. Not due to the truth being bad, for on hearing the truth there may be a conflict arising within your mind, you may become ill tempered and distrusting of me. You may feel hurt and betrayed. It often leads to troubled thoughts when one hears knowledge that may differ from that of their preconceived ideas. As you follow your path the revelations appear, and the Gnosis starts to come to you naturally. These revelations are a wonder to behold, I would not deny you of them. A truth found inside is more real and enlightening than a truth passed by another. You find here the tools to gain the answers yourself - within. Your path to Gnosis must be walked and you must walk it alone."

Meaning

If the truth is given out freely, most would just ignore it anyway and not agree with it. Others would get very angry at the person who told them, and reject it. Others might believe it, but because they are not mentally prepared for it, they would go insane.

I myself am asked repeatedly why so many secrets? Why levels to the Order. This teaching answers it perfectly. It doesn't matter if someone waves the truth in front of your face, if you are not ready to hear it, or see it, it will only do more harm than good.

Mary Magdalene - Teaching VII

James had spent the afternoon meditating. He walked towards the Temple where Mass was about to take place. He found Mary sat inside where the Temple Altars were being prepared.

James sat down beside her and said "Sister, today I meditated on the problems we are currently facing, and will pray this evening during Mass to send out healing energy. I feel this will help greatly."

Mary smiled and replied "Yes James, the meditation will help you remain calm and able to think clearly about solutions to solve our current problems, and the Mass will help spread that energy out to those attending. Please remember that it is not enough just to want or wish for change, we must also act to bring about those changes. The art of doing is the key to change, the art of meditation is the key to making sure those changes are positive and good for all."

Meaning

So many think that all they have to do to make changes in the world, is to do their own inner work. In truth both are necessary. When we do our inner work, we become more enlightened people, who are better equipped to make positive changes in the world. If we change ourselves, and then do nothing, we are not becoming the solution to the world, just ourselves. We might have inner peace from doing the inner work, but it does not reflect on the outside without action.

When we do our inner work, we become better, more balanced people.. who are better equipped to make the right decisions in life. However, just becoming a better person and wishing things were different in the world is not enough. We must take our Divine Wisdom from within and spread it out into the world by standing up and doing something about it.

Mary Magdalene - Teaching VIII

Simon Peter was aware that someone was interested in working to become a Priest. He felt jealous that this man joining the group would mean less time for himself with Mary. When the young man approached him Simon Peter said that we are not currently taking in new Seekers. The young man showed his disappointment, this left Simon Peter feeling guilty as he watched the young man slowly walk away.

Simon Peter could not sleep that night, and decided he would go to see Mary the next day.

He found Mary and asked "Sister, what can one do to dispel the feelings of guilt about ones actions?"

Mary answered saying "Brother, there is usually a way to put right that which makes you feel guilt is there not?"

Simon Peter thought for a moment, and then departed in a hurry. He searched through the whole village trying to find the young man he had discouraged the previous day. Eventually he found him. He put his arm round him and said "Brother, there is someone I would like you to meet." They returned to Mary where Simon Peter introduced him as a Seeker of Gnosis.

Mary smiled and said "How wonderful that you brought your Brother here, we will gladly receive him amongst us, Simon Peter I would be pleased if you would become his Mentor."

Simon Peter smiled, he felt proud to have been given this responsibility, and his new friend looked overjoyed at being given this honour.

A few months later Simon Peter was sat alone with Mary and confessed what he had done. "Sister, I did wrong to my new brother when first he came here looking for help on his path. I turned him away, and now he is here we have become the best of friends. I do not admire myself for my actions and felt the need to confess this."

Mary placed her hand on his shoulder saying "Brother, we all make mistakes. What is important is that you knew you had wronged him and you put it right. You have no reason to feel guilt any longer, your Higher Self guided you to what you knew must be done and all has come good. All those here are our Brothers and Sisters, and all are as important and have the right to take the path we are on if they so choose. To deny them, is to deny yourself. This is a lesson you have now learnt."

Meaning

Jealousy can make us do things we will regret, but if we listen carefully to our Higher Self, we will know our actions are wrong, and can aim to put them right.

It also teaches us to not feel guilty about our mistakes, we all make them and if we tried to put them right, then all the more we should learn from them and move on. We also can not allow ourselves to become obsessed with things from the past that we can not change, we must learn to forgive ourselves.

Mary Magdalene - Teaching IX

Food was plentiful in this village at the time and small loaves were being passed around. Everyone had become accustomed to this abundance that other villages would be thankful to receive once a week.

After they had all received a small loaf, Mary took out several large loaves and placed them on a table. She gave one to a weak elderly man, who was very grateful and happy to have received it.

John was envious of the old man for receiving a larger loaf. John stood up and protested "Sister, why have you given us small loaves when you have larger ones to share?"

Mary answered saying "Brother, you have not shown you are thankful for the small loaf, therefore why do you feel you should receive a larger loaf, would you not just take this for granted as well?"

John shouted angrily "This is not fair! We should all receive the same."

Mary replied "Envy is ugly, why do you begrudge this man a little more bread this day? When tomorrow you may have more than him? He has worked hard in the fields this day. I feel he needs more sustenance to replenish his energy. Rather than looking to what others have, be thankful that you have enough to sustain yourself. If you have that, you are truly blessed."

John thought for a moment and said "Sister you are right. I remember the day I was ill and lacking energy, you made sure I had more than enough to restore me. I am thankful for what I have received today, and everyday."

Meaning

Always, always be thankful that you have enough to sustain you, and never ever feel envy for those who have more than you. Sometimes people have more than you because they need it. Sometimes it is because they are lacking other things. Don't compare yourself to others in this way. It makes you spiteful and full of hate. Just learn to be thankful for what you do have and you will be truly happy.

Mary Magdalene - Teaching X

Bartholomew asked Mary "Sister, why do we have to perform rituals and meditate? Why do we have to work so hard at The Great Work? Why isn't it easier?"

Mary answered saying "Brother, you don't have to do anything. That which you do, you do because you choose to, if you do not wish to continue the work simply stop."

Bartholomew then said "Sister, how could I live a content and happy life, knowing if I had continued on the path a little further, I would have found all the answers I seek?"

Mary answered "Then you have your answer. Have you ever known anything of great significance being easily obtained?"

Bartholomew thought for a moment, then answered "No Sister, the gold that which is most sort, is always difficult to obtain."

Mary answered saying "The path is full of distractions and obstacles. If you can find a path with no obstacles, it probably leads to that which has no value. If you focus on only the problems, you will miss all the beauty."

Meaning

The Great Work isn't meant to be easy, it is hard, but the rewards are amazing and well worth it. If something comes too easy, you don't value it.

Mary Magdalene - Teaching XI

Matthew went to Mary and asked "Sister, when I was young I took that which was not mine. Likewise I insulted those I envied in order to upset them. Now I see how wrong this was. I feel so much guilt. How do I make amends for what I have done?"

Mary answered saying "Brother, if I told you that I once did something similar when I was young, would you forgive me? Or would you think so badly of me that you would never look at me the same way?"

Matthew didn't need to think for long before answering "Sister, I have come to know you over many years. I know there is nothing you would do to harm another, your heart is kind and true, you would do anything to help others. How could I ever think bad of you? It does not matter to me what was done in your past, as I know that is not who you are now."

Mary smiled and said "Brother, you are so quick to forgive me, and you tell me you know I am a good person. Then tell me, why can you not come to forgive yourself? You know yourself better than any other, and you know that you have learnt from you past mistakes and will not repeat them. Do you not think it is now time to forgive yourself?"

Matthew smiled "Sister you are so wise, of course you are correct. I forgive myself, I know that the past does not matter, it is who I am now that counts."

Meaning

I think this explains itself very well. We are not who we were, we are who we are now.

Mary Magdalene - Teaching XII

Simon was busy harvesting some of the Sacred Holy Herb, ready for use in making oil. He carried the gathered bundles inside. Mary was pouring some of the oil in to a small jar.

Simon asked "Sister, we use this herb in our ceremonies, but for what purpose do you use the oil derived from it?"

Mary answered saying "This oil heals, it is a precious and pure gift from the Great Mother, the most prized of all herbs, we are fortunate to have ample amounts available. Guard the secrets of this oil well, as there are those who would, for greed and control, destroy the crops and keep it from the people. It is more valuable than gold"

Simon asked "Why would they want to stop us using this healing oil?"

Mary answered saying "Those who seek power will use any means to gain control. That which is the most prized, they will attempt to turn against the people. Let the fools take gold for how it looks, for we have the real gold here and should they ever discover its true value, it will be taken from us."

Meaning

As Mary Magdalene says, once the Eagles found out about the Sacred Holy Herb they did take it from us as a means of controlling everyone. Now is the time for fighting to get it back.

Knowledge from the Underground Stream

Some prophecies and other information passed down through our families.

A new era will be brought forth when a female born under Pisces within the royal Serpent Bloodline, brings hope in every nation of the Earth at a time when the great truths are being revealed. She leads them forward towards Aquarius, and leaves behind the dying God of Pisces.

~*~

When the truth revelations quicken, and all horrors are uncovered. The people will be forlorn. At this time the new Aeon will be brought in by the Serpent bloodline, who will finally come out of the shadows, they will create a new Eden on Earth.

~*~

As the wheel forever turns, the past is set to repeat. The age of enlightenment will be brought forward after death has visited every land. The earth will be cleansed by fire. The end is as much the beginning, as the beginning is the end.

~*~

When the rivers and oceans have turned to poison, the skies have turned to fumes, the land raped of all its nature. Then the Great Mother shall weep and shake, purging herself of all disease, only then shall she heal.

~*~

The Eagles reign will be over, when the Serpents awaken and remember who they are.

~*~

The stream flows through our veins, the blood of the serpent is within.

~*~

Mana

The rituals and traditions of the Serpent families, involved the drinking of menstrual blood mixed with red wine to increase magickal power. Of course the High Priestess chosen as a Grail Goddess would be of pure bloodline and having reached Kether had become a Tau in her own right. In a state of spiritual and magickal ecstasy during the Dark Moon, the Priestess would produce the Mana or Elixir - The menstrual blood mixed with her own water (the ejaculatory fluid) which was collected in a chalice and ritualistically drunk by those wishing to experience a brief glimpse of the spiritual enlightenment achieved by the Priestess. Ingesting the chemicals released into the fluid, which are created in the pineal gland and the other glands of each chakra, the drinker would experience the magick powers the Priestess herself had.

A version of this, without all the knowledge of how the Elixir was created, was later used by the Taoists and the Ancient Egyptians. In Ancient Greece spring festivals included the spreading on the earth of corn mixed with menstrual blood to increase fertility.

The word 'ritual' comes from 'rtu' which is Sanskrit. Rtu, a fixed or appointed time, especially the proper time for sacrifice (yajna) in Vedic Religion. The traditions of blood sacrifice have their origin in the 'sacrifice' of Moon blood from women. However, the menstrual blood was given freely and then used to nourish the tribe or the earth in other ways and no-one suffered, unlike later more corrupted versions.

The blood from the womb which nourished the unborn child was believed to have 'mana' or 'breath of life'. The word menstruation comes from the Greek menus meaning both moon and power, and men meaning month. The Latin term came to be used to mean the Christian Eucharist. As the water and wine in the chalice of Christian ceremonies is also symbolic of the Moon Elixir of the High Priestess.

Within the Bloodline families a woman's bleeding is considered a wonderful, amazing, cosmic event, relating and connecting one to the Moon, the lunar cycles and the tides. She is at the height of her power at this time, and for this reason is encouraged to spend time listening to her inner voice, which brings wisdom which benefits the whole tribe.

The time of the dark Moon, or Moon time was later distorted by patriarchy, where women were told they were dirty and unclean. They were told to be separate from the others, and that anything she touched at this time is unclean and impure.

Men who touched their wife at this time had to ritually cleanse themselves. What a difference this is to how it was in the era of Goddess worship and the veneration of all things feminine.

Even today we use the words Lunatic or Lunacy, from the words Luna, meaning Moon - to represent someone who has lost their mind.

With all the shame put on to women in this patriarchal society, is it any wonder we suffer so much at this time of the month? When we should be happy that we are at our most magickal.

Secrets of the Serpent Bloodline - The Unveiling of Profound Esoteric Mysteries

Epilogue

In this book you have been told many secrets that have been passed down for generations in the Underground Stream. Where possible I have tried to show references from others who also have this information as we slowly released it to the public over time. But some of it has never before been known by the general public, and you as a reader of this book, are one of the few people in the world who now also has some of the knowledge.

As we have seen by the teachings of Mary Magdalene, some things should be left for you to discover for yourself when you start on your own path to illumination. Reading this book is a great start, starting on the path to become a Priest/ess in your own right is the next.

This is often met with disapproval from people, as they can only see what being a Priest in patriarchal religions has involved, but try to see it from the Gnostic point of view, you are simply empowering yourself with truth, wisdom, knowledge and reaching your true potential. It doesn't have to be a full time calling, it is something that once achieved can never be taken away from you and the skills you learn can help to enrich your life and the life of those around you.

In some parts of this book I have deliberately only hinted at things or only discussed them very briefly, and this is because you have so much to discover yourself. Plus this book has tried to cover a lot of topics and would have become impractically large if I hadn't showed some restraint. Esoteric subjects are something you study for the rest of your life, it is such a massive topic, but after reading this book you now have a grounding.

It is time for you to start your own - quest for the grail, to seek out more from within yourself.

Good luck on your journey.

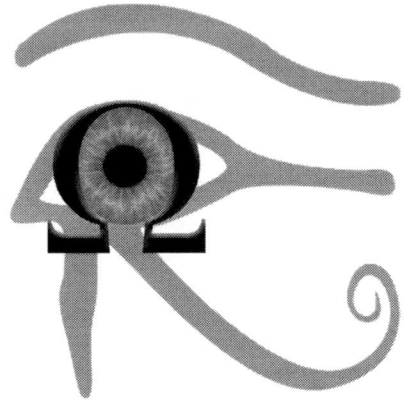

Secrets of the Serpent Bloodline - The Unveiling of Profound Esoteric Mysteries

Bibliography

- C.M. Bravi et als. "Characterization of Mitochondrial DNA and Y-chromosome Haplotypes In a Uruguayan Population Of African Ancestry," Human Biology 1997 Oct;69(5.:641-52.
- http://en.wikipedia.org/wiki/Skene's_gland
- http://davidpratt.info/sex2.htm
- http://en.wikipedia.org/wiki/Astrological_age
- J. Burger, S.Hummel And B.Herrmann, "Detection of DNA Single-Copy Sequences of Prehistoric Teeth. Site Milieu As A Factor For Preservation Of DNA," ANNALS OF ANTHROPOLOGY 1997.
- R. Scozzari, et als. "Differential Structuring of Human Populations For Homologous X And Y Microsatellite Loci," American J. Of Human Genetics 1997.
- Dunbar, Robin (2003). THE SOCIAL BRAIN: Mind, Language, and Society in Evolutionary Perspective.
- Ehrlich, Paul (2000). Human Natures: Genes, Cultures, and the Human Prospect. Washington, D.C.: Island Press. ISBN 1-55963-779-X.
- Stephen Jay Gould; Paul McGarr; Steven Peter Russell Rose (2007). "Challenges to Neo-Darwinism and Their Meaning for a Revised View of Human Consciousness". The richness of life: the essential Stephen Jay Gould. W. W. Norton & Company.
- Hugh Montgomery. The God-Kings of Europe: The Descendants of Jesus Traced Through the Odonic and Davidic Dynasties.
- Extended Y chromosome haplotypes resolve multiple and unique lineages of the Jewish Priesthood by M.F. Hammer, D.M. Behar, T.M. Karafet, F.L. Mendez, B. Hallmark, T. Erez, L.A. Zhivotovsky, S. Rosset, K. Skorecki, Hum Genet, published online 8 August 2009.
- http://www.eupedia.com/forum/showthread.php?24893-Do-modern-Europeans-partly-descend-from-Neanderthal
- http://en.wikipedia.org/wiki/Y-chromosomal_Aaron
- http://www.britam.org/DNA/BAMAD60.html
- http://en.wikipedia.org/wiki/Haplogroup_I2_(Y-DNA)
- La Momie de Ramsès II: Contribution Scientifique à l'Égyptologie (1985).
- Jean Bernard. Blood and History (1983).
- Peter Clayton, Chronicle of the Pharaohs, Thames & Hudson Ltd., 1994.
- http://www.ankhonline.com/revue/histoire_afrique_acquis_recherche_ankh.htm
- http://tim-theegyptians.blogspot.com/2011/03/coffin-of-weaver-nakht.html

- Mark Kurlansky, The Basque History of the World, Penguin Books, New York, 2001.
- http://www.aoi.com.au/matrix/Mat04.html
- http://www.reptilianagenda.com/research/r110199a.html
- http://www.cogs.susx.ac.uk/users/larryt/basque.faqs.htm
- http://www.geocities.com/ask_lady_lee/rhneg.html
- http://www.clan-blackstar.com/research/basque.html
- Robert J. Sawyer, Hominids, Tor Books, 2002.
- David Noel, Matrix Thinking, BFC Press, 1997. Chapter 104, Syston Boundaries and SIOS.
- Philip Lieberman, Eve Spoke: Human Language and Human Evolution, W W Norton, 1998.
- http://www.eirelink.com/alanking/collq1.htm#Pronunciation
- http://www.modernhumanorigins.com/neanderthalensis.html
- http://en.wikipedia.org/wiki/List_of_Neanderthal_sites
- http://www.betterbirth.com/rh-negative
- http://en.wikipedia.org/wiki/La_Chapelle-aux-Saints_1
- http://drpinna.com/neanderthals-and-basques-14808
- http://drpinna.com/neanderthal-genes-boosts-our-immune-system-23305
- Crowley, Aleister; Magick in Theory and Practice, ©1991 Castle Books.
- Stayskal, Byron. Ancient Greek Literature, WWU, Winter 2009.
- Hutton, Ronald (2009). Blood and Mistletoe: The History of the Druids in Britain. New Haven: Yale University Press. ISBN 0300144857
- Venn, J.; Venn, J. A., eds. (1922–1958). "Stukeley, William". Alumni Cantabrigienses (10 vols) (online ed.). Cambridge University Press.
- Stukeley, William (1980). The Commentarys, Diary, & Common-Place Book of William Stukeley & Selected Letters. London: Doppler Press.
- Stukeley, William (1740). Stonehenge, A Temple Restor'd to the British Druids. London: W. Innnys and R. Maney.
- Hawkins, Gerald S. (1965). Stonehenge Decoded.
- Newton's apple: The real story. New Scientist. 18 January 2010.
- Hutton, Ronald (2009). Blood and Mistletoe: The History of the Druids in Britain.
- Doyle White, Ethan (2010). "The meaning of "Wicca": A study in etymology, history and pagan politics". The Pomegranate (2). ISSN 1528-0268.
- The Rebirth of Witchcraft, Doreen Valiente.
- The Triumph of the Moon, Ronald Hutton.
- Bracelin, Jack (1960). Gerald Gardner: Witch. Octagon Press.
- Gardner, Gerald (1936). Keris and other Malay Weapons. Singapore: Progressive Publishing Company.

- Gardner, Gerald (1954). Witchcraft Today. Rider.
- Heselton, Philip (2000). Wiccan Roots. Capall Bann Publishing. ISBN 978-1-86163-110-7.
- Heselton, Philip (2003). Gerald Gardner and the Cauldron of Inspiration: An Investigation Into the Sources of Gardnerian Witchcraft. Capall Bann Publishing. ISBN 978-1-86163-164-0
- Heselton, Philip (2012a). Witchfather: A Life of Gerald Gardner. Vol 1: Into the Witch Cult. Loughborough, Leicestershire: Thoth Publications. ISBN 978-1-870450-80-5
- Heselton, Philip (2012b). Witchfather: A Life of Gerald Gardner. Vol 2: From Witch Cult to Wicca. Loughborough, Leicestershire: Thoth Publications. ISBN 978-1-870450-79-9
- Hutton, Ronald (1999). The Triumph of the Moon: A History of Modern Pagan Witchcraft. Oxford University Press. ISBN 978-0-19-285449-0
- Ruickbie, Leo (2004). Witchcraft Out of the Shadows. Hale.
- Lamond, Frederic (2004). Fifty Years of Wicca. Green Magic. ISBN 978-0-9547230-1-9
- Valiente, Doreen (1989). The Rebirth of Witchcraft. Hale.
- Farrar, Stewart (1983). What Witches Do. Phoenix Publishing. ISBN 0-919345-17-4
- Crowther, Patricia (1998). One Witch's World. London: Robert Hale.
- Sanders, O. Alexander (1984). The Alex Sanders Lectures. New York: Magickal Childe Publishing, Inc.
- Crowley, Aleister (1979). The Confessions of Aleister Crowley. London; Boston : Routledge & Kegan Paul.
- del Campo, Gerald. (1994). New Aeon Magick: Thelema Without Tears. St. Paul, Minnesota : Llewellyn Publications.
- Evans, Dave (2007). Aleister Crowley and the 20th Century Synthesis of Magick. Hidden Press, Second Revised Edition. ISBN 978-0-9555237-2-4
- Hymenaeus Beta (ed.) (1990) The Equinox: Vol.III, No.10. York Beach Samuel Weiser ISBN 978-0-87728-719-3
- Kaczynski, Richard. (2002). Perdurabo, The Life of Aleister Crowley. New Falcon Publications ISBN 1-56184-170-6
- King, Francis (1973). The Secret Rituals of the O.T.O. Samuel Weiser, Inc. ISBN 0-87728-144-0
- King, Francis (1978). The Magical World of Aleister Crowley. Coward, McCann & Geoghegan. ISBN 0-698-10884-1
- Dvorak, Josef (1998-12). "Carl Kellner". Flensburger Hefte (63). Retrieved 2011-04-26
- Neil Powell Alchemy, the Ancient Science, p. 127, Aldus Books Ltd., 1976 SBN 490-00346-X
- Free Encyclopedia of Thelema (2005). Carl Kellner. Retrieved May 24, 2005.

- See photographic reproduction of the "Notes of meeting proposing the formation of the Theosophical Society, New York City, 8 September 1875" on this page. File:St-1ata.jpg. Wikimedia Commons.
- U.S. Grand Lodge, Ordo Templi Orientis. Carl Kellner. Retrieved 6 October 2004.
- Rosicrucian Egyptian Museum & Planetarium at www.egyptianmuseum.org
- RC Salon - Mysterious Inventions of Dr. Lewis at www.rosicrucians.org
- Alchemy Journal Vol.4 No.1 at www.alchemylab.com
- Rosicrucian Order AMORC at www.rosicrucian.org
- Kessinger Publishing - Rare Reprints of Hard to Find Books at www.kessinger.net
- Lindgren, Carl Edwin, The way of the Rose Cross; A Historical Perception, 1614–1620. Journal of Religion and Psychical Research, Volume18, Number 3:141-48. 1995.
- Fra. A.o.C. (2002). A Short Treatise on the History, Culture and Practices of The Hermetic Order of the Golden Dawn. Retrieved August 3, 2007.
- Armstrong, Allan & R. A. Gilbert, eds. (1997). Golden Dawn: The Proceedings of the Golden Dawn Conference, London - 1997. Hermetic Research Trust.
- Cicero, Chic and Tabatha Cicero (1991). The New Golden Dawn Ritual Tarot. St. Paul, MN: Llewellyn Publications. ISBN 0-87542-139-3
- Colquhoun, Ithell (1975). Sword of Wisdom: Macgregor Mathers and the Golden Dawn. Neville Spearman. ISBN 0-85435-092-6
- Greer, Mary K. (1994). Women of the Golden Dawn. Park Street. ISBN 0-89281-516-7
- Greer, Mary K. & Darcy Kuntz (1999) The Chronology of the Golden Dawn. Holmes Publishing Group. ISBN 1-55818-354-X
- Gilbert, Robert A. (1983). The Golden Dawn: Twilight of the Magicians. The Aquarian Press. ISBN 0-85030-278-1
- Gilbert, Robert A. (1986). The Golden Dawn Companion. Weiser Books. ISBN 0-85030-436-9
- Gilbert, Robert A. Golden Dawn Scrapbook - The Rise and Fall of a Magical Order. Weiser Books (1998) ISBN 1-57863-037-1
- Howe, Ellic (1978). The Magicians of the Golden Dawn: A Documentary History of a Magical Order 1887-1923. Samuel Weiser. ISBN 0-87728-369-9
- Jenkins, Phillip (2000) Mystics and Messiahs: Cults and New Religions in American History. Oxford University Press. ISBN 978-0-19-512744-7
- King, Francis (1971). The Rites of Modern Occult Magic. New York: Macmillan Company. Library of Congress Catalog Card Number 76-158-933

- King, Francis (1989). Modern Ritual Magic: The Rise of Western Occultism. ISBN 1-85327-032-6
- King, Francis, ed. (1997). Ritual Magic of the Golden Dawn: Works by S. L. MacGregor Mathers and Others. Destiny Books. ISBN 0-89281-617-1
- Regardie, Israel (1982). The Golden Dawn. Llewellyn Publications. ISBN 0-87542-664-6
- Regardie, Israel, et al., eds. (1989). The Golden Dawn: A Complete Course in Practical Ceremonial Magic. Llewellyn. ISBN 0-87542-663-8
- Regardie, Israel (1993). What You Should Know About the Golden Dawn (6th ed.). ISBN 1-56184-064-5
- Runyon, Carroll (1997). Secrets of the Golden Dawn Cipher Manuscripts. C.H.S. ISBN 0-9654881-2-8
- Smoley, Richard (1999). Hidden Wisdom: A Guide to the Western Inner Traditions. Quest Books ISBN 978-0-8356-0844-2
- Suster, Gerald (1990). Crowley's Apprentice: The Life and Ideas of Israel Regardie. Weiser Books. ISBN 0-87728-700-7
- Wasserman, James (2005). The Mystery Traditions: Secret Symbols and Sacred Art. Rochester, VT: Destiny Books. ISBN 1-59477-088-3
- Blavatsky 1888. "Our Divine Instructors". Volume II: Anthropogenesis. pp 365–378. Phoenix, Arizona: United Lodge of Theosophists. 2005. Retrieved 2011-01-29.
- Blavatsky, Helena (1888). "The Three Postulates of the Secret Doctrine". The Secret Doctrine: The Synthesis of Science, Religion, and Philosophy. Volume I: Cosmogenesis. London: The Theosophical Publishing Company. OCLC 8129381. Phoenix, Arizona: United Lodge of Theosophists. 2005.
- Breglia, Lisa (2005): Monumental Ambivalence: The Politics of Heritage , University of Texas Press, Austin.
- Alfredo Barrera Vásquez in "The Book of Chilam Balam books" according to Luis E. Arochi in "The Pyramid of Kukulkan".
- Paredez as Luis E. Martinez Arochi in "The Pyramid of Kukulkan".
- Juan Francisco Molina Solís Review Yucatan Ancient History Discovery and Conquest of Yucatan. Merida, Yucatan, 1896.
- Anthropology and Religion: What We Know, Think, and Question By Robert L. Winzeler.
- J.M. Coles, E. S. Higgs (1969): The Archaeology of Early Man, New York: Frederick A. Praeger, 1969, p. 286-287.
- Lewis Binford (1981): Bones: Ancient Men and Modern Myths, New York: Academic Press, 1981, p. 10. A citation of F. C. Howell.
- http://www.drachenloch.ch/
- Marshack, Alexander (1991), The Roots of Civilization, Moyer Bell Ltd, Mount Kisco, NY.
- When the Drummers were Women by Layne Redmond, Publisher:

Three Rivers Press (1997), ISBN-10: 0609801287, ISBN-13: 978-0609801284.
- The Myth of the Goddess (Evolution of an Image), by Anne Baring and Jules Cashford.
- Beard, Mary, The Roman and the Foreign: The Cult of the 'Great Mother' in Imperial Rome, in Nicholas Thomas and Caroline Humphrey, eds., Shamanism, History, and the State (Ann Arbor, University of Michigan, 1994) pp. 164–90.
- Roller, Lynn E., "Attis on Greek Votive Monuments; Greek God or Phrygian?" Hesperia: The Journal of the American School of Classical Studies at Athens, Vol. 63, No. 2.
- Roscoe, Will, "Priests of the Goddess: Gender Transgression in Ancient Religion", History of Religions, Vol. 35, No. 3 (Feb., 1996), University of Chicago Press, pp. 195–230.
- Motz, Lotte, The Faces of the Goddess, Oxford University Press US, 1997. ISBN 0-19-508967-7
- Lane, Eugene, (Editor) Cybele, Attis, and Related Cults: Essays in Memory of M.J. Vermaseren, Brill, 1996.
- http://lilithgate.atspace.org/essays/algol.html
- http://www.thefreedictionary.com/incubi
- http://peacenews.info/node/3598/sign-times
- http://en.wikipedia.org/wiki/Evil_eye
- http://en.wikipedia.org/wiki/Hamsa
- http://www.masaru-emoto.net/english/index.html
- http://en.wikibooks.org/wiki/Cultural_Anthropology/Marriage,_Reproduction_and_Kinship
- http://www.reocities.com/newworldorder_themovie/theosophy.html
- http://www.kabbalaonline.org/
- http://www.dreamknow.com/page/13
- http://www.greatdreams.com/five/five.htm
- Kogan I (March 1968). "Information theory analysis of telepathic communication experiments". Telecommunications and Radio Engineering 23 (2): 122–125. ISSN 0040-2508
- Targ, Russel; Harold Puthoff (1974). "Information transmission under conditions of sensory shielding". Nature 251 (5476): 602–607. doi:10.1038/251602a0
- Marks, D. and Kammann, R., (1980) The Psychology of the Psychic, p26. Prometheus Books. ISBN 1-57392-798-8
- Hastings, A.C.; Hurt, D.B. (October 1976). "A confirmatory remote viewing experiment in a group setting". Proceedings of the IEEE 64 (10): 1544–1545. doi:10.1109/PROC.1976.10369.
- Whitson, T.W.; Bogart, D.N.; Palmer, J.; Tart, C.T. (October 1976). "Preliminary experiments in group 'Remote viewing'". Proceedings of the IEEE 64 (10): 1550–1551. doi:10.1109/PROC.1976.10371.

- Sergei Nechiporuk (2004-12-06). "CIA's remote viewers initiated quest for WMD in Iraq. Extrasensory agents helped the CIA arrest KGB spies and detect secret objects in the USSR".
- Joseph Rodes Buchanan, Manual of Psychometry : the Dawn of a New Civilization Boston, Frank H. Hodges (4th edition), 1893 p.3. ISBN 1-150-07724-7.
- Aleister Crowley, Lon Milo Duquette and Christopher S. Hyatt, Enochian World of Aleister Crowley/Enochian Sex Magick Scottsdale AZ: New Falcon Publications, 1991.
- Colin D. Campbell, "The Magic Seal of John Dee: The Sigillum Dei Aemeth." Teitan Press, 2009.
- The Written Law (The Torah).
- The Zohar.
- Wolfson, E.R. Venturing Beyond: Law and Morality in Kabbalistic Mysticism, Oxford University Press, 2006.
- Huson, Paul, (2004) Mystical Origins of the Tarot: From Ancient Roots to Modern Usage, Vermont: Destiny Books, ISBN 0-89281-190-0
- A Desert of Roses by Alan Chapman, Duncan Barford.
- Yes! 50 secrets from the science of persuasion by Robert Cialdini.
- Cognitive Dissonance by Leon Festinger.
- Prometheus Rising by Robert Anton Wilson.
- Daftary, Farhad (1998). A Short History of the Ismailis: Traditions of a Muslim Community. Edinburgh, UK: Edinburgh University Press. ISBN 978-1-84511-717-7. Retrieved September 15, 2010.
- http://psychology.wikia.com/wiki/Eugenics
- SS5-3: Rh Haemolytic Disease of the Newborn: A Major Public Health Problem. Alvin Zipursky MD, FRCP; Vinod Paul MD, PhD
- http://www.isogg.org/
- The First Americans- Retrieved 16th July 2003 from http://www.freerepublic.com/focus/f-news/946813/posts
- The Scotsman Publications Ltd: SCOTLAND ON SUNDAY 15/04/2001
- Type 1 diabetes among Sardinian children is increasing: the Sardinian diabetes register for children aged 0-14 years (1989-1999).
Casu A, Pascutto C, Bernardinelli L, Songini M.
Department of Internal Medicine, Azienda Ospedaliera Brotzu, Via Peretti, Cagliari, Italy.
- Type 1 diabetes among Sardinian children is increasing
-ncbi.nlm.nih.gov/pubmed/15220238
- DNA of Sardinians-
nature.com/ejhg/journal/v11/n10/full/5201040a.html
- Diabetic Disorders linked to Diabetes Type 1 –
generativemedicine.org/wiki/wiki.pl/Rhesus_(Rh)_Blood_Group

- SNP Rs2476601 -snpedia.com/index.php/Rs2476601
- Linking PTPN22 with HLA-B27 -http://europepmc.org/articles/PMC3224698/?report=abstract
- http://www.merckvetmanual.com/mvm/index.jsp?cfile=htm/bc/10203.htm
- http://www.endmemo.com/medical/bloodtype.php
- Are you a secretor or a non secretor? Source 3rd MAY 2009 http://proactivemedicine.blogspot.co.uk/2009/05/are-you-secretor-or-non-secretor.html
- Secretor Status: Source 2010 http://www.weight-tips.co.za/utlhealth/bloodtype-&-diet.htm

Images

1. Page 4 - Gnostic Theolalite Tau - Created by Tau Tia L Douglass, copyright Tau Tia L Douglass.
2. Page 6 - Serpent & egg illustration - The Orphic Egg by Jacob Bryant 1774, Permission - Public Domain.
3. Page 8 - Fleur de Lys, Permission - Public Domain.
4. Page 16 - Chartres labyrinth, Permission - Public Domain.
5. Page 24 - O Positive Symbol - Created by Tau Tia L Douglass, copyright Tau Tia L Douglass.
6. Page 24 - Vainest Blood Group Chart - Created by Tau Tia L Douglass, copyright Tau Tia L Douglass.
7. Page 25 - A Negative Symbol - Created by Tau Tia L Douglass, copyright Tau Tia L Douglass.
8. Page 28 - Vesica Piscis Diagram - Graphic Created by Tau Tia L Douglass, Permission - Public Domain.
9. Page 34 - Celtic Tree of Life - Unknown Artist, Permission - Public Domain.
10. Page 53 - Hitler Youth Photograph - Unknown Photographer, Permission - Public Domain.
11. Page 54 - Caduceus - Unknown Artist, Permission - Public Domain.
12. Page 56 - Blood Calculator Charts - Graphic Created by Tau Tia L Douglass, Permission - Public Domain.
13. Page 57 - Blood Comparability Chart - Graphic Created by Tau Tia L Douglass, Permission - Public Domain.
14. Page 58 - Risks During Pregnancy Chart - Created by Tau Tia L Douglass, copyright Tau Tia L Douglass.
15. Page 64 - Rh Negative Blood Chart - Created by Tau Tia L Douglass, Permission - Public Domain.
16. Page 68 - Rh Negative Eye Colours Chart - Created by Tau Tia L Douglass, copyright Tau Tia L Douglass.
17. Page 69 - General Eye Colours Chart - Created by Tau Tia L Douglass, copyright Tau Tia L Douglass.
18. Page 70 - Eye Genes Chart - Created by Tau Tia L Douglass, Permission - Public Domain.
19. Page 70 - Green Eyes Map - Created by Tau Tia L Douglass, Permission - Public Domain.
20. Page 71 - Evil Eye Pendent - Photographed by Tau Tia L Douglass, copyright Tau Tia L Douglass.
21. Page 91 - Sumerian Figures - Photographer unknown, Permission - Public Domain.
22. Page 91 - Neanderthal Skull - Project Gutenberg. http://www.gutenberg.org/files/2933/2933-h/2933-h.htm
23. Page 92 - Path of Aspirant - Graphic Created by by Tau Tia L Douglass, copyright Churchsmsj.org
24. Page 101 - Nigredo - Atalanta fugiens by Michael Maier 1617, Permission - Public Domain.
25. Page 102 - Albedo - Atalanta fugiens by Michael Maier 1617, Permission - Public Domain.
26. Page 103 - Citrinitas - From Andrea de Pascalis, Alchemy: The Golden Art, Permission - Public Domain.
27. Page 104 - Rubedo - Atalanta fugiens by Michael Maier 1617, Permission - Public Domain.
28. Page 116 - Vitriol - Basil Valentine, Chymical Wedding, mid seventeenth century, Permission - Public Domain.
29. Page 123 - Magick Numbers - Created by Tau Tia L Douglass, copyright Tau Tia L Douglass.
30. Page 132 - Honey Bee - Royalty Free Stock Phone, 123rf.com
31. Page 148 - Seal of Solomon - Permission - Public Domain.
32. Page 155 - Seven Pointed Star - Graphic Created by Tau Tia L Douglass, Permission - Public Domain.
33. Page 156 - Star of Babalon - Aleister Crowley, Permission - Public Domain.
34. Page 156 - Seven Hills of Rome Map - Unknown Artist, Permission - Public Domain.
35. Page 157 - Liber Oz Symbol - Aleister Crowley, Permission - Public Domain.
36. Page 157 - Elven Star - Unknown Artist, Permission - Public Domain.
37. Page 168 - Minotaurus Labyrinth - MAFFEI, P. A. "Gemmae Antiche," 1709, Pt. IV, pl. 31, Permission - Public Domain.
38. Page 170 - Venus of Laussel - Photo 120, œuvre dont l'auteur est mort depuis environ 25 000 ans, Permission - Public Domain.
39. Page 171 - Sumer Priests - Donald A. Mackenzie, Myths of Babylonia and Assyria (1915), Messrs. Mansell & Co., Permission - Public Domain.
40. Page 172 - Photographed in the Heraklion Museum 2005, Permission - Public Domain.
41. Page 172 - Egyptian Bee - Photographer unknown, Permission - Public Domain.
42. Page 172 - Bee Coin - Photographer unknown, Permission - Public Domain.
43. Page 172 - Merovingian Bees - Photographer unknown, Permission - Public Domain.
44. Page 172 - Bee Transformation - Unknown Artist, Permission - Public Domain.
45. Page 173 - Gold Seal - Unknown Artist, Permission - Public Domain.

46. Page 174 - Bee Keeping - Unknown Artist, Permission - Public Domain.
47. Page 174 - OMPHALOS STONE at Delphi, Greece. - Unknown Artist, Permission - Public Domain.
48. Page 176 - Artemis Statue - Photographer unknown, Permission - Public Domain.
49. Page 177 - Goddess Wearing Hacilar, ancient Turkey circa 8000 BCE. - Photographer unknown, Permission - Public Domain.
50. Page 178 - Mecca Black Stone - Photographer unknown, Permission - Public Domain.
51. Page 179 - Cybele wearing her Mitre - Unknown Artist, Permission - Public Domain.
52. Page 180 - Lilith by John Collier - Permission - Public Domain.
53. Page 183 - Hieros Gamos - Created by Tau Tia L Douglass, copyright Tau Tia L Douglass.
54. Page 187 - Peace Symbol - Graphic Created by Tau Tia L Douglass, Permission - Public Domain.
55. Page 187 - CND Symbol - Unknown Artist, Permission - Public Domain.
56. Page 188 - Algiz Rune Symbol - Graphic Created by Tau Tia L Douglass, Permission - Public Domain.
57. Page 189 - Crucified Serpent - Unknown Artist, Permission - Public Domain.
58. Page 189 - Dollar Symbol - Graphic Created by Tau Tia L Douglass, Permission - Public Domain.
59. Page 194 - Anatomical Man, an an inset page of Les Très Riches Heures du Duc de Berry, Permission - Public Domain.
60. Page 195 - Astrotheology Graphic - Created by Tau Tia L Douglass, copyright Churchsmsj.org.
61. Page 200 - Bloodline Map - Created by Tau Tia L Douglass, copyright Churchsmsj.org.
62. Page 202 - Chakra Body - Unknown Artist, Permission - Public Domain.
63. Page 254 - Très Riches Heures du duc de Berry, Folio 25, verso, Permission - Public Domain.
64. Page 261 - Tattvas Chart - Created by Tau Tia L Douglass, Permission - Public Domain.
65. Page 263 - Elemental Table - Created by Tau Tia L Douglass, copyright Tau Tia L Douglass.
66. Page 270 - Lotus Drawing - Created by Tau Tia L Douglass, copyright Tau Tia L Douglass.
67. Page 271 - Twirl Graphic - Unknown Artist, Permission - Public Domain.
68. Page 272 - Head and Leg Raises Graphic - Unknown Artist, Permission - Public Domain.
69. Page 272 - Back Arches Graphic - Unknown Artist, Permission - Public Domain.
70. Page 273 - The Table Graphic - Unknown Artist, Permission - Public Domain.
71. Page 274 - Cobra to Downward Dog - Unknown Artist, Permission - Public Domain.
72. Page 276 - Earth Pentagram - Created by Tau Tia L Douglass, copyright Tau Tia L Douglass.
73. Page 276 - Sign of Silence - Unknown Artist, Permission - Public Domain.
74. Page 280 - Sigillum Dei Aemaeth by John Dee, Permission - Public Domain.
75. Page 287 - Planetary Talisman, Mafteah Shelomoh, Permission - Public Domain.
76. Page 288 - Magick Sigil - Created by Tau Tia L Douglass, copyright Tau Tia L Douglass.
77. Page 289 - Magick Sigil - Created by Tau Tia L Douglass, copyright Tau Tia L Douglass.
78. Page 290 - Wheel of the Year - Unknown Artist, Permission - Public Domain.
79. Page 292 - Magick Sigil - Created by Tau Tia L Douglass, copyright Tau Tia L Douglass.
80. Page 298 - Genie - Created by Tau Tia L Douglass, copyright Tau Tia L Douglass.
81. Page 345 - Sine Line - Photographed by Tau Tia L Douglass, copyright Tau Tia L Douglass.
82. Page 361 - Viking Boat - Photographed by Tau Tia L Douglass, copyright Tau Tia L Douglass.
83. Page 379 - Magick Sigil - Created by Tau Tia L Douglass, copyright Tau Tia L Douglass.
84. Page 382 - IPoKHT Arms – Created by Tau Tia L Douglass, copyright IPoKHT.
85. Page 387 - Tau Staff Graphic - Created by Tau Tia L Douglass, copyright Tau Tia L Douglass, Permission - Public Domain.
86. Page 392 - The Church of St Mary & St John Seal - Created by Tau Tia L Douglass, copyright Churchsmsj.org.
87. Page 414 - Retable de l'Agneau mystique - Jan van Eyck (ca. 1390-1441) retable de l'Agneau mystique, Gand, Permission - Public Domain.
88. Page 416 - Madonna del Magnificat, Sandro Botticelli, painted in 1481, Permission - Public Domain.
89. Page 420 - Penitent Mary Magdalene, Nicolas Régnier, first half of 17th century, Permission - Public Domain.
90. Page 436 - Bee Hive - Unknown Artist, Permission - Public Domain.
91. Page 438 - Omega Eye - Created by Tau Tia L Douglass, copyright Tau Tia L Douglass.

Index

A

Aaron, 36, 38-39, 45
Abbess, 388
Abbot, 363, 388
Abducted, 375
ABO, 73
Abraham, 67, 366, 418
Abramelin, 313
Abstaining, 400
Abyss, 107, 124, 347, 390
AC, 79
Acana, 241
Acquisition, 138
Activation, 246, 339, 354
Activism, 37
Adam, 366, 378-379
Adamo, 59
Adams, 197
Addenbrooke, 83
Addison, 83
Adept, 119, 124, 330, 359
Adepts, 118-119
Adhvaryu, 359
Admônîy, 66
Adrenal, 155, 204
Adulterer, 365
Adulteress, 365
Adultery, 365
Adventurine, 204
Aegean, 180
Aemeth, 223
Aeon, 98-99, 124, 196-198, 243, 326, 384, 433
Aeons, 99, 124, 196, 198, 259
Aequilibrium, 334
Aeroplane, 360
Aesir, 142-143
Aesop, 294-295
Aethyr, 281, 304-305, 309, 315
Aethyrs, 138, 223, 281, 302, 304, 312
Aetiology, 84
Africa, 26, 38, 49, 74-76, 79, 88-89, 145, 212
Africans, 72, 75-76, 78
Afterlife, 97, 137, 147, 238

Agape, 158
Agaric, 36
Agasha, 242
Agate, 205
Agenda, 322, 324, 377
Agglutinate, 59
Agglutination, 59, 63
Agliz, 188
Agnes, 44
Agniveer, 357
Agnosticism, 133
Agrippa, 193
Âkâsha, 258
Akasha, 260
Akhenaten, 50, 386
Alatheia, 294
Alb, 98
Albany, 46
Albedo, 102-103
Albert, 165, 250
Alchemical, 101-104, 154, 183-184, 190, 198, 241
Alchemist, 104, 190, 381, 419
Alchemists, 102, 165, 193, 247, 311
Alchemy, 100, 129, 133, 136, 155, 190, 239, 247
Ale, 413
Alef, 386
Aleister crowley, 124-125, 136, 138, 145, 163-165, 193, 198, 242, 378
Aleph, 311
Aletheia, 294-295
Alexander, 42, 160, 163, 395
Alexandria, 180
Alexandrian, 133-135, 138, 146, 162-163
Algeria, 38, 152
Alice, 322
Alien, 17, 55, 375
Aliens, 199, 338-339, 375, 377, 390, 407
Allah, 140, 364-365
Allegoric, 236
Allegorical, 250
Allegory, 19, 32, 45-46, 138, 150, 154, 158-159

Allele, 56, 78, 83-84
Alleles, 30, 56
Aloeswood, 232
Alpha, 305, 386
Alphabet, 187, 193, 238, 241-243, 251
Alps, 81, 169
Altar, 139, 157, 171, 222, 263-268, 293-294, 312, 316, 405-406, 412
Altars, 157, 263, 326, 427
Altruism, 340
Alumbrados, 379
Amanita Muscaria, 36
Amber, 68, 232, 234
Ambergris, 233
Ambrose, 366
Ambrosiaster, 367
Amen, 318
Amenhotep, 133
Amenism, 133
Americans, 87, 186, 210
Amerind, 87
Amerinds, 86
Amethyst, 205
Amorc, 163-164, 166, 339
Amun, 50
Anally, 375
Anarchistic, 340, 409
Anarchy, 189, 340
Anatolia, 41, 180
Anatolian, 177
Androgynous, 252
Androgyny, 124, 197
Andromeda, 182
Anemia, 63
Angel, 107, 109-110, 124, 134, 192, 226, 263, 322, 413
Angelic, 55, 222, 237, 239, 241-242
Angels, 109, 134, 138, 140, 192, 220-223, 250, 264, 312, 339, 406, 413
Anglican, 161
Anglo, 40, 144, 152-153
Animalism, 134
Animism, 138, 144
Anise, 232
Anjou, 41
Ankh, 49, 134
Ankylosing, 48, 76-78, 85

Anointed, 153-154, 423
Anointing, 153, 165, 371
Anomaly, 81
Antenna, 186
Anthropological, 88
Anthropologists, 55
Anthropology, 42
Antibodies, 63, 73-74
Antibody, 73, 77, 84
Antigen, 49-50, 63, 65, 75-76
Antigens, 59-60, 63
Antioch, 395
Antoinette, 67
Anunnaki, 199
Ape, 64, 153
Aphrodite, 177
Apollo, 160, 174-175
Apollonia, 400
Apostle, 366-367
Apostles, 386
Apostolic, 21, 96, 139, 364, 370, 386-387
Apparition, 142
Apples, 192
Aqua, 278
Aquarius, 96-97, 196, 291, 411, 433
Aquatic, 359
Aquitaine, 170
Arab, 324
Arabian, 227
Arabic, 182
Arabs, 39
Aramaic, 40
Arcadian, 134
Arcana, 243, 250-252
Archaeological, 37, 161, 180
Archaic, 35
Archangel, 241
Archangels, 109
Archbishop, 388
Archegoniumel, 381
Archetypal, 188
Archetype, 183, 228
Archetypes, 109, 141, 252
Archipallium, 111
Architecture, 137, 338
Archives, 43, 67, 371

Argentium, 165
Aries, 96-97, 196, 291, 346
Arimathea, 395, 411
Armenia, 40
Armenian, 371
Aromatherapy, 161, 227, 229, 399
Artefact, 203
Artefacts, 85-86
Artemis, 174-175, 179-180, 399
Arthritic, 77
Arthritis, 48, 76-78, 82-85, 271, 316
Artisans, 228
Artist, 109, 252, 352, 417
Aryan, 143
Asana, 257, 264-268
Ascetic, 330
Asexually, 196, 402
Asia, 75, 175, 180, 214, 315, 399
Asians, 27, 41, 72, 78
Asiatic, 180
Aspartame, 407
Aspen, 324
Aspirant, 107-108, 118, 120-121, 223, 279
Aspirants, 118-119, 139, 397, 403
Assassin, 389
Assassination, 389
Assassinations, 211
Assassins, 389
Astral, 100, 109, 118, 145, 186, 193, 217, 219, 243, 263-269, 279, 312-313, 321, 330
Astrally, 186, 219
Astrological, 32, 97, 196
Astrology, 100, 136, 142, 239, 243, 247
Astronomers, 165, 167, 182
Astronomical, 411
Astronomy, 136
Astrotheology, 32, 35, 195, 338
Astrum, 165
Atbash, 33, 389
Aten, 133
Atenism, 133
Atenist, 133
Athame, 143, 146, 263, 294
Athanasius, 241
Atheism, 134

Atlantis, 17
Atman, 258
Aton, 134
Atone, 366
Atonism, 134
Attainment, 335-336, 342, 361, 387-388, 404
Attis, 181
Auburn, 25, 278
Auditory, 354-355
Augustin, 77
Augustine, 363, 365-366
Aura, 223, 258, 405
Auras, 118
Auriel, 263
Australia, 69-70
Australians, 72
Austria, 153, 398
Autism, 60, 407
Autistic, 51
Autoimmune, 51, 59, 77, 79, 82-85
Autosomal, 65
Autumn, 278, 346
Autumnal, 291, 411-412
Avebury, 161
Awakened, 184, 226
Aybss, 124
Azul, 17

B
Babalon, 156-157, 327
Babylon, 183
Babylonian, 136, 418
Bafomet, 33, 389-390
Bailey, 322
Balkan, 78
Balkans, 38-39, 41
Baltic, 38
Banished, 150, 316
Banishing, 108, 188, 223-224, 255-256, 258, 275-277, 281, 291, 293-294, 296
Baphomet, 33, 389-390
Baptise, 370
Baptised, 153-154, 190, 370
Baptism, 154
Baptisms, 388
Baptist, 393-395, 412

Baptiste, 142
Barbarian, 399
Bardic, 134
Bards, 161
Bartholomew, 430
Basilisks, 190
Basque, 19, 73, 75, 79, 152, 395
Basques, 53, 72-75, 79
Bayberry, 233
Beehive, 177
Beehives, 174
Beer, 247
Bees, 172-177, 180
Beetle, 173
Beings, 17-18, 20, 38, 64, 93-94, 103, 130, 133, 140, 173, 197, 287, 328, 330, 339, 385, 389-390, 396, 405, 409-410
Belgium, 41, 398
Beltane, 29, 291, 411
Benedict, 364, 368
Benzoin, 232
Betrothed, 365
Bible, 32, 98, 149, 176, 236, 364-365, 369-371, 394
Biblical, 237
Binah, 124, 240
Binary, 123, 182, 191
Bishop, 153, 386, 388, 398, 402
Bishops, 36, 45, 98, 181, 386, 402
Blackness, 101-102, 104
Blackstar, 79
Blavatsky, 165
Blessed, 79, 108, 130-131, 153, 296, 326, 364, 429
Blessing, 130, 153, 372
Blessings, 175, 334, 337
Blood, 85
Blooded, 26, 46
Bloods, 197
Bloodtype, 60
Blundellsands, 162
Boars, 65
Boleyn, 67
Bonfire, 266, 412
Bordeaux, 170
Botanical, 140
Botticelli, 417

Bottini, 82
Boudica, 67
Bovine, 180
Brahman, 359
Brahmanas, 360
Brahmin, 360
Brainwash, 349
Brainwashing, 409
Breath, 214, 258, 261, 273, 311
Bretons, 53, 65, 152
Britons, 40, 399
Brittany, 135
Bromance, 158-159
Broomsticks, 224
Brosseau, 162
Brotherhood, 165, 322, 385-386
Bubonic, 78
Buchanan, 216
Buckland, 144
Buddha, 135
Buddhism, 135, 147, 339, 357
Buddhist, 147, 203, 241, 253
Buddhists, 166
Buffy, 162
Bulgaria, 153, 395
Bull, 96-97, 174, 196

C
Caesar, 398
Calamities, 141
Calamus, 233
Calcium, 59
Caledonii, 135, 139
California, 75
Callimachus, 181
Cambridge, 83
Camphor, 232
Canadians, 72
Cancer, 76, 88, 196, 291, 373
Candida, 59
Candlemas, 411
Cannabis, 33, 389, 399
Capitalised, 162
Capricorn, 196
Caprine, 180
Carbohydrates, 59
Carbon, 131

Carcinogenic, 228
Cardamom, 232
Cardell, 162
Cardiac, 111
Cardinal, 250
Caribbean, 141
Carnelian, 204
Carpenter, 393
Carpocratian, 135
Carter, 163, 212
Cashford, 175
Cassia, 232
Caste, 36, 91, 117
Castile, 19
Castrated, 99, 181
Castrations, 399
Cataclysm, 153
Çatalhöyük, 180
Catastrophes, 169
Cathari, 400
Cathars, 46, 66, 379, 397-398, 400
Catholicism, 135, 400
Catholics, 30, 98, 390, 413
Caucasus, 81
Cavalier, 330, 335
Cave, 85-88, 169
Caverns, 180
Caves, 51, 87, 166, 169, 173, 175, 180, 196, 199, 284, 376
Cedar, 232-233
Celiac, 82, 84-85, 203
Celibacy, 99
Celibate, 378
Cell, 64, 76, 78, 82
Cells, 59, 64, 76, 78, 82, 217
Cellular, 173
Celtic, 99, 131, 134-135, 139, 143, 146, 257, 388, 390, 398, 400, 405-406, 411-413
Celts, 88, 186, 397-398
Censer, 264-268, 296
Ceremonial, 45, 98, 108, 133, 136, 140, 145, 163, 220, 225
Ceremonies, 19, 29, 33, 36, 120, 124, 146, 161, 166, 169, 171, 175, 197, 227-229, 291, 352, 354, 389, 399, 432

Ceremony, 223, 255, 292-294, 308, 313, 405-406, 411-413
Cernunnos, 390
Chad, 152
Chakra, 192, 203-205, 245, 268, 293, 339, 348, 385
Chakras, 30, 100, 155, 182, 192, 203, 289, 347-348
Chaldean, 136
Chalice, 66, 198, 263, 278, 396, 423
Chanting, 130, 224, 245, 259, 293
Chants, 248
Chaos, 107, 136
Chaotic, 23, 400
Chapelle, 79
Chapman, 316
Chariot, 237
Chastity, 395
Chesed, 240
Chestnut, 278
Chi, 258
Chiefs, 165, 213
Chieftains, 40
Chimpanzee, 26
Chimpanzees, 21, 35
Chimps, 152
China, 37, 76, 214, 227, 233, 258
Chokmah, 124-125, 240, 311-312
Choronzon, 124
Christeos, 283-284
Christianity, 31, 96-97, 140, 142, 145, 150, 155, 159, 164, 167, 239, 339, 363-364, 379, 389, 402
Christians, 98, 161, 166-167, 191, 379, 384, 401
Christos, 153-154
Chromosomal, 39
Chromosome, 30, 33, 39, 63-64, 81, 196
Chromosomes, 30, 64, 184
Chrysostom, 364, 368
Churches, 36, 119, 139, 218, 335, 363
Churchsmsj, 21, 96, 123, 131
CIA, 211-213
Cialdini, 375
Cincinnati, 216
Cinnamon, 232

Cipher, 33, 243, 389
Circumcised, 369
Citrine, 204
Citrinitas, 103
Civet, 233
Civilisation, 53, 251
Civilization, 180, 343, 398
Clades, 40
Clairalience, 207
Clairaudience, 207
Claircognizance, 207
Clairgustance, 207
Clairsensing, 206
Clairsentience, 207
Clairvoyance, 205-207, 209-210
Clairvoyant, 206-207
Clan, 40-41, 79, 191, 352-353
Clans, 52-53, 65, 353
Cleopatra, 67
Clergy, 99, 131, 363, 388, 396
Clergyman, 161
Cleric, 187
Cloak, 98, 278
Cloister, 367
Clones, 29
Cloning, 82
Clove, 233
Clovis, 46
Coalition, 86
Cobra, 274
Cochrane, 162
Cochranian, 162
Codename, 165
Coffin, 49
Cognitive, 35, 141, 203, 375
Cohen, 39, 45, 91, 177
Collier, 182
Colloidal, 321
Colostrum, 63
Comet, 178
Commander, 165
Communism, 37
Communities, 144, 197, 211, 367, 413
Concordia, 334
Conjure, 140
Conjurers, 140
Conqueror, 140, 160

Consciousness, 35, 100-101, 103, 138, 140, 144, 164, 175, 177, 186, 188, 196, 198, 211, 214, 224, 260, 329
Consecrated, 146, 388
Consecrates, 406
Consecration, 124, 146, 154, 387
Constellation, 182, 210
Copal, 232
Coriander, 232
Corinthians, 364, 367
Cornelius, 193
Cortex, 97
Cosmic, 129, 181, 252, 338, 402
Cosmological, 141
Cosmology, 238
Cosmos, 252
Coven, 162-163
Covenant, 141, 286
Covens, 119, 133-134, 138, 147
Covert, 53, 211
Craft, 224-225, 313, 353
Crafts, 399
Craniums, 72
Creed, 387
Crescent, 157, 179-180, 258, 260
Crests, 65
Crete, 172-174, 180, 395, 398
Cro-Magnon, 21, 26, 38, 46-47, 50-51, 64, 71, 87, 150, 152-153, 197, 199, 338, 386
Croatia, 39, 153
Crohn, 82, 85
Crone, 399
Crotona, 162
Crucified, 189
Crucifixion, 371
Crucify, 334
Crucis, 164
Cryptic, 250-251
Crystal, 130, 143, 146, 204-205, 219, 263
Crystals, 130-131
Cult, 97, 137, 142, 163, 179-181, 390
Cults, 36, 93, 138, 166, 324
Cunningham, 134
Curandera, 135
Cureandero, 135

Cursed, 371
Cybele, 175-176, 179-181
Cypress, 232
Czechs, 53

D

Daath, 124, 240
Daemon, 108, 124, 315
Daemons, 108-109, 222-223, 264, 307
Dagger, 275-278, 327
Damsel, 365
Danish, 40
Dardanelles, 180
Darpa, 211
Deacon, 395
Deacons, 388
Deborah, 176
Deborahs, 176
Debunked, 375
Decode, 167
Dee, 136, 138, 220-223, 239, 241, 283-284, 286
Deities, 134, 138-139, 142-143, 241, 370
Deity, 97, 108-109, 399
Delphi, 174
Delphic, 174
Demeter, 176, 180
Demigod, 394
Democritus, 164
Demon, 110, 159, 182, 185, 363
Demonism, 136
Demons, 52, 109, 136, 140, 307, 339
Denisovans, 75
Denmark, 41, 153
Denomination, 138, 144
Denominational, 236
Dervish, 144
Descendant, 42, 44, 66
Descendants, 41, 72, 176, 393-394
Desdemona, 159
Dettmann, 44
Deuteronomy, 365, 370-371
Devil, 19, 46, 52, 55, 304, 341, 347, 364, 366
Dharana, 258, 260

Dharma, 140
Diabetes, 59, 80-85
Diabetic, 80, 82, 85
Dianic, 137
Diasporas, 40
Dieties, 146
Disc, 203
Discarnate, 207
Disciples, 67
Disincarnate, 400
Disinformation, 41, 48-49, 63, 66, 210, 213
Disk, 50, 133, 287
Dissonance, 375
Divination, 142, 144, 174, 216, 250
Divinations, 188
Divine, 29, 31-32, 36, 52, 71, 93, 96, 98, 101, 104, 108, 110, 123-124, 133-134, 137, 139-145, 155, 171-172, 175, 178, 184, 188, 191, 197-198, 237, 239-241, 257, 259, 279, 292, 305, 311, 326-327, 330-331, 334, 338, 361, 364, 383, 386-387, 391, 393-397, 401-402, 405, 415, 422, 427
Divinities, 139
Divinity, 17, 188, 259, 359
DNA, 17, 19, 30, 33, 38, 40-46, 49, 65-66, 72, 81, 85, 87, 91, 127, 218, 339, 354
Doctrine, 119, 133-135, 139-141, 165, 387
Doctrines, 136, 140, 145, 236, 311
Dogma, 19, 119, 165, 323, 327, 408-410
Dogon, 98
Dollar, 189, 347
Dolphin, 303
Dolphins, 51, 278
Dolus, 295
Dordogne, 170
Douglas, 44
Douglass, 41-42, 79, 123, 139, 355, 361, 398, 415
Doves, 322
Doziaal, 304
Drachenloch, 169
Dracones, 190
Draconian, 137

Draconic, 137
Dragon, 46, 137, 150, 166, 190, 232, 304, 313, 330, 335
Dragonfly, 265
Dragons, 31, 65, 137, 149, 190, 278
Dragonsblood, 233
Dragoon, 213
Druid, 161-162
Druidic, 135, 161
Druidism, 166
Druidry, 134-135, 137, 161
Druids, 98, 161, 357
Dualism, 238
Dualist, 400
Dualistic, 103, 400
Duality, 141, 238
Dynastic, 399
Dynasty, 50, 133
Dyscalculia, 47
Dysfunctions, 59
Dyslexia, 47
Dyugarel, 263, 278

E

Eagle, 149-151, 185, 342, 354, 377
Eagles, 127, 150-153, 166, 348-349, 418, 424, 432-433
Ear, 302-303
Earlobes, 73
Ears, 67, 206, 274, 295
Earth, 17-18, 21, 32, 35, 37, 52-53, 55, 101-102, 127, 129, 137, 142-143, 149-150, 166, 169, 173, 177, 180-182, 192, 196-197, 204, 222-223, 226-227, 258-260, 263-265, 268, 272, 275-278, 282-284, 287, 291, 303, 311, 313, 315, 325, 328-329, 347-348, 351, 374, 385, 390-391, 399-400, 402, 407, 411, 424, 433
Earthly, 305, 316
Eastern, 40-41, 164, 241, 267, 319, 357, 386
Ebola, 65, 76
Ecclesiastes, 370
Ecclesiastical, 368, 386
Ecclesiasticus, 371
Eclectic, 134, 136-137, 139-140, 143, 145-146

Eclipsed, 101
Ecliptic, 31
Eden, 17, 52, 184, 192, 401, 433
Egypt, 19-20, 45, 48, 50, 96, 133, 152, 172-173, 180, 191, 196, 251, 386, 395
Egyptian, 48, 66, 77, 133, 136-137, 152, 164, 233, 239, 241, 251
Egyptians, 137, 311
Égyptien, 48
Égyptologie, 48
Egyptology, 136
Elders, 401
Electromagnetic, 207, 212, 216, 311
Element, 77, 137, 143, 212, 214, 222, 224, 241, 263, 369, 385, 411-413
Elemental, 135, 190, 203, 411
Elements, 35, 77, 129, 135, 137, 142, 169-170, 206, 212, 222, 226, 237, 241, 248, 252, 259, 268, 311, 353, 355, 372, 399, 406
Elemi, 232
Eleusinian, 158
Elf, 212, 293
Elfimp, 292-293
Eliphas, 251, 390
Elitist, 108, 226
Elixir, 104, 118-119, 153, 220, 423
Elixirs, 423
Elizabeth, 67, 220-221
Elk, 188
Elven, 157
Elynas, 46
Emanates, 331
Emanating, 278, 356
Emanation, 192, 216, 240-241
Emanations, 237, 239-240
Embalm, 173
Emerald, 278
Emeth, 259
Emigration, 40
Eminence, 369
Emperor, 67, 250, 399
Emperors, 156
Empire, 142, 179, 181, 183, 399
Empress, 125
Emptiness, 354
Enchant, 246

Enchantress, 183
Enchonian, 136
Encode, 84
Encodes, 167
Endocrine, 155, 204
Engels, 53
England, 38, 41, 133, 142, 152, 161, 221, 242, 395, 418
Enki, 32, 96, 196, 276
Enlightened, 30-31, 93, 96-97, 106-107, 109, 153, 184, 192, 332, 349, 354, 363, 387, 427
Enlightening, 426
Enlightenment, 21, 30-31, 33, 93, 96-99, 105-107, 111, 122-123, 135, 149-150, 153, 159, 164, 184, 190, 196, 198, 223, 316-317, 334, 340, 351, 378, 386-387, 398, 417, 421-423, 433
Enlil, 32, 96, 196
Enoch, 221
Enochian, 136, 138, 140, 145, 217, 221-223, 239, 241, 275, 279, 281-282
Entities, 109, 137, 186, 207, 264
Entity, 228, 340, 366
Entombed, 216
Enzymes, 48
Ephesia, 180
Ephesians, 179-180, 367
Ephesus, 179-180
Epiphanius, 367
Epitaph, 183
Equator, 347, 411-412
Equilibrated, 125
Equinox, 291, 411-412
Equinoxes, 142, 411-412
Era, 32, 35, 50, 67, 174, 190, 196, 433
Esoteric, 17-436
Esotericists, 193
ESP, 185, 206-211
Espionage, 207
Essene, 401
Essenes, 397-398, 401
Eternal, 103, 108, 127, 141, 259
Ether, 311
Ethic, 142
Ethiopians, 400
Etruscan, 145

Etymology, 175
Eucharist, 405-406
Eugenic, 62
Eugenics, 62
Eunuchs, 181
Europeans, 20-21, 41, 72, 74, 76, 78
Eve, 79, 366
Eves, 197
Evil, 71
Evokes, 137
Evoking, 134
Evolution, 26, 35-36, 79, 88, 95, 175, 190, 196, 215, 287
Exodus, 371
Exoteric, 119, 139, 142, 165, 386-387, 397, 402
Extinction, 62, 135
Extrasensory, 209
Eye, 71
Eyebrows, 73
Ezekiel, 237

F

Faery, 135, 137-138, 146
Fairies, 36, 135
Fairy, 46, 157, 199, 292-293
Fairyland, 199
Falcon, 303
Familiars, 175
Fantasy, 63
Faraday, 207-208
Feathers, 192, 294
Feminazi, 159, 178, 341
Feminism, 38
Feminist, 137
Feminists, 340, 367
Festinger, 375
Festival, 156, 181, 412-413
Festivals, 135, 139, 142, 352, 411
Figurine, 170-171, 180
Fisher, 96, 98, 196
Fjords, 303
Fleming, 42
Fleur, 65-66
Fluoride, 151, 407
Foetus, 33, 74, 177
Folklore, 138, 140, 146, 185

Foster, 324
Fourfold, 258
Frankincense, 227, 229, 233, 264-268, 316
Frater, 356, 383
Fraternal, 138, 161, 163
Fraternities, 158, 160
Freckles, 72, 88
Freemason, 160-161, 164, 319
Freemasonic, 161
Freemasonry, 50, 137-138, 155, 157-159, 162-166, 239, 339, 357
Freemasons, 162, 165, 319, 338, 378
Frequencies, 81, 207
Frescoes, 167
Freudian, 252
Friedrich, 53
Frigga, 143
Ftdna, 49
Funeral, 228
Fungi, 36
Fungicides, 249
Fythruel, 263, 278

G

Gabriel, 263
Gaea, 399
Gaelic, 40, 355
Gaels, 65, 152, 186
Gaia, 180
Galactic, 357
Galangal, 233
Galatia, 41
Galaxy, 287
Galbanum, 233
Galcottus, 250
Galilee, 394
Gallai, 181
Galli, 181
Gallos, 181
Gamos, 104, 123, 153, 183-184
Gandhi, 348
Gardner, 134, 138, 146, 162-163
Gardnerian, 133-135, 138, 144, 146, 162-163
Gargoyle, 390

Gaul, 390
Gauls, 400
Gautama, 135, 359
Geburah, 240
Gematria, 126, 223, 242, 328
Gematrix, 126
Gemini, 32, 96, 196
Gene, 19, 37-38, 49, 56, 65, 69-70, 72, 75-78, 82-83, 88-89
Genes, 17-21, 26, 30, 33, 37-38, 41, 46-47, 51-53, 55, 64-65, 69-71, 75-76, 79, 82, 84, 88, 90, 150-153, 197, 199, 338, 349, 424
Genesis, 67, 364, 371
Genetic, 25-27, 30, 33, 38, 40, 42, 55-56, 62, 64, 74, 78, 82-84, 88, 118, 141, 167, 199, 217-218, 345, 398, 405, 418
Genetics, 17, 26-27, 30, 55-56, 62, 65, 84, 91, 118-119, 142, 218, 418
Genoa, 169
Genocided, 51
Genome, 37
Genotype, 56
Genotyped, 84
Genotypes, 82-83
Genotyping, 84
Genuflection, 43
Geofu, 362
Geometry, 32, 191, 338
Georgia, 40
Germanic, 36, 315
Ghost, 142
Ghosts, 141
Ghoul, 182
Giants, 35, 91
Ginger, 88-89
Glastonbury, 395
Glucose, 82
Glycation, 82
Glycemia, 82
Glycemic, 82
Glycosylated, 82
Gnomes, 135
Gnosis, 33, 55, 96-98, 100, 127, 138, 165-166, 170, 182, 184, 192, 374, 386-387, 393, 405, 426, 428

Gnostic, 96, 98-100, 110, 131, 139, 153, 157, 257, 329, 331, 379, 385-388, 393, 398, 400, 405-406, 410-413, 435
Gnosticism, 135, 138, 239, 379
Gnostics, 45, 96, 157, 167, 193, 379, 384
Goddess, 29, 31-33, 45, 50, 99, 104, 133-134, 137-138, 142-143, 145, 153, 155, 157, 171-177, 179-181, 183, 191-192, 197, 217, 291-292, 294-296, 311, 318, 338, 355, 363, 386, 389, 399, 402, 413
Goddesses, 17-18, 91, 99, 126, 144, 175, 251, 287, 398, 401
Godform, 228
Godhead, 108, 239-240
Gods, 17-18, 20, 32, 35-36, 79, 91, 98-99, 137, 139-141, 143-145, 153, 156, 160, 173, 175, 180, 188, 197, 238, 287, 346, 359, 398, 400-401
Goetia, 223
Gold, 129, 133, 167, 173, 227, 278, 312, 315, 322, 330, 430, 432
Gorilla, 27
Gorillas, 21, 26, 152
Gospels, 394
Gout, 77
Grail, 17, 19, 21, 31, 66, 71, 118-119, 149, 386, 389, 393-396, 422, 435
Greco, 239
Greece, 38, 40-41, 139, 152, 159, 174-175, 177, 180-181, 239
Greeks, 31, 251, 370, 399
Grids, 222
Grimoire, 377
Groves, 119, 175
Guru, 337, 347, 354, 374, 376
Gurus, 94, 126, 186, 323, 334, 347, 352, 357
Gustatory, 355
Gutenberg, 251

H

Haemolysis, 63
Haemolytic, 61, 63, 74
Halloween, 220
Hallucinogenic, 36

Hamsa, 71
Haplogroup, 19, 38-41, 46, 49, 65, 81
Haplogroups, 19, 38, 40-41, 45, 65, 81
Haplotype, 39, 43-44, 49, 81
Haplotypes, 39
Harmonious, 173
Harmony, 17, 21, 32, 51, 53, 118, 137, 139, 141, 145, 149-150, 152-153, 159, 178, 197, 267-268, 287, 295, 328-329, 353, 377, 383, 397, 405
Harold, 211
Harps, 367
Harvey, 164
Hasan, 365
Hashashiyyin, 389
Hashish, 389
Hashishi, 389
Hashishin, 389-390
Hashishiyya, 389
Hassassin, 389
Hazel, 26, 68
Healer, 139, 141, 353, 381
Healers, 161
Heathens, 167
Heaven, 17, 52, 102, 181, 192, 307, 315, 328-329, 365, 394
Hebraic, 40, 124
Hebrew, 66, 141, 154, 223, 241, 243, 251, 259, 311, 355, 386, 398, 417-418
Hebrews, 40
Hecate, 174
Hecate, 174
Hecatine, 139
Hechiceria, 139
Hechiceros, 139
Heidelbergensis, 21, 26, 71
Heinrich, 193
Hellenes, 139
Hellenic, 139
Hellenism, 139
Hellenismos, 139
Hellenists, 139
Hemoglobin, 82
Hémoglobines, 48
Hemoglobins, 48
Henges, 169
Hephaestion, 160

Heraclitus, 164
Herb, 33, 142, 247, 371, 389-390, 432
Herbalism, 247, 399
Herbalists, 165, 247
Hercules, 160
Hereditary, 133, 135, 138, 163
Heresy, 384
Heretical, 236, 379
Heretics, 31, 390
Hermes, 174-176, 251
Hermetic, 136, 138, 164, 235, 239, 241, 243, 251
Hermeticism, 239
Hestia, 399
Heterosexual, 159
Heterozygote, 83
Hexagram, 124, 184
HGA, 124, 317, 322-323
Hierarchies, 343
Hierarchy, 165, 322
Hieroglyphic, 251
Hieroglyphics, 167
Hieroglyphs, 174
Hierophant, 322
Hieros, 104, 123, 153, 183-184
Highlanders, 53
Highlands, 40
Hilaria, 181
Himalayas, 165
Hindi, 140
Hindsight, 222
Hindu, 96, 196, 203, 241, 318, 339, 358-359
Hinduism, 140, 357-358
Hindus, 166
Hitler, 53
Hittite, 183
HIV, 78
Hive, 176-177
Hives, 175
HLA, 48-49, 65, 75-79, 83-85
Hod, 240-241
Holies, 182, 417
Holiness, 144
Hollywood, 224
Holographic, 305, 339
Homeland, 399

Hominid, 35
Hominids, 36, 72, 79
Homo Erectus, 21, 26, 47-48
Homosexuality, 159
Homosexuals, 378
Honey, 173, 175-177, 230-231, 278
Honeycomb, 175
Honourary, 198, 396
Hoodoo, 140
Horned, 134, 390
Horns, 174
Horus, 198
Hospitaller, 145, 383-385, 391, 396
Houston, 77
HPV, 76
Humanistic, 146
Humanitarian, 395
Hyacinth, 160
Hyacinthus, 160
Hydrophobic, 368
Hymn, 174, 176
Hyperborea, 17
Hyperthyroid, 271
Hypnosis, 186, 214

I

Iberia, 40
Iberian, 73, 81
Iceland, 142
Icke, 52, 190
Iconography, 144
Idaho, 87
Illicit, 211
Illuminati, 378-379, 396
Illumination, 96, 118, 142, 192-193, 235, 305, 378, 383, 386-387, 390, 397, 423, 435
Imbolc, 291, 411
Immigrated, 41
Immortality, 220
Immune, 48, 59, 63, 65, 75-77, 84, 190, 204
Immunization, 60-61
Immunomodulatory, 84
Immunoregulatory, 84
Imp, 293

Imperator, 164
Inanna, 183, 277
Inaugurated, 161
Incantations, 136, 138, 142, 223
Incense, 219, 227-232, 245, 263-268, 281, 291, 294, 296
Incubi, 185
Incubus, 185
India, 61, 251, 357
Indian, 85-87, 139-140, 233, 251-252, 318, 357-358
Indians, 27, 85-87
Indra, 359
Infinite, 140, 240, 326
Infinitus, 123, 145, 326, 328, 383, 396
Infinity, 122, 157
Inflammation, 59, 76-78
Inflammatory, 78
Initiatic, 100
Initiation, 118-119, 124, 138, 146-147, 170, 185, 243, 384
Initiations, 134, 157, 166, 169-170, 354
Initiators, 22
Initiatory, 133-134, 146, 162
Injected, 407
Injection, 60
Injections, 407
Innana, 173
Inquisition, 379, 385
Insight, 217
Insights, 238
Insulin, 82
Interbred, 75-76
Interbreeding, 76, 88
Intercourse, 185, 367
Intuit, 245
Intuition, 33, 46, 93, 103, 109, 186-187, 205, 209, 214, 323, 391, 397
Intuitive, 103, 134, 139, 393, 405
Invocation, 291, 294, 413
Iran, 40
Iranian, 214, 399
Ireland, 19, 135, 150, 152, 395
Isaac, 161
Isabella, 160
Isis, 32, 173, 179, 181, 191, 339
Islam, 67, 140, 144, 147, 339, 389

Islamic, 220, 364-365
Israel, 73, 91, 176, 235, 395, 418
Italian, 31, 143, 145, 250, 418
Italy, 38, 41, 80, 82, 152, 169, 418

J

Jainism, 140
Jamaican, 141
Janus, 181
Japan, 144, 325, 333
Jasmine, 234
Jehovah, 165
Jerusalem, 417-418
Jesuit, 165
Jesuits, 379
Jews, 39-40, 53, 91, 141, 166, 235-236, 384
Johannine, 393, 401
Johannines, 398, 401
Judah, 66, 371
Judaism, 140-141, 145, 339, 401
Judeo, 133, 140
Judgement, 282, 357
Jung, 141, 252
Jungian, 141
Juniper, 232
Jupiter, 205, 295

K

Kabbalah, 100, 141, 223, 417
Kabbalistic, 136
Karma, 140, 345
Kelley, 221-222, 239
Kelly, 136, 138, 163, 220
Kemet, 66
Kemetic, 141
Kennewick, 87
Kent, 242
Kether, 124-125, 164, 192, 226, 240, 311-312, 417
Khabs, 311
Khristós, 154
KHT, 275, 384, 396
Kinaesthetic, 354-355
Kings, 18-19, 21, 45, 98, 153, 165, 226, 391, 417, 423

Knight, 150, 315, 321-322
Knights, 145, 383-385, 389, 391, 396
Knosis, 174
Knossos, 173-174
Kony, 339, 377
Koran, 364-365, 367-368
Ku Klux Klan, 165
Kukulkan, 167
Kundalini, 30, 182, 184, 226, 387
Kurgans, 399

L

Labdanum, 230, 233
Laboratory, 78, 211, 381
Labyrinth, 166, 170
Labyrinths, 169-170
Lamentations, 418
Lancashire, 162, 406
Lance, 322
Lapis, 205
Laussel, 170
Lavender, 233-234
Lazarus, 394
Lazuli, 205
LBRP, 223-224, 256
Lemongrass, 234
Lennox, 42
Leo, 163, 196, 242, 291, 300
Leopard, 302
Leopards, 180
Leviticus, 369, 371
Libra, 125, 196
Libya, 152
Libyan, 214
Lightworker, 324
Lightworkers, 339
Lilac, 278
Lilies, 173
Lilith, 182-183
Lily, 183, 234
Lineage, 39, 134, 137, 383, 387, 402
Lineaged, 162
Lineages, 38-39, 225, 393-394
Lionheart, 67
Lions, 37, 65, 180, 183
Litha, 291
Lizards, 31

Logos, 244, 294
Loki, 143
Lotus, 183, 257, 264-268, 281, 305
Lovelock, 85-86
LSD, 36, 211
Lucid, 118, 332
Lucifer, 31, 191-192
Lughnasadh, 291
Luminary, 237
Luna, 18, 30
Lunatic, 376
Lupus, 77

M

Mabon, 291
Macaque, 74
Macgregor, 165, 251
Macrocosmos, 124
Madonna, 178, 417
Magdala, 394
Magdalene, 17-19, 52, 98, 104, 167, 184, 330, 393-394, 412, 415, 417-419, 421-432, 435
Magdalon, 394
Mage, 136, 140, 145
Magi, 136, 185
Magister, 312, 383
Magna, 180-181
Magnon, 21, 46-47, 50, 71, 150, 152-153, 197, 386
Magnons, 21, 26, 38, 47, 51, 64, 71, 87, 150, 197, 199, 338
Magus, 312
Mahomet, 389
Mali, 98
Malkuth, 240
Mana, 140, 434
Mantra, 257-259, 359
Mantras, 259, 323
Maria, 355-356
Marie, 67
Marijuana, 33
Martinism, 142
Mary Magdalene, 17-18, 21, 52, 67, 71, 96, 98-99, 104, 133, 139, 155, 167, 179-181, 184, 330, 355-356, 388, 393-398, 403, 405-406, 410-412, 415, 417-419, 421-432, 435

Maryland, 212
Mason, 339
Masonic, 138, 142, 164-165, 349
Masonry, 158, 164
Masons, 164
Mater, 180-181
Mathers, 165, 251
Matriarchal, 18, 51, 53, 66, 165, 362, 398-399
Matriarchy, 18, 29
Matrix, 79, 311
Mayan, 167
Mayans, 167
Maze, 166, 397
Mazes, 225
Mead, 173, 176
Meade, 212
Mecca, 178-179, 181
Mediaeval, 144
Medici, 160, 417
Medieval, 37, 66, 190, 251, 400
Meditate, 226, 241, 256, 289, 317, 430
Meditation, 100, 102, 104, 107, 142, 147, 203, 214, 217, 224, 226-227, 229, 256-258, 263-268, 271, 311, 427
Mediterranean, 39-40, 49, 175, 180
Mediumistic, 207
Medusa, 182
Megalithic, 161
Melanocortin, 65, 88
Melek, 192
Melissa, 176
Melissae, 175-176
Melissai, 175-176
Melusine, 46
Mena, 318
Menses, 368
Menstrual, 171, 358, 368
Menstruating, 29
Menstruation, 362, 368-369
Mercury, 102, 190, 205, 241, 407
Merkabah, 237
Mermaid, 46, 65-66, 303
Mermaids, 31
Merovingian, 45, 172
Merovingians, 45, 186
Mesopotamia, 32, 35

Messiah, 106, 141, 154
Metabolic, 59
Metaphysical, 236
Meteorite, 179-181
Meth, 259
Mexican, 135, 139
Microcosmos, 124
Microorganisms, 59, 77
Midnight, 308, 346
Midsummer, 412
Minoan, 96, 172-173, 175, 180, 196, 393, 398
Minoans, 173-174, 397-398
Miriam, 355-356
Miscarry, 74
Misogynist, 160, 198
Misogynists, 158, 162, 165
Misogyny, 153
Mithraism, 142
Mitochondrial, 72
Mitre, 45, 98, 155, 177, 179-181, 402
MK Ultra, 211
Molar, 47
Moldavia, 41
Monastery, 253
Monks, 192, 334, 357
Monotheistic, 140, 144, 239
Montgomery, 39
Moorish, 101
Moors, 321
Mormon, 165
Mormons, 357
Morocco, 19, 38, 152, 395
Mortals, 176
Moses, 97
Mounds, 51, 87, 166, 169, 199, 376
Mtdna, 19, 38, 41, 45, 49, 65, 81, 85
Muhammad, 67, 140, 364, 389
Mules, 63
Mundi, 390, 400
Murray, 137, 163
Muscaria, 36
Mushrooms, 29, 36, 196, 199
Musk, 233
Muslims, 140, 178, 181
Mutation, 30, 33, 42, 78, 88, 196
Mutations, 49, 242

Myathrel, 263, 278
Myrrh, 233

N
NADA, 79
Namaste, 357-358
Napier, 42-44
Napoleon, 242
Nasarean, 401
Natives, 150, 167
Navy, 210
Nazarene, 393
Nazarenes, 67
Nazareth, 154
Nazcan, 91
Nazis, 143
Neanderthal, 21, 26, 37-38, 41, 47-48, 50, 72-73, 76-77, 79, 87-88, 91, 151-152, 169, 197
Neanderthalensis, 72, 74, 79
Neanderthals, 21, 26-27, 35, 37, 41, 47, 64, 71-76, 78-79, 87-90, 150, 153, 169, 186, 196-197, 199
Necromancy, 142
Nectar, 173, 175
Nefesh, 237
Neocortex, 35-36, 186
Neolithic, 173-174, 227, 253
Neopagan, 144, 162-163, 239
Neoplatonic, 239
Neoplatonism, 239
Neptune, 205
Neshamah, 238
Netherlands, 38, 41
Netzach, 240
Neurotoxin, 407
Nevada, 85-86
Newton, 161
Nicene, 167
Nichols, 162
Nigredo, 101
Nile, 78, 191
Nirgantha, 140
NLP, 186
Nobility, 40
Noble, 97, 166, 360, 368, 385, 394-395

Nobleman, 395
Nomadic, 399
Nonsecretor, 59-60
Nordic, 37, 142
Nordics, 85
Nordvedt, 40
Norman, 40, 153
Normandy, 41
Normans, 152
Norse, 37, 142-143, 146
Norway, 41, 153, 303, 318, 362
Nostradamus, 220
Nucleotide, 72
Nucleotides, 72
Numegalogy, 123
Numerological, 242
Numerology, 238, 243
Nusku, 276
Nutmeg, 232
NWO, 324

O
Oath, 120-121, 149, 383
Oathbound, 134
Oathbreaker, 121
Oaths, 121, 134, 149, 338
OBOD, 161-162
Occultism, 239, 386
Occultist, 163, 184, 193, 390
Ochre, 170
Odin, 143
Odinism, 142-143
OIO, 145, 275, 306, 311-312, 326-327, 384, 391, 396
Olive, 26, 66, 68, 154
Olympians, 139
Olympic, 31
Om, 131, 275
Omega, 302, 305, 386
Omphalos, 174, 176-177
Onyx, 174
Opaque, 208, 250
Oprah, 358
Orator, 399
Orbit, 191
Ordination, 187, 387, 403

Ordo Infinitus Orbis, 123, 145, 326, 328, 383, 396
Oriental, 27, 136, 140, 145, 315, 333
Orientis, 155, 163-164
Orphic, 158
Orthodox, 236, 386
Orthodoxy, 400
Ostara, 291
Osteoarthritis, 76
Ostrander, 210
Otherworlds, 138
OTO, 155-158, 161, 163, 326, 339
Otra, 303, 318
Ovaries, 155, 204
Ovates, 161
Ovine, 180
Owl, 183
Ox, 311

P
Padma, 359
Paganism, 139, 142-144
Pagans, 139, 142-143, 157
Paiutes, 85-87
Palaeolithic, 35
Palestine, 67
Pantacle, 263
Pantheon, 135, 137, 142
Papal, 385
Paphos, 177
Paranormal, 210-211, 214-215
Parapsychological, 211, 221
Parapsychologists, 207
Parapsychology, 206, 214
Paris, 390
Parkinson, 271
Parthenogenesis, 29, 31, 33, 184, 196, 402
Parthenogenetic, 191
Patchouli, 233-234
Patriarch, 390
Patriarchal, 19, 29, 38, 46, 51, 66, 124, 155, 157-158, 161, 163, 165-166, 197, 339, 357-358, 363, 376, 385, 398, 410, 435
Patriarchs, 235
Patriarchy, 21, 29, 31, 36-37, 53, 99, 155, 161-162, 166, 183, 197, 330, 338-339, 357, 363, 376, 385, 394, 410
Peacock, 192
Penis, 122, 184
Pentacle, 31-32, 191, 223
Pentagram, 32, 124, 191, 223, 255-256, 258, 276-278, 304, 309, 311, 315
Pentagrams, 224, 276, 279
Perfume, 243
Perseus, 182
Persia, 160, 220, 395
Persians, 147
Phaedrus, 295
Phallic, 156, 363
Phallus, 370
Pharaoh, 50
Pharaohs, 49, 66
Phenotype, 82
Phi, 32, 191
Philosophers, 102, 136, 140, 145, 164-165, 190
Philosophia, 193
Philosophical, 140, 166, 239
Phoenix, 129, 328
Phrygian, 180
Phrygians, 41
Pict, 399
Picti, 399
Pictish, 19, 40, 45, 143, 146-147, 399
Picts, 19, 40, 65, 143, 146, 153, 186, 397-399
Pike, 165
Pillars, 100
Pineal, 30, 155, 205
Pinna, 72, 76
Pisces, 96, 98, 125, 181, 196, 346, 402, 433
Piscis, 181, 260, 338, 402
Pituitary, 155, 205
Pixies, 36
Plague, 78
Planetary, 127, 287
Plato, 136, 140, 145, 158
Polynesian, 140
Polynesians, 72
Polytheism, 139

Polytheists, 139
Pope, 250, 363-364, 367-368, 389-390, 402
Poppy, 385
Portal, 402
Portals, 332-333
Possessed, 52, 110
Potions, 142, 245-249
Prana, 258
Pranayama, 257-258, 261
Pranic, 145
Prayer, 130, 257, 359, 364, 367
Prayers, 180, 323, 367
Prechristian, 138, 412
Precognition, 206-207, 212
Precognitive, 118, 209
Predictive, 212, 214
Predictor, 49
Preestruscian, 143
Pregnancy, 33, 58, 74, 171
Prehistoric, 161, 166
Priest, 50, 97, 130-131, 134, 139, 143-146, 161, 163, 178, 183-184, 354, 359, 371, 388, 403, 405-406, 410, 419, 428, 435
Priestess, 30, 97, 139, 146, 174, 178, 183-184, 354, 386, 399, 402, 405-406, 410, 415, 417, 423
Priestesses, 29, 31, 99, 133, 143, 145, 166, 171-173, 175-176, 184, 196, 340, 370, 393-394, 398, 402
Priesthood, 39, 50, 134, 139, 181, 370, 378
Priestly, 36, 39, 91
Priests, 29-32, 36, 38, 45, 50, 91, 99, 133, 143, 145, 161, 167, 171, 177, 181, 359, 393, 395, 398
Primal, 192
Primates, 74
Primitive, 53, 227
Primitives, 349
Prince, 115, 165, 278
Princes, 98, 311, 423
Princess, 115, 418
Princesses, 98
Priory, 383-384
Probationer, 120-121, 384

Probed, 375
Profane, 188
Prometheus, 295
Prophecies, 433
Prophecy, 175
Prophet, 67, 126, 134, 140, 364-365, 389, 395
Prophetess, 176
Prophetic, 364
Prophets, 32, 126, 175, 235, 418
Protectress, 175, 181
Protestant, 365, 368, 418
Psalms, 66, 367
Pseudoscience, 376
Psi, 145, 188, 211-213, 221
Psilocybe, 36
Psilocybin, 187
Psoratic, 316
Psoriasis, 78, 85, 316, 321
Psoriatic, 48
Psychic, 95, 112, 205-206, 209-210, 212, 216, 307
Psychically, 219
Psychoactive, 36
Psychokinesis, 211-212, 214
Psychologist, 209
Psychometric, 216
Psychometry, 95, 216, 245
Psychopathic, 152
Psychopaths, 51, 165, 339
Psychopathy, 407
Psychotropic, 29
Psyops, 377
Pulmonary, 111
Purification, 102, 227, 229, 369
Pyrenees, 73, 81
Pythagoras, 164, 166
Pythagorean, 158, 328

Q

Qabalah, 235-239, 241-243, 251
Qabalist, 241
Qabalistic, 237-238, 241, 252
Qabalists, 235, 237-238
Qaballah, 318
Qabbalistic, 136
Qigong, 214

Qliphothic, 239
Queen, 50, 67, 96, 102, 104, 153, 165, 173, 176-177, 226, 294, 351, 359, 362, 387, 399, 423
Quran, 364

R
Ra, 50, 83, 286
Rabbinic, 236
Racist, 53, 349
Racists, 165
Rainbow, 155, 192, 203, 385
Ramases, 20, 386
Ramesses, 50
Ramses, 48-50, 67
Ramsès, 48
Rand, 361
Rankine, 242
Raphael, 263
Raphaelite, 322
Ratzinger, 364, 368
Reaper, 399
Rebirth, 127, 129, 143, 326, 345, 413
Reborn, 104, 166, 170
Recessive, 20, 56, 65, 77
Recessively, 21, 53
Red Haired, 19, 85-86, 400
Redhead, 400
Redheaded, 67
Redheads, 88-89, 400
Reincarnated, 97
Reincarnation, 117, 140, 177, 345-346
Reindeer, 36
Relic, 335
Remote, 26, 95, 206-207, 210-215, 330, 335
Remotely, 118, 211
Renaissance, 239, 250-251
Reptiles, 65, 149, 190, 341
Reptilian, 55, 79, 111
Resins, 228-229, 232, 294
Resurrection, 181
Revelation, 103, 315
Revelations, 165, 426, 433
Rh, 17-18, 20-21, 25-27, 38, 45, 49, 51, 53, 55, 58, 60-66, 68-69, 74-75, 77, 79-82, 85, 90, 328

Rhesus, 53, 56, 60, 73-74, 85, 400
Rheumatic, 77-78
Rheumatism, 77
Rheumatoid, 76-77, 82-85
Rhine, 208-209
Rhneg, 79
Rhogam, 51
Rite, 153, 164-165, 183-184, 271-274, 360, 378, 419, 421, 423
Rites, 141, 164, 173, 179, 181, 256, 271, 387
Ritual, 107, 136, 140, 145, 153, 169, 173, 177, 183, 217, 223-226, 228, 247, 251, 255-256, 258, 275, 279, 281, 291, 293-294, 309, 311, 313, 358-359, 411-413
Ritualized, 142
Ritually, 181
Rituals, 19, 99, 118, 127, 133-134, 137, 142, 146, 163, 173, 177, 224-226, 228-229, 246, 255-256, 264, 275, 309, 312, 323, 326-327, 341, 385, 387, 411, 419, 430
Robe, 98, 225, 255, 263, 294, 304, 310, 320, 366
Robed, 305, 328
Robes, 45, 98-99, 155, 385, 413, 415
Romania, 153
Romans, 152, 156, 179, 181
Rome, 67, 156-157, 175, 179, 181
Rootwork, 140
Rosae, 164
Rosalind, 88
Rosarium, 369
Rosecroix, 164
Rosicrucian, 162, 164-165
Rosicrucianism, 164, 239
Rosæ, 164
Rota, 303, 318
Rowan, 412
Royals, 19, 45-46, 67, 165
Royalties, 158
Royalty, 19, 21, 38, 41, 45, 50, 65, 67, 158, 199, 384, 394
Ruach, 238
Ruddy, 66
Rufus, 400

Ruickbie, 163
Rune, 188, 362
Runes, 188
Russia, 41, 70, 399
Russians, 210

S

Sabbats, 133, 146
Sacral, 204
Sacraments, 45, 153-154, 366, 388, 397
Sacrificial, 146, 359
Saffron, 233
Sage, 233, 359
Sages, 235
Sagittarius, 196, 291
Saint, 46, 142-143, 372, 390, 418
Saints, 79, 145, 372
Salamander, 190-191
Salamanders, 31, 190-191, 278
Salamandrae, 190
Salin, 46
Salvation, 190, 197, 393
Samhain, 291
Samson, 186
Sanctum, 182
Sandalwood, 232, 234
Sanders, 133-134, 146, 163
Sangre, 17
Sanguin, 48
Sanskrit, 203, 318
Santa, 36
Santería, 143, 145
Santeros, 143, 145
Santis, 82
Santo, 143
Sapiens, 35, 37, 47, 64, 72, 74, 88-89, 169
Sapphire, 237
Sardinia, 39, 80-82
Sardinian, 80-81, 83, 85
Sarmatians, 399
Satan, 32, 191, 339
Satanism, 143
Saturn, 101, 204, 294
Saul, 418
Savant, 47, 196
Saviour, 180

Saxon, 40, 46, 144
Saxons, 152-153
Scandinavia, 38-40, 69-70, 214
Scandinavian, 36, 38, 50
Scarab, 173
Scarlet, 415
Scientology, 165, 357
Sclerosis, 59, 82, 85, 271
Scorpio, 196, 291
Scots, 44, 67, 87-88
Scotsman, 89
Scottish, 53, 89, 135, 139, 147, 165, 252-253
Scribe, 237
Scripture, 358, 368, 395
Scriptures, 235
Scrolls, 393
Scry, 219, 223, 281, 309
Scryed, 319
Scryer, 216, 219-220
Scrying, 143, 146, 217, 219-221, 263, 281, 302-304, 309
Scythe, 399
Scythians, 186, 397-399
Seasonal, 142
Seax, 144
Secrecy, 338, 397
Secretive, 47, 94, 138, 394
Secretor, 59-60
Sect, 135, 389, 393
Sects, 140, 147
Seer, 134, 139, 385, 415, 419
Seers, 165, 174, 425
Sefirot, 237-238, 243
Semen, 369, 371
Seminary, 139, 397, 402-403
Semitic, 39, 183
Sepher, 251
Sephira, 124
Sephirah, 237, 240-241, 243
Sephirot, 243
Sephiroth, 124, 240-241
Septimontium, 155-156
Sermones, 250
Serum, 63
Seti, 50
Sexism, 358

Sexist, 162, 340
Shaman, 35, 146
Shamanism, 135, 142, 144, 146, 227
Shamanistic, 17, 29, 53, 135, 146, 192, 199, 206, 338, 385
Shamans, 21, 35, 38, 41, 150, 165, 186, 334
Shazam, 281, 286
Shell, 167, 263, 279
Shells, 65-66, 336
Shintoism, 144
Shofar, 196
Sicily, 172
Sickle, 399
Sigil, 189, 244, 288-289, 292-294, 304, 315-316, 326, 380-381, 385
Sigilisation, 244-245
Sigillum, 223
Sigils, 117, 127, 136, 189, 244, 381
Simian, 17-18, 51, 90, 150, 153, 338
Simians, 17, 26, 52-53, 64, 152
Simples, 150-153, 197, 327, 418
Sine, 346-347
Sinfarel, 263, 278
Sinistra, 31
Sinner, 370, 372
Sinners, 341, 372
Siren, 333
Sirius, 32, 173, 191
Skeletal, 78
Skeleton, 79, 86-87, 101
Skeletons, 77, 86, 91, 372
Skene, 29
Skull, 91, 169, 220
Skullcap, 187
Skulls, 73, 91, 169
Skyclad, 133, 138
Slavs, 53
Smallpox, 65, 78
Snowdrop, 411
Snowflakes, 130
SNP, 82-83, 85
Socrates, 158
Solitaire, 250
Solomon, 66, 390, 417
Solstice, 173, 191, 222, 291, 411-413
Solstices, 142

Sophia, 33, 97, 100, 165-166, 170, 182, 192, 386, 389, 393, 396, 405
Sorcerer, 221
Sorcerers, 162
Soror, 356, 383
Soviet, 208, 210-212, 214
Spain, 19, 73, 152, 379, 398
Species, 26, 35-36, 51, 55, 62-63, 72-74, 79, 88-89, 196-197, 369, 390
Sperm, 64
Sphere, 124, 223, 275
Spices, 248
Spikenard, 233
Spinal, 77-78
Spine, 30, 184, 203-204, 271, 273-274
Spiral, 105
Spiritualist, 242
SPM, 113-114
Stalactite, 169
Stargate, 213-214
Starseed, 55
Steeple, 363
Stellar, 129, 182
Steppenwolf, 320
Sterile, 63
Sterility, 125
Stewards, 41, 43-44
Stewart, 41-44
Stillbirths, 61
Stillborn, 74
Stonehenge, 161, 338
Storax, 233
Strawberry, 25, 302
Strega, 142-143, 145
Stregheria, 142-143, 145
Streptococcus, 77
Stuart, 42-43
Stukeley, 161
Subclades, 40, 81
Subconscious, 100, 120, 136, 217, 227, 288
Subgroup, 50
Subspecies, 72
Succubi, 185
Succubus, 185
Sufi, 144
Sufis, 339

Sufism, 144
Sulphur, 102, 104, 190
Sumer, 32, 96, 171, 196
Sumeria, 173, 183
Sumerian, 91
Summon, 109, 142, 146, 185-186, 360
Summoning, 108, 142
Supernatural, 238, 398
Supernova, 129
Superstitions, 163
Surnames, 42, 44, 355
Swans, 66
Swastika, 315
Sweden, 41, 153
Swirl, 291
Swiss, 141, 169
Switzerland, 386, 398
Swizz, 386
Sword, 66, 122, 198, 263, 278, 315, 322, 330, 335, 361, 396
Swords, 311, 320, 330, 335
Symbology, 142, 311
Synchronicities, 106
Syria, 180

T

Tactless, 379-380
Talisman, 71, 158, 287
Talmud, 190
Tamil, 140
Tanakh, 236
Tantra, 164, 203, 239
Tantric, 30, 153, 157, 164, 183, 340
Taoism, 144
Taoists, 144
Taro, 251, 303, 318
Tarot, 100, 125, 223, 239, 241, 243, 250-252, 309, 311-312, 317
Tattvas, 258, 260
Tau, 45, 98, 123, 139, 225, 242, 255, 263, 361, 372, 386-387, 415, 418
Taurus, 96, 182, 196, 291
Tawsi, 192
Teeth, 90
Telepathically, 220, 264
Telepathy, 95, 206-207, 209-210, 212
Telescope, 182

Tempe, 316
Templar, 98, 139, 383-385, 389, 391
Templars, 33, 46, 145, 379, 384-386, 389-390, 396
Templeoftheola, 94, 372, 377, 410
Templi, 155, 163-164, 312, 383, 390
Terrestrial, 390
Testament, 66, 141, 167, 417-418
Testes, 155, 204
Testosterone, 33, 340
Teutonic, 143
Thebes, 50
Thecla, 395, 413
Thelema, 158, 163-164, 166, 198, 326-327
Thelemic, 136, 140, 145, 165, 198, 239, 242, 326-327
Thelemite, 193
Thelemites, 124, 158, 193, 326
Theodism, 144
Theola, 93, 96, 145, 198, 259, 275, 326-327, 383, 391, 396, 406
Theolalite, 21, 65, 94-96, 104, 110, 126, 151, 329, 331, 386, 407, 410
Theolalites, 93-96, 98, 129, 139, 145, 149, 153
Theologian, 364, 366
Theologica, 369
Theology, 138-139, 346, 400, 403
Theomerla, 52, 353, 396, 408
Theosophical, 163, 165, 339
Theurgy, 136, 140, 145
Thistles, 371
Thor, 143
Thorns, 371
Thoroughbreds, 63
Thoth, 241, 251
Thrace, 400
Thracian, 19, 41, 153, 400
Thracians, 397-400
Thymus, 155, 204
Thyroid, 84-85, 155, 205
Tia, 50, 79, 123, 139, 286, 361, 372, 388, 398, 415
Tiamet, 277
Tibet, 334
Tibetan, 136, 234, 253, 256, 271

Tigris, 35, 66, 73-74, 152-153, 395
Tiphareth, 125, 240
Tirzah, 417, 419
Tomb, 101, 104, 173, 177, 361
Tombs, 174
Tombstones, 400
Tonsured, 187
Torah, 236
Transcend, 138, 400
Transform, 173, 423
Transformation, 100
Transformed, 103, 173
Transmutation, 133
Triangle, 184, 258, 260
Tribal, 86, 146, 151
Tribe, 17-18, 21, 36, 86-87, 98, 153, 197, 424
Tribes, 18-19, 21, 29, 41, 53, 86, 90, 152, 165, 196-197, 199, 315, 383, 398-400
Trigrammaton, 242-243
Trinity, 124, 259, 326, 338
Trismegistus, 251
Triwens, 259, 391
Troglodytes, 199
Tsunami, 333
Tuberculosis, 77
Turin Shroud, 66
Turkey, 40-41, 153, 177, 180, 308
Turkish, 371
Tuscany, 41
Twin, 67, 295, 417
Twins, 32, 96, 196, 417
Typhonian, 239
Typhoon, 212
Tzion, 417, 419

U
Ufism, 144
Ufos, 375
UK, 19, 60, 79, 83, 123, 152, 395, 406, 417
Ultraviolet, 88
Umbria, 41
Unction, 153
Unicorn, 66
Uninitiated, 214
Upanishad, 358
Upanishads, 203
Ur, 259
Uranus, 205
USA, 85, 164, 207, 388

V
Vaccination, 51, 60
Vaccinations, 47, 63
Vagina, 181, 192, 386, 402
Vampire, 112, 162
Vampires, 307, 309
Vampyre, 145
Vanilla, 232, 234
Vatican, 330, 335, 371
Vaults, 330, 335
Vecchia, 143, 145
Vedas, 359
Vedic, 140, 358
Venus, 31, 125, 170-171, 191-192, 204, 291-292, 311, 339, 362, 377
Veritas, 150, 198, 294-296, 334, 413
Vernal, 291, 411-412
Vertebra, 75
Vesica, 181, 260, 338, 402
Vestments, 36, 371
Vetiver, 233
Viking, 38-40, 362
Vikings, 152-153, 186
Virgin, 30, 155, 179-180, 183, 294, 322, 365, 395
Virginity, 179-180, 395
Virgins, 175, 360
Virgo, 196, 291
Virtue, 190, 294, 296
Virtues, 197-198, 238, 250, 294, 296
Vishnu, 252
Vodoun, 145-146
Vodu, 145
Voodoo, 140-141, 145
Voudon, 143, 145
Voudou, 145-146
Voudoun, 145-146
Vulva, 171

W

Wales, 41, 135, 395
Wand, 122, 263, 275, 318, 354
Wands, 224
Warpaint, 399
Warrior, 21, 142, 152, 198
Warriors, 383
Watchers, 35, 182
Watchtowers, 222
Wayseers, 339, 377
Weaver, 48-49
Weishaup, 378-379
Welsh, 137-138, 146
Westcott, 165
Whiteness, 102, 104
Whore, 415
Whores, 358
Wicca, 133-135, 137-138, 143-144, 146, 155, 157-158, 161-163, 166, 339
Wiccans, 98, 133-134
Wiccen, 162
Wita, 143, 146-147
Witans, 143, 146
Witch, 19, 62, 133, 137, 139, 142, 146, 162-163, 183, 192, 224
Witchcraft, 134-136, 138-139, 142-143, 145-146, 161-163, 166, 247
Witchery, 142
Witches, 19, 31, 52, 98, 133, 135, 138-139, 143, 152, 163, 169, 186, 193, 224, 357
Witta, 146-147
Wittan, 147
Womb, 30, 171, 338, 386, 402

Y

Yahweh, 356, 398, 418
Ychromosome, 30
Yellowness, 102-104
Yeshua, 401, 415, 417, 419
Yesod, 124-125, 240
Yetzirah, 251
Yezidis, 192
Yhaplogroup, 38
Yiskah, 418-419
Yitzirah, 237
Ylang, 234
Yochanan, 356
Yoga, 224, 226, 256, 274, 322-323
York, 79, 164-165
Yosef, 356
Yule, 291

Z

Zanzarah, 321
Zen, 147
Zeus, 160, 173, 175, 295
Zion, 417
Zohar, 236, 238
Zoroaster, 99, 142, 147
Zoroastrianism, 147

Web Sites

knightshospitallertemplar.org
churchsmsj.org
templeoftheola.org
tialdouglass.com
purplepeacockpublications.info
serpentbloodline.info
alchemistslaboratory.com
theomerla.weebly.com
ordoinfinitusorbis.com
gnosticchivalry.weebly.com

Blogs

churchsmsj.blogspot.co.uk
tialdouglass.blogspot.co.uk
rhnegativebloodsecrets.blogspot.co.uk

Facebook Pages

facebook.com/IPoKHT
facebook.com/TempleofTheola
facebook.com/ChurchSMSJ
facebook.com/Gnostic.Theolalite
facebook.com/WhatWouldMaryMagdaleneDo
facebook.com/Tau.Tia.L.Douglass
facebook.com/Tau.Graham.T.Suddick
facebook.com/BeTheSolutionMovement
facebook.com/RhNegativeBloodTypeSecrets
facebook.com/NeanderthalADA
facebook.com/Sapentia
facebook.com/tialdouglass
facebook.com/alchemistslaboratory
facebook.com/PurplePeacockPublications

Youtube Channels

youtube.com/user/TempleofTheola
youtube.com/user/rhnegbloodsecrets
youtube.com/user/OrdoInfinitusOrbis

Twitter

twitter.com/TauTiaLDouglass
twitter.com/Templeoftheola
twitter.com/RhNegBlood

Printed in Great Britain
by Amazon

12607388R00269